The READER'S Anthology

Globe Book Company, Inc.
New York/Chicago/Cleveland

The
READER'S
Anthology

Robert R. Potter

Robert R. Potter received his B.S. from the Columbia University School of General Studies and his M.A. and Ed.D. from Teachers College, Columbia University.

Dr. Potter has been a teacher of English in the New York City School System, a research associate for Project English at Hunter College, and a teacher of English at the Litchfield (Conn.) High School. He has held professorships at the State University of New York and at the University of Connecticut.

Dr. Potter is the author of Globe's *Myths and Folktales Around the World, The Reading Road to Writing, Making Sense, A Better Reading Workshop, Writing Sense, Writing a Research Paper, Language Workshop, Tales of Mystery and the Unknown, The American Anthology,* and co-author of *The World Anthology.*

Special thanks to Alice Delman who assisted Robert R. Potter.

Consultants

Nancy Garrison, English Teacher Albany High School, Albany, Georgia
Bernard Gordon, English Department Head Intermediate School 320, Brooklyn, New York
Sterling C. Jones, Supervisor Detroit Public Schools, Detroit, Michigan
Ruth D. McCubbrey, English Teacher Tamalpais High School, Tamalpais, California
Dorothy Smith, Former Language Arts Teacher Dallas Independent School District, Dallas, Texas

Project Editor: Carol Callahan
Editors: Patricia Walsh and Eden Force Eskin
Photo Editor: Adelaide Garvin Ungerland
Cover Design: Bill Gray
Text Design: Celine Brandes

Acknowledgments and credits appear on pages 403–404.

ISBN: 0-87065-333-4

Published simultaneously in Canada by Globe/ Modern Curriculum Press. Copyright © 1986 by Globe Book Company, Inc., 50 West 23rd Street, New York, NY, 10010. All rights reserved. No part of this book may be kept in an information storage or retrieval system, transmitted or reproduced in any form or by any means without the prior written permission of the publisher.

PRINTED IN THE UNITED STATES OF AMERICA   9 8 7 6 5 4 3 2

CONTENTS

UNIT 1:   LOOKING AT LOVE

UNIT II: TOWARD THE TWILIGHT ZONE

UNIT III: ZIGZAGS

U N I T IV: DISCOVERING THE SELF

U N I T V: WHAT IS A HERO?

SKILL DEVELOPMENT

INTRODUCTION

▶ Introductions are invitations—or they should be.
So WELCOME, reader. Come on in. Relax. Sit down and let a
top modern writer invite you to the pages that follow.

"I," SAYS THE POEM

by Eve Merriam

"I," says the poem arrogantly,
"I am a cloud,
I am a tree.

I am a city,
I am the sea,
I am a golden
Mystery."

How can it be?

A poem is written
by some someone,
someone like you,
or someone like me

who blows his nose,
who breaks shoelaces,
who hates and loves,
who loses gloves,
who eats, who weeps,
who laughs, who sleeps,

an ordinary he or she
extraordinary as you or me
whose thoughts stretch

as clouds in the sky,
whose memories
root deep as trees,

whose feelings choke
like city smoke,

whose fears and joys in waves redound
like the ocean's tidal sound,

who daily solves a mystery:
each hour is new, what will it be?

"I," says the poem matter-of-factly,
"I am a cloud,
I am a tree.

I am a city,
I am the sea.

I am a golden
Mystery."

But, adds the poem silently,
I cannot speak until you come.
Reader, come, come with me.

- **arrogantly** (AR uh gunt lee) in a very proud, almost rude, way
- **extraordinary** (ik STROR duh ner ee) beyond the ordinary; remarkable
- redound (ri DOUND) go forth, have an effect, and return

Did you like the poem on the opposite page? Whatever the case, you'll certainly agree that the poet's message is a true one: *No poem—or piece of writing of any kind—can "speak" until the reader's active mind brings it to life.*

Literature is a two-way process. The writer writes. The reader reads. Words on paper form a path from mind to mind. The words themselves are just little black squiggles on a white background. They mean nothing until you say, *Yes, I'll go down that path. I'll open my mind to the writer's ideas.*

Waiting in the darkness of the closed pages inside this book are more than 100,000 words. Each is part of an invitation—a story, a play, a poem, an article. Plan now to be an active reader who says *yes, maybe,* or even *no* to the writer's words. Plan to get involved in your reading.

Like most literature books, this one contains questions. Some are here to test your reading:

The poet in Eve Merriam's poem is imagined as being (a) a person with special powers. (b) a common person like you or me. (c) someone who wastes time with nonsense.

Other questions make you think:

At the end, the poem is said to *speak . . . silently.* How is this possible? What does it mean?

There are a number of other questions that will help you develop your reading and literature skills:

The term "speak silently" is a paradox. A **paradox** is created when two ideas or things that seem to be opposites can both be true at the same time. What is the paradox at the end of the poem's first column? How might it be explained?

In addition, you'll find exercises that will make you a better speaker and a better writer. You'll also be asked to review vocabulary words from time to time. To prepare for these, pay special attention to the words printed in **heavy black type.** On the bottom of the opposite page, for instance, **arrogantly** and **extraordinary** are the words to know.

Did you find some of the questions above quite hard? No great matter— for now. Come back to this page when you have finished reading the book. And when you do, you'll find that you're a better reader because you started by saying that magic word: *yes!*

UNIT · 1

LOOKING AT LOVE

Love is one of the strangest words in our language. The odd thing about the word *love* is that it has so many meanings. You can *love* a boy, a girl, a parent, or a piece of steel and plastic on four wheels. You can *love* dogs, cats, money, or sports. Some people even find themselves falling in *love* with *love*.

Love is a puzzling, fuzzy word. It's hard to define. The poet Emily Dickinson puts it this way:

> That Love is all—
> Is all we know of Love.

Love... Friendship... Brotherhood... Affection.... Call it what you will, it's the idea that holds this unit together. You'll start by reading a story that pits the force of love against the force of law. You'll end by reading thoughts about love as expressed by various poets. Along the way, you'll read about a young couple who grow in understanding and in respect for each other over a period of time.

There's much more, so get started now.

O. Henry (1862-1910)

A street in New York City in the year 1900

The lives of some writers are nearly as interesting as the stories they write. The career of the author known as *O. Henry* is a good example.

William Sydney Porter was born in North Carolina in 1862. He had little education. He worked here and there—in a drugstore, on a ranch, in a bank. He moved to Texas, got married, and began to find his true talents as a writer for a Houston newspaper.

Then his luck turned sour. He was charged with stealing money from the bank in Austin where he once worked. He fled to Honduras in Central America. After a few months, he learned that his wife was near death. He returned to her bedside. Soon he was arrested, tried, and given a three-year term in jail. Meanwhile, his wife died.

Another turn of events followed. To pass time in prison, Porter started writing short stories. He signed them O. Henry (Orrin Henry was one of the prison guards). Before long he was a popular author—and a free man again. He moved to New York, where he wrote hundreds of stories before his death, in 1910.

After such a life, it seems only natural that O. Henry has become famous as the master of the last-page surprise, or the tricky ending.

You might enjoy reading other stories by O. Henry in *Best Stories of O. Henry, The Complete Works of O. Henry*, and *Tales of O. Henry*.

A RETRIEVED REFORMATION

by O. Henry

▶ True love triumphs and brother saves brother in this well-known tale by the master of the last-page surprise. Get ready for a flip-flop!

A guard came to the prison shoe shop. There Jimmy Valentine was busily stitching shoes. He was taken to the front office, where the warden handed Jimmy his pardon. It had been signed that morning by the governor.

Jimmy took the pardon in a tired kind of way. He had served nearly ten months of a four-year sentence. He had expected to stay only about three months—at the longest. For Jimmy Valentine had friends on the outside. When such a man goes in the "stir," it is hardly worthwhile to cut his hair.

"Now, Valentine," said the warden, "you'll go out in the morning. Brace up. Make a man of yourself. You're not a bad fellow at heart. Stop cracking safes, and live straight."

"Me?" said Jimmy, in surprise. "Why, I never cracked a safe in my life."

"Oh, no," laughed the warden. "Of course not. Let's see, now. How was it you happened to get sent up on that Springfield job? Was it because you wouldn't prove that you didn't pull the job for fear of exposing someone in very high society? Or was it simply a case of a mean old jury that had it in for you? It's always one or the other with you innocent victims."

"Me?" said Jimmy. "Why, I never was in Springfield in my life!"

"Take him back, Cronin," the warden said, smiling. "And fix him up with clothes for the outside. Unlock him at seven in the morning. Better think over my advice, Valentine."

At a quarter past seven the next morning, Jimmy stood in the warden's outer office. Jimmy had on a suit of badly fitting, ready-made clothes and a pair of stiff, squeaky shoes. This is the outfit the state bestows on its "guests" as they leave prison.

The clerk handed him a railroad ticket and a five-dollar bill. With these, the law expected him to rehabilitate himself. The warden gave him a cigar and shook his hand. Valentine, 9762, was

---

- **retrieved** (ri TREEVD) got back again
- **reformation** (ref ur MAY shun) act of changing for the better
- **bestow** (bi STO) give in a formal way, as a gift
- **rehabilitate** (ree huh BIL i tate) to get back one's good health or reputation

entered on the books "Pardoned by Governor." Then Mr. James Valentine walked out into the sunshine.

Jimmy ignored the song of the birds, the waving green trees, and the smell of the flowers. He headed straight for a restaurant. There he tasted the first sweet joy of liberty—a broiled chicken. Then he had a cigar a grade better than the one the warden had given him. From there he strolled to the railroad station, where he boarded a train. Three hours set him down in a little town near the state line. He went to the café of one Mike Dolan. He shook hands with Mike, who was alone behind the counter.

"Sorry we couldn't make it sooner, Jimmy, me boy," said Mike. "But we had that protest from Springfield to fight against. And the governor nearly balked. Feeling all right?"

"Fine," said Jimmy. "Got my key?"

He took his key, went upstairs, and unlocked the door of a room at the rear. Everything was just as he had left it. There on the floor was Ben Price's collar button. It had been torn from that famous detective's shirt when they had overpowered Jimmy to arrest him.

Jimmy pulled out a folding bed from the wall. He slid back a panel in the wall and dragged out a dust-covered suitcase. He opened it and gazed fondly at the best set of burglar's tools in the east. It was a complete set, made of the finest steel. It had the latest designs in drills, punches, and clamps. In addition, there were two or three novelties, invented by Jimmy, himself. He took special pride in these. He had paid over $900 to have them made at _____, a place where they made things for the profession.

- **balk** (BAWK) refuse or hesitate
- **novelty** (NOV ul tee) something new or unusual

In half an hour, Jimmy went downstairs and through the café. He was now dressed in tasteful and well-fitting clothes. In hand was his dusted and cleaned suitcase.

"Got anything on?" asked Mike Dolan, smiling.

"Me?" said Jimmy, in a puzzled tone. "I don't understand. I'm with the New York Short Snap Biscuit Cracker and Frazzled Wheat Company."

A week after the release of Valentine, 9762, there was a neat job of safe burglary done in Richmond, Indiana. No clue to the burglar was found. A mere $800 was taken. Two weeks after that an improved, burglar-proof safe in Logansport was opened like a piece of cheese. A sum of $1,500 was removed. That began to interest the crime stoppers.

Then an old bank safe in Jefferson City became active. It threw out $5,000 worth of bank notes. The losses were now high enough to get Ben Price on the case. He compared notes. The methods of the burglaries were found to be very similar. Ben Price investigated the scenes of the robberies. He was heard to remark:

"That's dandy Jim Valentine's autograph. He's back in business. Look at that lock—jerked out as easy as pulling up a radish in hot weather. He's got the only tools that can do it. Jimmy never has to drill but one hole. Yes, I guess I want Mr. Valentine. He'll do his bit next time without any help at all from the governor."

Ben Price knew Jimmy's habits. He had learned them while working on the Springfield case. Long jumps, quick getaways, no helpers—these had helped Mr. Valentine become successful.

One afternoon Jimmy Valentine and his suitcase climbed out of the mail truck in Elmore. This was a little town five miles (eight kilometers) off the railroad in the back country of Arkansas. Jimmy went down the board sidewalk toward the hotel. He looked like an athletic young senior just home from college.

A young lady crossed the street. She passed him at the corner and entered a door over which was the sign "The Elmore Bank." Jimmy Valentine looked into her eyes. He forgot what he was and became another man. She lowered her eyes and blushed slightly. Young men of Jimmy's style and looks were scarce in Elmore.

Jimmy grabbed a boy that was loafing on the steps of the bank as if he were one of the stockholders. Feeding him dimes, Jimmy began to ask the boy questions about the town. By and by the young lady came out. She looked royally unaware of the young man with the suitcase as she went her way.

"Isn't that young lady Miss Polly Simpson?" asked Jimmy.

"Naw," said the boy. "She's Annabel Adams. Her pa owns the bank. What'd you come to Elmore for? Is that a gold watch chain? I'm going to get a bulldog. Got any more dimes?"

Jimmy went to the Planter's Hotel, registered as Ralph D. Spencer, and got a room. He leaned on the desk and told his tale to the clerk. He said he had come to Elmore to look for a place to go into business. How was the shoe business, now, in the town? He had thought of the shoe business. Was there an opening?

The clerk was taken with the clothes and manner of Jimmy. He, himself, was something of a model of fashion to the youth of Elmore, but he now saw his shortcomings. While trying to figure out Jimmy's manner of knotting his tie, he gave him some facts.

Yes, there ought to be a good opening in the shoe line. There wasn't a shoe store in the town. The clothing shops and the general stores were the only ones that carried shoes. Business in all lines was fairly good. Hoped Mr. Spencer would decide to locate in Elmore. He would find it a pleasant town. And the people were very friendly.

Mr. Spencer thought he would stay in the town a few days and look things over. No, the clerk needn't call for help. He would carry up his suitcase himself—it was rather heavy.

Mr. Ralph Spencer was the phoenix that arose from Jimmy Valentine's ashes. The ashes had been left by the flame of a sudden attack of love. So he remained in Elmore, and did well. He opened a shoe store and watched the profits roll in.

Socially he was also a success. He made many friends. And he gained the wish of his heart. He met Miss Annabel Adams, and became more and more taken by her charms.

At the end of a year the situation of Mr. Ralph Spencer was this: He had won the respect of the town. His shoe business was thriving. And he and Annabel were engaged to be married in two weeks. Mr. Adams, the typical country banker, approved of Spencer. Annabel's pride in him almost equaled her love. He was very much at home in the family of Mr. Adams and that of Annabel's married sister. He seemed as if he were already a part of the family.

One day Jimmy sat down in his room and wrote this letter, which he mailed to one of his old friends in St. Louis:

Dear Old Pal:

I want you to be at Sullivan's place in Little Rock, next Wednesday, at nine o'clock. I want you to wind up some little matter for me. And, also, I want to make you a present of my kit of tools. I know you'll be glad to get them—you couldn't copy the lot for a thousand dollars. Say, Billy, I've quit the old business—a year ago. I've got a nice store. I'm making an honest living. And I'm going to marry the finest girl on earth two weeks from now. It's the only life, Billy—the straight one. I wouldn't touch a dollar of another man's money now for a million. After I get married, I'm going to sell out and go west. There I won't be in so much danger of having old scores brought up against me. I tell you, Billy, she's an angel.

- phoenix (FEE niks) **A mythical bird of great beauty. Stories are told that it lived for about 500 years, then burned itself to death in a great funeral fire. From its own ashes, it arose again—younger and more beautiful than ever.**
- **thriving** (THRYV ing) doing very well

She believes in me. And I wouldn't do another crooked thing for the whole world. Be sure to be at Sully's, for I must see you. I'll bring along the tools with me.

Your old friend,
Jimmy

On the Monday night after Jimmy wrote this, Ben Price rode quietly into Elmore in a fancy buggy. He lounged about town until he found out what he wanted to know. From the drugstore across the street from Spencer's shoe store, he got a good look at Ralph D. Spencer.

"Going to marry the banker's daughter—are you, Jimmy?" said Ben to himself, softly. "Well, I don't know!"

The next morning, Jimmy had breakfast at the Adamses'. He was going to Little Rock that day to order his wedding suit and buy something nice for Annabel. That would be the first time he had left town since he came to Elmore. It had been more than a year now since those last "jobs." So he thought he could safely go to the big city.

After breakfast, quite a family party went downtown together—Mr. Adams, Annabel, Jimmy, and Annabel's married sister with her two little girls, aged five and nine. They came by the hotel where Jimmy still lived. He ran up to his room and brought along his suitcase. Then they went on to the bank. There stood Jimmy's horse and buggy and Dolph Gibson. Dolph was going to drive Jimmy over to the railroad station.

They all went past the high, carved oak railings that led into the banking room. Jimmy went too, for Mr. Adams's future son-in-law was welcome anywhere. The clerks were pleased to be greeted by the good-looking, nice young man who was going to marry Miss Annabel. Jimmy set his suitcase down. Annabel, whose heart was bubbling with happiness, put on Jimmy's hat and picked up the suitcase. "Wouldn't I make a nice salesman?" said Annabel. "My, Ralph, how heavy it is! Feels like it was full of gold bricks."

"Lot of nickel-plated shoehorns in there," said Jimmy coolly. "I'm going to return them. Thought I'd save express charges by taking them up. I'm getting awfully economical."

The Elmore Bank had just put in a new safe and vault. Mr. Adams was very proud of it. He made everyone inspect the vault. It was small, but it had a newly invented door. It fastened with three

• **lounge** (LOWNJ) pass time in an easy, idle way

solid steel bolts thrown by a single handle. And it had a time lock. Mr. Adams beamed as he explained its workings to Mr. Spencer. Jimmy showed a polite but not too intelligent interest. The two children, May and Agatha, were delighted. They loved the shining metal and funny clock and knobs.

While they were all busy, Ben Price strolled in and leaned on his elbow. He looked casually inside between the railings. He told the teller that he didn't want anything. He said he was just waiting for a man he knew.

Suddenly, there was a scream or two from the women, followed by an uproar. Unseen by the elders, May, the nine-year-old girl, had playfully shut Agatha in the vault. She had then shut the bolts and turned the knob of the lock, as she had seen Mr. Adams do.

The old banker sprang to the handle and tugged at it for a moment. "The door can't be opened," he groaned. "The clock hasn't been wound, nor the combination set."

Agatha's mother screamed again, hysterically.

"Hush!" said Mr. Adams, raising his shaky hand.

"All be quiet for a moment. Agatha," he called as loudly as he could. "Listen to me." During the following silence, they could just hear a faint sound. It was the child wildly shrieking in the dark vault in a panic of terror.

"My precious darling!" wailed the mother. "She will die of fright! Open the door! Oh, break it open! Can't you men do something?"

"There isn't a man nearer than Little Rock who can open this door," said Mr. Adams, in a weak voice. "My God! Spencer, what shall we do? That child—she can't stand it long in there. There isn't enough air. Besides, she'll die from fright."

Agatha's mother, frantic now, beat the door of the vault with her hands. Somebody wildly suggested dynamite. Annabel turned to Jimmy. Her large eyes were full of pain, but not yet hopeless. To a woman, nothing seems impossible for the powers of the man she worships.

"Can't you do something, Ralph—try, won't you?"

He looked at her with an odd, soft smile on his lips and in his keen eyes.

"Annabel," he said, "give me that rose you are wearing, will you."

Hardly believing that she heard him right, she unpinned the rose from her dress and placed it in his hand. Jimmy stuffed it into his vest pocket. He threw off his coat, and pulled up his sleeves.

With that act Ralph D. Spencer passed away, and Jimmy Valentine took his place.

"Get away from the door, all of you," he ordered.

He set his suitcase on the table, and opened it flat. From that time on, he seemed to be unaware of the presence of anyone else. He laid out the shining tools swiftly and neatly, whistling softly to himself as he always did when at work. Silent and unmoving, the others watched him as if under a spell.

Jimmy's pet drill was biting smoothly into the steel door. In ten minutes—breaking his own record—he threw back the bolts and opened the door.

Agatha, almost collapsed, but safe, was gathered into her mother's arms.

Jimmy Valentine put on his coat. He walked outside the railings toward the front door. As he went, he thought he heard a faraway voice that he once knew call "Ralph!" But he never hesitated.

At the door a big man stood somewhat in his way.

"Hello, Ben!" said Jimmy, still with his strange smile. "Got around at last, have you? Well, let's go. I don't know that it makes much difference, now."

And then Ben Price acted rather strangely.

"I guess you must be mistaken, Mr. Spencer," he said. "Don't believe I recognize you. Your buggy's waiting for you, ain't it?"

And Ben Price turned and strolled down the street.

ALL THINGS CONSIDERED

1. When the story opens, Jimmy Valentine is (a) in court. (b) on a business trip. (c) in prison.
2. Jimmy is released from prison because he (a) has been found innocent. (b) has friends in high places. (c) has served his time.
3. At first, Jimmy works as a (a) safecracker. (b) pickpocket. (c) con man.
4. Jimmy decides to settle in Elmore because he (a) falls in love. (b) likes the hotel. (c) plans to rob the local bank.
5. One of Jimmy's trademarks as a crook is his (a) fingerprints. (b) special tools. (c) habit of leaving a dollar in the safe.
6. Ben Price is after Jimmy because Jimmy (a) robbed Ben's bank. (b) double-crossed him. (c) is a criminal.
7. In Elmore, Jimmy works in (a) a bank. (b) his own shoe store. (c) a hotel.
8. Jimmy's letter to his friend shows that Jimmy (a) has really gone straight. (b) plans to rob Mr. Adams's bank. (c) plans to continue robbing banks after his marriage.
9. The Adams family sees Jimmy's burglar tools when (a) Ben Price tells them Jimmy is a burglar. (b) Annabel accidentally opens Jimmy's suitcase. (c) Agatha gets locked in the bank vault.
10. As the story ends, you can conclude that Jimmy will probably (a) return to safecracking. (b) return to prison. (c) marry Annabel.

THINKING IT THROUGH

Discuss the following items in class.

1. What clues lead Ben Price to think that Jimmy Valentine has gone back to his old trade? Name at least two.
2. (a) What does the author mean by the sentence, "Mr. Ralph Spencer was the phoenix that arose from Jimmy Valentine's ashes"? (b) Is that statement correct or incorrect, based on your reading of the end of the story?
3. At the end, what does Jimmy expect to happen when he walks up to Ben Price?
4. Jimmy Valentine and Ben Price do things in the story that show their very high respect for others. (a) What does each person do? (b) How might Jimmy's action change the way Ben thinks of him? (c) How might Ben's action change the way Jimmy thinks of him?

Literary Skills

Short Story

The term **short story** really defines itself. A short story is simply a *story* that is *short*. When the term is used in literature books, however, another idea is added. A *short story* is usually a made-up story, or a piece of **fiction** (FIK shun). Stories about events that happened in real life are usually called *true stories*, or **nonfiction.**

Plot

The events in a short story are called the **plot.** A story's plot is its skeleton—the framework that holds it together. Try to think of a plot as a series of problems that the main character has to overcome. For instance, at the beginning of "A Retrieved Reformation," Jimmy Valentine has a big decision to make: Should he go straight or return to a life of crime?

Here are three problems Jimmy meets in "A Retrieved Reformation." Write a few sentences to explain how each problem is solved. Then tell what further action the solution leads to. The first one is done as an example.

Problem 1: Should Jimmy go straight or return to a life of crime?

> Jimmy decides to return to crime. This decision finally leads him to Elmore, where he falls in love with Annabel.

Problem 2: Can Jimmy become an honest man and get Annabel to promise to marry him?

Problem 3: Should Jimmy open the safe to save Agatha's life, even though Annabel might learn his true identity?

Coincidence

In some stories, the events seem to follow one another as they do in real life. In other words, the plot seems natural. The solution to problem 1 leads to problem 2. The solution to problem 2 leads to problem 3. "Yes, that's the way life happens," we say when we read such a story.

But are all the stories we read really this true to life? Of course not. "Now, *wait* a minute!" we sometimes mutter. "Don't put me on! Who could be expected to believe *this*?" When thoughts like these leap into our minds, it's likely that the story has far too many *coincidences.*

A **coincidence** (koh IN si duns) occurs when two or more related events accidentally happen at the same time. In "A Retrieved Reformation," it is a coincidence that Annabel Adams appears on the street right after Jimmy arrives in town. It is also a coincidence that Annabel's father happens to own the bank Jimmy intends to rob.

Too many coincidences make a story hard to believe. Think about the ending of "A Retrieved Reformation." How many coincidences does it contain? Do you think the story could ever happen in real life? What events make the story believable or unbelievable? Discuss your answers to these questions in class.

Composition

Follow your teacher's instructions before completing *one* of these writing assignments.

1. Suppose you were a teacher preparing a short true-false test on the plot of "A Retrieved Reformation." Write five statements. Make two statements true, and two false. The other statement may be either true or false. Remember, the statements should be about the plot, or the happenings in the story.

2. Write a short paragraph called "Coincidences at the End of 'A Retrieved Reformation.'" In your paragraph, include at least three related events that must happen to allow the story to end as it does. (You can add others if you want to.) What are the chances of these coincidences occurring in real life? For you as a reader, do so many coincidences ruin the story? Explain.

Carl Sandburg (1878-1967)

A statue of Abraham Lincoln located in the Lincoln Memorial, Washington, D.C.

Perhaps more than any other American writer, Carl Sandburg was a poet of the people. The son of a blacksmith, he was born in Illinois, the nation's heartland. From the early age of 13, he had to earn his own living. A number of odd jobs—from laborer to milkman to farmhand—gave him firsthand knowledge of the people he grew to love. While still in his 20s, he started to write, first as a reporter and then as a poet. His poems were filled with wisdom and love of America and its people. Soon there was no stopping Sandburg. In 1950, a six-volume biography of Abraham Lincoln won him a Pulitzer Prize. He toured the country looking for folk songs, which he collected in *The American Songbag*. His book *The People, Yes* makes poetry of a Native American and a farmhand drawing circles.

Sandburg had a deep admiration for Abraham Lincoln and his Gettysburg's Address. "Of the people, by the people, and for the people"— that was Carl Sandburg.

You might enjoy reading other poems by Carl Sandburg in *Chicago Poems, Cornhuskers,* and *Good Morning, America* as well as in *The People, Yes.*

from *THE PEOPLE, YES*

by Carl Sandburg

The white man drew a small circle in the sand
and told the red man, "This is what the Indian
knows," and drawing a big circle around the
small one, "This is what the white man knows."
The Indian took the stick and swept an immense
ring around both circles: "This is where the
white man and the red man know nothing."

WAYS OF KNOWING*

1. Draw the three circles quickly on a piece of paper. Then shade the area that the Indian in the poem means by the word "This" (next to last line).

2. In your view, which circle in the poem is the most important? (a) The second circle drawn by the white man. (b) The circle drawn by the Indian.

3. The message of the poem clearly concerns brotherhood. Yet that message is hard to put into words. Which statement seems best to express the idea of the poem? (a) What you don't know won't hurt you. (b) All people are united by their ignorance. (c) A picture is worth a thousand words.

* **immense** (i MENS) huge

*"A poem is a way of knowing."—John Hall Wheelock

VOCABULARY AND SKILL REVIEW

Before completing the exercises that follow, you may wish to review the **bold-faced** words through page 14.

I. On a separate piece of paper, mark each item *true* or *false*. If it is *false*, explain what is wrong with the sentence.
1. Very shy people often act *arrogantly*.
2. An elephant is an *immense* animal.
3. It would be a *coincidence* for all four members of a certain family to have the same birthday.
4. You would probably be pleased if someone *balked* at your request.
5. On Sunday afternoons, many people like to *lounge* in front of the TV set.
6. A *thriving* business would probably make its owner happy.
7. If you were working on your *reformation*, you would try to do better in the future.
8. A *novelty* shop would sell many new or unusual products.
9. Made-up stories are properly called *nonfiction*.
10. It takes *extraordinary* skill to become a professional basketball player.

II. Some details about a story are important to the plot. Others are not. Here are ten statements about "A Retrieved Reformation." On a separate piece of paper, number from one to ten. Then mark **I** (important) or **N** (not important) next to each number.
1. Most of the story takes place in Elmore, Arkansas, not Staunton, Virginia.
2. Jimmy's first treat after his release is a broiled chicken.
3. Annabel Adams's father happens to own the local bank.
4. Jimmy robs exactly three safes between prison and Elmore.
5. Jimmy's success as a shoe merchant allows him to stay in Elmore.
6. Jimmy decides to give his tools away, rather than bury them.
7. Jimmy does not leave Elmore for even a day in over a year.
8. It's the five-year-old, not the nine-year-old, who gets locked in the vault.
9. Mr. Adams's vault has a time lock on it.
10. Ben Price happens to be present when Jimmy opens the vault.

15

UP ON FONG MOUNTAIN

by Norma Fox Mazer

Girl meets boy . . . girl loses boy . . . girl gets boy.
Boy meets girl . . . boy loses girl . . . boy gets girl.

▶ Either way, it's one of the oldest plots in the world. It's the skeleton used for hundreds and hundreds of stories. Here's how a gifted modern writer brings the old bones to life.

TO: All Students Taking English 10
MEMO FROM: Carol Durmacher—Feb. 3

Your term project will be to keep a weekly journal. Purchase a 7¾ x 5-inch ruled, wire-bound notebook. Date each entry. Note the day, also. Make a minimum of two entries each week. The journal must be kept to the end of the school year. It is to be handed in June 24th.

I will not read these journals—only note that they have been kept. There will be two marks for this project—Pass and Fail. Only those students not handing in a journal or disregarding the few rules I have set down will receive a Fail.

In writing in your journal, try to be as free as possible. This is your journal: express yourself. Use the language that comes naturally to you. Express your true feelings. Remember, I will not read what you have written (unless you ask me to). Once I record your mark I will hand the journal back to you. You may be present while I check.

These journals are for YOU. To introduce you to the joys of record-keeping. To help you think about your lives, the small events, the funny, sad, or joyful moments. Record these as simply and directly as possible.

A moment recorded is a moment forever saved.

- **journal** (JUR nul) a written daily record; diary
- **entry** (EN tree) thing written in a book or list
- **minimum** (MIN uh mum) smallest amount; lowest

February 6, Thursday

I don't know what to write really. I have never kept a journal before. Well, I better write something. I have to do this two times in the next three days. Miss Durmacher, you said, "Write your true feelings." My true feelings are that I actually have nothing to write. Well, I'll describe myself. My name is Jessie Granatstein. I'm 15 years old. My coloring is sandy (I think you would call it that). I ought to lose ten pounds. My eyes are brown. I have thick eyebrows that my sister Anita says I ought to pluck. My father says I'm stubborn as a bulldog.

February 8, Saturday

Anita and I made a *huge* bowl of popcorn tonight, then ate it watching TV. Then we were still hungry, so we made a pot of spaghetti. We had a good time till Mark came over, then Anita acted like I didn't exist.

February 12, Wednesday

Lincoln's birthday, also my parents' anniversary. Mom made a rib roast, baked Idaho potatoes, and strawberry shortcake. I stuffed myself like a pig. It half rained, half snowed all day. Why would anyone want to get married on Feb. 12, in the middle of winter? Mom just laughs when I ask her, and looks at Dad.

February 14, Friday

I don't have anything to write. I'm sorry, Miss Durmacher, but all I seem to be writing about is food. Mom says not to worry about my weight, that I'm "appealing." She's nice.

February 18, Tuesday

Yesterday I was talking to Anita and we got called to supper right in the middle of a sentence. "Girls!" That's my father.

But, anyway, that wasn't what I was going to write about today. I was going to write about Brian Marchant—Brian Douglas Marchant III. Kids call him BD. I'm pretty sure he was watching me in class today. Fairly sure, although not positive. What I am positive of is that *I* was watching *him*. In fact—well, I'm not going to write any more about it. I thought I wanted to, but I take it back. And that's all I have to say today.

Feb. 21, Fri.

Well, Miss D., it's a Friday, it's winter, I feel sort of depressed. I wish I had someone I could really talk to. It snowed again today. I've always loved snow. Today, for the first time ever I didn't like it. I *hated* it. And that depressed me even more.

And to tell the truth, Miss D., while we're on depressing subjects, I just can't believe this journal. Almost three more *months* of my real thoughts and feelings—that's depressing!

Monday, February 24

Brian Marchant borrowed paper from me, and winked at me. I have always hated winking boys.

Feb. 28, last day of the month, Friday

BD winked at me again.

I said, "Why are you winking at me?"

"What do you mean? I'm winking at you because I feel like winking at you."

"Don't," I said.

"Don't?" He looked at me in amazement. I mean it, Miss Durmacher, like nobody ever said *don't* to him before.

"I think winking is dumb," I said.

He stared at me some more. Then he gave me a double wink.

March 3, Monday

I saw BD in the cafeteria today. I said, "Hi." He said, "Hi." I said, "Have you given up winking?" He said, "What?" Then he laughed. He has a nice big laugh.

Tues. Mar. 4

BD and I ate lunch together today. No winking.

Thursday, March 6

Lunch again with BD. I forgot to bring mine, and didn't have any money with me. BD brings *enormous* lunches. Two peanut butter jelly sandwiches, one tuna fish with pickle relish, one salami with cheese, one bag of chips, an apple, an orange, a banana, plus he bought three cartons of milk and two ice cream sandwiches. And parted with one of the pbj's for me. Also, he gave me half his apple.

And that makes *three* entries for this week, Miss Durmacher. Not bad, huh?

Tuesday, March 11

BD walked home with me and came in for cocoa. Then we went outside and he looked up at the tallest tree around. "I think I could climb that, Jess," he said.

"Don't, BD," I said.

"Why not? I like to climb trees."

"I don't like heights, and it might be slippery."

"*You* don't have to climb it," he said. And up he went.

When he got nearly to the top he yelled, "Jess-eee! Jess-eee!" I yelled back, "I hear you, Beee-Deee!" Then he came down, laughing all the way.

Wednesday, March 12

Anita said she thought BD was funny-looking. I said I didn't think he was any funnier-looking than most human beings.

She said, "You have to admit he's shorter than you. Green pop eyes, like a frog. Also, a big mouth which looks like he could swallow your whole face when he kisses you."

"How do you know he kisses me, Anita?"

"Well, sister, I hope he kisses you!" She laughed.

Are you reading this, Miss Durmacher? Don't, please. The truth is, I have only been kissed a few times—well, not even a few. Three to be exact—at parties. But I'm not going to tell Anita that.

March 21, Friday

Anita doesn't stop making cracks about BD's looks. I just don't understand it. Her boyfriend, Mark Maloff, is supposed to

be super-good-looking, but I really can't stand him. He wears pink ties and has a little green ring on his left hand. It's true BD looks as if he never thinks about what he's wearing. Nothing ever matches. But something about him really pleases me.

Saturday night, March 22

Miss Durmacher, don't read this—you said you wouldn't. I think I love BD!

Wednesday, March 26

Mom thinks she and I are alike. She's always saying it. *But I'm not like her at all. I'm not sweet.* I became aware of this because of BD. I have been noticing that he likes things his own way. Most of the time he gets it. I have noticed, too, that I don't feel sweet about this at all!

March 29, Sat. afternoon

BD came over last night and said we were going bowling. I said why didn't we do something else, as we went bowling last week. He said he liked bowling and what else was there to do, anyway? I said we could go roller skating. I like roller skating. BD said, "Jessie, why are you being so picky? Why are you being hard to get along with?" I thought, Right! Why am I?

And we went bowling. And then, later, I realized he had talked me out of what I wanted to do and into what he wanted to do.

Monday, March 31, last day of the month

I don't even mind writing in here anymore, Miss Durmacher. I have plenty to write all the time. That favorite subject, Myself.

Also, today, I noticed that BD is another one whose favorite subject is—myself. That is—*himself.* The thing is, I really like to listen to him because, mainly, I like him. But if he never wants to listen to me, I get this horrible lonely feeling. I think that's it. A lonely feeling. Sad.

April 2, Tuesday, no I mean, Wednesday

A dumb fight with BD today. He got going on his ancestors who came over here about 200 years ago. *Pioneers,* he said with a big happy smile. As if because they got on a boat about 150 years earlier than my family this made them really special. So I said, "Well, BD, I think there's another word for your ancestors. *Thieves.*"

"Thieves!" His cheeks puffed up.

"They stole Indian land, didn't they?" (I have just become aware of this lately from history class.)

BD whipped out a map of the Northeast. He stabbed his finger about a dozen places all over Maine and Vermont. "Here's Marchantville, Jessie. Marchant River. Marchant's Corners. East Marchant! West Marchant, and Marchant's Falls!" He looked at me very triumphantly.

"BD," I said, "I've seen all that before." I burst out laughing.

"You think thieves were the founders of all these places, Jessie? You think that's why all these rivers and towns were named after the Marchants? They were *pioneers*, Jess—" And he got that happy look on his face again at the mere sound of the word. "*Pioneers*, people who had the intelligence and foresight to go to the new country, the unexplored—"

"Now listen, BD," I said. I had to talk loud to slow him down. "Suppose a boatload of people came over here tomorrow from China and pushed us all out. And they say to us, 'From now on, we're going to call this Fong City after our leader, Mao Tze Fong. This river here, this is going to be Fong River, and over here we've got Fong Mountain—'"

"Jessie, that's dumb," BD yelled. "That comparison just won't work—"

Well! I can yell, too. "*Like I was saying,* BD, although we don't know it, the Chinese have developed this ray gun. Instant death. Okay? Now—"

"No, it's not okay. We've got atomic weapons, an army, police—"

"So here comes Mao Tze Fong," I went on, "and all the others with him. They've got these ray guns which we can't do *anything* against. They kill off a bunch of us, take over our houses and land, and the rest of us run to hide in the mountains—"

"Fong Mountain, I presume?" BD said.

"Right! We're up on Fong Mountain. From there we would try

• **mere** (MEER) *nothing else but; simple*

21

to get our homes back. But after a few years, we'd have to agree to anything they said. Because, remember, we have just a few old hunting rifles against their ray guns. They, after a while, would let us have some land they didn't care about, some swamps and stuff. They'd stick us all on it and call it a reservation. And meanwhile, *meanwhile*—BD, are you listening?—they'd have been wiping out all the old maps and making new ones. With Fong Mountain, East Fong, West Fong, Fong's Corners. And that's it, BD, if you don't want to understand the point of what I'm saying!"

April 3, Thursday

In class today: "How're your famous ancestors, BD?"

"How're things up on Fong Mountain, Jessie?"

April 6, Sunday

I talked to BD on the phone. We were peaceful. That's good. Because we have been fighting a good bit lately.

April 12, Saturday

Mom came into my room with a sweater she'd washed for me. "Oh, by the way, honey," she said (which is always the signal that she's going to be serious), "aren't you and Brian seeing an awful lot of each other?"

"Me and BD?" I said. "You don't have to worry, Mom. No one is going to carry me away."

Tuesday, April 15

Thinking about me and BD. At this point in my life, the way I feel is—I don't think I have to know why. It's just the way I feel.

Sunday, April 20

A fight with BD last night. Please don't read this, Miss Durmacher! It's private and personal. BD said I was being mean. He said I was being selfish, and also unfair. I didn't know what to say in return, so I just got mad. He won't even let me get mad in my own way!

Monday, April 21

Miss Durmacher, you didn't say how long or short the entries had to be. I'll describe the weather today. Gray air and the smell of garbage everywhere.

Tuesday, April 22

Today, in school, I saw BD in the halls, and I saw him in class, and I saw him in the cafeteria. We looked at each other. He didn't say anything, and I didn't say anything.

After school I started home. After a few blocks I felt someone was following me. I turned around. There was BD behind me. I started walking again. Then I turned around. He was right behind me. He grabbed me in a big hug, knocking my books every which way and said, "Kiss! Kiss!" I was sort of shocked, but I couldn't help kissing him back. And then he laughed and laughed.

Wednesday, April 30

Today I tried to talk to BD. He says it's my fault we fight so much. He says I pick the fights, that he's peaceful. This might be true. He *is* peaceful when he gets his way. He says I'm a prickly character. He's started calling me Porky, short for porcupine.

Sunday, May 4

Last night BD and I went out. I had the feeling that I was up there on Fong Mountain again. And I was all alone. And I thought, Oh! I wish I had someone to talk to.

Saturday, May 10

I have kind of a problem here. What I want to write about is BD and me, but I keep thinking you'll read this, Miss Durmacher. So this is going to be my second entry for the week.

Friday, May 16

Oh, BD, you mix me up . . . I love you . . . but . . .

Friday, May 23

BD came over last night. I thought we could just walk around, buy ice cream, and maybe talk. Be restful with each other. It was a nice night, warm, and I didn't feel like doing anything special.

But the minute we set foot on the sidewalk, BD said, "We're going to the movies," and he starts walking fast, getting ahead of me.

So I just kept walking along at my usual pace. I said to his back, "How do you know that's what I want to do?"

"There's a new movie at the Cinema," he said. "You'll like it."

"How do you know that?"

He turned around, gave me one of his smiles. He really has the nicest smile in the world! But he uses it unfairly. "Oh, listen, Jessie, if I like it, you'll like it. Right?"

"Wrong!" I yelled.

"Say it again, Porky. They couldn't hear you in Rochester."

"Very funny, BD. And I told you not to call me *Porky!* I don't believe I'm going to any movie," I said. "I haven't made up my mind what I want to do tonight. Nobody asked me what I wanted to do, only told me what they wanted to do."

"They," BD said. "There's only one of me."

"Oh, BD," I said, "no, you're a whole government. You're a president, vice-president, and secretary of defense all rolled into one."

"What are you talking about?"

"You know what I'm talking about, BD. How you always have to be Top Banana. The Big Cheese. Always telling me. You're a regular Mao Tze Fong! We're going to do this. We're going to do that. We're going here. We're eating this. Don't you think I have a mind of my own?"

"You're being difficult tonight," he said. He was smiling. Only not his regular beautiful smile, more of a toothy mean smile, as if he would like to really bite off my arm instead of talking to me. "You've been difficult just about every time we see each other lately. Now, do you want to see that movie, or don't you?"

"I don't care about the movie," I said. "What I care about is that I have a mind of my own. I am a free person also, and I don't want to be in any dictatorship relationship!"

"Dictatorship relationship," he said. And he laughed. Hee-hee-hee. "You mean a *dictatorial* relationship. *Dictatorial,* not *dictatorship.*"

I stared at him. Then I turned around and walked in the other direction. And he didn't come after me, and I didn't go back after him.

Wednesday, May 28

I guess everything really is over with BD and me. We really

* **dictatorial** (dik tuh TOR ee ul) **forcing one's beliefs upon someone else**

have broken up. I never would have thought it—breaking up over grammar!

June 2, Monday

I know I missed making a couple of entries, Miss Durmacher, but I was sort of upset. I'll make some extra ones to make up for it. Anita has a job after school at the telephone company. Mom has been going over every day to help Aunt Peggy, who just had her fifth baby. I don't have anything to do except hang around the house, feeling crummy.

June 4, Wednesday

Sometimes, thinking about BD, I think I was the biggest fool in the world. I never loved a boy the way I loved BD. Then I go over everything in my mind, and I don't see what else I could have done.

June 5, Thursday

Why should I miss someone who all I could do was fight with, anyway?

Friday, June 6

I'm sick of hanging around the house. I'm sick of thinking about BD. Two whole weeks is enough. I'm going to get a job.

Saturday, June 7

Everyone at every place I go says, "Leave your name, we'll call you." Or else, "Fill out this application." Then they ask you a hundred questions about your whole life for a job which they don't mean to give you, anyway.

Sunday, June 8

I got a job!

It happened just by accident, this way. Yesterday, I stopped into Dippin DoNuts. Just out of habit I told the lady behind the counter I was looking for work.

She looked me over. I sat up straighter. She said, "Are you prepared to start next week, and then work all summer?"

I said, "Sure!"

She looked me over again. She asked me how old I was. She asked me where I lived. She said she was Mrs. Richmondi and she owned the place. She needed someone right away. I start tomorrow afternoon.

Sunday, June 15

I've worked a whole week, every day after school from four to seven. (Then Mrs. Richmondi comes in for the last three hours and to close up.) And I worked all day Saturday. I'm a little bit tired today, but I like working. Yesterday morning I got up at five o'clock. Everyone was asleep. I crept around the house and let myself out as quiet as I could. The streets were empty. Not even one car. And the houses all quiet. It was nice. I was never out early in the morning like that.

Monday, June 16

I have to wear a horrible uniform, orange with white trim. But other than that, I really like my job. Mrs. Richmondi is nice, too, but she *hates* bare feet. She's got a sign on the door: NO BARE FEET.

Wednesday, June 18

I see BD every day in school and we never say a word. We just look at each other and then keep walking.

Mom came in to Dippin DoNuts today and ordered coffee and a jelly doughnut. Then a bunch of kids came pouring in yelling orders. Before I'd really taken in who was there, I thought—BD's here! And my hands got sweaty.

Thursday, June 19

BD came into the doughnut shop today.

It was 6:30. At first I almost didn't recognize him. He was wearing a funny-looking hat that was too big for him. And huge red-and-white sneakers.

He sat down at the counter. I wiped my hands down the sides of my uniform. "Yes?" I said, just like I did to anyone who came in. "Can I help you?"

"Cupacawfee," he said.

I poured coffee into the orange mug. "Would you like a doughnut?" I said.

"Yup," he said.

I was nervous. Some of the coffee spilled. I wiped it up. "Cinnamon, plain, sugar, jelly, chocolate, banana, peach, orange, cream, or cinnamon-chocolate?"

"What kind would you recommend?"

"Whatever you like."

"What do *you* think is the best?"

"That depends on your taste," I said.

"Well, what is your taste? What is your favorite?"

"The cinnamon-chocolate."

"Then that's what I'll have," BD said. "Cinnamon-chocolate."

"I thought you didn't like chocolate, BD," I said, putting the doughnut down in front of him.

"Everyone needs an open mind in this world," he said. "I haven't eaten chocolate in quite a few years, so I might just as well try it again. Don't you agree, Jessie?"

I stared at him. I wanted to say, "BD, is that you?" I had missed BD an awful lot. I had thought about him nearly every single day. Sometimes I had loved him so much that I could hardly stand it. Sometimes I had hated him just as hard. Now here he was, not more than two feet from me. And all we were talking about was doughnuts.

"Cooperation, ma'am," he said, putting on a Western accent. "We strive to co-op-erate. For instance, how do you like my hat?"

"Your hat?"

He took off the hat, twirling it on his fingers. "My hat. This antique, genuine gangster hat. You don't like it, do you?"

"Well—"

"No, I can tell. You don't have to say anything. You think it's an ancient, grungy piece of junk. Okay, Jessie, if that's what you think, then I don't want to wear this hat." And he opened the door and flipped the hat through. I could see it sailing out into the parking lot. "That's what I mean by cooperation, Jessie."

"You dope, BD," I said. "I liked that hat all right, it's your sneakers I'm not so wild about."

"My sneakers? These genuine red-and-white All-Americans? Jessie! That's all you have to say." He kicked off his sneakers and sent them sailing into the parking lot where they joined his hat.

"You're crazy, BD," I said. "You're really impossible."

And just then my boss, Mrs. Richmondi, parked her car outside in the lot. I looked down at BD's bare feet and then at the sign tacked on the door. NO BARE FEET.

"BD, here comes my boss," I said, sort of fast. "You better leave." My voice was froggy. I felt kind of sick. Because BD and I

• **grungy** (GRUN jee) shabby or dirty

27

hadn't said anything real. "My boss hates bare feet. BD, you better just go."

Mrs. Richmondi was coming to the door now.

"But, Jessie—"

"BD, she's coming!"

Mrs. Richmondi pushed open the door with her shoulder. And the first thing she saw was BD's feet. "Young man! You have bare feet. You shouldn't have let him in, Jessie. I've told you, no bare feet!"

"I didn't come in with bare feet," BD said.

Mrs. Richmondi glared at him. "Out!" She pointed to the door.

"I'm going," BD said, "but don't blame—"

"Out!"

BD left. I watched him through the window, cutting across the parking lot. Mrs. Richmondi was talking to me.

"I'm sorry, Mrs. Richmondi," I said. "Excuse me, please." I bolted through the door. I snatched up BD's sneakers and hat and ran after him. "BD! BD!" I thrust the sneakers into his hand

- **bolt** (BOLT) run away fast
- **thrust** (THRUST) push with force

and clapped the hat on his head. "Perfectly good sneakers, BD," I said, which wasn't what I wanted to say, at all.

"If you don't like 'em, Jessie, I don't want 'em."

Oh, BD, I thought. Oh, BD! I knew I had to go back in the shop. Mrs. Richmondi was watching us through the window. But we still hadn't said *anything*. Neither of us. And we were just standing there, looking at each other.

"BD," I said. "BD, do you want to be friends?"

"That's what I mean," he said. And then he gave me a smile, that terrific smile which I'd missed all this time. "That's what I really mean, Jessie."

Friday, June 20

Today I hand in my journal.

When I started writing it way back in February, I didn't even know BD. It's funny. Odd, I mean. So much has happened. And now, this is the last time I'm writing here. I'm not going to do it anymore. I don't care about the past that much. Not when there's tomorrow to look forward to! So, Miss Durmacher, this is it. Please remember your promise not to read this journal. I trust you, Miss Durmacher.

Pass
Carol Durmacher

ALL THINGS CONSIDERED

1. Miss Durmacher intends to grade the journals by using (a) A, B, C, D, F. (b) Pass—Fail. (c) numbers on a curved scale.

2. When Jessie begins writing in her journal, she (a) starts the first entry with a description of BD. (b) writes the same sentence over and over. (c) has trouble knowing just what to write.

3. In writing her journal, Jessie (a) puts down only what a teacher would like to read. (b) often tries to fool herself with half-truths. (c) is usually honest about how she feels.

4. Which statement could *not* be used to describe BD? (a) He is confident. (b) He is shy. (c) He is stubborn.

5. Quite early in the story, Jessie begins to dislike herself for (a) going only where BD wants to go on dates. (b) trying to make BD jealous. (c) forcing BD to be the boy she wants him to be.

6. From history class, Jessie has come to learn that (a) more women should have become famous. (b) the Indians, or Native Americans, were treated unfairly. (c) the pioneers deserve more credit than we give them.

7. The break up between BD and Jessie comes when (a) BD refuses to diet. (b) Anita makes remarks about BD's looks. (c) BD corrects Jessie's grammar.

8. The *main* reason Jessie gets a job is (a) that she's bored and wants to get her mind off BD. (b) to earn money for college. (c) to show BD that she's a serious person.

9. When BD comes into the doughnut shop, Jessie (a) is surprised by the things he says. (b) becomes angry. (c) asks his forgiveness for being wrong.

10. The person who changes most at the end of the story is (a) Jessie. (b) BD. (c) Anita.

THINKING IT THROUGH

Discuss the following items in class.

1. What do you think are Miss Durmacher's purposes in having the class members keep journals? Some are given in her handout that starts the story. Can you think of any others?

2. (a) How does Jessie feel about the journal assignment at first? (b) Do you think Jessie's feelings about the journal change while writing it? Explain.

3. Over and over, Jessie writes something like "Please don't read this, Miss D." Why does Jessie worry so much about Miss D. reading her journal?

4. Think of two sentences that best describe BD. Then for each sentence, give an example of one event in the story that proves your opinion is correct.

5. (a) As a modern love story, does "Up on Fong Mountain" seem real to you? (b) Give an example of *anything* in the story that strikes you as really believable. (c) Give another example of something you find less easy to believe.

6. Think about the title. (a) Why does Jessie invent the "Fong Mountain" idea? (b) Here's a harder but most important question: In what way does the "Fong Mountain" idea apply to Jessie herself?

Literary Skills

Conflict

There's an old story that goes like this:

> Three bandits were sitting around a campfire. And one of the robbers said to another, "Bandit, tell us a story." The bandit thought a minute and began like this:
> Three bandits were sitting around a campfire. And one of the robbers said to another, "Bandit, tell us a story." The bandit thought a minute and began like this:
> Three bandits were sitting around . . .

On and on and on . . . The plot of this story could hardly be called interesting. In fact, it's downright boring. It lacks any *conflict*.

A **conflict** (KON flikt) develops when two opposite forces meet. For example, two robins want one worm. Ben Price wants Jimmy Valentine back in jail, while Jimmy wants to stay free. Jessie wants to go roller skating; BD insists on going bowling. All good stories have an interesting conflict at the very center of the plot. In truth, without a conflict there is no plot—and no story worth reading.

There are four kinds of conflicts. A story can contain more than one kind, but usually only one is the *main* conflict.

A. Conflict between people. (One person against another, one person against a group, or one group against another.)

B. Conflict within a single person. (Should Ben Price arrest Jimmy Valentine after he opens the vault or should he pretend he doesn't know him?)

C. Conflict between people and things. (Will Jimmy Valentine open the vault in time to save Agatha?)

D. Conflict between people and nature. (Will the woman make it through the storm to warn her friends of trouble?)

1. Reread the four kinds of conflicts listed above. Then think about "Up on Fong Mountain." Which kind is the *main* conflict in the story? On a separate sheet of paper, list at least two situations in the story that are examples of the main conflict.

2. What *other* kind of conflict is involved in the story? In a few sentences, give an example. (Hint: You should be able to find a good quote on page 25 to support your example.)

Sentence Meaning

The Right Word

"The difference between the right word and the almost right word," wrote Mark Twain, "is the difference between lightning and the lightning bug."

Mark Twain was certainly correct. Good authors choose words that blaze with brilliance in the reader's mind.

In the same way, the author Norma Fox Mazer has Jessie write, "I had the feeling that I was *up there on Fong Mountain* again." This says a lot more than words like *depressed, terrible,* or *defeated.*

Here are four sentences from the story. Each contains a word (or words) that makes the selection more colorful. Try to explain why these words are better than the words in brackets.

1. She said, "You have to admit he's shorter than you. Green pop eyes, like a frog [protruding green eyes]."
2. BD whipped [took] out a map of the Northeast.
3. "You know what I'm talking about, BD. . . . You're a regular Mao Tze Fong [much too bossy].
4. My voice was froggy [broken and thick].

Composition

Follow your teacher's instructions before completing *one* of these writing assignments.

1. Write four sentences about "Up on Fong Mountain." In each sentence, include the three words given after each number below. Try to include at least one or two descriptive words of your own that will make your sentence more interesting to the reader.
   Example: *father, stubborn, Jessie's*
   Sentence: *Jessie's father* said she was as *stubborn* as a bulldog.
   (1) BD, Jessie, winked   (3) movie, argument, characters
   (2) job, doughnut, school (4) ancestors, pioneers, towns
2. The story seems incomplete to some readers. It simply stops when the journal has to be handed in. What do you think happened to Jessie and BD after June 20th? Explain your ideas in a short paragraph. Be sure to give reasons for your opinions.

▶ Look around you. What do you see? Joy, love, and sharing? Hate, war, and sorrow? A little of each, probably.

The world is a large subject for a poet to take on successfully. Here's how two poets managed it well.

The questions below call for some deep thinking. Before trying to answer them, read the poems on page 34 at least three times. First read them at your normal speed. Then look at them for deeper meanings and originality. Finally, read them aloud to catch the *sound* of the words.

WAYS OF KNOWING

1. One of the poems you will read was written by a very well-known American poet, Langston Hughes. The other was penned by a student. After reading the poems, use a separate sheet of paper to explain which is which, in your opinion. Give at least two reasons.*

2. Regardless of your answer to number 1, tell which poem you prefer. In a few sentences, explain why.

3. Both poems are about the state of the world, but they hardly say the same thing. In the best sentence you can think of, state the difference in meaning between the two poems after you have read each poem at least three times.

*See bottom of page 83 for the answer, but your own answer *must* come first!

I DREAM A WORLD

I dream a world where man
No other man will scorn,
Where love will bless the earth
And peace its paths adorn.
I dream a world where all
Will know sweet freedom's way,
Where greed no longer saps the soul
Nor avarice blights our day.
A world I dream where black or white,
Whatever race you be,
Will *share* the bounties of the earth
And every man is free,
Where wretchedness will hang its head,
And joy, like a pearl,
Attends the needs of all mankind.
Of such I dream—
Our world!

REFLECTIONS

If the world looked in a looking glass,
It'd see back hate, it'd see back war and it'd see
          back sorrow,
it'd see back fear.
If the world looked in a looking glass, it'd run
     away with shame, and hide.

- **adorn** (uh DORN) decorate
- **sap** (SAP) weaken
- **avarice** (AV ur is) greed
- **blight** (BLYT) weaken; deform; ruin
- **bounty** (BOUN tee) gift; good thing
- **attend** (uh TEND) take care of; wait on

SPRING OVER BROOKLYN

by Zachary Gold

▶ "Love is eternal," an old saying goes. Yet the *ways* of love have always changed with the times. Here's a boy-meets-girl story that readers have loved for nearly 50 years. Get ready to jump back into the world of trolley cars, five-cent phone calls, and a lovable, crazy nut named Willie.

"Hello, Dolly," I shouted into the telephone.

"Who is this?" Dolly said. "Where are you?"

"I'm in a phone booth." I looked out and saw the corner of a counter and medicine bottles piled in a pyramid and a poster with shades of red smeared on it and a sign that read: BE BEAUTIFUL. "I'm in a drugstore," I said.

"Who is this?"

"Willie," I said. "You remember. Willie."

"Willie?"

"I live two blocks away from you. The house with the shutters."

"Willie?"

When did you see her last, Willie? I said to myself. The church bazaar? A school dance? A family bingo game? I couldn't remember.

"Nice Willie," I said.

"Oh," said Dolly. "Crazy Willie."

"That's a fine thing to say to me. That's a fine thing to hear over a telephone."

"What do you want, Willie?"

"Come out with me, Dolly. I looked through my little black book today, because it's spring; and, Willie, I said, who'll you see tonight, who'll you make happy? Come out with me, Dolly, and let me hold your hand, because it's spring and I haven't seen you in three years."

"I'll go out with you," said Dolly.

"You won't regret it," I said and hung up.

From the drugstore to my house it's two blocks, and from my house to Dolly's it's two blocks; and I hadn't seen Dolly in three years. That's the world for you; that's Brooklyn.

Two blocks and three years. In three years I could walk from my house to San Francisco and halfway back; but I couldn't walk two blocks.

After supper I went upstairs to get dressed. Wear a bow tie, Willie, I said to myself. Don't ask me why. Don't ask me if Dolly likes bow ties; I don't know. Wear your sport slacks, Willie. Wear your porkpie hat with the yellow brush.

- **bazaar** (buh ZAHR) special event where things are sold
- **porkpie** (PORK py) snap-brim hat with flat top

I washed and shaved and looked in the top drawer of my bureau. I had two dollars and eighty cents in the little glass. Spend it all, Willie, I said to myself; do it right. I folded the bills into my wallet and dropped the change into my pocket.

"So long, Ma," I called, and closed the door easy.

"Remember you work tomorrow," Ma said.

I should worry about Caesar and Company. I should worry about the shipping department. Who is Dolly, what is she? That's like a song, I thought. I walked down the street and I clipped the hedges as I passed and I banged the wires around the front lawns.

It was so clear you could see Coney Island; I swear you could see Coney Island. You could see the sky, too, all the way up; not a cloud, just blue, all blue from Avenue N to Coney Island. And from Coney Island to Sandy Hook, and from Sandy Hook to Europe, I bet. But I should worry about the color of the sky in Europe. I should worry about anything except that it was spring and the sky was blue and the lawns were fuzzy with green and the trees weren't brown any more and Dolly was only two blocks away.

When I got to the house I checked with my little black book. This is the place, Willie, I said.

"Dolly," I said, when the door opened, "Dolly, you're beautiful."

"I'm not Dolly," the girl said. "I'm her sister."

"I'm sorry," I said. "I haven't seen Dolly in three years and I forgot what she looks like."

That was a mistake, all right, but I should cry over spilt milk. I took off my hat and sat down on the porch swing. I whistled awhile and looked at my wrist watch. It was 7:38. My watch is never wrong. It is an heirloom. My brother gave

- **heirloom** (AIR loom) something handed down in a family, usually from parent to child

it to me last year. I don't know where he got it.

This time it was Dolly. She was blond and she had a smile and she wasn't too fat and she wasn't too skinny. That was Dolly, all right. Don't ask me how I knew. I just knew.

"Let's go, Dolly," I said.

Dolly said good-by to her ma and pa, and I said hello and good-by; and I said good-by and I'm sorry to her sister, Janet, and I got Dolly into the street in five minutes.

"Dolly," I said, "you have a wonderful family. I always loved them."

"You never saw them before," Dolly said.

"Didn't I?"

"No."

"I think they're swell. I think you're swell. I've seen you before."

"At a party once," Dolly said. "You never took me out."

That's the world for you; that's Brooklyn. Three years and two blocks, and I never took her out before. Willie, I said to myself, you're slipping.

We did it right that night. Loge seats in the movies, forty cents per; soda afterward, twenty cents per.

"Dolly," I said, "would you like a chocolate bar; would you like some candy drops, some chewing gum?"

"No, thanks."

"I have a dollar sixty to burn. What do you want to do?"

"Save it, Willie," she said. "Let's go home."

The sky was like a blot of blue-black ink.

"Home?" I said. "I don't want to go home. Let's take a walk in the park."

We got in the Ocean Avenue entrance and we walked around past the zoo and the boathouse, past the rose garden and the lily pool, under the covered bridge.

"I'm tired," I said. "Let's sit down."

Out on a point in the lake I found a bench and we sat down. "Dolly," I said, "this is the life. This reminds me of college. We used to sit on the steps of the frat house and sing songs. Those were the times. Willie, they'd say to me, tell us how you made that touchdown. Willie, did you hit that home run on a curve or a straight ball? That was a great game of basketball you played tonight, Willie. Those were the times."

"You never went to college," Dolly said.

"Be technical," I said. "It sounds nice, doesn't it? It could have been. What do you want me to say?"

"I don't know," Dolly said.

"The only reason I said it was because I wanted to get around to holding your hand. It works too. Ask me; I know."

"You can't hold my hand."

"That's a fine thing to tell me now. Why didn't you say that on the phone? Aw, come on, Dolly. It's spring and it's Willie asking."

- loge (LOJ) expensive front section of a theater balcony
- **frat** (FRAT) short for "fraternity," a club for men in college
- **technical** (TEK ni kul) very detailed

"I'll let you hold my hand when you see a seal waiting for a trolley car," Dolly said, and laughed.

"You're not giving me a runaround?"

"No."

"Come on home, Dolly," I said.

So we walked back the way we came, past the rose garden and the lily pool and the zoo, out on to Ocean Avenue, and the first thing we saw was a trolley stalled on the tracks.

"What's the matter, bud?" I said to a fellow.

"Go look," he said. "How should I know?"

That's the world for you; that's Brooklyn.

I pushed through the crowd, and there was an animal sitting on the tracks.

"What is it?" I said to the fellow next to me.

"It's a seal," he said. "Escaped from the zoo."

"What's he doing here?" I said.

"He's waiting for a trolley car, bright boy."

"I believe you," I said.

So all the way home I held Dolly's hand.

"You're not sore at me?" I said.

"No."

I wanted to sit on the porch swing awhile, but Dolly said: "Go on home, Willie. You're not so tired that you need a rest, and it's only two blocks anyway."

When I got home I didn't feel like sleeping. Read a book, Willie, I said to myself. So I went down to the bookcase and I looked through every shelf, and I'd read them all. I looked through all the magazines, and I'd read them too. Willie, I said to myself, you read too much. So all I did was make a lettuce and tomato sandwich and eat it, looking out of the window, waiting for a car to pass, so I'd know I wasn't the last one in New York to go to sleep. When a car passed I got into bed.

The next morning the sun was shining. Lord, it was a beautiful day. It was a baseball day; it was a day to go swimming. It was a day for anything except work.

"Ma," I said at breakfast. "I could call up the place and tell them I was sick. I could tell them I broke my arm or something."

"You go to work, Willie," Ma said.

"Why can't I tell them, Ma? They'll never know."

"It's a lie," Ma said.

"You don't understand about lying, Ma. Sometimes you have to lie. Sometimes things aren't just right and a lie helps straighten it out. Sometimes things sound nicer when you lie. Suppose you're out with a girl. Do you have to tell the truth all the time?"

"If you're serious about the girl," Ma said.

"I want you to know the truth, Ma. I was out with a girl last night."

"Get out," Ma said. "Go to work."

I slapped Ma on the back and pulled her apron loose, and while she was still laughing I went out. On the way to the subway I stopped at the telegraph office and wrote a telegram.

MEET ME SAME PLACE STOP SAME TIME
STOP URGENT
                    WILHELM

It cost me thirty cents. I addressed it to Dearest Dolly.

When I got to the shipping room of Caesar and Company, I felt good. "Buck," I said to the head clerk, "I'm going to ship out the whole place by myself today."

"That's fine," Buck said.

"Buck, you don't know how to say things. It's wonderful. It'll be the most stupendous thing that ever happened in Caesar and Company. Today I'm Atlas. I'm Hercules. I'm Tarzan.* I'm Willie the Giant Killer."

"What's the matter with you?"

"How should I know?" I said. "How should I know."

I worked like a demon. I tied; I packaged. I sent things out so fast the top of the shipping table burned from the friction. Don't ask me why; I don't know. Willie, I said to myself, you're terrific, you're a one-man department.

I went to the park and sat down on the bench at the point. You're sad, Willie, I said to myself; you're deep in sorrow.

By the time Dolly came, I really felt sad. I felt terrible. Nobody ever felt the way I did.

"What's the matter, Willie?" Dolly said. "Your telegram scared me."

"It's come, Dolly," I said. "It's come. Be brave."

"For heaven's sake, tell me what's the matter."

"The company," I said. "A secret mission. I may never come back. But don't take it too hard, Dolly. I'm not worth it."

● **stupendous** (stoo PEN dus) **amazing**

*Atlas, Hercules, and Tarzan: famous strong men of story and legend.

"A secret mission?" Dolly said. "You may never come back? Willie, you're not just making it up?"

"Dolly!"

"I knew it," Dolly said. "I knew it. Wilhelm. Of all the silly things."

I felt better. I didn't have to feel sad any more. "Well, it was for your sake I did it," I said.

"My sake?"

"It's spring," I said. "Let me hold your hand and hug you, because it's spring and it's Willie asking."

"You can hold my hand," Dolly said.

"Suppose I were really going away? Suppose you might never see me again?"

"You're not going away."

"What's a hug?" I said. "You talk as if it was the most important thing in the world."

"When the stars fall down," Dolly said laughing. "I'll hug you."

"That's a fine thing to tell me," I said.

I looked up into the sky. "Look," I said. "Make a wish. It's a falling star. Make two; there's another."

They came down fizz and bang; gone.

"Dolly," I said.

"Yes."

"They fell down."

"What?"

"You said stars. You didn't say all the stars. You just said stars. Two stars are stars."

So I hugged her.

I was glad I wore my crepe-soled shoes and my hand-painted tie. I was glad I wore my tab-collar shirt. Willie, I said to myself, you look swell. Willie, I said to myself, you feel swell too.

"You're not sore?" I said to Dolly.

"No."

Walking home from Dolly's that night I met old Mr. Pranzer. "Hello, sir," I said. "It's a beautiful night."

"I have hay fever," said Mr. Pranzer.

That night I dreamt about my little black book. I dreamt I tore out all the pages. I tore out Lily's and Flo's; Jane and Jean and Helen, Phyllis, Corinne, Dorothy, Joan and Norma and Anne. The only page left was Dolly's.

As soon as I got up I looked for the book. It was there, and so were all the pages. That was close, Willie, I said to myself; be careful of the little black book.

That morning I didn't feel like working. That's how it goes. I was going to take a taxi downtown, but I only had a quarter with me. I asked the taxi driver about it and he told me I could go take a jump. I told him I'd pay him off a nickel a week.

I heard the train coming and ran for the turnstile. I just made the station as the doors were closing. A fat lady held it open for me.

"Thanks," I said to her.

"I couldn't help it," said the lady; "somebody was trying to push me off the train."

- **turnstile** (TURN styl) turning gateway, often made to turn only when charge is paid

That's the world for you; that's Brooklyn.

Lunch time I went out and had a roll and coffee. I used a nickel to call Dolly.

"This is Jay Freling Matton," I said, "counselor-at-law. We have just received word that you are the beneficiary of a large estate left by a Mr. Dubelo, of Kansas, China. If you will meet us in front of the lions at the Public Library, we will be happy to further discuss the matter with you."

"Willie?" said Dolly. "Is that you, Willie?"

"You'll come?" I said.

"I didn't say that."

"Remember, it is to your benefit."

"The Public Library?"

"No," I said, remembering the nickel I had left. "I'll pick you up at home."

I heard Dolly say, "Willie—" just as I hung up.

"Why do you lie to me?" Dolly said. "Why do you make up all these stories?"

"It isn't lying," I said. "Why can't you have an uncle in Kansas or in China?"

"I haven't. That's all. I haven't."

"Dolly, you're wonderful. You're beautiful. Your eyes are like stars. Your mouth is a red, red ruby. Your hair is like spun gold. Your hands are like pale pieces of jade."

"Jade is green."

"There's white jade, too."

"Well, my hands aren't like jade," Dolly said.

"I said they are."

"You read it in a book, Willie."

"No, I didn't. It was in a movie. The girl was in Malay and the fellow who told it to her was an international thief. It was a wonderful, wonderful scene."

"I don't like it," Dolly said.

"All right. You make up something better."

"I don't want to make up anything. I want you to tell the truth."

"I was going to tell you that your mouth was like a ripe melon. I was going to say that if I could kiss you once, just once, ah, then death would be sweet. There's a speech."

"Why don't you just ask for a kiss?"

"You will?" I said. "Oh, Dolly!"

"I didn't say that."

"There. There you have it. I suppose if I said, 'How about it, Babe?' it would have been all right?"

"No."

"That's fine," I said. "You just won't kiss me. That's fine. Aw, Dolly, it's spring and it's me, Willie, asking. Come on."

"No."

"What if I see a seal waiting for a trolley car?"

"No."

"If the stars fall down?"

"No."

"What then?"

- counselor-at-law (KOUN suh lur at LAW) lawyer
- **beneficiary** (ben uh FISH ee er ee) one who receives benefits, such as property or money
- **jade** (JADE) kind of jewel-like stone, usually green

You're in the groove, Willie, I said to myself. You did it, Willie, you did it.

I reached down and tore off a snowball from the bush in the lawn. "Here, keep it," I said. "This is a night to remember."

"Willie—"

"What?"

"Do you love me, Willie?"

"I don't know, Dolly. It's spring; and sure I love you. Kiss me again, because it's spring and it's Willie asking."

"You better go home, Willie."

"I'm Don Juan," I said. "You're standing on a balcony and I'm serenading you. I'm singing you a love song. I'm Casanova* and I'm sitting beside you whispering poetry in your ear."

"You better go home, Willie."

"Is something the matter?" I said. "Did I say something?"

"Go home, Willie." And she got up and she was crying. And before I could say anything she was in the house and the door was locked and I was standing on the porch all alone.

Willie, I said to myself, be sad; you've got a right to be sad now.

Walking home, I met Mr. Pranzer. "The trouble with you, Willie," he said, "is that you've never had hay fever. If you'd ever had hay fever you'd know how it's possible to be sad in the spring."

Dolly laughed and leaned over. "Because you're such a crazy loon, Willie."

"That's a fine thing to say to me," I said.

But I kissed her.

Wonderful. Like running a strike right down the alley; like clicking off a rack in pool; like a cannon-ball ace in tennis.

- **loon** (LOON) **fish-eating bird**
- **ace** (ASE) **perfect serve in tennis**
- **serenade** (ser uh NADE) **sing a love song to**

*Don Juan and Casanova: both famous lovers in legend and history.

"Go jump in the lake, sir," I said courteously.

You do your best. You make everything nice. You think of things to say. You try to be different. You try to be romantic and glamorous. What happens?

She runs into the house crying.

You're a fool, Willie, I said to myself. You're a crazy fool. I should worry about one girl. I have a million girls. I have a choice, anyone I want. They're all mine. Brooklyn is full of girls. Look in the little black book, Willie, I said to myself.

It was no good. I looked in the little black book and I got out a number. "Hello," I said. "Is Joan home?"

"This is Joan talking."

"This is Willie. How are you?"

"Fine. And you, Willie?"

"Fine."

And then it was no good. Joan has knock-knees, I said to myself. Joan talks with a lisp.

"What is it you wanted, Willie?" Joan said.

"I'm working for the telephone company," I said. "I'm just testing the connection. Good-by, Joan," I said, and hung up.

The same with Phyllis. Ditto on Anne. Corinne has hair like wet grass. Jane always sings. Lily has a job and a boss. Flo wanted classical music.

There was something wrong with all of them.

I took out the little black book and I tore out all the pages except Dolly's. I tore them all out and scattered them in the wind. What's the good of a little black book if you don't like any of them?

Ma said I didn't sleep enough. Buck told me I looked like the devil. Every time I ran for a train I missed it. When I went out to eat lunch I wasn't hungry.

It was Dolly all right.

Dolly was the one.

A week later I wrote her a letter:

DOLLY: He had your name on his lips; I who am his closest friend have undertaken the sacred duty of telling you what he said.

However, do not grieve, since I know it was his wish that we who knew him should continue to carry on in the carefree happy way he knew, despite the fact that he no longer will be with us.

But I feel that all of us must feel that something fine, something grand has disappeared now that Willie has left.

So it is with both grief and the happiness he wanted us to continue to feel that I write you this news. Be brave, my dear, be brave.

His friend,
CARTER WAINWRIGHT, JR.

P.S. Willie asked me specially to convey to you certain matters too personal for the pages of this letter. So if you will meet me in front of the Public Library (I am sure you know the lions) I will be glad to divulge this information to you.

C. W., JR.

- **convey** (kun VAY) carry; communicate
- **divulge** (di VULJ) make known

I went all the way up to the Bronx to mail it.

I waited three hours and ten minutes, on my brother's watch, in front of the lions, and when Dolly came, I was good and angry.

"That's it," I said to her, "keep me waiting. I don't matter at all."

"You didn't say what time to meet you in the letter," Dolly said.

"What letter? I never sent you any letter."

"Please, Willie," Dolly said. "What is it you wanted?"

"Marry me, Dolly," I said. "I'll give you a penthouse and a limousine. I'll shower you with diamonds and furs.

You'll live in a house of flowers. I will be your slave. Step on me. Do as you will with me. But marry me."

"No," Dolly said.

"You let me hold your hand," I said.

"That was because of the seal."

"You let me hug you."

"The stars fell down."

"I kissed you."

"I liked your crazy talk, Willie."

"You cried over me."

"That was because I thought you didn't love me."

"I do," I said. "I do. Why won't you marry me, Dolly?"

"Willie," Dolly said. "Oh, Willie. I'll let you hold my hand and hug me because you're lucky; and I'll let you kiss me because I like you. But I won't marry you."

"I'll give you everything you want. Luxuries. Anything. Just ask for it."

"No, you won't. You know you can't do that, Willie."

So that was it. And maybe she wasn't wrong. Maybe I was wrong. Maybe, Willie, I said to myself, you're not good enough for her. I felt all washed up. I felt like the stone lions must feel in a rain.

"Dolly," I said, "you're right. I can't give you anything. I work in a shipping room and I make twenty-two-fifty a week. I haven't got any money in the bank and I'm always lying. Don't ever believe me, Dolly. All I have is myself. That's all I can give you."

"No limousine?" Dolly said.

"No."

"No furs?"

"No."

"No diamonds?"

"No."

"Just you?"

"Just me, Dolly."

"And you'd like it that way: Just you and me?"

"Oh, Dolly!" I said.

"Without lies or stories?"

"Dolly," I said, "you're breaking my heart."

"How much do you make a week, again?" Dolly said.

"Twenty-two-fifty."

"I make eighteen," Dolly said. "What do you think?"

"Dolly," I said. "Dolly!"

"Crazy Willie," Dolly said. "Who wants all those things?"

Imagine that. Furs, diamonds, limousines, penthouses—pouf, in the garbage pail; all in exchange for me—Willie. There's a girl for you.

I didn't know what to do. "Hey, lions," I yelled.

"Willie," she said. "Willie, kiss me, because it's spring and it's me, Dolly, asking."

That's the world for you; that's Brooklyn.

ALL THINGS CONSIDERED

1. The title of the story gives you some ideas about (a) famous lovers in history. (b) the time and place of the story. (c) Willie's weak points.

2. Willie's little black book contains information on (a) girls he's met. (b) jokes he wants to remember. (c) vocabulary words.

3. Willie is employed as a (a) salesperson. (b) joke writer. (c) shipping clerk.

4. At the beginning of the story, Willie (a) is engaged to Dolly. (b) has had an argument with Dolly. (c) hasn't seen Dolly in three years.

5. Perhaps the most interesting thing about Willie is his (a) imagination. (b) physical strength. (c) habit of giving up too soon.

6. Dolly and Willie are alike in that they both have (a) very successful careers. (b) an interest in sports. (c) a sense of humor.

7. The most unusual happening in the story is (a) the seal waiting for a trolley. (b) the falling stars. (c) Dolly running into the house in tears.

8. A high point in the story is when Dolly cries and runs into the house. She does this because (a) she's not sure that Willie really loves her. (b) her parents are looking out the window. (c) she realizes suddenly that she doesn't like Willie.

9. It seems clear that the "lions" referred to in the story are (a) in the zoo where Willie and Dolly meet. (b) stone statues in front of the Public Library. (c) in a famous painting.

10. At the end, Willie learns that one most often gets what one wants by (a) pretending to be something you're not. (b) trusting to luck. (c) being honest.

THINKING IT THROUGH

Discuss the following items in class.

1. Many readers like the story because they are constantly surprised. The first surprise comes when Willie arrives at Dolly's house. (a) What is this surprise? (b) Name one other surprise in the story that you especially enjoy.

2. Willie says he worked like a "demon" in the shipping room the day after his first date with Dolly. Why do you think he worked so hard?

3. Near the end of the story, a week passes without Willie and Dolly seeing each other. (a) What happens to Willie during this period? (b) What are Dolly's feelings about Willie?

4. Throughout most of the story, it seems to be Willie who gets things started and forces the action. But at the end, it's Dolly's turn to take control. (a) What does she do to turn things around? (b) What lesson does Willie learn from Dolly at the end?

Literary Skills

Rising Action and Climax

First, let's review what we know about the *plot* of a story. We know that the plot involves a series of *problems* that the main character has to solve. The solution to each problem leads to still another problem. We know that the plot must have one or more *conflicts:* two robins and one worm.

All good authors want to keep the reader's interest. Short-story writers know that each plot problem must be more interesting than the last. This is called **rising action.** If a certain plot problem is less interesting than the one before it, the reader yawns and puts the book down. Readers expect that a good story will have *rising action* that leads to a climax.

The **climax** of a story is the most exciting part at or near the end. The action at the climax involves the solution to the final plot problem. The climax of "Spring Over Brooklyn" is the last scene, where Willie changes in an honest way and Dolly agrees to marry him.

Study the following diagram carefully. The longer slanted lines stand for five plot problems. The circles stand for yes-or-no answers. Copy the diagram on a separate sheet of paper. Use your knowledge of the story to fill in the other questions and answers.

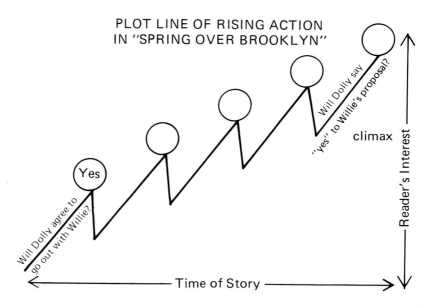

PLOT LINE OF RISING ACTION
IN "SPRING OVER BROOKLYN"

Sentence Meaning

The Right Word

Good authors seem to have a sixth sense: the sense of always knowing just the *right word* for what they want to say. Often these right words arouse the reader's five senses. They make the reader *see* and *hear* things. They involve the senses of *touch, taste,* and *smell.*

Look back at the first page of "Spring Over Brooklyn." Notice that the story starts with a roar: Willy *shouts* into the phone. A few lines later, the reader is looking at *smears of red* on a poster.

Here are five items from the story. On a separate piece of paper, copy the word or words in each item that arouse the reader's senses: *sight, hearing, touch, taste,* and *smell.* Then tell which sense or senses are involved. Thus, the first answer would be **1.** *shouted* (*hearing*).

1. "Hello, Dolly," I shouted into the telephone.
2. I whistled awhile and looked at my wrist watch.
3. So all the way home, I held Dolly's hand.
4. So all I did was make a lettuce and tomato sandwich. . . .
5. I felt like the stone lions must feel in the rain.

Composition

Follow your teacher's instructions before completing *one* of these writing assignments.

1. In two or three sentences, explain why Dolly referred to Willie as "Crazy Willie." Was he really crazy? If not, what did Dolly mean?
2. "Spring Over Brooklyn" was written in 1939. How do you think the plot differs from the plot of a modern love story? To help you find out, make a list of five of the mistakes that you think Willie made while dating Dolly. Then make another list of the things a modern teenager might do in the same situation.

   In a short paragraph, explain how the plot of a modern story would differ from "Spring Over Brooklyn."

VOCABULARY AND SKILL REVIEW

Before completing the exercises that follow, you may wish to review some of the **bold-faced** words on pages 16 to 43.

I. On a separate sheet of paper, write the *italicized* term that best fills the blank in each sentence. Use each term only once.

> *minimum   adorn   entry   bazaar*
> *heirloom   jade   convey   technical*

1. Carmella tried to make a(n) _____ in her diary every day.

2. Many starting jobs pay only the _____ wage.

3. Jobs that require _____ training usually pay more than others.

4. Tom's watch is a(n) _____ that once belonged to his grandfather.

5. You can sometimes find real bargains at a(n) _____.

6. A letter of sympathy should _____ some comforting thoughts.

7. We plan to _____ the living room with streamers for the party.

8. _____ is a kind of precious stone often used for jewelry.

II. Read the short poem and answer the questions that follow on a separate sheet of paper:

GREYDAY

by Maya Angelou

> The day hangs heavy
> loose and grey
> when you're away.
>
> A crown of thorns
> a shirt of hair
> is what I wear.
>
> No one knows
> my lonely heart
> when we're apart.

1. Clearly, the poet has managed to find just the right words to express her feelings. Yet one of the **stanzas** (groups of lines) is written in quite ordinary language. Which stanza is this?

2. The poet appeals to at least two of the reader's senses. One is the sense of sight. What is the other?

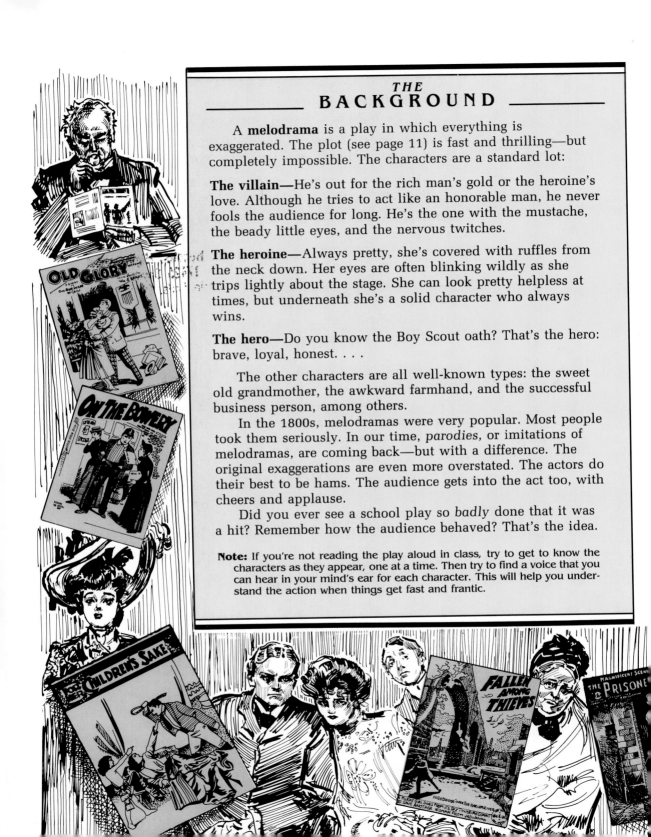

THE BACKGROUND

A **melodrama** is a play in which everything is exaggerated. The plot (see page 11) is fast and thrilling—but completely impossible. The characters are a standard lot:

The villain—He's out for the rich man's gold or the heroine's love. Although he tries to act like an honorable man, he never fools the audience for long. He's the one with the mustache, the beady little eyes, and the nervous twitches.

The heroine—Always pretty, she's covered with ruffles from the neck down. Her eyes are often blinking wildly as she trips lightly about the stage. She can look pretty helpless at times, but underneath she's a solid character who always wins.

The hero—Do you know the Boy Scout oath? That's the hero: brave, loyal, honest. . . .

The other characters are all well-known types: the sweet old grandmother, the awkward farmhand, and the successful business person, among others.

In the 1800s, melodramas were very popular. Most people took them seriously. In our time, *parodies*, or imitations of melodramas, are coming back—but with a difference. The original exaggerations are even more overstated. The actors do their best to be hams. The audience gets into the act too, with cheers and applause.

Did you ever see a school play so *badly* done that it was a hit? Remember how the audience behaved? That's the idea.

Note: If you're not reading the play aloud in class, try to get to know the characters as they appear, one at a time. Then try to find a voice that you can hear in your mind's ear for each character. This will help you understand the action when things get fast and frantic.

HE AIN'T DONE RIGHT BY NELL

adapted from an old melodrama

by Wilbur Braun

▶ Hiss the villain!
Cheer the hero!
And in general, ham it up!!!

CHARACTERS

Kenston High School
17425 Snyder Road
Chagrin Falls, Ohio 44022-5496

Nell Perkins, *the heroine*
Granny Perkins, *the woman who has raised Nell*
Lolly Wilkins, *a neighborhood busybody*
Hilton Hays, *the villain, manager of a mill*
Burkett Carlton, *the mill owner*
Vera Carlton, *Burkett's daughter*
Jack Logan, *the hero, a mill worker*

(The scene is Granny Perkins's dining and living room. She lives in a small town. It is 1890. As the curtain rises, Granny and Lolly are sitting and talking.)

Lolly: Where's Nell?

Granny: Taking a walk.

Lolly: I think she's visiting Hilton Hays. I don't know what she sees in him.

Granny: He's a fine gentleman. He lets Nell work in the mill when he needs extra workers.

Lolly: I don't trust him.

Granny: Why not?

Lolly: He's from the city. He's got a fancy house and fancy clothes. He has rich friends. Why would he want to marry Nell?

Granny: Everyone loves Nell. Sunshine lives in her eyes. Why shouldn't she marry Hilton Hays—or any other rich man?

Lolly: We all thought she would marry Jack Logan. He's a real man. His hands are strong from honest work.

Granny: But Jack is poor. His wife would wear herself out working too hard.

HILTON

Lolly: Have you told Nell about . . . ? (*She stops.*)
Granny: About what?

(*Hilton Hays enters the front door without knocking. The women don't notice him. When he hears Lolly speak, he hides in a corner.*)

Lolly: Does Nell know you aren't her real grandmother?
Granny: No. She must never know.
Lolly: Where did you find her?
Granny: Pa Perkins found her in a basket outside our door. No one claimed her, so we treated her as our own. Pa was working on his invention then. He said it would make us rich. He died before he could sell it. But I still have his papers.

(*Hilton smiles.*)

Lolly: Where are they?
Granny: Never mind. I'll give them to Nell for a wedding present.

(*Hilton rubs his hands together greedily.*)

Lolly (*rising*)**:** Remind Nell to be in church on Sunday. She is to sing in the choir.
Granny (*rising*)**:** I sure will. She has the voice of an angel.

(*Lolly goes out the front door. Granny leaves the room. Hilton walks out of his corner. He starts to look for the papers. He hears a knock—and opens the door. Vera Carlton enters.*)

Hilton: Vera! Are you spying on me again?
Vera: Why haven't you answered my letters?
Hilton (*softly*)**:** If you leave here now, I'll marry you soon.
Vera: I don't believe you. I know about you and Nell Perkins.
Hilton: You don't think I would marry a nameless nothing, do you?
Vera: What do you mean?
Hilton: Her name isn't Perkins. Who knows what it is? As a baby, she was found outside in a basket.
Vera: Then why are you spending time with her?

Hilton: Remember the money you got from your father and gave to me?

Vera (*sadly*): How could I forget? I lied to my father for the first time in my life.

Hilton: I lost the money in the stock market. So I came here to run your father's mill. It's not easy being the only person in my rich family who must work.

Vera: Poor Hilton.

Hilton: I knew you'd trust me.

Vera: What about Nell?

Hilton: I felt sorry for her. I gave her a part-time job at the mill. Now I've learned that she will soon own papers for a valuable invention. Once I get those papers, I won't have to work. We'll be free, Vera!

Vera: Hilton, forgive me. I thought I couldn't trust you.

Hilton: You're the only woman for me. How much money do you have in your purse?

Vera: About $50.

Hilton: Let me have it. When I see Nell, I'll buy the invention from her.

Vera: Will we be married soon, Hilton?

Hilton: As soon as I get that invention. Now run along. (*She turns to leave.*) Vera, haven't you forgotten something?

Vera (*shyly*): Oh, Hilton, I can't kiss you good-bye until after we're married.

Hilton: I meant the $50.

Vera (*giving him the money*): Oh, yes.

Hilton: Thanks. (*She leaves.*) I hope I never see her again.

Granny (*entering*): Is that you, Nell?

Hilton (*to the audience*): Maybe I can get the old woman to sell the invention!

Granny: Oh, Mr. Hays! I thought you were Nell.

Hilton: I'm pleased to be taken for such a beautiful person. I suppose you've noticed that I've been paying attention to your Nell.

Granny: Yes.

Hilton (*pretending to be shy*): I . . . I love her, and I want to marry her.

Granny: Are you sure you will be good to Nell?

Hilton: I give you my word.

Granny (*tearfully*): I'm going to lose my little girl.

VERA

NELL

Hilton: You'll be gaining a son. (*He twirls his mustache.*) I know you can't afford to buy a wedding present for Nell. So I'll give you some money to buy her something.

Granny: But I have a present for Nell.

Hilton: You mean the invention that Pa Perkins left?

Granny: Who told you?

Hilton: That worthless Jack Logan was talking about it at the mill. He plans to marry Nell—just to get the invention.

Granny: I can't believe it!

Hilton: You can't trust that man. I have an idea! Give me the papers for the invention. I'll guard them until you give them to Nell.

Granny: Well, all right. (*Pause.*) No, I'd better keep them until you and Nell are married.

Hilton (*to the audience*)**:** The old witch! (*He smiles at her.*) Suppose I give you $10 to buy a dress for the wedding. Then you'll know that I mean well. Then you'll trust me with the papers.

Granny: You want me to spend $10 on a dress? What a waste of money!

Hilton: You'll never have to worry about money again.

Granny (*happily*)**:** I can't believe my Nell is going to marry a billionaire.

Hilton: Granny, where are the papers?

Granny: They're in the . . . No, I want the thrill of giving them to Nell myself. All the money in the world can't change a woman's mind once it's made up. Now, I must feed the lambs. (*She leaves through a side door.*)

Hilton: I must find a way to get those papers! (*He follows Granny.*)

(*Nell enters the front door. She is small and pretty.*)

Nell (*happily*)**:** It's so good to be home after walking through the woods. My old home looks so pretty today. I wish Jack Logan would visit us the way he used to.

(*There is a knock. Nell opens the front door. Jack Logan enters. He is tall and handsome. He wears work clothes.*)

Jack (*shyly*)**:** Hello, Nell. I brought you some wild flowers. (*He hands her some flowers.*) Is Granny home?

Nell (*putting the flowers on a table*)**:** She's here some place. You haven't visited in weeks. We've missed you. I mean, Granny missed you.

Jack: I didn't think you'd want me around. After all, you and Mr. Hays are keeping steady company.

Nell: I'll bet Lolly Wilkins told you that! Mr. Hays and I are friends. But we are not keeping steady company. I would never get mixed up with a city fellow.

Jack: Do you mean that?

Nell: Of course.

Jack: Nell, I have a lot to tell you. But I was afraid you didn't want to talk to me.

Nell (*eagerly*): What do you want to say, Jack?

Jack: I'm going to give up my job at the mill. I'm going to start a farm.

Nell: Oh, Jack, that's wonderful!

Jack (*shyly*): I'll build a house on the farm. Then maybe we can be married.

Nell: Do you mean it? Oh, this is all so sudden! I've only known you since I was a baby.

Jack: I can't give you the money that Hilton Hays can. I'm a poor boy who must make his own way in the world. But if you wait for me, I'll try to make you happy.

Nell: I'll wait forever.

JACK

(*Jack holds out his arms. Nell is about to hug him—when Granny enters. She is followed by Hilton.*)

Granny: What is the meaning of this? (*Jack quickly puts his arms down.*) Hilton has been waiting to see you, Nell.

Hilton: I'd wait my whole life to see someone as pretty as you, Miss Perkins.

Nell (*nervously*): I'd better get some water for these flowers. (*She picks up the flowers and leaves the room.*)

Hilton (*to Jack*): I've been wanting to talk to you, Logan. You've been telling the mill workers that I don't pay them enough.

Jack: Yes. I *know* they don't earn enough. I work at the mill, too.

Hilton: So you're disloyal to the company that pays for your food!

Jack: You've cut the workers' pay. They are starving. You ride around in fancy carriages. Your horses are better fed than the mill workers!

Hilton: Is it true that you're telling the workers to go on strike?

Jack: They told me to tell you they need more pay. If they don't get it, they will go on strike tomorrow.

Hilton: I won't raise their pay by a penny! And if they strike, they'll never work at the mill again.

Jack: I'd rather be a poor man with a conscience than a rich man without a heart! (*He walks out the front door.*)

(*Nell enters from the side door. She carries a tin can filled with flowers.*)

Granny (*angrily*): I'm glad that no good Jack Logan is gone! (*She turns to Nell.*) Now, you listen to Mr. Hays. He plans to do right by you. (*She leaves the room.*)

Hilton: Those flowers are pretty, Miss Perkins. But they aren't half as pretty as you.

Nell (*coldly*): Save your fine speeches for those who want to hear them.

Hilton (*surprised*): What do you mean?

Nell: I'm through with you! I know you've asked Vera Carlton to marry you!

Hilton (*sneering*): You're not through with me yet, my proud beauty!

Nell: I'm going to marry Jack Logan.

Hilton: I'll make sure that never happens!

Nell: Leave this house!

Hilton: Some day you will apologize to me for this. (*He grabs Nell's wrist.*)

Nell: Let go! That hurts!

Hilton: Marry me! Otherwise, I'll tell everyone that no one knows who your real parents are.

Nell: What do you mean?

Hilton (*grinning*): Jack told me that Granny isn't your real grandmother. You were found outside in a basket. (*He lets go of her wrist.*) Your real parents didn't care enough to keep you. Or they were too poor.

Nell: It can't be true!

Hilton: Granny will tell you it's true. But I'm still willing to marry you.

Nell (*trying not to cry*): I would never marry someone as cruel as you.

Hilton (*to the audience*): My, the girl has courage. (*He turns back to Nell.*) Marry me. Or I'll tell everyone that your real parents were worthless.

Nell: Then the stories Granny told me about my wonderful parents aren't true.

Hilton: But if you marry me, no one will find out the truth.

Nell: Granny wouldn't lie. (*She touches a locket which hangs around her neck.*) Granny says the picture in this locket is of my ma.

Hilton: Anyone can buy a locket and put a picture in it. Ask Granny for the truth.

Nell: I will. But I'll never marry you. I'll only marry Jack Logan.

Hilton: He doesn't want to marry you. He only wants the plans for Pa Perkins's invention. Once he gets them, he'll leave you.

Nell (*suddenly weeping*): I'm not Granny's Nell! Jack doesn't really love me! Is there anyone I can trust? (*She runs out of the room.*)

Hilton (*grinning*): My plan is working. (*He twirls his mustache.*) Now where are those papers? (*He looks around. He takes a teapot off a shelf. He reaches inside and pulls out some papers. He looks at them—and grins.*) Now I'll get rid of Vera. (*He walks out the front door.*)

(*Nell and Granny enter from a side door. They both look sad.*)

Granny (*gently*): This will be our secret.

Nell: Lolly Wilkins will find out. Then everyone will know. (*She puts on a long cape.*)

Granny: Where are you going, child?

Nell: To start a new life.

Granny: Don't go! Stay here and marry Hilton Hays.

Nell: I would rather die than become his wife. (*She looks around the room.*) Good-bye, dear home.

Granny: Nell, wait! I've always wanted to give you Pa Perkins's invention as a wedding present. You might as well have it now. (*She goes to the teapot and reaches inside.*) The papers are gone!

Nell: Who could have taken them?

(*There is a knock. Nell opens the door, while Granny leaves to look for the papers. Jack enters.*)

Jack: Nell, where are you going?

Nell: I'm leaving forever. You have just been playing a game with me.

Jack: That is not true!

Nell: You told Hilton that I'm a nameless stranger. No one knows who my real parents are.

Jack: It isn't so! He's doing this to split us up!

Nell: I asked Granny. It's true. I'm not really a Perkins.

Jack: Then you'll become a Logan. We'll be married right away.

Nell: Do you mean it?

Jack: Of course I mean it. I love you.

(*Lolly enters the front door without knocking.*)

Lolly: Nell, is it true? Hilton Hays says you're going to marry him.

Nell: It's not true!

Lolly: I'm glad of that. Jack, Hilton says he fired you from the mill because you're dishonest.

Jack: I'll force those words down his throat!

(*Hilton enters the front door without knocking.*)

Hilton: Nell, I have great news for you.

Granny (*entering from a side door*)**:** I can't find those papers anywhere!

Jack (*to Hilton*)**:** You lied about me to my future wife. Take back your words!

Hilton: Are you trying to start a fight to cover up your own dishonesty?

Lolly: You should be ashamed of yourself, Hilton Hays. You just make trouble.

Hilton: You keep out of this. Everybody knows you're just an old busybody.

Lolly: Don't call me names, you city slicker!

Hilton (*ignoring her*)**:** Granny, did you say some papers were missing?

Granny: Yes. Someone has taken the plans for Pa Perkins's invention.

Hilton: I know where they are. Logan, you took those papers!

Jack: Take back those words before I kill you! (*He grabs Hilton around the neck and forces him to his knees.*)

Hilton: Let me up!

Jack: Not until you tell the truth and clear my name!

(*There is a knock. Granny opens the door. Vera Carlton and her father, Burkett Carlton, enter.*)

Vera (*surprised*): Hilton!

Burkett (*angrily*): Let go of him, Logan! (*Jack lets go of Hilton.*)

Hilton (*standing up*): Mr. Carlton, what are you doing here?

Burkett: I'm taking over my mill. You've been using money from the mill to buy stocks.

Hilton (*nervously*): That isn't so. You want to get rid of me because I'm so popular with the workers.

Burkett: They hate you. Who told you to cut their pay?

Hilton: I did it to save you money.

Burkett: *You* took the money. I went over the accounts at the mill. Only you could have taken that money.

Hilton: I'm not going to stay here and listen to lies! (*He hurries out the door.*)

Jack: Come back here! (*He follows Hilton outside.*)

Vera (*to Nell*): This is my father, Miss Perkins. Dad, this is the girl I was telling you about. Hilton was begging her to marry him—while he was engaged to me. Nell convinced me he was being dishonest.

Nell (*to Mr. Carlton*): I'm pleased to meet you, sir.

Burkett (*staring at Nell*): Those eyes! That hair! Who are you, girl?

Nell (*sadly*): Nobody knows my real name.

Burkett: Where did you get that locket?

Granny: It was around her neck when we found her outside in a basket. That was 18 years ago.

Nell (*handing the locket to Burkett*): Have you ever seen it before?

Burkett (*opening the locket*): That's a picture of my daughter Grace! It was taken just before she was married. Her husband left her after they had a baby. He took the baby with him. He sent her a letter, telling her to bring him $5,000. Then she could get her baby back.

Nell: What happened?

Burkett: She took the money out of the bank. She went looking for her husband, but she never found him. Six months later, she died of a broken heart. The baby was not found—until today. You are Gracie's daughter!

Granny: I always knew Nell came from a rich family.

Burkett: This locket proves you are my granddaughter. (*He hugs her.*) I'll try to make up for the years we've been apart. I'll take care of Granny, too.

Granny: I hope Hilton Hays doesn't get away. I knew all along he was no good.

Lolly: I've known that since he kicked Nell in the head.

Burkett (*shocked*)**:** He kicked you in the head, Nell?

Nell (*smiling*)**:** He kicked a bloodhound named Nell.

Burkett: Well, the sheriff will get him. He's waiting outside. Now, Nell, anything you wish shall be yours. What would you like first?

Nell: I would like to marry Jack Logan.

Burkett: I'll make Jack the head of the mill. I'll give him Hays's job.

(*Jack enters the front door, waving some papers.*)

Jack: These fell out of Hays's pocket as he climbed a tree. (*He hands the papers to Granny.*)

Granny: These are the plans for Pa Perkins's invention.

Burkett: What's he doing up a tree?

Jack: Nell, the bloodhound, chased him up there. Now the sheriff is trying to get the dog away. I bet Hays is sorry he kicked that dog. I bet he wishes he had done right by Nell. (*He hugs Nell. The others smile, as the curtain falls.*)

Copyright ©, 1935, by Samuel French
Copyright ©, 1962 (In Renewal) by Samuel French

ALL THINGS CONSIDERED ——————————

1. As the introduction states, the plot of this play is (a) very lifelike. (b) completely impossible. (c) slow and drawn out.

2. We learn early in the play that (a) Nell Perkins's father was an inventor. (b) Granny Perkins is dishonest. (c) Nell and Granny are not really related.

3. Hilton Hays has lost money (a) paying the mill workers too much. (b) buying presents for Nell. (c) investing in the stock market.

4. Hilton, unlike characters in modern plays, (a) speaks directly to the audience. (b) never leaves the stage. (c) wins the heroine and remains a villain.

5. The picture inside Nell's locket is of (a) her mother. (b) Granny Perkins. (c) no importance to the plot.

6. The person who steals the plans for Pa Perkins's invention is (a) Burkett. (b) Hilton. (c) Jack.

7. A high point in the play is a fight that develops between (a) Burkett and Jack. (b) Lolly and Granny. (c) Jack and Hilton.

8. It turns out that Nell is, in fact, (a) Burkett's grandchild. (b) Hilton's sister. (c) Burkett's daughter.

9. A second character named Nell is a (a) city friend of Vera's. (b) baby left on a doorstep. (c) dog.

10. As the introduction states, the characters in this play are (a) based on persons known by the author. (b) well-known types in melodramas. (c) copies of Shakespeare's characters.

THINKING IT THROUGH

Discuss the following items in class.

1. Amazing things can happen in a melodrama. For instance, characters always manage to arrive on the stage just when they are needed. They leave when they are no longer useful to the plot. What is one other happening in the play that you would find hard to believe in real life? (You might think about the finding of the lost invention papers.)

2. In several ways, Jack Logan and Hilton Hays *contrast* with one another. In other words, they are opposites. For example, Jack is from the country, Hilton from the city. How many other contrasts can you find? Give at least two.

3. When watching a melodrama, the audience is supposed to laugh at some lines and hiss at others. Suppose you were watching this play put on by an excellent cast of actors. What, in your opinion, would get the biggest laugh? The loudest hiss?

4. Underneath the laughter and the hisses, the play does have a serious meaning that relates to the theme of this unit: Only people of a certain kind can fall in love with each other, marry, and "live happily ever after." What kind of people are these? Think about the qualities of Nell and Jack.

Oral Interpretation

Dramatic Reading

Oral interpretation means reading aloud with expression. It is an important reading skill. Even when you can't actually say the words—in study hall, for instance—you can manage to have the words ringing in your mind's ear.

A play like "He Ain't Done Right by Nell" demands to be read with expression for full enjoyment. The person who reads all the parts in the same way cannot possibly bring life to the characters. The play just lies dead on the page. Consider this brief exchange:

Granny: Are you sure you will be good to Nell?
Hilton: I give you my word.
Granny (*tearfully*)**:** I'm going to lose my little girl.
Hilton: You'll be gaining a son. (*He twirls his mustache.*)

Can you read these lines as the author intended them to be read? Can you exaggerate them enough to get a few laughs from your audience?

Creating a Character

Choose one of the major characters in the play as your specialty, or study the part assigned by your teacher. Then read that character's part for the entire play. Finally, practice reading the part aloud. The following tips will help.

1. Keep the relationships between the characters clear. Know how they feel about each other in every line.

2. Try to picture the characters on the stage. Where are they standing? What actions go with the speeches?

3. As you practice your lines, add gestures and facial expressions. Try to hold the book with one hand.

4. Don't rush through your lines. Pauses often add meaning. If you expect a laugh, stop for it.

5. As you continue to practice, you'll find yourself really getting into your character. Your voice, eyes, head, and body will start to work

together. Some actors find that they are not really acting. The character seems to take over.

6. Continue to think about every speech. How can you make it sharper? Is your facial expression just right?

7. Be willing to accept suggestions from others. Remember, even the best movie, TV, and stage actors need good directors.

Relationships

Comparison and Contrast

A **comparison** usually shows how two (or more) things are alike. A **contrast,** on the other hand, shows how things are different.

We find comparisons and contrasts everywhere. Every piece of literature in this book is full of them. Consider the play you have just read. Think, for example, about the characters of Granny and Nell. Both are women. Both live in the same small town, even in the same house. Both are on the side of the good guys in the play. But in other ways the two contrast with each other. Granny is old, Nell young. Granny is fooled by Hilton, but Nell is not. Granny knows certain facts about Nell of which the girl is totally unaware.

Here are ten statements about the play. On a separate sheet of paper, tell whether each contains a comparison, a contrast, or both.

1. Hilton and Jack are employed by the mill, but one is the manager and the other a worker.
2. Hilton and Vera come from the city.
3. Jack says, "I'd rather be a poor man with a conscience than a rich man without a heart!"
4. Burkett realizes the truth when he sees the resemblance between Nell and his daughter.
5. Granny says (about Nell), "She has the voice of an angel."
6. Jack speaks the truth, but Hilton doesn't.
7. Nell is a major character, Vera a minor character.
8. In this play, the curtain rises at the start and falls at the end.
9. Vera and Nell have the same opinion of Hilton at the play's end.
10. In spite of the "ain't" in the title, the grammar in the play is fine.

Composition

Follow your teacher's instructions before completing *one* of these writing assignments.

1. Imagine you are a reporter on a local newspaper. You are sent to interview Hilton Hays when he climbs down from the tree. Write three questions you think would be most important to ask him.

2. Suppose that your class decided to present the play "He Ain't Done Right By Nell" in a school assembly. Which character would you choose to play? What would you do to prepare for the role? Tell how you would speak and use gestures to make the character come alive. Put your ideas in a short paragraph.

M. E. Kerr (Born 1927)

Have you read any books by M. E. Kerr lately? Here's a not-so-hidden secret: M. E. Kerr, the teenage favorite, is also Vin Packer, writer of hard-boiled mysteries. She is also Laura Winston, the romance writer. Sounds confusing? It isn't, really. These are all *pen names* of the talented Marijane Meaker. This selection is from her autobiography (life story), *Me Me Me Me Me*.

WHERE ARE YOU NOW, WILLIAM SHAKESPEARE?

by M. E. Kerr

▶ What does the word *love* mean to a ten-year-old? Can you remember? Here's a true story by a topflight writer who most definitely *can* remember.

My very first boyfriend was named William Shakespeare. This was his real name, and he lived over on Highland Hill, about a block from my house.

I often went to his house to get him, or I met him down in the empty lot on Alden Avenue, or over at Hoopes Park, where we caught sunfish and brought them from the pond in bottles of murky water with polliwogs.

Marijane is ten [my father wrote in his journal]. *She plays with boys and looks like one.*

This was true.

My arms and knees were full of scabs from falls out of trees and off my bicycle. I was happiest wearing the pants my brother'd grown out of, the vest to one of my father's business suits over one of my brother's old shirts, Indian moccasins, and a cap. Everything I said came out of the side of my mouth, and I strolled around with my fists inside my trouser pockets.

This did not faze Billy Shakespeare, whose eyes lit up when he saw me coming, and who readily agreed that when we married we'd name our first son Ellis, after my father, and not William after him.

"Because William Shakespeare is a funny name," I'd say.

"It isn't funny. It's just that there's a famous writer with the same name," he'd say.

"Do you agree to Ellis Shakespeare then?"

"Sure, if it's all right with your father."

"He'll be pleased," I'd tell Billy.

Around this time, I was always trying to think of ways to please my father. (The simplest way would have been to wear a dress and a big hair ribbon, stay out of trees, stop talking out of the side of my mouth, and act like a girl . . . but I couldn't have endured such misery even for him.)

Billy Shakespeare accepted the fact,

- murky (MUR kee) **clouded; unclear**
- journal (JUR nul) **daily record; diary**
- **stroll** (STROHL) **walk in a leisurely way**
- faze (FAYZ) **confuse; weaken**
- **endure** (en DOOR) **put up with**

66

early in our relationship, that my father was my hero. He protested only slightly when I insisted that the reason my father wasn't President of the United States was that my father didn't want to be.

That was what my father told me, when I'd ask him why he wasn't President. I'd look at him across the table at dinner, and think, He knows more than anybody knows, he's handsome, and he gets things done—so he ought to be President. If he was, I'd think, there'd be no problems in the world.

Sometimes I'd ask him: "Daddy, why aren't you President of the United States?"

His answer was always the same.

"I wouldn't want that job for anything. We couldn't take a walk without Secret Service men following us. Do you think we could go up to the lake for a swim by ourselves? No. There'd be Secret Service men tagging along. It'd ruin our lives. It'd end our privacy. Would you want that?"

Billy Shakespeare would say, "He's not President because nobody elected him President."

"He won't let anyone elect him," I'd answer. "He doesn't want Secret Service men around all the time."

"I'm not sure he could *get* elected," Billy would venture.

"He could get elected," I'd tell Billy. "He doesn't want to! We like our privacy."

"Okay." Billy'd give in a little. "But he never tried getting elected, so he really doesn't know if he could."

I'd wave that idea away with my dirty hands. "Don't worry. He'd be elected in a minute if he wanted to be. You don't know *him.*"

Billy Shakespeare's other rivals for my attention were movie stars. I'd write Clark Gable and Henry Fonda and Errol Flynn, and they'd send back glossy photos of themselves and sometimes letters, too.

These photographs and letters were thumbtacked to the fiberboard walls of a playhouse my father had built for me in our backyard.

When I did play with a girl, the game was always the same: getting dinner ready for our husbands. I had an old set

- **venture** (VEN chur) proceed onward; risk
- **rival** (RY vul) one who wants the same thing as another person
- fiberboard (FY bur bord) **building material made from compressed wood chips**

of dishes back in the playhouse, and my girl friend and I played setting the table for dinner. During this game, Billy Shakespeare was forgotten. When my husband came through the playhouse door, he would be one of the movie stars pinned to the wall.

I played this game with Dorothy Spencer, who lived behind our house.

She was a tall redhead who looked like a girl, and who always had it in her head to fix meat loaf with mashed potatoes for a movie star named Spencer Tracy.

I changed around a lot—the menu as well as the movie star—but Dorothy stuck to meat loaf with mashed for Spencer.

I'd be saying, "Well, Clark is a little late tonight and the turkey is going to be overdone," or "Gee, Henry isn't here yet and the ham is going to be dried up." But Dorothy would persist with "Spencer's going to love this meat loaf when he gets here. I'll wait until I hear his footsteps to mash the potatoes."

Billy Shakespeare was jealous of this game and tried his best to ruin it with reality.

He'd say, "What are two famous movie stars doing living in the same house?"

He'd say, "How come famous movie stars only have a one-room house with no kitchen?"

But Dorothy Spencer and I went on happily playing house, until the movie *Brother Rat* came to town.

That was when we both fell in love with the movie star Ronald Reagan.

- **persist** (pur SIST) say over and over; keep on going
- **reality** (ree AL uh tee) actual fact

Suddenly we were both setting the table for the same movie star—different menus, but the same husband.

"You've always stuck to meat loaf and mashed for Spencer!" I said angrily. "Now you want my Ronald!"

"He's not *your* Ronald," she said.

"It's my playhouse, though," I reminded her.

"But I won't play if I can't have Ronald," she said.

"We both can't have Ronald!" I insisted.

We took the argument to her mother, who told us to pretend Ronald Reagan was twins. Then we could both have him.

"He isn't twins, though," Dorothy said.

"And if he is," I put in, "I want the real Ronald, and not his twin."

Our game came to a halt, but our rivalry did not. Both of us had written to Ronald Reagan and were waiting for his reply.

"No matter what he writes her," I told Billy Shakespeare, "my letter from him will be better."

"You might not even get a letter," Billy said. "She might not get one either."

"She might not get one," I said, "but I will."

"You don't know that," Billy said.

"Do you want to know why I know I'll get one?" I asked him.

I made him cross his heart and hope to die if he told anyone what I'd done.

Billy was a skinny little kid with big eyes that always got bigger when I was about to confess to him something I'd done.

"Crossmyheartandhopetodie," he said very fast. "What'd you do?"

"You know that Ronald Reagan isn't like any of the others," I said.

"Because Dorothy Spencer likes him, too."

"That's got nothing to do with it!" I said. "He's just different. I never felt this way about another movie star."

"Why?"

"*Why?* I don't know why! That's the way love is."

"Love?" Billy said.

"Yes. What did you think made me write him that I was a crippled child, and had to go to see him in a wheelchair?"

"Oh migosh!" Billy exclaimed. "Oh migosh!"

"I had to get his attention somehow."

"Oh migosh!"

"Just shut up about it!" I warned him. "If word gets out I'll know it's you."

Dorothy Spencer was the first to hear from Ronald Reagan. She didn't get a letter, but she got a signed photograph.

"Since I heard from him first," she said, "he's my husband."

"Not in my playhouse!" I said.

"He wrote me back first," she said.

"Just wait," I said.

"I don't have to wait," she said. "I'm setting the table for him in my own house."

- **rivalry** (RY vul ree) **competition; trying to get the same thing as another**

"It's not even your house, it's your father's," I said. "At least when he's married to me, we'll have our own house."

"He's married to me now," she said.

"We'll see about that," I said.

I was beginning to get a panicky feeling as time passed and no mail came from Ronald Reagan. You'd think he'd write back to a crippled child first. . . . Meanwhile Dorothy was fixing him meat loaf and mashed at her place.

I had pictures of him cut out of movie magazines scotch-taped to my bedroom walls. I went to sleep thinking about him, wondering why he didn't care enough to answer me.

The letter and photograph from Ronald Reagan arrived on a Saturday.

I saw the Hollywood postmark and let out a whoop, thereby attracting my father's attention.

"What's all the excitement?"

I was getting the photograph out of the envelope. "I got a picture from Ronald Reagan!"

"Who's he?"

"Some movie star," my mother said.

By that time I had the photograph out. My heart began to beat nervously as I read the inscription at the bottom. "To a brave little girl, in admiration, Ronald Reagan."

"What does it say?" my father said.

"Nothing, it's just signed," I said, but he already saw what it said as he stood behind me looking down at it.

"Why are you a brave little girl?" he asked.

"How do I know?" I said.

"There's a letter on the floor," said my mother.

"That's my letter," I said, grabbing it.

"Why are you considered a brave little girl?" my father said again. "Why does *he* admire *you?*"

I held the letter to my chest. "Those are just things they say," I said.

"They say you're *brave?*" my father said.

"Brave or honest or any dumb thing," I said weakly.

"Read the letter, Marijane," said my father.

I read the letter to myself.

Dear Marijane,
   Thank you for your letter.
   Remember that a handicap can be
      a challenge.
   Always stay as cheerful as you are
      now.

                    Yours truly,
                    Ronald Reagan

"What does it say?" my mother asked.

"Just the usual," I said. "They never say much."

"Let me see it, brave little girl," my father said.

"It's to me."

"Marijane . . . " and he had his hand out.

After my father read the letter, and got the truth out of me concerning my correspondence with Ronald Reagan, he told me what I was to do.

What I was to do was to sit down immediately and write Ronald Reagan, telling him I had lied. I was to add that I thanked God for my good health. I was to return both the letter and the photograph.

No Saturday in my entire life had ever been so dark.

My father stood over me while I wrote the letter in tears, convinced that Ronald Reagan would hate me all his life for my deception. I watched through blurred eyes while my father took my letter, Ronald Reagan's letter, and the signed photograph, put them into a manila envelope, addressed it, sealed it, and put it in his briefcase to take to the post office.

For weeks and weeks after that, I dreaded the arrival of our postman. I was convinced a letter'd come beginning,

   Dear Marijane,
      How very disappointed I am in
         you. . . .

"I don't think he'll write back," Billy Shakespeare told me. "I don't think he'll want anything more to do with you."

That ended getting dinner for movie stars in my playhouse.

I told Dorothy Spencer that I'd outgrown all that.

Three years after I wrote Ronald Reagan that letter, I slumped way down in my seat in humiliation as I watched him lose a leg in the movie *King's Row.* . . . I was sure he thought of the little liar from upstate New York who'd pretended she was crippled.

- **correspondence** (kor uh SPON duns) exchange of letters
- **deception** (di SEP shun) trick; act of deceiving

Many, many years later, the man I always thought should be President of the United States was dead, and Ronald Reagan was President of the United States.

I didn't vote for him.

I heard Dorothy Spencer got married, and I envision her making meat loaf and mashed for her husband.

The only remaining question is, Where are you now,

William Shakespeare?

ALL THINGS CONSIDERED

1. The main character in the story is named (a) Ronald. (b) William. (c) Marijane.

2. Early in the selection, the writer describes herself as a (a) tomboy. (b) good athlete. (c) tall redhead.

3. The writer believes that her father could easily be (a) a movie actor. (b) a writer like Shakespeare. (c) president of the United States.

4. Dorothy Spencer and the writer spend a lot of time (a) arguing about Billy Shakespeare. (b) playing house. (c) riding bicycles and climbing trees.

5. The two girls also write to (a) people in politics. (b) each other. (c) movie stars.

6. Marijane lies when she writes that she is (a) old enough to vote. (b) a crippled child. (c) a friend of William Shakespeare.

7. The girl is punished for her lie by her (a) mother. (b) father. (c) friend Dorothy Spencer.

8. At the end of the story, Marijane dreads (a) her father's continuing anger. (b) that Dorothy may learn the truth. (c) getting a second letter from Ronald Reagan.

9. The selection was written (a) during the events it describes. (b) right after these events. (c) many, many years after the events.

10. The author's purpose in writing the selection is probably to (a) teach the reader not to lie. (b) make Shakespeare more popular. (c) tell a funny true story.

• envision (en VIZH un) **picture in the mind**

THINKING IT THROUGH

Discuss the following items in class.

1. An **autobiography** is a person's account of his or her own life. What do the three parts of the word—*auto, bio,* and *graph*— mean? Use a dictionary to help you understand the word parts.

2. We learn early in the selection that the author's father had kept a journal about the doings of family members. (a) Why might he have done this? (b) How might this journal have helped his daughter years later?

3. In your opinion, does the ten-year-old girl in the selection seem true to life? Support your answer with at least one fact from the story.

4. It is sometimes said that "girls should be girls" and "boys should be boys." Yet in real life, this is usually not so. Give one way in which the ten-year-old behaves like a (a) "girl" and like a (b) "boy."

5. The author writes Billy's "Crossmyheartandhopetodie" as one word. Why?

6. (a) How does the mother in the story try to arrange for both girls to have the same imaginary husband? (b) Does this make sense to you?

7. (a) What is the girl's punishment for the lie in the letter? (b) In your opinion, is this punishment fair? Explain.

8. In a sense, there are two "Marijanes" in the story. One is the ten-year-old girl. The other is the adult author. (a) Which Marijane did not know that Ronald Reagan would become president? (b) To which Marijane is the story a big laugh?

9. Think about the three pen names mentioned in the introduction. Clearly, *Vin Packer* sounds like a tough-guy writer. *Laura Winston* sounds romantic. *M. E. Kerr* is nearly the author's real name (Meaker). Suppose you wanted to become a famous pen-name author. What kind of stories would you choose to write? What right-sounding name do you think would lead to big sales?

10. The girl in the story seems to love at least four people: Billy Shakespeare, Dorothy Spencer, her father, and Ronald Reagan. (a) In your opinion, which of these loves depends mostly on her imagination? (b) Which love does she always try to please? (c) Which love is the most long lasting throughout her adult life? Explain your answers.

Inferences

An **inference** is an understanding of, or an idea about, something that is not stated directly by the writer. For instance, M. E. Kerr does not use terms like *miserable* or *embarrassed* to tell the reader directly how she felt when her parents learned about her letter to Reagan. Instead, she writes sentences like "No Saturday in my life had ever been so dark." By **reading between the lines** (making inferences), we can tell that the girl was very upset.

Unstated Ideas

1. Early in the selection, the author writes, "Everything I said came out of the side of my mouth, and I strolled around with my fists inside my trouser pockets." What kind of person was the author trying to look and act like?
2. The author never states directly that Dorothy Spencer was *more feminine* than she was. What gives the reader the idea that Dorothy was more feminine?
3. We are never told directly that Ronald Reagan was in a movie called *Brother Rat.* What leads us to make this inference?
4. The word *strict* is never used to describe the father. What leads us to make this inference?
5. In the short addition at the end of the selection, the author refers to "the man I always thought should be President of the United States. . . . " Who was this man?

Composition

Follow your teacher's instructions before completing *one* of these writing assignments.

1. Suppose you were a teacher preparing a short "Who Am I?" test on the selection. Write sentences starting with "I" about five characters. For instance, your first sentence might be "I told my daughter to pretend Ronald Reagan was twins." (Character: Dorothy's mother)
2. Pretend you are Marijane. Write the letter to Ronald Reagan that your father tells you to write. Before you begin, look back to see just what the letter *must* contain. Add anything else you want, to make it an appealing, interesting letter.

Gwendolyn Brooks (Born 1917)

Children at play below the elevated train structure on the south side of Chicago, Illinois, 1941

Like Carl Sandburg (see page 13), Gwendolyn Brooks deserves the title of people's poet. The poems of both writers are filled with insights into the kinds of people you might see on the street any day. The two poets were born among quite ordinary people (Brooks's father was a janitor). Both happened to grow up in Illinois. They were good students, but neither graduated from a four-year college. In later years, both went on to win the Pulitzer Prize, the highest honor for a writer. When Carl Sandburg died in 1967, the title Poet Laureate (honored poet) of Illinois was given to Gwendolyn Brooks.

Gwendolyn Brooks's mother had been a teacher. Her father loved great literature. The girl was urged to do well in school. She published her first poem at age 13. She wrote to Langston Hughes (see page 293), and he encouraged her to work on her writing. When success finally came, she tried hard to share it with others. Perhaps no one has done more to help young black writers get their names in print.

▶ Is a family really *a way of feeling?* With kids like Andre and Otto, you bet!

ANDRE

by Gwendolyn Brooks

I had a dream last night. I dreamed
I had to pick a Mother out.
I had to choose a Father too.
At first, I wondered what to do,
There were so many there, it seemed,
Short and tall and thin and stout.

But just before I sprang awake,
I knew what parents I would take.

And *this* surprised and made me glad:
They were the ones I always had!

OTTO

by Gwendolyn Brooks

It's Christmas Day. I did not get
The presents that I hoped for. Yet,
It is not nice to frown or fret.

To frown or fret would not be fair.
My Dad must never know I care
It's hard enough for him to bear.

WAYS OF KNOWING

1. The poem "Andre" makes a little dream-play out of the boy's feelings. If you had to state his feelings in a sentence, what would that sentence be?
2. In "Otto," exactly why didn't the boy get the presents he had wished for?
3. Compare the feelings of Andre and Otto about their families. In other words, in what ways are they alike?

VOCABULARY AND SKILL REVIEW

Before completing the exercises that follow, you may wish to review some of the **bold-faced** words on pages 50 to 72.

I.
1. A statement about the differences between two things is best called a (a) *contrast.* (b) *comparison.* (c) *deception.*

2. If you *strolled* to school this morning, it means that you (a) got a ride from someone. (b) walked fast. (c) took your own sweet time.

3. When people *endure* a lot of teasing, it means that they (a) like to tease others. (b) fight and tease back. (c) put up with it.

4. "Nothing *ventured,* nothing gained" is an old saying. In other words, (a) nothing risked, nothing won. (b) nothing bet, nothing lost. (c) nothing avoided, nothing gained.

5. A *melodrama* is a(n) (a) love story. (b) exaggerated play. (c) true-to-life drama.

6. Two students who compete for the best mark can correctly be called (a) *villains.* (b) *contrasts.* (c) *rivals.*

7. *Correspondence* always involves (a) seeing. (b) talking. (c) writing.

8. Magic has been called "the art of (a) *deception.*" (b) *reality.*" (c) *enduring.*"

9. "Come down to *reality*" means to (a) get in touch with actual facts. (b) forget a *rivalry.* (c) *persist* in your old ways.

10. It is not surprising that the word *journal* appears in the titles of many (a) records. (b) textbooks. (c) newspapers.

II. Read the two poems that follow and answer the questions.

WHAT IS ONCE LOVED

by Elizabeth Coatsworth

What is once loved
You will find
Is always yours
From that day.
Take it home
In your mind
And nothing ever
Can take it away.

SOME PEOPLE

by Rachel Field

Isn't it strange some people make
   You feel so tired inside,
Your thoughts begin to shrivel up
   Like leaves all brown and dried!

But when you're with some other ones,
   It's stranger still to find
Your thoughts as thick as fireflies
   All shiny in your mind!

1. In a way, both are love poems. Both also hit home with many readers. (a) Which stanza (of the three) has the most meaning for you? (b) Briefly describe an experience in your own life that your favorite stanza seems to describe.

2. Which poem makes the most use of *contrast*?

3. Is *comparison* also used in the poem you used to answer question 2? If so, how? Remember, comparison usually shows how two things are alike.

4. Do the poems demand that the reader make a lot of *inferences?* In other words, do the poets state their feelings directly, or do they expect the reader to look between the lines?

III. Read the two poems that follow and answer the questions.

CHRISTMAS MORNING I

by Carol Freeman

Christmas morning i
got up before the others and
ran
naked across the plank
floor into the front
room to see grandmama
sewing a new
button on my last year
ragdoll.

SPRING

by Carole Gregory Clemmons

the second man I love,
we'll find the wishbone
and make our wishes,
I won't even try for the strongest end,
because this time when the bone breaks
either way I'll be in.

1. Again, both can be called love poems. (a) Who is loved in "Christmas morning i"? (b) What does the author of "Spring" hope for in "the second man I love"?

2. How many *contrasts* can you find between the two poems? In other words, in what ways are they different? For instance, do the persons described in the poems seem to be the same age? Is the loved one in both poems remembered from the past?

3. Why might Carol Freeman have chosen to refer to herself with a small "i"?

4. Both poems demand that the reader make *inferences*. "Spring" is the more demanding of the two. The last three lines, especially, do not state the poet's real meaning directly. What is this real meaning? Try to put it in a sentence.

5. Compare the poem "Otto" on page 76 with "Christmas morning i." Think about how each child feels on Christmas morning and how he or she handles those feelings.

UNIT REVIEW

I. Match the terms in Column A with their definitions in Column B.

A	B
1. climax	a) opposite forces acting against each other
2. stanza	
3. plot	b) understanding of something not directly stated
4. conflict	
5. coincidence	c) exciting high point at end of story
6. inference	d) made-up literature, not reported from real life
7. oral interpretation	
	e) group of lines in a poem
8. autobiography	f) a person's account of his or her life
9. comparison	g) examination of ways in which two or more things are alike
10. fiction	
	h) the act of reading aloud with expression
	i) skeleton, or framework, around which a play or a story is built
	j) two or more related events that accidentally happen at the same time

II. As the introduction to this unit states, the word *love* is hard to define. Some dictionaries offer 15 or more meanings. Here are just four of them.

1. Romantic love, an overpowering feeling for a person of the opposite sex

2. Deep affection, as for a parent, child, or friend

3. Concern for the well-being of others, as a love of one's neighbors

4. Strong liking for something, as for a certain sport, job, or food

This unit, "Looking at Love," contains examples of all four definitions. Use a separate piece of paper to do the following: For each definition, name one selection that has an example of that type of love. First, write the title of the selection. Then write the definition that applies to it. Next, write at least one sentence showing how that particular kind of love is illustrated in that selection.

III. It's sometimes fun to pretend that stories are real happenings that might be reported in newspapers. For instance, the *Daily Blah* might have covered "A Retrieved Reformation" like this:

EX-CON SAVES DOOMED CHILD

ELMORE, ARK.—James Valentine, an ex-convict and a master safe-cracker, pried open a bank vault here yesterday to save the life of a trapped five-year-old girl.

"I was only doing the right thing," Valentine told reporters. . . .

On a separate piece of paper, write a headline. Then write a one-sentence summary for any other selection in this unit.

Following each Unit Review in this book, there is a selection for you to practice reading aloud. Reading aloud before a group helps you develop self-confidence and improve your acting ability. Most of all, it can be fun. Try to keep these tips in mind.

1. Hold the book in one hand, or put it on something in front of you. This leaves at least one hand free for gestures.
2. Start by feeling comfortable and confident. Speak loudly and clearly. If you happen to make a little mistake, forget it. Get on with your acting.
3. If the selection calls for you to play a role, pretend actually *to be* that character. Soon the gestures, the expressions on your face, your tone of voice—all will come naturally.
4. Don't be afraid to play either a male or a female role. This is all part of the fun.
5. Rehearse. Rehearse. Rehearse. Put everything you have into the act—your voice, your body, your eyes.

The selection that follows is a **monologue** (MON uh lawg), or an entertaining talk by a single speaker. Start by reading the monologue silently, trying actually to see and to be the character in action.

Dear Mr. or Ms. Loveletter

(Enter carrying a bunch of letters. Sit down at the desk and spread them out in front of you. Arrange to have a member of the class introduce you as Mr. or Ms. Loveletter, a newspaper writer.)

Good evening, ladies and gentlemen. I am here to solve your love problems. Your problems are my specialty. I probably know more about your problems than you know yourselves. Why, every day I get hundreds of letters like these.

(Read from a letter) "Dear Mr. (Ms.) Loveletter: A girl in a far off country writes that she is as graceful as an antelope, as busy as a bee, and as patient as an elephant. Do you think I should go to visit the girl?" *(look up, shrug)* You'd save money by visiting a zoo.

(Read from another letter) "Dear Love-Expert: My boy friend insists on calling me by the pet name of Snooky. Snooky, Snooky, Snooky—all day long he calls me Snooky. If there's anything I hate, it's the name Snooky." *(look up, wave letter)* It's signed—"Snooky." *(shrug, toss letter aside)*

(Read) "My girl friend owns an oil well, but I am very poor. What difference do you think this makes?" *(look up, shrug)* Offhand, I'd say about $100,000.

(Read) "One of my boy friends hasn't called me for about six weeks. My question is—how can I keep it this way?" *(shrug, crumple letter)*

(Read) "My boy friend insists on showing off by walking down the street on his hands. What should I do?" *(look up)* The least you could do is buy him a pair of heavy gloves.

(Read) "My girl friend insists on buying me a pair of heavy gloves. . . ." *(Frown at letter, toss it aside)*

(Read) "The other day I met a charming man who says he's madly in love with me. But I think he cares only for my money. How can I be sure?" *(look up)* Just send *me* your money and see what happens.

(Read) "Dear Ms. (Mr.) Loveletter: Whatever gave you the idea that you're an expert on love letters?" *(rise, shrug)* Frankly, I haven't the slightest idea! *(bow, exit)*

WRITING YOUR OWN PLOT

The photograph shown was taken not long ago in a stadium in a large city. Suppose the photo had been taken to illustrate a *short story.* What might be the *plot* of the story?

Start with the present time and ask yourself some questions. Then list the questions with possible answers. What's happening in the picture? For instance, study the girl. What's her name? How old is she? Why did she bring her pet rabbit? Who is the man on the left? Is he related to the girl? What might the uniformed guard be saying? Think of other questions. Then answer them in detail.

Next, think about the past and the future. Has the ball team been winning or losing? Is the girl a fan of the team? Most important, what will happen in today's game? What will be the girl's reaction? Answer these questions, too. Add them to your list.

When you have decided on the past, present, and future, you are ready to plan the plot of a story on a piece of paper. (1) List the event that led up to the scene shown in the picture. (2) List details you might use to tell what happens at the game. (3) Describe what might happen at an exciting *climax* near or at the end of the story.

"I Dream a World" is by Langston Hughes, the famous poet (with William Grant Still). Vanessa Howard, the author of "Reflections," was a junior-high student at the time she wrote the poem. (Answer to question one, page 33)

U N I T · 2

TOWARD THE TWILIGHT ZONE

All that we see or seem
Is but a dream within a dream.
　　　　　—Edgar Allan Poe

Read Poe's words again. Try to think your way into their meaning. Could they be true? Could all our *see*ing really be *seem*ing? Could everything that we seem to do really be just a dream?

In fact, all of us live in a real world of the *here* and *now*. Some stories, however, let us enter a different and unusual world. Then, we move toward the twilight zone.

Anything can happen in the twilight zone! In this unit, you'll meet some spirits and even a visitor from outer space. Get ready to stretch your imagination to the snapping point.

85

APPOINTMENT AT NOON

by Eric Frank Russell

▶ Henry Curran was a tiger of a man—always on the go. He was rich and powerful. He pushed buttons and people jumped. He shouted and people shook. Then, one day, he finally met his match. . . .

Henry Curran was big, busy, and successful. He had no patience with people who weren't successful. He had the build of a fighter and the soul of a tiger. His time was worth a thousand bucks an hour. He knew of nobody who was worth more.

And crime did not pay? "Bah!" said Henry Curran.

The law of the jungle paid off. Henry Curran had learned that nice people are soft people, and that smiles are made to be slapped.

Entering his large office with the fast, heavy step of a big man in fighting shape, Henry threw his hat onto a hook. He glanced at the wall clock. He noted that it was ten minutes to twelve.

Seating himself in the large chair behind his desk, he kept his eyes on the door. His wait lasted about ten seconds. Frowning at the thought of it, Curran reached over and pushed a red button on his big desk.

"What's wrong with you?" he snapped when Miss Reed came in. "You get worse every day. Old age creeping over you or something?"

She paused. She was tall, neat, and steady. She faced him across the desk, her eyes showing a touch of fear. Curran hired to work for him only people he knew too much about.

"I'm sorry, Mr. Curran, I was—"

"Never mind the excuse. Be faster—or else! Speed's what I like. SPEED—SEE?"

"Yes, Mr. Curran."

"Has Lolordo phoned in yet?"

"No, Mr. Curran."

"He should be through by now if everything went all right." He looked at the clock again, tapping angrily on his desk. "If he's made a mess of it and the mouthpiece comes on, tell him to forget about Lolordo. He's in no position to talk, anyway. A little time in jail will teach him not to be stupid."

"Yes, Mr. Curran. There's an old—"

"Shut up till I've finished. If Michaelson calls up and says the *Firefly* got through, phone Voss and tell him without delay! And I mean without delay! That's important!" He thought for a moment. Then he finished, "There's that meeting downtown at twelve-twenty. God knows how long it will go on. If they want trouble, they can have it! If anyone asks, you don't know where I am. You don't expect me back before four."

"But, Mr. Curran—"

"You heard what I said. Nobody sees me before four."

"There's a man already here," she got out in an apologetic voice. "He said you have an appointment with him at two minutes to twelve."

"And you fell for a joke like that?" He studied her with a cutting smile.

"I can only repeat what he said. He seemed quite sincere."

"That's a change," snapped Curran. "Sincerity in *my* office? He's got the wrong address. Go tell him to spread himself across the tracks."

"I said you were out and didn't know when you would return. He took a seat and said he'd wait because you would be back at ten to twelve."

Without knowing it, both suddenly stared at the clock. Curran lifted an arm and looked at his wristwatch to check the instrument on the wall.

"That's what the scientific bigbrains would call precognition. I call it a lucky guess. One minute either way would have made him wrong. That guy ought to bet money on the horses." He made a gesture of dismissal. "Push him out—or do I have to get the boys to do it for you?"

- **mouthpiece** (MOUTH pees) slang for criminal lawyer
- **apologetic** (uh POL uh JET ik) filled with apology; suggesting that one is sorry
- **sincerity** (sin SER uh tee) honesty; quality of being sincere
- **precognition** (pree kog NISH un) knowledge of future events

"That wouldn't be necessary. He is old and blind."

"I don't care if he's armless and legless—that's *his* tough luck. Give him the rush."

Obediently she left. A few moments later she was back. She had the sorrowful look of a person whose job forced her to face Curran's anger.

"I'm terribly sorry, Mr. Curran. He insists that he has a date with you for two minutes to twelve. He is to see you about a personal matter of great importance."

Curran scowled at the wall. The clock said four minutes to twelve. He spoke with purpose.

"I know no blind man and I don't forget appointments. Throw him down the stairs."

She hesitated, standing there wide-eyed. "I'm wondering whether—"

"Out with it!"

"Whether he's been sent to you by someone else, someone who'd rather he couldn't tell who you were by sight."

He thought it over and said, "Could be. You use your brains once in a while. What's his name?"

"He won't say."

"Nor state his business?"

"No."

"H'm! I'll give him two minutes. If he's trying to get money for some church or something he'll go out through the window. Tell him my time is valuable and show him in."

She went away and brought back the visitor. She gave him a chair. The door closed quietly behind her. The clock said three minutes before the hour.

Curran sat back and looked at his guest, finding him tall, thin, and white-haired. The old man's clothes were black, a deep, somber black. They set off the bright, blue, unseeing eyes staring from his colorless face.

Those strange eyes were the old man's most noticeable feature. They were odd, as if somehow they could look *into* the things they could not look at. And they were sorry—sorry for what they saw.

For the first time in his life, Henry Curran felt a little alarmed.

- **scowl** (SKOUL) frown and look angry
- **somber** (SOM bur) gloomy and dark; very sad

He said, "What can I do for you?"

"Nothing," replied the other. "Nothing at all."

His voice was like an organ. It was low, no more than a whisper, and with its sounding a queer coldness came over the room. He sat there unmoving and staring at whatever a blind man can see. The coldness increased, became bitter. Curran shivered despite himself. He frowned and got a hold on himself.

"Don't take up my time," advised Curran. "State your business or get out."

"People don't take up time. Time takes up people."

"Just what do you mean? Who are you?"

"You know who I am. Every man is a shining sun to himself, until he is dimmed by his dark companion."

"You're not funny," said Curran, freezing.

"I am never funny."

The tiger light blazed in Curran's eyes as he stood up. He placed a thick, firm finger near his desk button.

"Enough of this nonsense! What d'you want?"

Suddenly holding out a lengthless, dimensionless arm, the man whispered sadly, "You!"

And Death took him.

At exactly two minutes to twelve.

   • **dimensionless** (duh MEN shun les) **without dimensions, or size that can be measured in length, height, or width**

ALL THINGS CONSIDERED

1. Miss Reed works for Curran and obeys him because (a) he pays her a double salary. (b) she is a close relative. (c) he knows something about her that she doesn't want others to know.

2. Curran's discussion of possible phone calls shows that he (a) is involved in criminal activities. (b) never uses the phone himself. (c) is worried about death.

3. Miss Reed has difficulty telling Curran about (a) the morning mail. (b) an old man waiting to see him. (c) a broken typewriter.

4. The appointment is not actually "at noon" but at (a) 11:58 A.M. (b) 12:02 P.M. (c) 4:00 P.M.

5. Curran finally agrees to see his visitor because he (a) suddenly remembers making the appointment. (b) feels sorry for any blind person. (c) thinks the old man may have been sent by someone important.

6. The old man is dressed in (a) bright blue. (b) black. (c) white.

7. The most noticeable thing about the old man is his (a) eyes. (b) hair. (c) smile.

8. The sentence "Time takes up people" means that (a) killing time is wrong. (b) most people take too much time. (c) after a certain period, death comes to everyone.

9. The old man represents (a) the force of law. (b) Curran's guilt. (c) death.

10. Suppose Miss Reed goes back into her boss's office at noon. It is reasonable to believe she will discover that (a) Curran is dead. (b) the visitor is dead. (c) nothing unusual happened.

THINKING IT THROUGH

Discuss the following items in class.

1. (a) At what point in your reading did you know who the old man really was? (b) Look back at the last section of the story. What are some helpful clues?

2. The old man's eyes are described as "odd, as if somehow they could look *into* the things they could not look at." What does this mean?

3. The meaning of the story can be expressed quite simply in a short sentence. On a separate sheet of paper, try to put that meaning in the best complete sentence you can write.

4. What do you think would have happened if Curran had refused to see his visitor?

Literary Skills

Characterization

A character, of course, is someone in a story or a play. When you finish reading a story, you know pretty well what the main characters are like. How do you know? The author's *characterization* has brought them to life for you.

The word **characterization** (kar ik tur i ZAY shun) means the ways in which authors bring the people in their stories to life. There are four main methods of characterization:

A. The direct statements made by the author.
(*Tizzie was a dishonest person.*)
B. The speeches and the thoughts of the character.
(*"I never lie to anyone," Tizzie said.*)
C. The actions of the character.
(*Tizzie avoided Ms. Breen's stern glance.*)
D. The reactions of other characters to the character.
(*"Tizzie, I think that's just another lie of yours," Ms. Breen barked.*)

I. Here are five items from "Appointment at Noon." On a separate sheet of paper, write A, B, C, or D to show which method of characterization is used.

1. Henry Curran was big, busy, and successful.
2. She [Miss Reed] faced him across the desk, her eyes showing a touch of fear.
3. "That's a change," snapped Curran. "Sincerity in *my* office? He's got the wrong address."
4. He [Curran] looked at the clock again, tapping angrily on his desk.
5. A few minutes later she [Miss Reed] was back. She had the sorrowful look of a person whose job forced her to face Curran's anger.

II. Now look back at the story. Find four other items you could use as examples of methods A, B, C, and D above. Write them on your paper.

Composition

Follow your teacher's instructions before completing *one* of these writing assignments.

1. Suppose you were telling a friend about "Appointment at Noon." On a separate sheet of paper, write three sentences that accurately describe different sides of Henry Curran.

2. The easiest method of characterization for an author to use is A, to simply tell the reader directly what a character is like. Write a short paragraph explaining why most good writers try to avoid this method by using the others instead. (Hint: Think about what a story would be like if only method A were used.)

Edgar Allan Poe (1809-1849)

Edgar Allan Poe, like O. Henry, (see page 2), lived a life that was a story in itself. It is not surprising that his specialty was the horror story. That a life such as his could produce a writer of great genius seems incredible.

Edgar Poe never knew his father, an actor who walked out on his family and was not heard from again. Death claimed Poe's mother when the boy was two. He was adopted by a man named John Allan, but father and son never got along well. Later, Poe was forced to drop out of college because of gambling debts. He was a talented editor, but he kept losing jobs because of a drinking problem. His hair-raising stories did not bring in enough money for him to avoid poverty and hunger. One day in 1849, he was found in a weakened, insane condition on the floor of a tavern in Baltimore, Maryland. Four days later he was dead.

The subject of death fascinated Poe. In his stories, people are buried alive, and spirits of the dead return to take over the bodies of the living. Horror follows horror. Corpse follows corpse. As you read "The Oval Portrait," remember that in a way, *death* became Poe's *way of life* as a writer.

THE OVAL PORTRAIT

by Edgar Allan Poe

▶ A gloomy old castle in Europe. . . . Midnight candles flickering among the shadows. . . . And on the wall, a painting of a young woman that looked more real than life itself.

My servant and I forced our way into the old castle. It was one of those piles of gloom and grandeur that have long frowned among the mountains of Europe. I was wounded. So it was a better place to pass a night than in the open air. The castle appeared to have been only recently abandoned.

We settled into one of the smaller apartments. It lay in a distant tower of the building. Its decorations were rich, yet tattered and old. Its walls were hung with tapestry. There were a great number of modern paintings in frames of rich gold. These paintings hung not only on the larger walls but in the many nooks and corners. I took a great interest in these paintings, perhaps due to my excited state of mind.

I told Pedro to close the heavy curtains at the windows. It was already night. I told him to light the tongues in the tall candles that stood by the head of my bed, and to throw open the heavy black curtains that surrounded the bed. I wanted to study the pictures and read a small notebook I found on the pillow. The notebook told the history of the paintings.

Long, long I read—and long, long I

- **oval** (OH vul) egg-shaped
- **grandeur** (GRAN jur) greatness
- **tapestry** (TAP is tree) cloth with a picture or design woven into it, used as a wall hanging
- **nook** (NOOK) place set off from the rest of a room

gazed. The hours flew by. Deep midnight came. The position of the candle holder displeased me. I reached out with difficulty. I placed it so that it would throw more light upon the pages.

But the action had an effect I had not expected. The light of the many candles (for there *were* many) now fell upon a previously hidden nook. I thus saw in clear light a picture I had not noticed before. It was the portrait of a lovely girl, almost a woman. I glanced at the painting hurriedly. I then closed my eyes. I do not know why I did this. I ran over in my mind my reason for shutting them. It was a sudden movement to gain time for thought. I wanted to make sure my eyes were not fooling me. I wanted to calm my imagination for a more careful look. In a few moments I again looked at the painting.

The portrait was that of a lovely girl.

It was a head-and-shoulders painting. Something artists call a *vignette.* The arms, the head, and even the ends of the radiant hair melted softly into the vague shadows of the background. The frame was oval. It was richly covered with gold. I had never seen a finer painting. Yet it was not the skill of the painter nor the beauty of the face that excited me. Nor had my imagination mistaken the head for that of a living person. I knew that it was a painting. I lay for an hour, half sitting, half lying down with my eyes always on the portrait.

At length I fell back into the bed. I understood what had alarmed me. I had found the portrait to be *absolutely lifelike.* It wasn't just a picture! It was the girl herself! This fact first startled me, then amazed me, then confused me. I had a deep sense of wonder. I replaced the candle holder to its former position. The painting was shut from view. I reached for the notebook that discussed the history of the paintings. I turned to the section on the oval portrait. I there read the strange words that follow:

She was a maiden of the rarest beauty. She was as full of happiness as she was beautiful. Evil was the day when she saw the painter. And evil was the day when she loved and wedded him. He loved his art and could not love another.

She was all light and smiles. She

- **vignette** (vin YET) small, pleasing picture that shades off gradually into the surrounding paper
- **vague** (VAYG) unclear

was as playful as a fawn. She loved all the things except the Art that was her rival. She dreaded the paints and brushes and other things that deprived her of the face and friendship of her lover. It was thus a terrible thing for her to hear the artist speak of his desire to paint his young bride.

Because she was sweet and obedient, she sat sweetly for many weeks. She sat in the high dark tower room. The light dripped in only from a single window overhead. She longed for the out-of-doors. But he, the painter, took glory in his work. He went on from hour to hour, from day to day. He was excited, and wild, and moody. He became lost in his own thoughts and did not think of his bride.

The artist would not see that the light that fell from the single window was withering the health and spirits of his bride. She looked worse and worse to all but him.

Yet she smiled without complaining, because she saw how much the painter took a pleasure in his job. She loved him, yet grew daily weaker and weaker. Some people who saw the portrait thought it was proof that the artist loved her. He painted her surprisingly well. They talked in low words of its lifelike beauty.

At length, as the work drew to a close, the artist allowed no other people to the tower. For the painter had grown wild with the love of his work. He rarely turned his eyes from the portrait. He rarely looked at the face of his wife. He would not see that the colors that he spread upon the portrait were drawn from the cheeks of her who sat beside him.

Many weeks had passed. Little remained to do. There was only one brush upon the mouth and one spot of color upon the eye. The spirit of the lady leaped up, like the flame in a dying candle. And then the artist applied the brush. The spot was placed.

For one moment the artist stood spellbound before the portrait he had painted. In the next moment, still gazing at the portrait, the artist began to shake and grow very pale. He cried out in a loud voice, "This is indeed Life itself!" He turned suddenly to look at his wife. *She was dead!*

ALL THINGS CONSIDERED

1. The narrator, or the person who tells the story, takes shelter in the castle because he is (a) very familiar with it. (b) invited in by the owner. (c) wounded.
2. The walls of the apartment are covered with (a) moss and slime. (b) tapestries and paintings. (c) designs in brilliant colors.

- **rival** (RY vul) one who wants the same thing as another
- **spellbound** (SPEL bound) seeming to be caught in a spell

3. The servant is told to "light the tongues in the tall candles. . . ." The word *tongues* probably means (a) the wicks of the candles. (b) the candlesticks. (c) human tongues.

4. The notebook found on the pillow contains the history of the (a) castle. (b) tapestries. (c) paintings.

5. The narrator does not notice the oval portrait at first because it is (a) in a dark corner. (b) just a head-and-shoulders painting. (c) shaped like an egg.

6. The narrator's *first* reaction upon seeing the portrait is to (a) close his eyes. (b) cry out in wonder. (c) blink in disbelief.

7. What most impresses the narrator about the portrait is (a) the painter's skill. (b) the young woman's beauty. (c) its lifelike quality.

8. One point of the story is that the painter loves (a) death more than life. (b) his art more than anything else. (c) money more than art.

9. At the end, the young woman (a) forgives the painter. (b) is delighted with her portrait. (c) is dead.

10. The main point of the story is that (a) the artist murders his wife. (b) the artist punishes his wife. (c) the life goes out of the wife and into the painting.

THINKING IT THROUGH

Discuss the following items in class.

1. "Some people who saw the portrait thought it was proof that the artist loved her." (a) Do you think these people were correct? (b) If not, what *was* the portrait proof of?

2. The author of the notebook seems to praise the young woman for continuing to love the painter and not complaining. (a) Do you agree that the young woman deserves praise? (b) If not, what is the notebook writer telling us (between the lines) about the social standing of women in those days?

3. "The Oval Portrait" is really two stories. First comes an "outer story" about the narrator. Then comes an "inner story" about the artist and his bride. The inner story is certainly the more important. In fact, the author could have told it by itself, without using the outer story. (a) Why do you think Edgar Allan Poe chose to write the outer story? (b) How does it help to have the tale of the painter and his bride come from a notebook found by the narrator? (Hint: An inner and an outer story are often used for mysterious tales.)

Literary Skills

Setting

What do we mean by the **setting** of a story? The *place* it happens, you might answer. That's a good reply, but it's usually more than that. The setting also includes the *time,* since the same place can differ greatly from one time period to another. The setting includes certain *natural events* as well, such as the weather, a mountain slide, or a tree falling across the road.

The following questions are about "The Oval Portrait" in terms of its setting.

1. (a) Where does the story happen? (b) Would the story be different if the setting were a modern house in a big city?
2. (a) When, would you say, does the story take place? (b) Why is this time period better for the story than the present?
3. What event has happened to the narrator that forces him into the building?
4. (a) What part of the setting (an object) does the narrator find on the pillow? (b) Would it be possible to tell the story without it?
5. (a) What is odd about the shape of the room? (b) How does this add to the story?
6. (a) At what hour does the climax of the *outer story* occur? (b) Why is this a better time for the climax than, say, midday?

Composition

Follow your teacher's instructions before completing *one* of these writing assignments.

1. Suppose the story had no title. Think of three possible titles of your own and write them on a sheet of paper. Place a check mark beside the one you think is best. Use two checks if you think your title is better than the author's.
2. Write a paragraph entitled "The Importance of the Setting in 'The Oval Portrait.'" Include *at least* the answers you gave to questions 1–6, above.

VOCABULARY AND SKILL REVIEW

Before completing the exercises that follow, you may wish to review the **bold-faced** words on pages 87 to 95.

I. On a separate sheet of paper, write the term in each line that means the same, or nearly the same, as the word in *italics*.

1. *vignette:* musical number, small picture, glass, bird
2. *grandeur:* contest, noble woman, greatness, applause
3. *apologetic:* truly sorry, shaky, diseased, intelligent
4. *tapestry:* tape measure, instrument, magic, wall hanging
5. *sincerity:* social skill, coolness, funny feeling, honesty
6. *vague:* dishonest, unclear, athletic, harsh
7. *scowl:* use a farm tool, be fierce, suggest, frown
8. *rival:* competitor, unpleasant person, kind of writing, small boat
9. *somber:* reddish, gloomy, strange, amusing
10. *dimensionless:* not measurable, insane, unspoken, foolish

II. As you've learned, *plot, character,* and *setting* must all work together in a good short story. If one of these three is weak, the whole story will be weak. In fact, if you take a well-known plot and deliberately change the characters or the setting, the result is often laughable. Read the following news story:

Food is not wasted at the John Sprat home, 127 Main Street. Sprat, 36, eats only lean meat. His wife, Dora, 32, favors fat. "This way, we never have any leftovers," Sprat told reporters.

What has happened here? An old nursery rhyme has simply been transferred to modern times. It still has the "Jack Sprat" who "would eat no fat." It still has a wife who "would eat no lean." However, the setting has been moved from the never-never land of nonsense to a modern American city. Characterization has been added in the form of a quote from Sprat in present-day language.

Two more examples follow. Read the news stories and answer the questions on a separate sheet of paper.

NAB BLONDE, 8, AS PORRIDGE THIEF

An eight-year-old, blue-eyed blonde has been turned over to local juvenile authorities on charges of malicious mischief.

The complaint was signed yesterday by Fred Bear, father of a family of three who live in a wooded area on the city's R. F. D. route. Bear charges that the youngster broke into his house while the family was out walking, stole food, broke his child's chair, and ransacked the bedrooms.

The suspect ran from the house when the Bear family returned from their walk. Bear later identified her from mug shots.

Police said the girl may be responsible for a series of rural break-ins during the past two months.

1. The original story is (a) "Cinderella." (b) "Goldilocks and the Three Bears." (c) "Little Red Riding Hood."
2. How has the vague setting of the original story been changed? Try to think of at least two ways.
3. How have the characters been changed? Remember, this is a modern news story about Fred Bear and his family.
4. In this case, the plot has been changed as well. How?

- **malicious mischief** (mul LISH us MIS chif) **intentional damage to or destruction of another's property**
- **ransack** (RAN sak) **search furiously**
- **mug** (MUG) **person's face**

99

Two of three pig brothers were devoured by a wolf yesterday. The tragedy is expected to spur a full-scale probe of substandard house-construction practices in the city.

The wolf, still at large, evidently destroyed the new homes of the victims before murdering them. Detectives sifting through the wreckage this morning said they have found evidence that the dwellings did not meet local building-code requirements.

A third pig brother, identified as a stonemason, told police that the wolf also made an attempt on his life. The pig escaped injury.

The surviving brother vowed revenge and told authorities that he would capture the wolf in a large pot when the wolf "tries to come down my chimney." He also claimed that the wolf "huffed and puffed and blew down" the homes of his brothers.

The pig has now been confined for observation.

5. What is the original story? If you can't think of the exact title, do your best.

6. (a) In your opinion, what has been changed most—the plot, the characters, or the setting? (b) Give one example of such a change.

7. The story lacks a headline. Think of a good one. Write it in big block letters on your paper.

8. Here's a harder question: What does the story have to do with the theme of this unit? The last paragraph of the story may help you.

- **devour** (di VOUR) eat up greedily
- **probe** (PROBE) investigation
- **evidently** (EV i dunt lee) clearly
- **confine** (kun FYN) shut in

100

OF MISSING PERSONS

by Jack Finney

▶ Imagine a world where everyone lives a happy life. Impossible, you say? Well, suppose someone offered you a ticket to just such a place. What would you do?

*W*alk in as though it were an ordinary travel agency. That's what the stranger I'd met at a party told me. *Ask a few ordinary questions about a vacation or something. Then hint about The Folder. But whatever you do, don't mention it straight out. Wait till he brings it up. If he doesn't, you might as well forget it. If you can. Because you'll never see it. You're not the type, that's all. He'll just look at you as though he doesn't know what you're talking about.*

I went over it all in my mind, again and again. But what seems possible at midnight at a party isn't easy to believe on a raw, rainy day. I felt like a fool, searching the store fronts for the street number. It was noon, West 42nd Street, New York. I walked with my head bent into the slanting rain. This was hopeless.

Anyway, I thought, who am I to see The Folder, even if there is one? Charley Ewell, a young guy who works in a bank. A teller. I don't like the job. I don't make much money, and I never will. I've lived here for over three years and haven't many friends. I see too many movies, and I'm sick of meals alone in diners. I have ordinary abilities, looks, and thoughts. Do I qualify?

Now I saw it, the address in the 200 block, an old office building. I pushed into the dirty lobby. The name was second on the list, "Acme Travel Agency" between "A-1 Copy Shop" and "Ajax Magic Supplies." I pressed the bell for the rickety elevator. I almost turned and left—this was crazy.

But upstairs, the Acme office was bright and clean. Behind a counter stood a tall man with a dignified look. He nodded at me to come in. My heart was pumping—he fitted the description exactly.

"Yes, United Air Lines," he was saying into the phone. "Flight"— he glanced at a paper—"seven-oh-three. I suggest you get there forty minutes early."

I waited, leaning on the counter, looking around. He was the man, all right. Yet this was just an ordinary travel agency. Big bright posters on the walls. Racks full of folders. Again I felt like a fool.

"Can I help you?" he said.

"Yes." Suddenly I was terribly nervous. "I'd like to—get away," I said. You fool, that's too fast, I told myself. Don't rush it! I watched in a kind of panic, but he didn't flick an eyelash.

"Well, there are a lot of places to go," he said politely. He brought out a folder: "Fly to Buenos Aires—Another World!"

I looked at it long enough to be polite. Then I just shook my head. I was afraid to talk, afraid I'd say the wrong thing.

"Something quieter, maybe?" He brought out another folder: "The Unspoiled Forests of Maine." "Or"—he laid a third folder on the counter—"Bermuda is nice just now."

I decided to risk it. "No," I said. "What I'm really looking for is a new place to live." I stared right into his eyes. "For the rest of my life." Then my nerve failed me, and I tried to think of a way to get out of it.

But he only smiled and said, "I don't know why we can't advise you on that." He leaned forward. "What are you looking for? What do you want?"

I held my breath, then said it. "Escape."

"From what?"

"Well—" Now I wasn't sure. I'd never put it into words before. "From New York, I'd say. And all cities. From worry. And fear. And the things I read in my newspapers. From loneliness." And then I couldn't stop, though I knew I was talking too much. "From never doing what I really want to do or having much fun. From selling my days just to stay alive." I looked straight at him and said softly, "From the world."

Now he was studying my face, staring at me. I knew that in a moment he'd shake his head. "Mister," he'd say, "you better get to a doctor." But he didn't. He kept staring. He was a big man, his lined face very intelligent, very kind. He looked the way ministers should look. He looked the way all fathers should look.

He lowered his gaze. I had the sudden idea that he was learning

---

- **Buenos Aires** (BWAY nus AIR eez) **capital city of Argentina in South America**
- **Bermuda** (bur MEW duh) **islands in the Atlantic Ocean, east of South Carolina, popular with tourists**
- **nerve** (NURV) **courage**

a great deal about me. More than I knew myself. Suddenly he smiled. "Do you like people?" he asked. "Tell the truth. I'll know if you aren't."

"Yes. It isn't easy for me to relax, though, and be myself, and make friends."

He nodded. "Would you say you're a pretty decent kind of man?"

"I guess so. I think so." I shrugged.

"Why?"

This was hard to answer. "Well—at least when I'm not, I'm usually sorry about it."

He grinned. "You know," he said casually, "we sometimes get people in here who seem to be looking for pretty much what you are. So just as a sort of little joke—"

I couldn't breathe. This was what I'd been told he would say if he thought I might do.

"—we've had a little folder printed. Simply for our own amusement, you understand. And for a few customers like you. So I'll have to ask you to look at it here, if you're interested."

I could barely whisper, "I'm interested."

He brought out a long, thin folder, the same size and shape as the others. He slid it over the counter toward me.

I looked at it, pulling it closer with a fingertip—I was almost afraid to touch it. The cover was dark blue, the shade of a night sky. Across the top in white letters it said, "Visit Enchanting Verna!" The cover was sprinkled with stars. In the lower left was a globe, the world, with clouds around it. At the upper right, just under the word "Verna" was a star larger and brighter than the others. Across the bottom it said, "Romantic Verna, where life is the way it *should* be."

> • **casually** (KAZH oo uh lee) **as if it were not important; in an off-hand way**

Inside were pictures, so beautiful they looked real. In one picture you could see dew shining on the grass, and it looked wet. In another, a tree trunk seemed to curve out of the page. It was a shock to touch it and feel paper instead of bark. Tiny human faces, in a third picture, seemed about to speak.

I studied a large picture taken from the top of a hill. The valley was covered with forest. Curving through it, far below, ran a stream, blue as the sky with spots of foaming white. It seemed that if you'd only look closely, you'd be sure to see that stream move. In clearings beside the stream were rough cabins. Under the picture were the words, "The Colony."

"Fun fooling around with a thing like that," the man said. "Eases the boredom. Nice-looking place, isn't it?"

I could only nod, staring at that forest-covered valley. This was how America must have looked when it was new. And you knew this was only a part of a whole land of unspoiled forests, where every stream ran pure.

Under that picture was another, of six or eight people on a beach. They were sitting, kneeling, or squatting in an easy way. It was morning, just after breakfast. They were smiling, one woman talking, the others listening. One man had half risen to skip a stone out onto the surface of the water.

You knew this: that they were spending twenty minutes or so down on that beach after breakfast before going to work. You knew they were friends, and that they did this every day. You knew—I tell you, you *knew*—that they liked their work, all of them, whatever it was. I'd never seen anything like their faces before. They were ordinary enough in looks. But these people were *happy*. Even more, you knew they'd *been* happy, day after day, for a long time. And that they always would be, and they knew it.

I wanted to join them. I *longed* to. And I could hardly stand it. I looked up at the man, and tried to smile. "This is—very interesting," I said.

"Yes." He smiled back. "We've had people so interested, so carried away, that they didn't want to talk about anything else." He laughed. "They actually wanted to know prices, details, everything."

I nodded. "And I suppose you've worked out a whole story to go with the folder?" I said.

"Oh, yes. What would you like to know?"

"These people," I said softly, touching the picture of the group on the beach. "What do they do?"

"They work. Everyone does." He took a pipe from his pocket. "Some study. Some of our people farm, some write, some make things with their hands. Most of them raise children, and—well, they work at whatever it is they really want to do."

"And if there isn't anything they really want to do?"

He shook his head. "There's always something for everyone. It's just that here, we so rarely have time to find out what it is." He looked at me gravely. "Life is simple there, and it's serene. In some ways, the good ways, it's like the life of early American pioneers. But without the drudgery that killed people young. We have electricity, washing machines, vacuum cleaners, modern bathrooms, and modern medicine.

"But there are no radios, televisions, telephones, or cars. People live and work in small villages. They raise or make most of the things they use. They build their own houses, with all the help they need from their neighbors. They have a lot of fun, but there's nothing you buy a ticket to. They have dances, card parties, weddings, birthdays, harvest parties, swimming, and sports of all kinds. People talk with each other a lot, and visit, and share meals. There are no pressures. Life holds few threats. Everyone is happy." After a moment, he smiled. "That's how the story goes in our little joke," he said, nodding at the folder.

THE COLONY

"Who are you?" I lifted my eyes from the folder to look at him.

"It's in the folder," he said. "The people of Verna—the original ones—are just like you. Verna is a planet of air, sun, land, and sea, like Earth. The weather's about the same. There are a few small bodily differences between you and us—but nothing important. We read and enjoy your books. We like your chocolate, which we didn't have, and your music. But our thoughts, and aims, and history—those have been very different from Earth's." He smiled. "Amusing fantasy, isn't it?"

"Yes." I knew I sounded abrupt. "And where is Verna?"

- **gravely** (GRAYV lee) **in a serious way**
- **serene** (suh REEN) **calm; peaceful**
- **drudgery** (DRUJ uh ree) **dull, tiring work; boring labor**
- **fantasy** (FAN tuh see) **daydream; idea created by the imagination**
- **abrupt** (uh BRUPT) **sudden; a little rude**

"Light years away, by your measurements."

I was suddenly annoyed. I didn't know why. "A little hard to get to then, wouldn't it be?"

He turned to the window beside him. "Come here," he said, and I walked around the counter to stand beside him. "There, off to the left, are two apartment buildings, built back to back. See them?"

I nodded, and he said, "A man and his wife live on the fourteenth floor of one of those buildings. A wall of their living room is the back wall of the building. They have friends on the fourteenth floor of the other building. A wall of *their* living room is the back wall of *their* building. In other words, these two couples live within two feet of one another.

"But when the Robinsons want to visit the Braedens, they walk from their living room to the front door. Then they walk down a long hall to the elevators. They ride fourteen floors down. Then, in the street, they must walk around to the next block. And the city blocks there are long. In bad weather, they've sometimes actually taken a cab. They walk into the other building, then go on through the lobby. They ride up fourteen floors, walk down a hall, ring a bell, and finally go into their friends' living room—only two feet from their own."

He turned back to the counter, and I walked around to the other side again. "All I can tell you," he said, "is that the way the Robinsons travel is like space travel. But if they could only step through those two feet of wall—well, that's how we travel. We don't cross space, we avoid it." He smiled. "Draw a breath here—and exhale it on Verna."

I said softly, "That's how they arrived, isn't it? The people in the picture. You took them there." He nodded, and I said, "Why?"

He shrugged. "If you saw a neighbor's house on fire, would you rescue his family if you could?"

"Yes."

"Well—so would we."

"You think it's that bad, then? With us?"

"How does it look to you?"

I thought about the headlines every morning. "Not so good."

He just nodded and said, "We can't take you all. We can't even take very many. So we've been choosing a few."

"For how long?"

• **light year** (LYT YEER) **huge distance in space**

106

"A long time." He smiled. "One of us was a member of Lincoln's cabinet."

I leaned across the counter toward him. "I like your little joke," I said. "I like it very much. When does it stop being a joke?"

For a moment, he studied me. Then he spoke. "Now, if you want it to."

You've got to decide on the spot, the man at the party had told me. *Because you'll never get another chance. I know. I've tried.*

Now I stood there thinking. There were people I'd hate never to see again, and a girl I was just getting to know. This was the world I'd been born in. Then I thought about going back to my job, back to my room at night. And finally I thought of the deep-green valley in the picture, and the beach.

"I'll go," I whispered. "If you'll have me."

He studied my face. "Be sure," he said sharply. "Be certain. We want no one there who won't be happy. If you have any least doubt, we'd prefer that—"

"I haven't."

After a moment, he slid open a drawer under the counter and brought out what looked like a railroad ticket. The printing said, "Good for ONE TRIP TO VERNA. Not transferable. One-way only."

"Ah—how much?" I said, reaching for my wallet.

"All you've got. Including your small change." He smiled.

"I don't have much."

"That doesn't matter. We once sold a ticket for $3,700. And we sold another just like it for six cents." He handed the ticket to me. On the back were the words, "Good this day only" and the date. I put $11.17 on the counter. "Take the ticket to the Acme Depot," he said. Leaning across the counter, he gave me directions.

It's a tiny hole-in-the-wall, the Acme Depot. You may have seen it. It's just a little store front on one of the narrow streets west of Broadway. Inside, there's a worn wooden counter and a few battered, chrome-and-plastic chairs. The man at the counter glanced up as I stepped in. He looked for my ticket. When I showed it, he nodded at the last empty chair. I sat down.

There was a girl beside me, hands folded on her purse. Rather pretty, she looked like a secretary. Across the way sat a young man in work clothes. His wife, beside him, was holding their little girl in

Trip to **VERNA**
GOOD for ONE TRIP TO VERNA.
Not transferable. One way only.
ONE WAY

• **depot** (DEE poh) station

her lap. And there was a man of around fifty. He was expensively dressed. He looked like the vice-president of a bank, I thought. I wondered what his ticket had cost.

Maybe twenty minutes passed. Then a small, battered old bus pulled up at the curb outside. The bus had dented fenders and tires with worn tread. It was just the sort of little bus you see around, ridden always by shabby, tired, silent people, going no one knows where.

It took nearly two hours for the little bus to work south through the traffic. We all sat, each wrapped in thought. We stared out the rain-spattered windows. I watched wet people huddled at city bus stops. I saw them rap angrily on the closed doors of full buses. At 14th Street I saw a speeding cab splash dirty water on a man at the curb. I saw the man's mouth twist as he cursed. I saw hundreds of faces, and not once did I see anyone smile.

I dozed. Then we were on a shiny black highway somewhere on Long Island. I slept again and woke up in darkness. I caught a glimpse of a farmhouse. Then the bus slowed, lurched once, and stopped. We were parked beside what looked like a barn.

It *was* a barn. The driver walked up to it. He pulled the big sliding door open and stood holding it as we filed in. Then he let it go, stepping inside with us. The big door slid closed of its own weight.

The barn smelled of cattle. There was nothing inside on the dirt floor but a bench of unpainted pine. The driver pointed to it with the beam of his flashlight. "Sit here, please," he said quietly. "Get your tickets ready." Then he moved down the line, punching tickets. His beam of light moved along the floor. I caught a glimpse of tiny piles of round bits of cardboard, like confetti. Then he was at the door again. He slid it open just enough to pass through. For a moment, we saw his outline against the night sky.

"Good luck," he said. "Just wait where you are." He let go of the door. It slid closed, snipping off the beam of his flashlight. A moment later, we heard the motor start and the bus lumber away.

The dark barn was silent now, except for our breathing. Time ticked away. I felt an urge to speak. But I didn't quite know what to say. I began to feel embarrassed, a little foolish. I was very aware

- **lurch** (LURCH) **tip to one side suddenly**
- **lumber** (LUM bur) **move heavily**

108

that I was simply sitting in an old barn. The seconds passed. I moved my feet restlessly. Soon I was getting cold.

Then suddenly I knew! My face blushed in violent anger and shame. We'd been tricked! We'd been swindled out of our money. How? By our pitiful desire to believe an absurd fairy tale. Now we were left to sit there as long as we pleased. Finally, we'd come to our senses. Then we'd make our way home, like others before us, as best we could.

It was suddenly impossible to understand how I could have been so stupid. I was on my feet, stumbling in the dark across the uneven floor. I had some idea of getting to a phone and the police. The big barn door was heavier than I'd thought. But I slid it back and stepped through. Then I turned to shout back to the others to come along.

As I turned, the inside of that barn came alight. Through every wide crack of its walls and ceiling and windows streamed light. It was the light of a brilliantly blue sky. I opened my mouth to shout. Suddenly, the air was sweeter than any I had ever tasted. Then dimly, through a dusty window of that barn, I saw it. For less than the blink of an eye. I saw a deep, forest-covered valley, a blue stream winding through it, and a sunny beach. That picture was imprinted in my mind forever.

- **absurd** (ab SURD) silly; making no sense
- **imprint** (im PRINT) print on; have a lasting effect (on)

Then the heavy door slid shut. My fingernails scraped along the wood in a desperate effort to stop it. I failed. I was standing alone in a cold, rainy night.

It took four or five seconds, no longer, to get the door open again. But it was four or five seconds too long. The barn was empty, dark. There was nothing inside but a worn pine bench. By the light of a match, I saw tiny drifts of what looked like confetti on the floor. I knew where everyone was. They were laughing out loud in that forest-green valley, and walking toward home.

I work in a bank, in a job I don't like. I ride to and from it in the subway, reading the daily news. I live in a rented room. In my battered dresser, under a pile of handkerchiefs, is a little square of yellow cardboard. Printed on its face are the words, "Good for ONE TRIP TO VERNA." Stamped on the back is a date. But the date is gone, long since.

I've been back to the Acme Travel Bureau. The tall man walked up to me and laid $11.17 on the counter. "You left this the last time you were here," he said. He looked me right in the eyes and added blankly, "I don't know why." Then some customers came in. He turned to greet them, and there was nothing for me to do but leave.

Walk in as though it were an ordinary travel bureau. You can find it, somewhere, in any city you try! Ask a few ordinary questions about a vacation, anything. Then hint about The Folder. But whatever you do, don't mention it straight out. Give him time to size you up and offer it. And if he does, if you can believe—then make up your mind and stick to it! Because you won't ever get a second chance. I know, because I've tried. And tried. And tried.

ALL THINGS CONSIDERED

1. Charley Ewell goes to the Acme Travel Agency because (a) he wants to see a certain folder. (b) he's planning a business trip. (c) his boss asks him to go.

2. He knows he will not be successful unless he (a) is the right type. (b) has enough money. (c) gets his girlfriend to go, too.

3. One of Charley's reasons for wanting to leave Earth is his (a) small apartment. (b) boring job. (c) noisy neighbors.

4. One picture of Verna shows people (a) on top of a hill. (b) in a barn. (c) on a beach.

5. One thing people do *not* have on Verna is (a) sports. (b) cars. (c) electricity.

6. The most important thing about life on Verna is that people are (a) young. (b) happy. (c) wealthy.

7. The man in the travel bureau sells tickets to Verna in order to (a) make lots of money. (b) cheat people out of their savings. (c) give people a chance to live a better life.

8. While sitting in the barn waiting to go to Verna, Charley suddenly decides he's (a) not properly dressed. (b) afraid to go. (c) the victim of a swindle.

9. As Charley leaves the barn, he catches a brief sight of (a) the other people laughing at him. (b) a spaceship. (c) Verna.

10. Charley's other efforts to get to Verna (a) seem to be working. (b) are totally unsuccessful. (c) fail because of lack of money.

THINKING IT THROUGH

Discuss the following items in class.

1. What kind of people get chosen to go to Verna? Try to give at least three qualities such people must have.

2. What does Charley like about work and jobs on Verna?

3. Is the man in the travel agency originally from Verna or is he from Earth? Prove your answer.

4. Read again the description of the people waiting in the depot for the bus (pages 107–108). What is the author suggesting here?

5. (a) What are the confetti-like bits of cardboard on the floor of the barn? (b) What does this suggest?

6. Imagine that Verna is a real place. How do you think the people in the barn actually get to Verna?

7. Now the big question: Would you go to Verna if given the chance? Explain in detail.

Literary Skills

Mood and Suspense

The **mood** of a story is the feeling it gives the reader. Some stories make us laugh and laugh. These put the reader in a happy, fun-filled mood. Other stories create a mood of fear, or even terror. Still others put the reader in a sorrowful mood.

What about the mood of a story like "Of Missing Persons"? Humorous? Fearful? Sorrowful? No, none of these. The mood of "Of Missing Persons" is one of *suspense*. **Suspense** is a condition of doubt or uncertainty. A *suspenseful* story keeps us wondering what will happen in the next paragraph or on the next page. Detective stories, for instance, nearly always have a mood of suspense. The reader often has to wait until the very last page to learn how the plot turns out.

Here are ten items from "Of Missing Persons." Each is intended to create suspense—to put an urgent question in the reader's mind. Read each item carefully. Then write those questions that come to mind on a separate sheet of paper. The first one is done as an example.

1. *Then hint about The Folder.* (page 101)
(What is so special about the folder, and why is it capitalized?)

2. Behind a counter stood a tall man. . . . My heart was pumping—he fitted the description exactly. (page 101)

3. He brought out a long thin folder. . . . He slid it over the counter toward me. (page 103)

4. "Who are you?" I lifted my eyes from the folder to look at him. (page 105)

5. "There, off to the left, are two apartment buildings, built back to back. See them?" (page 106)

6. *You've got to decide on the spot,* the man at the party had told me. (page 107)

7. It *was* a barn. The driver . . . pulled the big sliding door open and stood there holding it. . . . (page 109)

8. "Good luck," he said. "Just wait where you are." (page 109)

9. As I turned, the inside of that barn came alight. (page 109)

10. I've been back to the Acme Travel Bureau. (page 110)

Sentence Meaning

Multiple Meanings

Some words in sentences can have more than one meaning. For instance, early in the story this appears: "Wait till he brings it up." The right meaning here is "Wait till he suggests it." The reader who waits for someone to *carry* or *lift something up* will wait forever.

All readers question the meaning of a sentence now and then. You know the feeling. Halfway through a sentence you suddenly think, "Wait a minute! This sentence *can't* mean what I take it to mean!" Test yourself now on eight sentences from "Of Missing Persons." On a separate sheet of paper, write either **(a)** or **(b)** for the correct meaning of each sentence.

1. He looked the way ministers should look. (page 102)
   (a) looked at something the way a minister might look at it
   (b) had the appearance of the perfect minister

2. I studied a large picture taken from the top of a hill. (page 104)
   (a) picture that was brought down from a hilltop
   (b) photo that was shot from a hilltop

3. I wanted to join them. (page 104)
   (a) connect them together
   (b) be with them

4. They have a lot of fun, but there's nothing you buy a ticket to. (page 105)
   (a) there isn't anything happening
   (b) there's free admission to all events

5. *You've got to decide on the spot,* the man at the party had told me. (page 107)
   (a) decide on the specific place
   (b) decide right at that time

6. It's a tiny hole in the wall, the Acme Depot. (page 107)
   (a) a small opening in the side of a room
   (b) not a very large place

7. He was expensively dressed. (page 108)
   (a) had to pay to have a dress put on
   (b) had on costly clothing

8. It slid closed, snipping off the beam of his flashlight. (page 108)
   (a) causing the light to be cut off when the door closed
   (b) and the door acted like scissors by cutting off the tip of the flashlight

Composition

Follow your teacher's instructions before completing *one* of these writing assignments.

1. Jack Finney, the author of "Of Missing Persons," uses incomplete sentences (or sentence fragments) at times. Find five of these incomplete sentences in the story. Copy them on your paper. Then, rewrite each as a complete sentence.
   Example: And tried. (page 110)
       I know, because I've tried and tried.

2. The mood of the story is in contrast to the mood of the people of Verna. The author makes the mood of the story one of suspense. At the same time, he creates a different mood for Verna. In four or five sentences, describe the mood of the people of Verna. Write the sentences on a separate sheet of paper.

SOUTHBOUND ON THE FREEWAY

by May Swenson

A tourist came in from Orbitville,
parked in the air, and said:

The creatures of this star
are made of metal and glass.

5   Through the transparent parts
you can see their guts.

Their feet are round and roll
on diagrams—or long

measuring tapes—dark
10   with white lines.

They have four eyes.
The two in the back are red.

Sometimes you can see a 5-eyed
one, with a red eye turning

15   on the top of his head.
He must be special—

the others respect him,
and go slow,

when he passes, winding
20   among them from behind.

They all hiss as they glide,
like inches, down the marked

tapes. Those soft shapes,
shadowy inside

25   the hard bodies—are they
their guts or their brains?

WAYS OF KNOWING

1. After reading the poem once, you probably realize that the "tourist" from outer space made a big mistake. In a single sentence, what was this mistake?

2. Now go back and look at the poem line by line to find a number of other mistakes. In Earth language, tell what the tourist means by (a) "creatures"—line 3. (b) "transparent parts"—line 5. (c) "feet"—line 7. (d) "diagrams"—line 8. (e) "measuring tapes"—line 9. (f) "eyes"—line 11. (g) "a 5-eyed one"—lines 13-14. (h) "soft shapes"—line 23.

3. Finally, try to answer the question that ends the poem. Give reasons for your choice. If you wish, you can tell how the "soft shapes" might be *both* "guts" and "brains."

Harriet Beecher Stowe (1811-1896)

One of the homes of Harriet Beecher Stowe—in Hartford, Connecticut

About halfway through the Civil War, Harriet Beecher Stowe visited the White House. President Abraham Lincoln welcomed her with outstretched arms. His greeting was a warm one: "So you're the little woman who wrote the book that made this great war."

Harriet Beecher Stowe was "little" only in height. Lincoln was referring to the book *Uncle Tom's Cabin* (1852). It is still one of the most historically important novels ever written by an American author.

Uncle Tom's Cabin described the evils of slavery in a way that fired up the feelings of millions of people. It was a huge success. In a single year, more than 300,000 copies were sold. Turned into a play, it drew sell-out crowds for years. The book may not have "made" the Civil War all by itself, but it was certainly a story *about* slavery that helped put an end *to* slavery.

Harriet Beecher Stowe lived in Maine for many years. She knew its people well. (Readers of "The Cradle Will Rock" should know that she lost a son by drowning.)

She also fought hard to get the vote for women. She worked for better laws to control liquor sales. A "little woman" indeed!

THE CRADLE WILL ROCK

from a narrative by Harriet Beecher Stowe, dramatized

by Clay Franklin

▶ Life on the coast of Maine was far from easy 150 years ago. Fishing was the chief industry. The men sailed out to sea in small wooden boats without radios, electric lights, or even motors. Meanwhile, the women waited, for days, for weeks— sometimes for the rest of their lives.

CAST OF CHARACTERS

Lois Toothacre—*A tall, hardy woman*
Polly Clark—*A fidgety neighbor*
Sarah Wilson—*A fragile-appearing spinster*

Scene—A kitchen-sitting room in a Maine house.

Time—An autumn evening some years ago. (Nineteenth century)

- **hardy** (HAR dee) strong; tough
- **fidgety** (FIJ i tee) restless; uneasy
- **spinster** (SPIN stur) old-fashioned term for an unmarried woman, especially one who is not likely to marry

The furnishings of the room are rugged. A round table is at center. On it is a lighted oil lamp, two cups and saucers, and a sewing basket. Right and left of table are two chairs. A wooden clothes tree is down right.* An unseen door to the outdoors is up right. At left is a rocking chair and below it a cradle. Several logs are down left before an imaginary fireplace.

Lois is seated left at table mending a man's shirt. Polly is seated right busily knitting a muffler.

Sound—The wind is heard in the background.

Polly: (*After a few moments*) Jes' listen to that wind screechin'.

Lois: (*Calmly*) All we can do, Polly, is keep our fingers busy. Frettin' about it won' make it go away. (*They knit and stitch away a few moments.*) Abner will be tickled with that muffler. It'll feel warm as a lamb.

Polly: It's fer his birthday. Next Thursday it be. An' I hope to put around his neck myself.

Lois: 'Course ya will. I have a feelin' in my bones their ship will bring 'em back any day now.

Polly: Oh, Lois. Ain' you a sunbeam. (*She puts down knitting and crosses up to look out window.*) I get the fidgets every time yer Cal an' my Abner go out in them fishin' boats. I keep wonderin' if the tide will bring 'em back.

Lois: Hush. Ya mustn' plague yerself with sech thoughts. (*She puts down mending.*) Nothin' can put cheer in ya like another cup of tea. (*As she crosses left she glances down at cradle.*) There's li'l Matt fas' asleep.

Polly: (*Crosses toward her*) Oh, pshaw! I plum forgot to bring along them ginger cookies. I baked 'em this mornin'. (*She glances fondly at the figure in cradle.*) My. Sleepin' like a li'l angel. An' what a comfort he be—while ya wait fer the wind to bring back yer man.

- **clothes tree** (KLOZE tree) **upright pole with hooks for clothing**
- **plague** (PLAYG) **pester; annoy**

*The term *down right* means "front right." Some stages slant slightly toward the audience, so that the rear of the stage is actually higher than the front. Thus, *down* means "front" and *up* means "back."

(*Lois has reached down for tea kettle behind the logs and moves back to table.*)

Polly: An' to think ya found this cradle out there on the shore—jes' afore l'il Matt come.

Lois: (*Pouring two cups of tea*) Yer tea is better for ya when it's pipin' hot.

Polly: (*Returns to her place by the table*) I cain' forget the night of that awful storm. The wind was howlin' somethin' fierce—like a baby cryin' out there.

(*Lois crosses and places kettle down left.*)

Lois: (*As she returns to table*) Polly, I jes' as soon talk 'bout somethin' else.

Polly: (*Disregarding the remark*) An' when Abner listen he hear it too. So nex' mornin' he look aroun'—but no hide or hair of a baby. Then you find that cradle out there an'—

Lois: (*Interrupts firmly*) Again I say, nuff of that.

Polly: My, yer touchy about it. (*They sip their tea.*)

(*Sound—The wind is heard again.*)

Polly: I ain' seen yer sister, Sarah, fer a spell. Has she fleshed up any?

Lois: Naw. Sarah is still scrawny as ever—an' feelin' poorly.

Polly: (*With sympathy*) Aw. A pity she never got herself a feller. But then she be sorta strange—seein' spirits aroun' that no one else can see. Guess that can scare away a man.

Lois: Don' we all have a cross to bear? Anyhow, Sarah keeps busy doin' things at church.

(*Sound—The wind is louder this time.*)

(*Polly glances toward the cradle and notices that it is rocking. She screams and bangs down her tea cup.*)

- **flesh up** (FLESH UP) slang for put on weight
- **poorly** (POOR lee) in bad health
- **bear** (BAIR) carry. A "cross to bear" is some kind of misfortune to put up with.

Lois: (*Startled*) Mercy, Polly. What's ailin' ya?

(*Frightened, Polly points to cradle.*)

Lois: (*She glances at cradle. Casually*) Aw, that. Every time the wind come up it do that. I pay it no mind.

Polly: Mercy. It's jes' as if somebody were settin' by the cradle an' rockin' it.

Lois: (*Firmly*) Now Polly, don' have a fit jes' because—

Polly: (*Interrupts*) It's spooky, I tell ya.

Lois: Stop actin' so foolish. It ain' nothin' to get in a tizzy about.

Polly: (*Rises*) Well, I ain' gonna set here an' watch it. (*She picks up knitting and hurries over to clothes tree and removes her shawl.*)

Lois: (*Severely*) Aw, Polly, don' be sech a fraidy cat.

Polly: (*Hotly, as she puts shawl over her head and shoulders*) 'Tain' only that, Lois Toothacre. I don' like the way ya sass me back. (*She flounces toward door up right but stops suddenly.*)

Lois: What now?

Polly: Lan' sakes! Sounds as if someone is comin' by.

(*Lois rises, crosses up as Sarah Wilson enters. She is slightly built with sensitive features.*)

Lois: (*Pleased surprise*) Sarah! What brings ya by—when a storm is brewin'?

Sarah: Somehow I jes' felt like comin' over.

Lois: (*Crosses to Sarah*) Anyhow, glad to see ya. Ya know Polly. She live across the way.

(*Sarah nods.*)

Polly: Jes' been askin' about ya. But I can see yer tuckered out walkin' a mile to get here.

Lois: (*Takes Sarah's cape and bonnet*) My, them things is cold.

Polly: (*Crosses toward door*) Well, I'm on my way.

- tizzy (TIZ ee) **state of excitement**
- flounce (FLOUNS) **make quick, angry movements**
- slightly built (SLYT lee BILT) **slender and small in build**
- **sensitive** (SEN si tiv) **tender; easily influenced**
- brewing (BROO ing) **getting ready to happen**

Lois: When ya get home, Polly, sing a hymn. It'll make ya feel better.

Polly: (*Saucily, at doorway*) Hmm! An' you should stitch yer tongue. (*She hurries off.*)

(*Sound—Wind howls.*)

(*The cradle rocks again.*)

Lois: (*Crosses to clothes tree and hangs up wraps.*) It's good ya come by. Polly an' me were 'bout to have a spat. Now go over there by the fire an' warm yerself.

Sarah: (*Crosses left*) An' li'l Matt—is he asleep? (*She notices the cradle rocking.*) Oh.

Lois: Pay no mind to that rockin'. It do that when the wind is high. Go on, Sarah, set on that chair. I'll bring Matt fer ya to hold. It's 'bout time for his feedin'. (*Sarah crosses toward rocking chair then stops.*) What's wrong now?

Sarah: (*Points to rocker*) Who—who is that woman settin' there?

Lois: Why, sister, there ain' nobody there.

Sarah: But I see her. She's settin' there—leanin' over—an' rockin' the cradle.

Lois: (*Kindly*) Foolish talk, Sarah. Reckon that long walk in the wind done tire ya out. Go in the other room an' rest a spell.

● **saucily** (SAW si lee) rudely; disrespectfully

Sarah: (*Not hearing*) Her face is so sad an' pale—an' her long black hair is hangin' down.

Lois: Now, Sarah. Come, set over here. (*She leads Sarah away and sets her left at table.*)

Sarah: (*Her eyes still on the rocking chair*) She's wearin' a silk dress. Now she looks at me as if to say somethin'.

Lois: (*Behind the table, after a pause*) Well?

Sarah: Poor lady. Her eyes are so pitiful.

Lois: Don' fret so. I'll bring ya a cup of tea.

Sarah: (*More excited*) Now she's standin' up an' walkin' to the cradle.

Lois: What!

Sarah: She stoops over—as if to pick up li'l Matt.

Lois: (*With spirit as she crosses to cradle*) Naw! Naw, she don'. She won' tech my baby. (*She reaches down, grasps the tiny bundle in her arms, then hurries to front of table.*) Where—where is she now?

Sarah: The lady turns away. She's cryin'.

Lois: (*Angrily*) An' she should. Tryin' to steal my baby. (*She sits right at table.*)

Sarah: I pity her. Perhaps she—Oh. She—she melted away.

Lois: An' she can stay away.

Sarah: (*Faces her*) Sister, remember that awful storm—when ya found that cradle the nex' mornin'?

Lois: (*Nods*) It would take a heap of forgettin' not to.

Sarah: Mebbe a ship wen' down—an' that lady an' her baby done drown. An'—

Lois: (*Interrupts sharply*) Well, I don' want her back. I want no sech doin's in my house. (*Reaching a decision, she rises and crosses to Sarah.*) Here, Sarah, take the baby.

Sarah: (*As she takes the bundle*) Lois, what are ya doin'?

Lois: (*Determined, as she strides to fireplace.*) I wanna be sure that spook lady won' come back. (*She picks up an ax that is beside the logs.*) That cradle done rock fer the last time.

Sarah: (*Rises in alarm and crosses to her*) Sister, don'! It ain' right! (*She extends a restraining hand.*)

Lois: Let me be. I'm choppin' it up fer kindlin'. (*With a few strokes of the ax the cradle falls apart. Then she throws pieces in the fireplace.*) There. Let it burn. An' the spook lady with it.

(*Sarah moans as Lois takes baby from her and crosses to her chair by table. Sarah slowly returns to her chair by table and sobs softly. For a few moments the women sit there. Lois is patting the baby as her body rocks.*)

(*Sound—A baby's cry is heard from fireplace area.*)

Lois: (*Alarmed*) Sarah, ya hear that? (*Sarah, still sobbing, nods*) It come from the fire.

(*Sound—The baby's cry becomes louder over the sound of wind.*)

Lois: (*She trembles with fright.*) Laws a-mercy! How that poor baby is cryin'!

(*Lights—dim to blackout*)

Curtain

• **restraining** (ri STRAYN ing) **holding back by force**

ALL THINGS CONSIDERED ────────────────

1. We learn early in the play that the return of the men at sea depends on the (a) tides and the wind. (b) power of their boats. (c) wishes of the boat owners.

2. The cradle has been found (a) in an attic. (b) beside a river. (c) on the shore.

3. Compared with Lois, Polly is (a) more humorous. (b) less inclined to worry. (c) much more jittery.

4. It is very important to the plot that Sarah is introduced as a character who (a) never married. (b) can see spirits. (c) is Lois's sister.

5. Lois tells Polly that the cradle starts to rock (a) only when she touches it. (b) when there's a draft in the room. (c) every time the wind blows hard.

6. At first, Lois's reaction to the rocking cradle is (a) surprisingly calm. (b) one of great fear. (c) to blame it on Polly.

7. Lois decides to (a) sell the cradle. (b) nail the cradle to the floor. (c) chop up and burn the cradle.

8. The two sounds that end the play are (a) the wind and the screech from a rocking cradle. (b) Sarah's scream and the screech from a rocking cradle. (c) the wind and a baby's cry.

THINKING IT THROUGH ────────────────

Discuss the following items in class.

1. The play takes place around 1834. Find and list three things in the play that would be done, used, or said differently today.

2. The play uses a lot of *dialect* (words spelled and used the way the people of a place say them). The author wants the reader to know how the characters would actually speak. However, the dialect makes some lines hard to read. How do you think the dialect helps in your understanding of the play? Explain.

3. The characters in a play often *contrast* with one another. Give one difference between (a) Lois and Polly, and (b) Lois and Sarah.

4. Suppose your class decided to put the play on in the auditorium. (a) How would you make the sound of the wind? (b) How might you make the cradle rock?

5. "The Cradle Will Rock" is supposed to be a play about the supernatural. Is there any natural way to explain any of the strange events? If so, explain.

Literary Skills

Foreshadowing

Good authors know the value of a big surprise. They know the power that a bolt from the blue can have. But surprises in literature are seldom *completely* unforeseen, or without warning. If they were, the reader would be shocked into disbelief. To prevent this, authors often drop hints or clues about a surprise before one happens.

Foreshadowing (for SHAD oh ing) is the providing of hints or clues as to what might happen in a story or a play. Good foreshadowing prepares the reader to accept the surprise when it finally comes.

1. Turn back to page 119. Find Polly's speech that starts, "I cain' forget the night. . . . " Read this speech and the two that follow. What surprise later in the play is foreshadowed by these speeches?
2. Now, on page 119, find Polly's speech that starts, "Aw. A pity she never . . . ." For what surprise does this foreshadowing prepare the reader?

Composition

Follow your teacher's instructions before completing *one* of these writing assignments.

1. A writer can add more information to a sentence to give the reader a fuller picture. Choose five sentences of eight words or less from the play. Rewrite each of them by adding at least three words of your own to make each sentence more interesting. Write your answers on a separate piece of paper.
2. Imagine you are the editor of a magazine called *School Plays.* Write Clay Franklin a business letter accepting his play. In your letter, propose one or two small changes that you believe will improve the play. Give good reasons for the changes without insulting the author. You will have to make up the address for the magazine and the address for Mr. Franklin.

VOCABULARY AND SKILL REVIEW

Before completing the exercises that follow, you may wish to review the **bold-faced** words on pages 102 to 123.

I. On a separate piece of paper, mark each item *true* or *false*. If it is *false*, explain what is wrong with the sentence.

1. It is *absurd* to think that people can live for ten years without eating.
2. Becoming a millionaire is a *fantasy* for most people.
3. "*Sensitive*" is the opposite of "tender."
4. "*Fidgety*" is the opposite of "calm."
5. It takes a lot of *nerve* to ride a loop-the-loop roller coaster.
6. A person who speaks *gravely* wants to be laughed at.
7. Many farm workers spend their lives in *drudgery*.
8. Football players have to be *hardy* people.
9. Fire drills sometimes bring classes to an *abrupt* end.
10. "*Bear*" means the same thing as "throw."

II. Sentences with words that are poorly chosen or placed can cause a lot of confusion. The following sentences are real-life examples. They actually appeared on bulletin boards, in student papers, and in other places. Rewrite each of them so that it has only one clear meaning that makes sense.

1. On Super Bowl Sunday, Mom looked longer than Dad.
2. There will be a short teachers' meeting after school.
3. Lying in the gutter I saw a woman's purse.
4. The kids were happy because they were having Grandpa for dinner.
5. MAN REFUSES TO GIVE UP BITING DOG.
6. Shakespeare went to London where he worked in a theater and became a good play boy.
7. Rather than read about Macbeth's downfall, I would prefer to see him fall apart on the stage.
8. More and more milk drinkers are turning to powder as the cost of bottled milk rises.
9. Owners of all dogs in the city of Metropolis are required to be on a chain.
10. ALBANY—The Assembly passed a bill requiring dog owners in New York City to clean up after their pets. The bill also applies to Buffalo.

▶ Only the boy's mother knew the strange secret. To others, he was simply a

BOY IN THE SHADOWS

by Margaret Ronan

Is it true that love is stronger than death? That the human spirit can survive the grave? Perhaps the answer can be found in the strange experience of Irene and Ernest Platt.

The Platts had always lived in cities, but when Ernest retired, they decided they wanted to spend the rest of their lives in the country. They bought a small house tucked away on the lower slopes of the Ozarks. Irene at once planted a vegetable garden. With what she could grow, and a trip once a week to the supermarket in the nearest town, they should have all the food they needed.

Food was the first thing she thought of when she saw the boy. She had been working in the garden when she became aware that someone was watching her. She raised her eyes, and there, standing at the edge of the field, was the boy—a thin, hollow-eyed boy wearing faded jeans and no shoes.

Irene raised her hand and waved, but the boy did not wave back. Perhaps he doesn't have the strength to wave, she thought to herself. He was very thin, and his ribs showed plainly.

The boy stood there a few more minutes. Then, as if he had seen all he wanted to, he turned and slipped away—vanishing among the thicket of trees at the edge of the field.

Two days later he was back. With him was a haggard-looking woman of about 40. When she saw Irene, she came straight up to the fence. The boy lagged slightly behind, head hanging listlessly.

"Are you the lady who bought this place?" the woman asked.

"I'm Mrs. Platt," replied Irene. "What can I do for you?"

"I've come about what we can do for you, Ma'am," replied the woman firmly. "This here's my son, Jayse. He's a good worker and a lot stronger than he looks.

- **Ozarks** (OH zarks) name of mountains that run through Arkansas, Missouri, Oklahoma, and Illinois
- **thicket** (THIK it) bushes or small trees growing close together
- **haggard** (HAG urd) thin and worn from too much worry or pain
- **listlessly** (LIST les lee) in a tired, inactive way

127

He'll work for you, do your garden and your chores, for two dollars a day."

Irene was about to say that she didn't need any help, that she enjoyed doing her own chores. But the sight of Jayse's thin, dangling arms and hollow-cheeked face stopped her.

"He's very young—and he doesn't look strong," she began, but the woman held up a work-scarred hand to stop her.

"He's 16," she said, "but he's small-ish and looks younger. And he's a lot stronger than he looks, like I said. You won't have no cause for complaint. Jayse's a good worker."

"All right," said Irene. Two dollars a day wasn't much, and having Jayse on her own ground would give her a chance to feed him properly. "All right. That will be fine. Jayse can come at ten every morning and go home at five. I'll give him his dinner at noon." She turned to the boy. "Will that be all right with you, Jayse?"

Jayse didn't answer. Irene wondered if he had even heard her, for he kept his head down, never raising his eyes. His mother beckoned Irene to one side and spoke in a low voice. "No, Ma'am. I don't want Jayse traveling back and forth. We live a fair distance from here. He can sleep in that little shed there. And don't you be worrying about feeding him. I'll come every day and bring his food. He's got a finicky stomach. I know just what he can eat and I'll fix it for him. When I come, you can give me his two dollars."

"But what about Jayse?" Irene asked. "If he's working for the money, shouldn't I pay it to him?"

- **finicky** (FIN uh kee) fussy; very hard to please

128

The woman shook her head. "You don't understand. I need that money to feed my other children. Jayse's pa is dead, and now the boy is the only one who can go out to work. He wants to do it to help us out. You won't be sorry you took him on. He's a good worker, is Jayse. He never gets tired, never complains. You'll see."

"Well, all right, but I don't think he should sleep in the shed. I could fix up a room in the house."

"No, Ma'am. Jayse wouldn't care for that. He's a poor sleeper and he wouldn't want to think he might disturb you. The shed will be fine."

So Jayse came to work for the Platts. Irene soon found that the claims his mother had made were true. Jayse never complained and never seemed to get tired. No matter how early Irene and Ernest got up in the morning, the boy was already at work, feeding the chickens, tending the garden. Gradually, Irene let him take over some of the cleaning chores in the house, and once she showed him what she wanted done, she never had to remind him to do it.

"He's a wonder," she told Ernest, "but he's not like a boy at all. He's like . . . like a machine. Do you know he's never said a word to me. He never even looks at me, only at the ground."

Ernest grunted. "All I know is that the kid gives me the creeps. Maybe he can't talk. And if you ask me, he's not all there mentally."

Irene shook her head. "No, he isn't stupid. It's more as though he's walking around in his sleep."

"Well, the price is right," said Ernest. "In fact, it's wrong—two dollars a day is ridiculous for the work he's doing. Let's raise it to four. I'm not crazy about having Jayse around, but let's see if a raise gets some reaction from him."

Why should it? Irene wondered. Jayse never touched the money he earned. Every day, shortly before noon, he would stop what he was doing. Then he would stand, eyes lowered, head turned slightly to one side as though listening. A few minutes later his mother would appear from the wooded thicket, carrying his dinner in a covered tin plate. She would wait until Irene handed her Jayse's daily wages, then lead him to the shed and sit with him while he ate.

"Why won't she let me feed him?" Irene asked furiously. "I've seen the stuff she brings him—it's some kind of mush. That's not decent food for a boy who works as hard as he does. I think he's even thinner than he was when he first came here."

Ernest had to agree. The bones of Jayse's face were more prominent. When the boy bent over the hoe in the garden, his knobby spine was plainly outlined under his thin T-shirt.

- **creeps** (KREEPS) feeling of fear or horror
- **prominent** (PROM uh nunt) easy to see; standing out
- **knobby** (NOB ee) lumpy

Irene decided to try again. "I want to give Jayse a hot meal every day," she told his mother. "Otherwise I can't let him go on working here the way he does. He's getting thinner all the time. I'm afraid he'll get sick."

There was a frightened glitter in the woman's eyes. "You don't understand, Mrs. Platt. Jayse's like his father. He can't eat the food you and I can eat. He can't take salt—his system can't handle it. Please, Ma'am, let things be. Don't say you won't let him stay. He's the only one the kids and I can depend on. Without what he earns here, his brothers and sisters will starve."

Irene gave in. "All right, he can stay. I must admit he's a wonderful worker—but he doesn't seem happy about being with us. He never smiles or laughs. And he's never said a word to either my husband or myself."

The woman shrugged. "It don't mean anything, Ma'am. Jayse's different. He don't feel things the way most kids do. All he cares about is helping me and the other kids. Don't worry about him. He's doing what he wants to do."

But *is* it what he wants? Irene wondered. She stood at her bedroom window later. She could see the shed where Jayse slept—but he wasn't asleep. He was sitting in the doorway, arms resting slackly on his knees, staring unmovingly into the moonlit night.

"Something's wrong," she said aloud.

"What are you talking about?" her husband asked sleepily.

"Jayse. I've been watching him for half an hour. He's never moved so much as a muscle. With the day he's put in, you'd think he'd have gone to sleep hours ago. But no—he's just sitting there."

Ernest got up and came to stand at her side. "I could have told you that. He always sits there at night. As far as I know, he never sleeps. I'll admit he's one spooky kid—but he's not really bothering anyone, is he?"

No one but me, Irene thought. As the days wore on, the sight of the boy wrung her heart. His skin, which had been pale, was now yellow and shiny. There were discolored patches on his forehead, cheekbones, and along the ridge of his nose. Even more disquieting, his movements seemed to be slower and more labored.

"Aren't you feeling well, Jayse?" she asked. But the boy only ducked his head and brushed past her. Uneasily, she went to her husband. "Look at Jayse. I think he's sick. He's moving around like an old man."

Ernest peered at Jayse, who was slowly cutting grass. "You're right. What are those dark patches on his skin?"

"I don't know, but I'm sure of one thing. He's going under from

- **slackly** (SLAK lee) loosely
- **disquieting** (dis KWY i ting) **disturbing; worrisome**
- **labored** (LAY burd) **not easy; done with effort**

malnutrition. I don't care what his mother says—I'm going to get some decent food into him. Tomorrow you can drive him into town to see the doctor."

Protein! Irene thought. Jayse needed some high-grade protein, and fast. She went into the kitchen and began to prepare a hearty meal of ham and eggs. That, plus plenty of milk and apple pie, should help.

When it was ready she called Jayse and brought him into the kitchen. "Sit down at the table," she told him. "I've made you a special dinner because you've been here three months today. That's cause for celebration."

Jayse took one bite of the food, then another. He chewed the ham slowly, and swallowed. Then he put down his fork and rose from the table.

"What's the matter?" Irene asked anxiously. "Where are you going?"

But he had already gone. The kitchen door closed behind him. Irene ran to the door and flung it open. The boy had already reached the line of trees that bordered the property. He was moving with long, steady strides. She called his name, but he never looked back.

"Leave him alone," said Ernest, who had just come into the kitchen. "He's going home. His mother was probably right. You shouldn't have given him that food."

Irene slept badly that night. She was up before dawn, walking about the garden. As she feared, Jayse had not come back. But shortly before noon, his mother appeared.

She walked straight up to Irene, her mouth fixed in a hard line. "You did it, didn't you? You fed my boy after I told you not to. What did you give him to eat?"

"Ham and eggs," replied Irene. "Good food, the kind he needed."

- **malnutrition** (mal noo TRISH un) **poor health condition caused by not having enough of the right kinds of food**
- **stride** (STRYD) **long step**

"Ham . . . " the woman whispered, "so salty. . . . " Then her voice rose to a shriek. "You're a fool, a meddling fool! Why couldn't you leave well enough alone?"

"I'm sorry if my cooking made Jayse sick," Irene retorted angrily, "but he was starving to death in front of me. I couldn't let it go on. My husband and I will pay any medical bills and see that a doctor takes care of him. Now I want you to take me to him or we will have to notify the authorities."

For a moment the woman was silent, then she began to laugh mirthlessly. "Yes, Ma'am. I'll take you to him. You come with me and see what you've done."

She turned and Irene followed her through the stretch of woods. For half an hour they climbed through the scraggy foothills. Finally they came to a shabby house where three young children sat listlessly on the stoop. But when Irene stopped, the woman took her arm and pulled her on.

"Isn't that your home?" asked Irene. "Isn't Jayse there?"

The woman shook her head and went on. Presently they came to another stand of trees. Beyond lay an open space with grass-covered mounds. Some of the mounds had wooden markers; others had none.

"What is this place?" Irene cried frantically.

"Old graveyard," replied the woman. "Nobody—hardly nobody uses it anymore. Over here, Ma'am." She pointed to one mound. Irene saw with horror that great tufts of grass had been torn from it, and that someone had tried to scoop a hollow in the dry dirt underneath.

Nothing could have made her go close to the mound. But from where she stood she could see what lay in it—a shriveled, withered something dressed in worn jeans and a stained T-shirt.

"There's Jayse," said the woman. "There's where you sent him. He and his pa died two years ago, that bad winter, of pneumonia. I wished them back, but only Jayse came. He knew I needed him, you see. He wanted to take care of me. He was a good boy, always."

"I don't understand," Irene said.

But the woman wasn't listening. She talked on, as if to herself. "I had to take special care of him. You can't feed the dead salt, you know. It makes them forget everything but the last place they rested. That's why Jayse had to come here. Now he won't leave it again, ever."

- **authority** (uh THOR i tee) **person with official power or right**
- mirthlessly (MURTH les lee) **without humor**
- scraggy (SKRAG ee) **rough and uneven**
- **tuft** (TUFT) **bunch of grass or hair, etc.**
- shrivel (SHRIV ul) **dry up**
- **pneumonia** (noo MOHN yuh) **disease of the lungs**

ALL THINGS CONSIDERED

1. Jayse's job is arranged by (a) Ernest Platt and Jayse's father. (b) Jayse and Irene Platt. (c) Irene Platt and Jayse's mother.

2. One of the strange things about Jayse is that he (a) never speaks. (b) tires very easily. (c) forgets orders almost at once.

3. Jayse's food is provided by (a) the Platts. (b) his mother. (c) both Irene Platt and his mother on different days of the week.

4. Soon after Jayse starts work, Ernest Platt suggests that he (a) may be a thief. (b) is smarter than he looks. (c) should be paid higher wages.

5. As the days pass, Jayse (a) laughs more at things. (b) expresses interest in school. (c) grows even thinner.

6. Talking about Jayse, Ernest Platt says, "As far as I know, he never (a) eats." (b) reads." (c) sleeps."

7. Irene Platt's big decision in the story is to (a) increase Jayse's wages. (b) get rid of Jayse. (c) feed Jayse better food.

8. The "shriveled, withered something" on the grave, at the end of the story, is (a) Jayse's clothing. (b) an animal. (c) Jayse's body.

9. We learn at the end of the tale that the dead (a) must be in their graves by midnight. (b) can't eat salt. (c) always haunt the living.

10. Reading between the lines, we can tell that Jayse (a) gets lazier each day. (b) loves his family. (c) grows to love Irene Platt as a mother.

THINKING IT THROUGH

Discuss the following items in class.

1. No date is given for the story. (a) In your opinion, could it be set in today's world? (b) Tell why or why not.

2. (a) What were the reactions of Irene and Ernest Platt to Jayse's conduct? (b) In your opinion, were these the reactions of normal human beings? Explain.

3. Jayse's mother may not have told the whole truth, but did she ever lie about her son? Think carefully.

Inferences

Making Predictions

A **prediction** (pri DIK shun) is a judgment about what will happen in the future. So-called weather reports, for instance, are really predictions: *showers tonight and much colder tomorrow.* People often make predictions about sports events or elections. You probably make a prediction about your mark every time you finish taking an important test.

Sometimes the purpose of *foreshadowing* (page 125) is to enable the reader to make predictions. Good readers make predictions constantly. Reading is more fun when you make predictions while you read.

Here are six items from "Boy in the Shadows." Three help the reader make predictions about the end of the story. The other three do not. On a separate sheet of paper, write the numbers of the items that help with predictions and what can be predicted from each.

1. Irene at once planted a vegetable garden.
2. Irene shook her head. "No, he isn't stupid. It's more as though he's walking around in his sleep."
3. There was a frightened glitter in the woman's eyes. "You don't understand, Mrs. Platt. Jayse's like his father. He can't eat the food you and I can eat. He can't take salt. . . . "
4. Ernest got up and came to stand at her side. "I could have told you that. He always sits there at night. As far as I know, he never sleeps. I'll admit he's one spooky kid. . . . "
5. Protein! Irene thought. Jayse needed some high-grade protein, and fast.
6. For half an hour they climbed through the scraggy foothills.

Relationships

Paragraph Signals

When writers begin new paragraphs they send signals to the reader. The message is always the same: *some sort of change is taking place.*

The change signaled by the start of a new paragraph usually includes one or more of the following:

A. A change in subject or idea.

B. A different person speaking or thinking.

C. A jump from one time period to another.

Good readers react to these signals almost automatically, usually with the first sentence of a new paragraph. Then they go on to grasp the central *purpose* of the new paragraph.

Look back at the third paragraph of "Boy in the Shadows" (page 127). The new paragraph signals a change in subject. Paragraph two tells about the Platts' move to the Ozarks. The purpose of paragraph three is to describe Irene's first encounter with the boy.

Examine the paragraphs from the story that begin with the items below. For each, write on a separate sheet of paper (a) the reason (or reasons) for the new paragraph (A, B, or C, above) and (b) the purpose of the new paragraph.

1. Two days later he was back. . . . (page 127)
2. "I've come about what we. . . ." (page 127)
3. Why should it? Irene wondered. . . . (page 129)
4. But he had already gone. . . . (page 131)
5. Irene slept badly that night. . . . (page 131)
6. "Ham and eggs," replied Irene. . . . (page 131)
7. "Old graveyard," replied the woman. . . . (page 132)

Composition

Follow your teacher's instructions before completing *one* of these writing assignments.

1. Suppose that "Boy in the Shadows" were a story that had just made first-page news in your local paper. Write the best headline you can think of for that story. Limit: ten words.

2. You learned earlier that a *prediction* (page 134) is a judgment about the future. Now that Jayse has returned to the grave, predict what will happen to his mother, brothers, and sisters. Answer in three or four sentences on a separate sheet of paper.

Sara Teasdale (1884-1933)

The wonders of nature—a favorite theme for Sara Teasdale's poems

Sara Teasadale wrote *great* poetry. But what does *great* really mean?

A *great* poem makes you see and think about things in a new light. Each word seems to be just the *right* word. Each is placed exactly where it should be placed. When read aloud, the sound seems to support the meaning. A great poem gives the reader the feeling that it could have been written in no other way.

Sara Teasdale could do all these things—and more. Her poetry has sent shivers of delight through readers for over 50 years, yet she makes the writing of poetry seem as easy as leaving a note for a friend. Anyone who doubts this should look in other books for some of her best-known poems: "Barter," "The Falling Star," "The Long Hill," "Wisdom," and "I Shall Not Care."

In a sense, Sara Teasdale gave her life to poetry. Born in St. Louis, Missouri, she published her first poems while she was still a girl. Her first complete book appeared before she was 25. Seven more books followed, each as solid as the one before it. She put into poems the love, the hope, and the happiness that she could not find in her personal life. And sadly, she put an end to that life before she was 50.

I STOOD UPON A STAR

by Sara Teasdale

I stretched my mind until I stood
　　Out in space, upon a star;
I looked, and saw the flying earth
　　Where seven planets are.

Delicately interweaving
　　Like fireflies on a moist June night,
The planetoids among the planets
　　Played for their own delight.

I watched earth putting off her winter
　　And slipping into green;
I saw the dark side of the moon
　　No man has ever seen.

Like shining wheels in an opened watch
　　They all revolved with soundless motion;
Earth sparkled like a rain-wet flower,
　　Bearing her petals, plain and ocean.

WAYS OF KNOWING

1. (a) In the first stanza, what does the poet claim she has done? Put this in a single sentence, starting with "She imagined. . . . " (b) Can you imagine yourself doing the same thing? (Try it!)

2. In the second stanza, to what are "the planetoids" compared?

3. The third stanza contains a mistake. (a) What is it? (b) What has happened to make that a mistake?

4. Is it the "Earth," the "rain-wet flower," or both that we see "Bearing her petals" in the last line?

- **delicately** (DEL uh kit lee) very carefully
- **interweaving** (in tur WEEV ing) weaving, or moving, in and out in a pattern
- **planetoid** (PLAN i toid) asteroid, or small planet-like body
- **bearing** (BAIR ing) carrying

▶ A **narrative poem** is a poem that tells a story. Here's one of the best-known narrative poems ever written. Read it through once for the meaning. Then read it a second time for the sound of the words and the rhythm of the lines.

THE LISTENERS

by Walter de la Mare

"Is there anybody there?" said the Traveller,
    Knocking on the moonlit door;
And his horse in the silence champed the grasses
    Of the forest's ferny floor:
5   And a bird flew up out of the turret,
    Above the Traveller's head:
And he smote upon the door again a second time;
    "Is there anybody there?" he said.
But no one descended to the Traveller;
10   No head from the leaf-fringed sill
Leaned over and looked into his grey eyes,
    Where he stood perplexed and still.
But only a host of phantom listeners
    That dwelt in the lone house then
15   Stood listening in the quiet of the moonlight
    To that voice from the world of men:
Stood thronging the faint moonbeams on the dark stair,
    That goes down to the empty hall,
Hearkening in an air stirred and shaken
20   By the lonely Traveller's call.
And he felt in his heart their strangeness,
    Their stillness answering his cry,
While his horse moved, cropping the dark turf,

- champ (CHAMP) **bite or chew, usually impatiently**
- turret (TUR it) **small tower on top of a building**
- smote (SMOHT) **pounded; struck**
- perplexed (pur PLEKST) **confused; puzzled**
- host (HOST) **large group**
- thronging (THRONG ing) **crowding; jostling**
- **cropping** (KROP ing) **biting off the tops**
- turf (TURF) **short grass**

    'Neath the starred and leafy sky;
25   For he suddenly smote on the door, even
      Louder, and lifted his head:—
    "Tell them I came, and no one answered,
      That I kept my word," he said.
    Never the least stir made the listeners,
30   Though every word he spake
    Fell echoing through the shadowiness of the still house
      From the one man left awake:
    Ay, they heard his foot upon the stirrup,
      And the sound of iron on stone,
35   And how the silence surged softly backward,
      When the plunging hoofs were gone.

• **surge** (SURJ) roll; swell up

ALL THINGS CONSIDERED

1. The setting of the poem is (a) in front of a house in the woods at night. (b) before a castle on top of a sunny hill. (c) behind a small cabin on a dark night.

2. The man comes to the building (a) to spend the night. (b) to investigate ghosts. (c) because of some promise he has made.

3. The listeners seem like living beings in that they (a) speak to the man. (b) move rapidly about. (c) seem to hear things.

4. During most of the poem, the man's horse (a) is very excited. (b) eats grass. (c) seems to know exactly what is going on.

5. The poem ends when the man (a) threatens the listeners. (b) leads his horse away. (c) rides off rapidly.

THINKING IT THROUGH

Discuss the following items in class.

1. What is the *mood* (see page 112) of the poem? Try to think of two words that correctly describe the mood.

2. More than most poems, this one is full of sounds. Name at least three places in the poem that have to do with sounds.

3. To whom or what do both the words "Stood" (line 17) and "Hearkening" (line 19) refer?

4. Line 24 ends with the term "leafy sky." How can a sky be "leafy"?

5. Trace the man's feelings throughout the poem. (a) At what point is he curious? (b) At what point is he confused? (c) At what point does he feel the spell of almost supernatural mystery?

6. Try to explain the last two lines in the poem. (a) Can a person really "hear" silence? (b) If not, try to put lines 35 and 36 in your own words.

Oral Interpretation

Choral Reading

Choral (KO rul) **reading** is reading aloud together, with different groups or individuals sometimes taking different parts. Narrative poems like "The Listeners" are best when they're read aloud to bring out the sounds. In planning your reading, remember the following.

1. Before trying to read the poem aloud, practice hearing the words clearly in your mind's ear. To do this, you will have to read the poem at least three more times silently. Remember, don't come to a complete stop at the end of a line unless the punctuation mark shown is a period.

2. Try to stress the *sounds* in the poem as much as possible. For instance, make the first four words sound like a real question. Take advantage of repeated sounds at the beginning of words ("forest's ferny floor"). Make the "loud" lines (like line 25) sound different from the "soft" lines (like line 29). Try to say "the silence surged softly backward" so that the reader can almost hear the event described.

3. It's often hard to understand a large group of people reading aloud together. For this reason, it's better to assign different parts to small groups or individuals. The number of different parts, of course, will depend on the size and make-up of your class.

4. It's best to stand up. If you wish, think of some actions to go with your performance. For example, the speaker(s) might step forward before reading. Someone might knock on the door or indicate listening by a cupped hand behind an ear.

5. Practice. Practice. Practice! As you do so, remember this: SLOW DOWN. Don't follow the temptation to speed up as you remember the lines better. Most of this mysterious poem should be read quite slowly. Keep in mind that your audience will be hearing it for the first time.

Composition

Follow your teacher's instructions before completing *one* of these writing assignments.

1. Without looking back, try to tell the story of "The Listeners" in just a few sentences. You need not include everything, only the main points.

2. Add to the story by making up details about (a) exactly why the man comes to the house, and (b) exactly how he feels as he leaves.

THE PROVENÇAL TALE

by Ann Radcliffe

▶ Stories of mysterious horror are a dime a dozen nowadays. But who invented the modern horror story? That honor probably goes to Ann Radcliffe (1764–1823). The wife of an English newspaper editor, Ann Radcliffe escaped an otherwise quiet life by following her imagination far into the twilight zone.

There once lived, in the province of Bretagne, a noble baron, famous for his riches and his kindness to guests. His castle was more splendid than those of many kings. Beautiful ladies and brave knights came from far-off countries to feast in the great hall of his castle. The baron's eight musicians, the banners that waved along the roof, the huge paintings, the gold and silver dishes, the piles of tasty food, the costly uniforms of the many servants—all combined to form a scene of magnificence such as we may not hope to see in these dull modern days.

The following adventure is told about the baron. One night, having stayed late at the dinner table, he went to his bedroom. A few minutes after he had told his servants to go, he was surprised by the sudden appearance of a man he had never before seen. The stranger's face was sorrowful. The baron believed this person had been hiding in his apartment, since he could hardly have just entered without being seen. Calling loudly to his servants, the baron drew his sword, which he had not yet removed from his belt. The stranger, slowly moving forward, told him that there was nothing to fear. He had come in friendship, he said, and wanted only to disclose a terrible secret, which it was necessary for the baron to know.

- **province** (PROV ins) **big division of a country, similar to a U. S. state**
- Bretagne (bruh TAN yuh) **northwestern region of France; now called Brittany**
- baron (BAR un) **lord; nobleman**
- **magnificence** (mag NIF i suns) **greatness**
- **disclose** (dis KLOHZ) **make known**

142

The baron was impressed by the polite manner of the stranger, and looked at him for some time in silence. Then he returned his sword to his belt, and asked how the man had gotten into the apartment, and the purpose of his unusual visit.

The stranger said he could not then explain himself. But, if the baron would follow him to the edge of the forest a short distance from the castle, he would there prove to him that he had something important to communicate.

This suggestion alarmed the baron again. He could hardly believe that the stranger meant to take him to such a lonely spot, at this hour of the night, without planning to kill him. He refused to go. He stated that if the stranger were up to any good, he would here and now explain the reason for his visit.

While the baron spoke this, he examined the stranger still more carefully than before. But he noticed no change in his face, nor anything that might hint at an evil plan. His visitor was dressed like a knight. He was tall and proud, and had polite manners. Still, however, the stanger refused to tell the reason for his visit in any place but the one he had mentioned. At the same time he gave hints about the secret. Finally, the baron grew curious enough to agree to the stranger's request.

"Sir knight," said he, "I will go with you to the forest, and will take with me only four of my servants."

To this, however, the knight objected.

"What I want to communicate," said he seriously, "is for you alone. There are only three living persons to whom the secret is known. It is of more importance to you than you realize. In future years, you will look back to this night with satisfaction or sorrow, depending on what you now do. If you would be happy in the future, follow me. I promise you on my honor as a knight that no evil shall come to you. If you are content to doubt me, remain here in your room, and I will leave as I came."

"Sir knight," replied the baron, "how is it possible that my future peace can depend upon what I decide now?"

"That is not now to be told," said the stranger. "I will explain myself no more. It is late. If you follow me it must be quickly."

The baron paced his room for some time in silence. He was impressed by the words of the stranger. But the unusual request he feared to agree to, and feared also to refuse. At length he said, "Sir knight, you are completely unknown to me. Tell me yourself, does it make sense that I should trust myself alone with a stranger, at this hour, in the forest? Tell me, at least, who you are, and who helped you hide yourself in this room."

The knight frowned at these words, and was a moment silent. Then, with a stern look, he said, "I am an English knight. I am called Sir Bevys of Lancaster, and my deeds are not unknown in the world. I was returning to my native land, when night fell in the forest."

"Your name is not unknown to fame," said the baron. "I have heard of it. But why, since my castle is known to entertain all passing knights, didn't you come to my gate? Why didn't you appear at the feast, where you would have been welcomed? Why did you choose to hide yourself in my castle, and sneak into my room at midnight?"

The stranger frowned, and turned away in silence. But the baron repeated the questions.

"I come not," said the knight, "to answer questions, but to communicate facts. If you want to know more, follow me. Again I give you the honor of a knight that you shall return in safety. Be quick to decide—I must be gone."

After thinking some more, the baron decided to follow the stranger, and to see the result of his unusual request. He therefore drew his sword, and taking a lamp, told the knight to lead on. The stranger

obeyed. Opening the door, they passed into another room, where the baron was surprised to find his servants asleep. He was about to punish them for their carelessness, when the knight waved his hand and shook his head, and they passed on.

The knight, having gone down a staircase, opened a secret door, which the baron had believed was known only to himself. They proceeded through several narrow and winding passages. At last they came to a small gate that opened beyond the walls of the castle. Noticing that these secret passages were well known to the stranger, the baron wondered if he shouldn't turn back. Didn't the adventure now promise some danger? Then, remembering that he carried his sword, and noticing again the polite and noble manner of his guest, he regained his courage. He blushed that it had failed him for a moment.

He now found himself on the great steps before the gates of his castle. Looking up, he saw lights shining in the windows of the guests, who were now going to bed. As he shivered in the wind and looked on the dark scene around him, he thought of the comfort of his warm room and his cheerful fire.

The wind was strong, and the baron watched his lamp carefully, expecting every moment to see it go out. But though the flame grew dim, it did not disappear. He continued to follow the stranger, who often sighed as he went, but did not speak.

When they reached the edge of the forest, the knight turned and raised his head, as if he meant to say something. But then, closing his lips, in silence he walked on.

As they entered the dark woods, the baron, now worried again, wondered whether to go on. He asked how much farther they were to go. The knight replied only by waving his hand, and the baron, with slow steps and a suspicious eye, followed through a dark and difficult path. When they had gone quite a way, he again demanded where they were going. This time he refused to walk another step unless he was told. As he said this, he looked at his sword, and then at the knight.

"A little farther is the place where I would lead you," said the stranger. "No evil shall come to you—I have promised on my honor as a knight."

The baron, feeling better, again followed in silence. They soon arrived at a deep valley in the forest, where the dark trees entirely shut out the sky. The knight sighed deeply as he walked on, and sometimes paused. Finally he reached a spot where the trees crowded into a knot. Here he turned, and with a terrific look, pointed to the ground. The baron saw there the body of a man, stretched out at length and swimming in blood. A ghastly wound was on the forehead, and death appeared already to have changed the face.

The baron, on seeing this sight, drew back in horror. He looked at the knight for explanation. Then he started to lift the body, to see if there were any remains of life. But the stranger, waving his hand, gave him so sad a look that he stopped.

But what were the baron's feelings next! Holding the lamp near the head of the corpse, the baron discovered the exact face of the stranger—at whom he now looked up in surprise and shock. As he stared, he saw the face of the knight change and begin to fade. Soon the stranger's whole form slowly vanished before him. While the baron stood fixed to the spot, a voice was heard to say these words:

"The body of Sir Bevys of Lancaster, a noble knight of England, lies before you. He was this night robbed and murdered as he journeyed towards his native land. Respect the honor of knighthood, and the laws of all lands. Bury the body in your castle ground, and cause his murderers to be punished. If you do this, peace and happiness shall be with you and your court forever!"

The baron, when he recovered from the shock into which this adventure had thrown him, returned to his castle. Soon the body of Sir Bevys was carried from the forest. On the following day it was buried, with the honors of knighthood, in the chapel of the castle, attended by all the noble knights and ladies who were the guests of the great Baron de Brunne.

- promise (PROM is) **give reason to expect**
- ghastly (GAST lee) **horrible**
- knighthood (NYT hood) **rank of a knight**

ALL THINGS CONSIDERED

1. At the beginning of the story, we are told that the baron is famous chiefly for his (a) interest in mystery. (b) courage. (c) riches and his kindness to guests.

2. The baron's first reaction to the stranger is (a) amusement. (b) fear. (c) kindness.

3. The mysterious visitor turns out to be quite (a) polite. (b) rude. (c) dishonest.

4. When the stranger first makes his request, the baron is (a) eager to help. (b) afraid but curious. (c) angry beyond belief.

5. The baron refuses at first to go with the visitor because he (a) already knows the visitor's secret. (b) is worried about his own life. (c) feels very sleepy.

6. When he finally goes with the knight, the baron takes (a) four servants. (b) a map of the forest. (c) a lamp and a sword.

7. The baron becomes even more disturbed when the knight seems to know (a) the castle's secret passages. (b) the servants' names. (c) the entire history of the castle.

8. At the end of the trip, the baron (a) sees the corpse of a man. (b) imagines the corpse of a man. (c) kills the stranger.

9. The visitor differs from the dead man in having (a) no ghastly wound on his forehead. (b) heavier clothes. (c) a softer voice.

10. The big mystery in the story is this: how a person can be both (a) young and old. (b) rich and poor. (c) dead and alive.

THINKING IT THROUGH

Discuss the following items in class.

1. After reading the end of the story, it is easy for us to know why the visitor did not tell the baron the real reason for his strange request. Suppose the visitor had chosen to tell the truth. (a) What would the visitor have told the baron? (b) What would the baron's reaction have been?

2. Explain how each of the following words describes the baron at different times in the story: (a) *fearful,* (b) *curious,* (c) *suspicious,* (d) *angry,* (e) *terrified.*

3. The story was written about 200 years ago. Yet the events it describes are set much earlier, during the Middle Ages. The year A.D. 1250 might be a good date. Explain three ways in which life in the Middle Ages differed from life today. Use details from the story to support your statements.

Literary Skills

Understanding Fantasy

A **fantasy** (FAN tuh see) is a very strange tale that could probably not happen in real life. Most of the stories in this unit can be called fantasies.

Writers of fantasies tend to follow a two-part rule: (a) There must be only *one* impossible element in a fantasy. (b) Other than that, the story must be as realistic as possible.

There are good reasons for this rule. If many impossible things happen, the reader will never come near to believing the story, even in fun. If, except for the impossible element, most of the story is as real as possible, the reader will come closer to belief. This is why fantasies are often crowded with realistic detail. Think about "Of Missing Persons," for instance. That story is cluttered with realistic details of city life. Except for the one fantastic element, it is about the most true-to-life story ever written.

Now consider "The Provençal Tale" in light of the above rule. On a separate sheet of paper, answer the following questions.

1. Ann Radcliffe wrote long before the rule about fantasies had been developed. Did she follow the rule? Explain your answer.
2. What is one impossible element in the story?
3. What are three details about the age of knighthood that make the story seem real?

Composition

Follow your teacher's instructions before completing *one* of these writing assignments.

1. Look back at the story. Find three sentences that contain realistic details. Write each sentence on a separate piece of paper. For each sentence, tell why it makes the story seem real.
2. Write a short composition comparing Ann Radcliffe's "The Provençal Tale" with another story in this book. Don't just tell what happens in the stories. Instead, explain your likes and dislikes. Give as many reasons as you can. Go into detail. Don't use words like "interesting" or "boring" without backing them up.

VOCABULARY AND SKILL REVIEW

Before completing the exercises that follow, you may wish to review the **bold-faced** words on pages 127 to 146.

I. On a separate sheet of paper, write the *italicized* term that best fills the blank in each sentence. Each term should be used only once.

disclose	*prominent*	*thicket*	*province*	*listlessly*
pneumonia	*delicately*	*finicky*	*bearing*	*malnutrition*

1. A _____ is similar to a U.S. state.

2. A _____ eater is very particular about his or her diet.

3. The Sears Tower is a _____ feature of the Chicago skyline.

4. A poor food supply caused many people to suffer from _____ .

5. A lot of rabbits live in the _____ behind our house.

6. The doctor listened to her lungs and said the sick girl had _____ .

7. The tired people sat _____ around the room.

8. Maria _____ removes the piece of soot from my eye.

9. Santa Claus enters the room, _____ presents for all.

10. The senator refuses to _____ her age to the press.

II. The paragraph that follows should really be nine paragraphs. Write the numerals 1 to 9 on your paper. After each, write the first two words of a new paragraph. Start with 1. *Do you.* Your next answer will be 2. *A certain.*

Do you like nonsense stories? Some people do; others do not. The story below will help you answer this question. A certain woman was once walking across the desert. Her walk was not an easy one. It was very hot. The dry sand stretched out for miles on all sides. She saw nothing until she spotted three small figures working their way through the heat waves toward her. Half an hour later the traveler could see the three figures clearly. They were three women. One carried a loaf of bread. Another carried a bottle of water. The third carried a car door. "Why do you carry that loaf of bread?" the woman asked when she was close enough to be heard. "So that if I am hungry, I may eat." "Why do you carry that bottle of water?" she asked the second. "So that if I am thirsty, I may drink." "And you," the woman asked the third. "Just why do you carry that car door?" "Why," came the answer, "so that if it gets really hot out here, I can just roll down the window."

UNIT REVIEW

I. Match the terms in Column A with their definitions in Column B.

A	B
1. characterization	a) person who tells a story
2. fantasy	b) giving hints about what might
3. foreshadowing	happen
4. narrator	c) the act of making people in a
5. narrative	story seem real
6. mood	d) unreal and weird story
7. suspense	e) story
	f) condition of doubt or anxiety
	g) feeling reader gets from a
	piece of literature

II. One reason for learning literary terms is that they help you evaluate literature. Without the terms, it's often difficult to state why a story strikes you as "interesting," "boring," or just "so-so."

Your job now is to write a composition explaining exactly why a certain story in this unit struck you as interesting, boring, or so-so. The following questions will help you to think about and to explain your reactions to your chosen story.

Plot

1. Is the *conflict* in the story clear and exciting?

2. Are the *plot questions* clear in the reader's mind as the story moves along? (If not, you find yourself just "reading words" without quite knowing why.)

3. Does the *climax*, or most exciting part, come toward the end? (If not, your interest falls off.)

4. Are there too many *coincidences* in the story?

5. Should more *foreshadowing* have been used to make the surprise in the story more acceptable?

Characters

6. Do the characters seem real, or are they just empty people with names?

7. Which methods of *characterization* (see page 91) does the author use successfully? (Or, which methods should the author have used to bring the characters to life?)

Setting

8. Does the story happen in the best possible place and time?

9. Could the author have made better use of the weather or other natural events?

10. Did the author include enough realistic details about the setting to make the story seem true-to-life?

SPEAKING UP

▶ The story that follows is an old American folktale. Like all folktales, it started as a spoken—not a written—story. Practice reading it aloud until you can read it well. For example, read the cats' conversations in a way that builds fear and excitement. Saying the last line with expression is especially important.

WAIT TILL MARTIN COMES

retold by Maria Leach

That big house down the road was haunted. Nobody could live in it.

The door was never locked. But nobody ever went in. Nobody would even spend a night in it. Several people had tried but came running out pretty fast.

One night a man was going along that road on his way to the next village. He noticed that the sky was blackening. No moon. No stars. Big storm coming for sure.

He had a long way to go. He knew he couldn't get home before it poured.

So he decided to take shelter in that empty house by the road.

He had heard it was haunted. But shucks! Who believed in ghosts? No such thing.

So he went in. He built himself a nice fire on the big hearth, pulled up a chair, and sat down to read a book.

He could hear the rain beating on the window. Lightning flashed. The thunder cracked around the old building.

But he sat there reading.

Next time he looked up there was a little gray cat sitting on the hearth.

• hearth (HARTH) **the floor of a fireplace**

151

That was all right, he thought. Cozy.

He went on reading. The rain went on raining.

Pretty soon he heard the door creak and a big black cat came sauntering in.

The first cat looked up.

"What are we goin' to do with him?"

"Wait till Martin comes," said the other.

The man went right on reading.

Pretty soon he heard the door creak and another great big black cat, as big as a dog, came in.

"What we goin' to do with him?" said the first cat.

"Wait till Martin comes."

The man was awful scared by this time, but he kept looking in the book, pretending to be reading.

Pretty soon he heard the door creak and a great big black cat, as big as a calf, came in.

He stared at the man. "Shall we do it now?" he said.

"Wait till Martin comes," said the others.

The man just leaped out of that chair, and out the window, and down the road.

"Tell Martin I couldn't wait!" he said.

- saunter (SAWN tur) walk in a slow, easy, relaxed way; stroll

152

Remember that a photograph can be turned into a story that happens over a period of time. Now think of a plot, and then write a whole story built around the photograph shown. Your story should be at least as long as "Wait Till Martin Comes" (Page 151).

The *setting* is very important in this picture. What natural event has happened—and is still happening? What time might it be? Which two people have probably just arrived in the boat? Think about *characterization*. How will you bring the characters to life for your readers? What are the names of the people? Which of the characters might be related? How are they related to each other?

Now go back to the plot. Suppose you start your story an hour before the time of the scene pictured. How will the action begin? What exciting plot question will hold the reader's interest? Finally, what *prediction* will you make about what will happen in the future? Where will the characters be an hour from now? How will they feel about their experience and about each other?

UNIT · 3

ZIGZAGS

In life, most people don't like to be caught napping.
Events that creep up from behind and knock us for a loop
aren't often welcomed. It's positively painful to
have our eyes pop out or our hair stand on end.
Between the covers of a book,
however, it's a different story.
Just for fun, look at the picture below
while you slowly turn
this book upside
down.

Surprised? Did you mind it? Not at all. Most readers
like to be staggered now and then. They like plots
that take sudden turns, do loop-the-loops,
and trace out zigzags. They love
authors who can pack
a punch that sends
them spinning.
Get set—for the
unexpected!

THE GETAWAY

by John Savage

▶ The surprises in this story seem to zigzag right off the page. Fasten your seat belts before you read this one.

Whenever I get sleepy at the wheel, I always stop for coffee. This time, I was going along in western Texas and I got sleepy. I saw a sign that said GAS EAT, so I pulled off. It was long after midnight. What I expected was a place like a bunch of others, where the coffee tastes like copper and the flies never sleep.

What I found was something else. The tables were painted wood, and they looked as if nobody ever spilled the ketchup. The counter was spick-and-span. Even the smell was OK, I swear it.

Nobody was there, as far as customers. There was just this one old boy—

really only about forty, getting gray above the ears—behind the counter. I sat down at the counter and ordered coffee and apple pie. Right away he got me started feeling sad.

I have a habit: I divide people up. Winners and losers. This old boy behind the counter was the kind that they *mean* well. They can't do enough for you, but their eyes have this gentle, faraway look, and they can't win. You know? With their clean shirt and the little bow tie? It makes you feel sad just to look at them. Only take my tip: Don't feel too sad.

He brought the coffee steaming hot, and it tasted like coffee. "Care for cream and sugar?" he asked. I said, "Please," and the cream was fresh and cold and thick. The pie was good, too.

A car pulled up outside. The old boy glanced out to see if they wanted gas, but they didn't. They came right in. The tall one said, "Two coffees. Do you have a road map we could look at?"

"I think so," the old boy said. He got their coffee first, and then started rooting through a pile of papers by the telephone, looking for a map. It was easy to see he was the type nothing's too much trouble for. Tickled to be of service.

I'm the same type myself, if you want to know. I watched the old boy hunting for his map, and I felt like I was looking in a mirror.

After a minute or two, he came up with the map. "This one's a little out of date, but . . ." He put it on the counter, beside their coffee.

The two men spread out the map and leaned over it. They were well dressed, like a couple of feed merchants. The tall one ran his finger along the Rio Grande and shook his head. "I guess there's no place to get across, this side of El Paso."

He said it to his pal, but the old boy behind the counter heard him and lit up like a light bulb. "You trying to find the best way south? I might be able to help you with that."

"How?"

"Just a minute." He spent a lot of time going through the papers by the telephone again. "Thought I might have a newer map," he said. "Anything recent would show the Hackett Bridge. Anyway, I can tell you how to find it."

"Here's a town called Hackett," the tall one said, still looking at the map. "It's on the river, just at the end of a road. Looks like a pretty small place."

"Not any more. It's just about doubled since they built the bridge."

"What happens on the other side?" The short one asked the question, but both of the feed-merchant types were paying close attention.

"Pretty fair road, clear to Chihuahua. It joins up there with the highway out of El Paso and Juarez."

The tall man finished his coffee, folded the map, put it in his pocket, and stood up. "We'll take your map with us," he said.

The old boy seemed startled, like a new kid at school when somebody pokes him in the nose to show him who's boss. However, he just shrugged and said, "Glad to let you have it."

The feed merchants had a little conference on the way out, talking in whispers. Then they stopped in the middle of

- **root** (ROOT) **dig or search around**
- feed merchant (FEED MUR chunt) **person who buys and sells food for animals**
- Rio Grande (REE oh GRAND) **river that separates the state of Texas from Mexico**
- El Paso (el PASS oh) **a city in western Texas, near the border of Mexico**
- Chihuahua (chi WAH wah) **city in northern Mexico**
- Juarez (WAH rez) **Mexican city across the Rio Grande from El Paso**

the floor, turned around, reached inside their jackets, and pulled guns on us. Automatic pistols, I think they were. "You sit where you are and don't move," the tall one said to me. "And *you,* get against the wall."

Both of us did exactly what they wanted. I told you we were a lot alike.

The short man walked over and pushed one of the keys of the cash register. "Every little bit helps," he said, and he scooped the money out of the drawer. The tall man set the telephone on the floor, put his foot on it, and jerked the wires out. Then they ran to their car and got in. The short man leaned out the window and shot out one of my tires. Then

they took off fast.

I looked at the old boy behind the counter. He seemed a little pale, but he didn't waste any time. He took a screwdriver out of a drawer and squatted down beside the telephone. I said, "It doesn't always pay to be nice to people."

He laughed and said, "Well, it doesn't usually cost anything," and went on taking the base plate off the telephone. He was a fast worker, actually. His tongue was sticking out of the corner of his mouth. In about five minutes he had a dial tone coming out of the receiver. He dialed a number and told the rangers about the men and their car. "They did?" he said. "Well, well, well. . . . No, not El

Paso. They took the Hackett turnoff." After he hung up, he said, "It turns out those guys robbed a supermarket in Wichita Falls."

I shook my head. "They sure had me fooled. I thought they looked perfectly all right."

The old boy got me another cup of coffee, and opened himself a bottle of pop. "They fooled me, too, at first." He wiped his mouth. "Then I got a load of their shoulder holsters when they leaned on the counter to look at the map. Anyway, they had mean eyes, I thought. Didn't you?"

"Well, I didn't at the time."

We drank without talking for a while, getting our nerves back in shape. A pair of patrol cars went roaring by outside and squealed their tires around the Hackett turnoff.

I got to thinking, and I thought of the saddest thing yet. "You *knew* there was something wrong with those guys, but you still couldn't keep from helping them on their way."

He laughed. "Well, the world's a tough sort of place at best, is how I look at it."

"I can understand showing them the map," I said, "but I'd never have told about the bridge. Now there's not a chance of catching them. If you'd kept your mouth shut, there'd at least be some hope."

"There isn't any—"

"Not a shred," I went on. "Not with a car as fast as they've got."

The way the old boy smiled made me feel better about him and me. "I don't mean there isn't any hope," he said. "I mean there isn't any bridge."

ALL THINGS CONSIDERED

1. The narrator, or the person telling the story, stops at the eating place because he's (a) afraid to drive alone after midnight. (b) sleepy. (c) awfully hungry.
2. At first, the narrator forms the opinion that the man behind the counter is a (a) winner. (b) loser. (c) crook.
3. When the two men enter, they are most interested in getting (a) a map. (b) change for a dollar. (c) something to eat.
4. It is clear that the two men want to (a) improve their Spanish. (b) get out of Texas and into Mexico. (c) drive across all the bridges on the Rio Grande.

• nerve (NURV) courage

5. The man behind the counter learns that the two men are armed when they (a) enter with their hands in their pockets. (b) order only two cups of coffee. (c) lean over to look at the map.

6. Before they leave, the two men (a) pay their bill. (b) make a phone call. (c) empty the cash register.

7. After the two men leave, the man behind the counter works fast to repair the (a) cash register. (b) telephone. (c) flat tire.

8. Toward the end of the story, the reader learns that the two men are (a) rangers. (b) feed merchants. (c) robbers.

9. The patrol cars are streaking toward (a) El Paso. (b) Wichita Falls. (c) Hackett.

10. The biggest surprise in the story comes when the man behind the counter says, (a) "Well, I didn't at the time." (b) "Anyway, they had mean eyes, I thought." (c) "I mean there isn't any bridge."

THINKING IT THROUGH

Discuss the following items in class.

1. The story contains more than one surprise. (a) The first big surprise happens about halfway through the story. What is the first surprise? (b) Another big surprise comes at the end. What is that surprise? (c) The reader can infer, or guess, one surprise that will take place after the end of the story. Who will be surprised and why? (d) Are there any other events or statements in the story that surprised you?

2. At first, the narrator assumes that the man behind the counter is a loser. Near the end of the story, the narrator changes his opinion of the man. Why?

3. Toward the end of the story, the man behind the counter laughs twice and smiles. Why?

Sentence Meaning

Figurative Language

The short introduction to "The Getaway" states that the surprises "seem to zigzag right off the page." It advises you to "fasten your seat belts" before reading. Obviously, the words don't *really* mean what they seem to say.

Language used in this way is called **figurative** (FIG yur uh tiv) **language.** The words do not mean exactly what they seem to say. You use figurative language every day. Suppose you tell a friend, "This headache is *killing* me!" In truth, are you anywhere near death's door? Of course not. The term *killing* is figurative—as is *death's door.*

The following sentences from "The Getaway" contain five examples of figurative language. On a separate sheet of paper, copy the figurative terms that are in *italics.* Then write the author's real meaning for each term.

1–2. What I expected was a place . . . where the coffee tastes *like copper* and *the flies never sleep.*

3. I watched the old boy hunting for his map, and I felt *like I was looking in a mirror.*

4. . . . the old boy . . . *lit up like a light bulb.*

5. We drank . . . *getting our nerves back into shape.*

Composition

Follow your teacher's instructions before completing *one* of these writing assignments.

1. Here are five figurative expressions you have probably heard many times. Choose two of them. Try to think of a fresher way to say the same thing. Write that on paper. (Hint: Some expressions can be made fresher by changing just one or two words.)
   (a) I'm so hungry I could eat a horse.
   (b) It was raining cats and dogs.
   (c) You could have knocked me over with a feather.
   (d) Those people have money to burn.
   (e) She eats like a bird.

2. Write a paragraph that explains the end of the story. What will happen to the two men when they get to Hackett?

SHERLOCK HOLMES
AND THE
SPECKLED BAND

by Arthur Conan Doyle
dramatized by Alice Delman

▶ What do gypsies, a lady in danger, and a baboon have in common? They're all part of this mystery from the files of Sherlock Holmes, the great detective of English fiction. The clues are all here. Can you solve the crime before Holmes does?

CHARACTERS

Sherlock Holmes, *the famous detective*
Dr. Watson, *his friend*
Helen Stoner, *the lady in danger*
Julia Stoner, *her sister*
Dr. Grimesby Roylott, *her stepfather*

SCENE 1

TIME: About 1900.
SETTING: The parlor in Holmes's *apartment on Baker Street, London, England.*

AT RISE: A woman dressed in black and wearing a veil is seated on the window seat in the parlor. The room is comfortably filled with sofas, chairs, old furniture, and the usual belongings of the bachelor detective: books, newspapers, slippers, magnifying glass, pipe rack, various hats, and a violin among them. Holmes *and* Dr. Watson *enter. The lady rises to greet them.*

Holmes: Good morning, Madam. I'm Sherlock Holmes. (*nodding toward* Watson) My close friend, Dr. Watson. You can speak freely in front of him. Please sit down by the fire. I'll order coffee, since I see that you're shivering.

• **at rise**—at the start of the scene; when the curtain rises

162

Helen (*changing her seat*)**:** Not from cold.

Holmes: What then?

Helen: Fear, Mr. Holmes. Terror.

(*She raises her veil to reveal a face tired and gray. She looks about 30, but her hair already shows traces of gray. Her eyes are restless and frightened. She looks like a hunted animal.* Holmes *studies her face.*)

Holmes: Don't be afraid. Just leave everything to me. Now . . . what sent you all this way by train? And so early in the morning, too.

Helen: How did you know I . . . ?

Holmes (*breaking in*)**:** There's the second half of a return ticket in the palm of your left glove. Plain as day. Please relax. That drive in the dogcart must have been difficult.

(Helen *gives a start of surprise. She stares at* Holmes.)

Holmes: It's no mystery, my dear madam. The left arm of your jacket has mud spots in seven places. The marks are fresh. Only a dogcart splashes mud in that way.

Helen: Well, whatever your reasons, you're right. Mr. Holmes, I can't stand this strain any longer! I'll go mad. I have no one else to turn to, except . . . well, someone who cares for me, but can't help. I've heard of you, Mr. Holmes. Can you help me? I . . . right now, I can't pay you. But in a month or so, I'll be married, and then . . .

Holmes (*breaking in*)**:** Madam, my work is its own reward. I'll be happy to help you. Now, tell us everything. Everything.

Helen: I'm afraid that . . . that's the horror of it. It's . . . so vague. My fears—they come from small things that might seem like nothing to you. Even my fiancé thinks it's all just nerves.

Holmes: He says so?

Helen: No, but it's in his soothing answers. And the way he turns his eyes from me. But you, Mr. Holmes—I've heard you can see all

- dogcart (DOG cart) **light, two-wheeled vehicle with two seats back to back, pulled by a horse**
- **vague** (VAYG) **not clear; hazy**
- fiancé (fee on SAY) **husband-to-be**
- **soothing** (SOOTH ing) **calming**

the evils that lie in the human heart. I'm surrounded by danger. Can you help me?

Watson: Yes!

Holmes: Thank you, Watson. Now, Madam—start with your name.

Helen: It's Helen Stoner.

Holmes: And you live . . . ?

Helen: With my stepfather. He's the last member of one of the oldest families in England, the Roylotts of Stoke Moran.

Holmes: Yes, I've heard the name.

Helen: The family was once very rich. But they were ruined in the last century. Nothing's left but a few acres and the ancient house. And that's crushed under a mortgage. The last Roylott lived out his life there—a horrible life as a penniless nobleman. But his only son—that's my stepfather—he saw that things had to change. He borrowed some money. He got a medical degree and went out to India. He built a large practice there.

Holmes: But he came back to England? Why?

Helen: A string of robberies in his house in India. He got into a fit of anger about them and beat his native butler to death. They almost hanged him. He spent a long term in prison. Then he came back to England. A sad man. A very disappointed man.

Holmes: And your mother, his wife?

Helen: He married my mother in India. She was the widow of a Major-General Stoner. My sister Julia and I were twins. We were only two years old when my mother remarried.

Holmes: Hm. Was she well-off at the time?

Helen: Well, yes. She had quite a bit of money—at least £1000 a year. And she gave it all to Dr. Roylott while we lived with him. Julia and I were to each get a certain amount a year when we married.

Holmes: Is your mother still living?

Helen: She died soon after we came to England—eight years ago. A railway accident.

Holmes: And you went on living with your stepfather?

Helen: Yes, he gave up trying to practice medicine. He took us to live in the family house at Stoke Moran. The money my mother

- **mortgage** (MOR gij) **loan given to purchase a house**
- practice (PRAK tis) **the business of a doctor or lawyer**

164

left was more than enough. We had all we needed to be happy.

Holmes: But?

Helen: It was my stepfather. A terrible change came over him. At first, the neighbors were so happy to see a Roylott back in the old family home. But instead of making friends, he shut himself up in the house. He hardly ever came out, except to get into fights with anyone who crossed his path. He has a terrible temper. As a matter of fact, some of his ancestors showed traces of . . . well, madness. In his case, it got worse because of those years in India.

Holmes: What happened?

Helen: A series of brawls. Two ended in the police court. He became the terror of the village. People would run when they saw him coming.

Holmes: Is he dangerous?

Helen: Well, he's a man of huge strength. And when he's angry, he's just out of control. Last week he threw the blacksmith over a bridge into a stream. I had to pay all the money I could get in a hurry to keep it quiet.

Holmes: He has no friends, then?

Helen: Only the gypsies. He lets them camp on his land. And they give him the hospitality of their tents. Sometimes for weeks on end. Oh, and he also has animals—Indian animals.

Holmes: Really?

Helen: Yes. They're sent over to him by a man in India. He's got a cheetah and a baboon. They just wander loose on the grounds. They scare people almost as much as he does! You can imagine what our life was like, Julia's and mine. No great pleasure. Julia was only 30 when she died, but her hair had already started to turn white. Like mine.

Holmes: Your sister is dead, then?

Helen: She died just two years ago. It's her death that I came to see you about.

Holmes: Go on.

Helen: Well, living the life we did, Julia and I met very few people our own age. But we had an Aunt Honoria, who lives near

---

- **brawl** (BRAWL) *noisy fight*
- **cheetah** (CHEE tuh) *wild cat in the tiger family*

Harrow. We went to visit her sometimes. Julia was there at Christmas two years ago, and she met a major of the marines. They got engaged.

Holmes: What did your stepfather think of that?

Helen: He didn't object. But within two weeks of the date set for the wedding . . . *(She is very upset.)*

Holmes: Please go on.

Helen: The terrible event that . . .

Holmes *(breaking in)***:** Please be precise. Details! I must have details.

Helen: That's easy. It's all burned in my memory.

(She appears about to cry.)

Holmes: Take it easy. Go ahead.

Helen: The house, as I said, is very old. We use only one wing. The bedrooms are on the ground floor. The first is Dr. Roylott's, the second my sister's, and the third is mine. No connecting doors. But all three rooms open into the same hallway. Is that clear?

Holmes: Perfectly.

Helen: The windows of the three rooms open out on the lawn. That night—the night she died—Dr. Roylott had gone to his room early. But we knew he hadn't gone to bed.

Holmes: How?

Helen: Because my sister smelled the strong Indian cigars he smokes. So she left her room and came into mine. We sat for a while, talking about the wedding. Then we said goodnight. I remember it all so vividly. She got up to go. . . .

SCENE 2

SETTING: Helen's bedroom in the Roylott mansion.

AT RISE: Julia *and* Helen Stoner *are seated on the bed. They kiss each other goodnight.* Julia *walks to the door, then pauses, turning to look back at* Helen.

Julia: Helen, have you ever heard anyone whistle in the dead of the night?

- **precise** (pri SISE) very exact
- **vividly** (VIV id lee) very clearly; as if lifelike

Helen: No! Why?

Julia: You couldn't be whistling in your sleep, could you?

Helen: No! What are you talking about?

Julia: It's just that the last few nights, I've heard a strange whistling. At about three o'clock in the morning! A low, clear whistle. I'm a light sleeper, and it wakes me up. I can't tell where the sound comes from—the next room, the lawn, I don't know.

Helen: It must be the gypsies.

Julia: I guess so. But if it's on the lawn, I wonder why you didn't hear it too.

Helen: Oh, I sleep like a log.

Julia: Well, it doesn't matter, anyway. Good night.

SCENE 3

SETTING: The parlor in Holmes's *apartment.*

AT RISE: Holmes, Watson, *and* Helen Stoner *are sitting as before.* Helen *goes on with her story.*

Helen: She smiled at me and closed my door. I heard her key turn in the lock.

Holmes: Her key? Did you usually lock yourselves in at night?

Helen: Always.

Holmes: Why?

Helen: Remember—the cheetah and the baboon! We didn't feel safe unless our doors were locked at night.

Holmes: Right. Go on.

Helen: I couldn' sleep that night. It was wild weather, howling wind. The rain beat against the windows. Suddenly I heard a scream— a woman's scream. I knew it was my sister's voice. I rushed into the hall. Then I seemed to hear a low whistle—just as my sister had described it. Then there was a clanging sound, like metal falling. My sister's door was unlocked—and it started to open slowly. I stared at it. I didn't know what would come out! It was Julia. Her face was white with terror. Her hands were groping for help. She swayed as if she was drunk. I ran to her and threw my arms around her, but her knees gave way and she fell to the

---

• **grope** (GROHP) feel about blindly

ground. She was twisting in terrible pain. I bent over her. Then suddenly, she shrieked—I'll never forget her voice! "Oh! Helen! It was the band! The speckled band!"

Holmes: That's all? She didn't explain?

Helen: She tried to say more. She stabbed her finger in the air towards the doctor's room. But then she choked and couldn't get the words out. I called out for my stepfather. But when he got to my sister's side, she was unconscious.

Holmes: Didn't he do anything to bring her around?

Helen: He sent for medical help from the village. But it was useless. She died without speaking again.

Holmes: One moment. Are you sure about this whistle and this metallic sound? Could you swear to it?

Helen: I don't know. I felt strongly that I heard it. But with the wind crashing, and the creaking of an old house—I don't know.

Holmes: Was your sister dressed?

Helen: No, she was in her nightgown. And she had a burnt match in one hand and a matchbox in the other.

Holmes: So she struck a match and looked about her when it happened. That's important. And what did the coroner find was the cause of death?

Helen: He was very careful because Dr. Roylott had caused so much trouble in the neighborhood. But he couldn't find the cause of death.

Holmes: Could anyone have entered her room?

Helen: The door was locked on the inside. The windows have old-fashioned shutters with broad iron bars, and they were locked every night. The walls are solid all around. So is the floor. The chimney's wide, but it's barred. My sister had to be alone when it happened. Besides, there were no marks of violence on her.

Holmes: Poison?

Helen: The doctors examined her for it. There wasn't any.

Holmes: What do *you* think your sister died of, then?

Helen: I think she died of pure fear and nervous shock. But what could have frightened her? I can't imagine.

Holmes: The gypsies—were they on the grounds that night?

Helen: Yes, there are nearly always some there.

Holmes: Ah. And what did you think she meant by her last words about a band—a speckled band?

Helen: I don't know. Sometimes I've thought it was just wild talk— she was dying. Or maybe it meant . . . some band of people. Perhaps the gypsies. Because of the spotted handkerchiefs they wear—she might have called them "the speckled band."

(Holmes *shakes his head. Clearly, he is far from satisfied.*)

Holmes: We're in deep waters here. Please tell us the rest.

Helen: That was two years ago. My life became lonelier than ever— until lately. About a month ago, a friend—a dear friend I've known for years—asked me to marry him. My stepfather hasn't objected. So we're going to be married in the spring.

Holmes: Then what brings you here?

Helen: Two days ago, some repairs were started in the west wing of the house. My bedroom wall has been ripped up. So I've had to move into the room where my sister died. And sleep in the bed she slept in. It was terrifying. Last night, I lay awake thinking

---

- **coroner** (CAWR uh ner) public officer who investigates deaths that may not be due to natural causes

about her. Her terrible death. I suddenly heard—it was very quiet—I heard the low whistle. Just like the whistle on the night she died. I jumped up and lit the lamp. But there was nothing in the room. I was too shaken to go to bed again. So I got dressed. As soon as it was daylight, I came here.

Holmes: Very wise. But have you told me everything?

Helen: Yes. Everything.

Holmes: You have not, Miss Roylott. You're protecting your stepfather.

Helen: Why, what do you mean?

(Holmes *leans toward* Helen *and pushes back the bit of lace that covers her hand.*)

Holmes: Ah. Five little black-and-blue spots. Just the sort of spots made by four fingers and a thumb. You've been treated cruelly.

Helen (*embarrassed*)**:** He's a hard man. Perhaps he doesn't really know his own strength.

(*A silence.* Holmes *leans his chin on his hands and stares into the fire.*)

Holmes: This is a very deep business. I have to know a thousand details before I decide what to do. But we haven't a moment to lose. If we come today to Stoke Moran, will we be able to look over these rooms? Without your stepfather knowing?

Helen: Well, yes. As a matter of fact, he said he'd be going into town today. He'll probably be away all day.

Holmes: Good. You wouldn't mind the trip, Watson?

Watson: I'd love it.

Holmes: Then we'll both come.

Helen: Thank you. I feel better already. I'll be waiting for you this afternoon, then.

(Helen *drops her veil back over her face and exits.*)

Holmes: Well, what do you think of it all, Watson?

- **treat** (TREET) **deal with**
- **deep** (DEEP) **hard to understand**

Watson: Hm. Seems to be a dark, evil business.

Holmes: Yes, it does.

Watson: But the floor and the walls were all solid. The door, the windows, and the chimney were all blocked. If she's right about that, then her sister must have been alone when she fell ill.

Holmes: Then what about those whistles? And what about the "speckled band"?

Watson: I really couldn't say.

Holmes: Well, let's put a few things together. First, the whistles at night. Second, the band of gypsies—very friendly with the old doctor. Third, the fact that the doctor has an interest in stopping his stepdaughter's marriage. And finally, the metallic clang. A sound that *might* have been caused by one of the metal bars on the shutters falling into place. I think we can wrap things up along those lines.

Watson: But how could the gypsies have done it?

Holmes: I haven't the faintest idea.

Watson: Holmes, I can think of quite a few objections to this theory.

Holmes: So can I. That's why we're going to Stoke Moran today. We'll see if the objections make sense. Or if they can be explained away.

(*The door has burst open. A huge man stands in the doorway. He wears a black top hat. He has on a long coat and carries a riding whip. He has a wrinkled, sun-burned face, which looks angrily at* Holmes *and* Watson *in turn.*)

Roylott: Holmes?

Holmes: Here. And you?

Roylott: Dr. Grimesby Roylott, of Stoke Moran.

Holmes (*very pleasant*)**:** Have a seat, doctor.

Roylott: I won't. My stepdaughter's been here. I've traced her. What's she been saying to you?

Holmes: It's a little cold for this time of year, isn't it?

Roylott (*yelling*)**:** What has she been saying to you?

Holmes (*still pleasant*)**:** But I've heard the crocuses are doing well.

- **theory** (THEE uh ree) **guess based on reasoning**
- crocus (KROH kus) **spring flower**

Roylott: Hah! You put me off, do you? (*He takes a step forward and shakes his riding whip at* Holmes.) I know you, you dog! I've heard of you before. Holmes, the meddler.

(Holmes *smiles.*)

Roylott: Holmes, the busybody!

(Holmes *smiles even more broadly.*)

Roylott: Holmes, the Scotland Yard puppet!

Holmes: Talking with you is very entertaining. When you go out, please close the door. There's a draft.

Roylott: I'll go when I've had my say. Don't you *dare* meddle with my business. I know she's been here. I traced her! I'm a dangerous man to go up against!

(*So saying,* Roylott *picks up an iron poker and bends it over double.*)

Roylott: See that you keep out of my grip.

(Roylott *hurls the poker into the fireplace and stomps out.*)

Holmes (*laughing*): He seems friendly. Larger than I am, of course.

- **meddler** (MED ler) one who butts in to other people's business
- Scotland Yard (SKOT lund YARD) detective department of the London police

But still, too bad he didn't hang around. We could have matched grips.

(*So saying,* Holmes *picks up the poker and straightens it out again.*)

Holmes: He's rude, though. Imagine thinking I'm—I—a puppet of the police! But this little visit makes the job more interesting, though, doesn't it? I only hope Miss Stoner won't be hurt by her carelessness—letting this brute trace her here. Now, Watson, let's have some breakfast. Then I'll do a little detecting.

SCENE 4

SETTING: Holmes's *parlor, later that day.*

AT RISE: Watson *is studying a medical book as* Holmes *returns.* Holmes *holds in his hand a sheet of blue paper. On it are written a bunch of notes and numbers.*

Watson: Find anything?

Holmes: I've seen the will of the dead wife, Miss Stoner's mother.

Watson: And?

Holmes: Not an easy job! I had to work out the present prices of all these investments. But the result is—at the time she died, the total income was almost £1100 a year. Now, with the fall in farm prices, it's only about £750. Each daughter was to get about £250 if she married.

Watson: What does that mean for Roylott?

Holmes: It means that if both girls had married, the old hulk would have had very little for himself. Even one marriage would be a serious blow for him.

Watson: So he has a strong motive for standing in the way of their marriages.

Holmes: Right.

Watson: What now?

Holmes: Get your revolver. An Eley's Number 2 is an excellent argument with gentlemen who can twist steel pokers into knots. That and a toothbrush should be all you need. Then—let's go!

- **motive** (MO tiv) reason to act
- **Eley's Number 2** (EE leez) old make of pistol

173

CHECKPOINT ─────────────────

> Answer these questions before going on. The answers are important to understanding the play. If you don't know an answer, look back and find it.
>
> 1. A hobby of Dr. Roylott is (a) telling fortunes. (b) keeping animals from India. (c) collecting fireplace pokers.
> 2. Helen's sister, Julia, dies about two weeks before (a) she is to be married. (b) the speckled band holds a concert. (c) her father quits practicing medicine.
> 3. Not long before she dies, Julia (a) has an argument with Helen. (b) decides to sleep in another room. (c) hears a mysterious whistle.
> 4. If Helen gets married, Dr. Roylott would (a) certainly return to India. (b) probably be pleased. (c) lose money.
> 5. Helen is now being forced to (a) swear she will never marry. (b) sleep in Julia's bed. (c) be friendly with the gypsies.

SCENE 5

SETTING: A hallway in the mansion at Stoke Moran.

AT RISE: Holmes *and* Watson *are received* by Helen Stoner.

Helen: I've been waiting. It's turned out very well. He's gone to town. And he's not likely to be back before dark.

Holmes: Yes, we had the pleasure of meeting the doctor. He followed you to my office. Demanded to know what your business was. Then he threatened us with a poker.

Helen: Good heavens! You weren't hurt?

Holmes: Certainly not.

Helen: He's so tricky. I never know when I'm safe from him. What will we do when he gets back?

Holmes: Better ask what *he'll* do. He'll have to be on guard. Because now he's got someone more cunning than he is on his track. *You* must lock yourself in tonight. If he's violent, we'll take you to your aunt's at Harrow. Now, let's examine the outside and then the rooms.

SCENE 6

SETTING: Outside the house.

AT RISE: Holmes is walking slowly. He examines the outsides of the windows.

Holmes: This window belongs to the room where you used to sleep. The center one is your sister's room, and the one next to the main building is Dr. Roylott's. Correct?

Helen: Exactly. But now I'm sleeping in the middle room.

Holmes: Ah, the alterations. I notice there doesn't seem to be any urgent need for repairs there.

Helen: There isn't. I think it was an excuse to move me from my room.

Holmes: That's important. Now, on the other side of this narrow wing is the hallway. All three rooms open off it. There are windows in the hallway, of course?

Helen: Yes, but very small ones. Too narrow for anyone to get through.

Holmes: Anyway, you both locked your doors at night. So your rooms couldn't have been entered from that side. Now, you've bolted these shutters?

Helen: Yes, they're locked from the inside.

(Holmes examines the shutters very closely, trying every way to open them. He tests the hinges with a magnifying glass.)

Holmes: No one could pass these shutters—if they were bolted. Hm. This brings up a few problems with my theory.

SCENE 7

SETTING: A bedroom in the mansion.

AT RISE: The bedroom is furnished with fireplace, bed, chest of drawers, dresser, and two chairs. Holmes sits in one of them. He looks over every detail of the room. Helen and Watson stand watching him.

• **alteration** (awl tuh RAY shun) change made to a building

Watson: This is the room where your sister died?

Helen: Yes. And where I'm sleeping now.

(Holmes *points to a thick bell-rope that hangs down beside the bed. The end of the rope lies on the pillow.*)

Holmes: This bell-rope—where does the bell ring?

Helen: In the housekeeper's room.

Holmes: This rope looks newer than the other things.

Helen: Yes, it was put there only a couple of years ago.

Holmes: Your sister asked for it, I suppose.

Helen: No, I never heard of her using it. We always used to get what we wanted ourselves.

Holmes: Hm. Then why was such a nice bell-rope put in? Excuse me while I satisfy myself about this floor.

(Holmes *throws himself face down on the floor. He has his magnifying glass in his hand. He crawls swiftly backward and forward. He examines the cracks between the boards. Then he jumps up and examines the woodwork on the walls. Then he stares at the bed closely. Finally, he takes the bell-rope and yanks it.*)

Holmes: It's a dummy!

Watson: Won't it ring?

Holmes: No. It's not even attached to a wire. Interesting. It's tied to a hook just above the little opening for the ventilator.

Helen: How absurd! I never noticed that before.

Holmes (*pulling the rope*): Very strange. There are one or two odd points about this room.

Watson: What are they? I don't see anything odd.

Holmes: Well, the builder must be a fool to open a vent into another room. With the same trouble, he could have opened it to the outside.

Helen: The ventilator's quite recent, too.

Holmes: Done about the same time as the bell-rope?

- bell-rope — rope that is attached to a bell that is used to call a servant
- ventilator (VEN tuh lay tur) opening to allow fresh air into and stale air out of a room

Helen: Yes.

Holmes: *Very* interesting. Dummy bell-ropes. Ventilators that don't ventilate.

Watson: What does it mean?

Holmes: Let's carry on in Dr. Roylott's room, please.

SCENE 8

SETTING: A slightly larger bedroom.

AT RISE: The room is plainly furnished. A cot, a shelf of books, an armchair beside the bed, a plain wooden chair, and a round table are the main pieces. There is also a large iron safe. Holmes walks slowly around the room. He examines everything. Helen and Watson look on.

Holmes (*tapping the safe*)**:** What's in here?

Helen: My stepfather's business papers.

Holmes: Oh. You've seen inside, then?

Helen: Only once. Years ago. I remember a lot of papers in it.

Holmes: There isn't a cat inside, for example?

Helen: No! What a strange idea!

Holmes: Well, look at this.

(Holmes *lifts up a saucer of milk that stands on top of the safe.*)

Helen: We don't keep a cat. But there's the cheetah. And the baboon.

Holmes: Ah, yes, of course. Well, a cheetah is just a big cat. But a saucer of milk won't do much to satisfy its appetite. There's one thing. . . .

(Holmes *squats down in front of the wooden chair and examines the seat.*)

Holmes: Good. That's settled.

Watson: What's settled? Holmes, what have you . . . ?

Holmes (*breaking in*)**:** Hello! Here's something interesting.

(Holmes *picks up a small dog leash hanging on one corner of the bedpost. The leash is curled to make a loop, and tied.*)

Holmes: What do you make of that, Watson?

Watson: It's a common enough leash. But I don't know why it's tied that way.

Holmes: That's not so common, is it? Oh, it's a wicked world. When a clever man turns his brains to crime, it's the worst of all. I think I've seen enough. (Holmes's *face is stern.*) Miss Stoner, you *must* follow my advice. In every way.

Helen: Of course I will.

Holmes: This is too serious for dilly-dallying. Your life may depend on it.

Helen: Believe me—I'm in your hands.

Holmes: Good. In the first place, both my friend and I must spend the night in Julia's room.

(Watson *and* Helen *look at* Holmes *in amazement.*)

Holmes: I'll explain. (*looking out the window*) Is that the village inn over there?

Helen: Yes, the Crown.

Holmes: Good. Your windows could be seen from there?

Helen: Yes.

Holmes: All right, here's what you do. Stay in your room. When your stepfather comes back, say you've got a headache. Then when you hear him go to bed, open the shutters of your window. Undo the lock. Put your lamp there as a signal to us. Then take everything you need, and go back to your old room. Even with the repairs, you can manage there for one night, can't you?

Helen: Oh, yes, easily.

Holmes: Leave the rest to us.

Helen: But what will you do?

Watson: Yes, what *will* we do?

Holmes: We'll spend the night in that room and find out what caused this whistling noise.

Helen: I think you already know, Mr. Holmes.

Holmes: Perhaps.

Helen: Then please tell me. What caused my sister's death?

Holmes: I'd rather have proof before I answer that.

Helen: At least tell me if I'm right—did she die from some sudden shock?

Holmes: No, I don't think so. I think there was something else. Something more . . . some *thing*. Now, Miss Stoner, we must leave. If Dr. Roylott came back and found us, our trip would have been useless. Be brave. If you do as I've said, we'll soon solve everything.

SCENE 9

SETTING: A room at the Crown.
AT RISE: Holmes is looking out a dark window. Watson sits nervously.

Holmes: Here comes Roylott. Huge monster, isn't he? He's roaring at the poor driver. Look at him shaking his fists! (*turning to* Watson) You know, Watson, I don't know if I ought to take you tonight. It could be dangerous.

Watson: Will I be any help?

Holmes: Possibly a great deal.

Watson: Then I'll come.

Holmes: Very kind of you.

Watson: You say danger. You must have seen more in those rooms than I did.

Holmes: I didn't *see* more. I *deduced* more. I imagine you saw everything I did.

Watson: I didn't see anything unusual. Except the bell-rope. And what could that be for? I can't imagine.

Holmes: What about the ventilator?

Watson: Well, yes, but I don't think that's so unusual—a small opening between two rooms. It was so small, a rat could hardly get through it.

Holmes: Even before we got here, I knew there'd be a ventilator.

Watson: What!

Holmes: Oh, yes. Remember what she told us? Her sister could smell Dr. Roylott's cigar? So there had to be an opening between the two rooms. Nothing was said about it at the coroner's inquest. So it had to be small. Therefore—a ventilator.

Watson: But what harm could that do?

Holmes: Well, at the very least, it's an odd coincidence. A ventilator

---

- deduce (di DOOS) **figure out by reasoning**
- inquest (IN kwest) **legal investigation into the cause of death**
- **coincidence** (ko IN si duns) **two related events accidentally happening at the same time**

is made. A cord is hung. And a lady who sleeps in the bed dies. Doesn't that strike you?

Watson: What's the connection? I can't see any.

Holmes: Notice anything odd about that bed?

Watson: No.

Holmes: It was clamped to the floor. Ever see a bed bolted down like that before?

Watson: Can't say I have.

Holmes: She couldn't move her bed. It had to stay there right under the ventilator and the rope. We might as well call it a rope, since it was never meant to be used as a bell-rope.

Watson: Holmes! I'm beginning to guess. If that's it, then . . . Why, we're just in time to prevent a horrible crime. A clever, horrible crime.

Holmes: Clever enough. And horrible enough. Watson, when a doctor goes wrong, he makes a first-rate criminal. He has nerve, and he has knowledge. Don't *you* ever turn your mind to crime!

Watson: Never! What a horrible idea!

Holmes: Believe me, we'll have plenty of horror before the night is over. Would you hand me my pipe, please? Might as well have a few cheerful hours first.

SCENE 10

SETTING: The same, later.
AT RISE: Holmes, *looking out the window, sees a single light appear across the way.*

Holmes: That's our signal!

(*The two hurry out.*)

SCENE 11

SETTING: Julia's bedroom.
AT RISE: The room is dark. Holmes *and* Watson, *their shoes off, enter.* Holmes *carries a candle and a cane.*

Holmes (*whispering*)**:** The least sound would be fatal to the plan.

(*Watson nods.*)

Holmes (*whispering*): We have to sit without light. He'd see it through the ventilator.

(Watson *nods again.* Holmes *blows out the candle. Darkness.*)

Holmes (*whispering*): Don't go to sleep. Your *life* may depend on it. Have your pistol ready.

(Holmes *motions to* Watson *to sit in the chair.* Holmes *sits on the edge of the bed.* Watson *takes out his pistol.* Holmes *places his cane on the side of the bed. They wait. Total silence. Then a bird cries suddenly outside, and the two jump. Then they go back to waiting. A clock strikes twelve.*)

SCENE 12

SETTING: The same.

AT RISE: Holmes *and* Watson *are sitting in the same places. They are slumped over, showing signs of tiredness.* Watson *shakes his head to keep his eyes open. A clock strikes three. Suddenly, there is the sound of something moving. Then comes a gentle, soothing sound—like the sound of steam coming out of a kettle.* Holmes *strikes a match. He springs from the bed. Then he begins lashing the bell-rope with his cane.*

Holmes (*yelling*): You see it, Watson? You see it?
Watson: What? What?

(There is the sound of a low, clear whistle. Holmes *stops striking the bell-rope. He watches it closely. After a moment, a horrible cry is heard off-stage. It becomes louder and louder. It is a hoarse yell of pain and fear and anger.* Watson *and* Holmes *look at each other. The scream finally dies away.*)

Watson: What does it mean?
Holmes: It means it's all over. Probably for the best, too. Take your pistol, Watson. We'll go into Dr. Roylott's room.

SCENE 13

SETTING: Dr. Roylott's *bedroom.*

AT RISE: Holmes and Watson, *with his pistol ready, enter the room. They see the iron safe, with its door ajar. Next to it, on a chair, sits* Dr. Roylott, *in his bathrobe. The dog leash is across his lap. Rigid, he stares at the ceiling. Around his brow is a yellow band, with brownish speckles. It seems to be bound tightly around his head.*

Holmes: There's the speckled band!

(Watson *takes a step forward. The speckled band begins to move! It lifts up a diamond-shaped head. It reveals the puffed neck of a deadly snake.*)

Holmes: A swamp adder! The deadliest snake in India. Ten seconds after he was bitten—he died! It was obvious. The rope had to be there as a bridge for something passing through the hole and coming to the bed.

Watson: But who'd think of a snake?

Holmes: I thought of it right away. Remember, the doctor had pets from India. We knew that. A snake seemed just the sort of weapon he'd choose. A kind of poison no test could discover. Then, too, it would take effect so quickly. A big advantage from his point of view.

Watson: A wicked point of view, you mean.

Holmes: Wickedly clever. Only a sharp-eyed coroner would find the two little punctures left by the fangs. Of course, there was also the whistle. That was a clue.

Watson: I've been wondering about that. Snakes don't whistle, do they?

Holmes: Don't be silly, Watson. The *doctor* whistled. The point is, he had to call back the snake before morning. He must have trained it—probably with milk—to return to him when he whistled. He'd put it through the ventilator. He knew it would crawl down the rope and land on the bed.

Watson: But how could he be sure the snake would bite?

Holmes: It might or it might not. She might escape every night for a week. But sooner or later . . .

Watson: Horrible. Yes, I can see now how he must have done it.

Holmes: Oh, I figured that out before I even went into his room. Then looking at his chair—that settled it.

Watson: The chair?

Holmes: Scuff marks. He'd been in the habit of standing on it. He'd have to in order to reach the ventilator. Then there was the speckled band. Let's put this thing back in its den. Then we can get Miss Stoner out of here and get the police in.

(Holmes *picks up the dog leash and throws it around the snake's neck. He carries the deadly reptile at arm's length, throws it into the safe, and locks the door.*)

SCENE 14

SETTING: *The parlor in* Holmes's *apartment. The next day.*

AT RISE: Holmes *and* Watson *sit, having tea.*

Holmes: I'm afraid I'd had the wrong idea about the case all along, Watson.

Watson: You too?

Holmes: That shows you how dangerous it is to reason without having *all* the facts.

Watson: A natural mistake. After all, the gypsies, the word "band"—it was logical to suspect them.

Holmes: Not at all. Sloppy thinking. There's only one thing *I* can say in my defense. That is, I instantly changed my mind when I saw the room couldn't be gotten at from outside.

Watson: You were very clever to notice the ventilator and the bell-rope. I didn't. But even when you pointed them out, I was at sea.

Holmes: Surely, Watson, after I showed you that the bell-rope was a dummy, you must have guessed . . . safe, the saucer of milk, the loop of cord for a leash. Elementary, my dear Watson.

Watson: Wait a second. What about that metallic clang heard by Miss Stoner? What was that?

Holmes: Her stepfather closing the safe, of course. And don't forget the softer noise—that was the snake's hiss. As soon as I heard it, I attacked the thing with my cane.

Watson: To drive it back through the ventilator.

Holmes: Exactly. And also, frankly, I had another purpose. My attack roused the snake's temper. Made it fly at the first person it saw.

Watson: Dr. Grimesby Roylott!

Holmes: Mmm. You might even say I sort of indirectly caused his death. Can't say it's likely to weigh very heavily on my mind. Will you pass me some toast, please, Watson?

THE END

ALL THINGS CONSIDERED

1. Helen Stoner comes to see Holmes because she fears that her (a) sister will die in a strange way. (b) life is in danger. (c) stepfather will be arrested.

2. Helen tells Holmes that her stepfather killed (a) a man in India. (b) his wife. (c) a thief.

3. When Helen describes the sounds she heard on the night her sister died, she does *not* mention a (a) whistle. (b) metallic clang. (c) hiss.

- **logical** (LOJ i kul) **based on reasoning**
- **elementary** (el uh MEN tuh ree) **simple; easy to understand**

184

4. At first, Helen thinks the "speckled band" may be a group of (a) musicians. (b) gypsies. (c) cheetahs.

5. Dr. Roylott has an interest in stopping Helen's marriage because he knows she will (a) no longer be his housekeeper. (b) inherit some of her mother's money, which he now has. (c) marry someone who is richer than he is.

6. Dr. Roylott bursts into Holmes's parlor and (a) offers him money to drop the case. (b) says he'll report Holmes to the police. (c) threatens Holmes with brute force.

7. One of the things Holmes notices in Julia's bedroom is (a) scuff marks on a chair. (b) a dummy bell-rope. (c) a loose floorboard.

8. In examining the doctor's room, Holmes does *not* point out the (a) scuff marks on one of the chairs. (b) saucer of milk. (c) strange loop on the leash.

9. An important clue is the (a) baboon. (b) clock. (c) ventilator.

10. At the end, Dr. Roylott is killed by (a) a heart attack. (b) Watson's gun. (c) a snake.

THINKING IT THROUGH

Discuss the following items in class.

1. Helen Stoner tells Holmes that she has come to see him because she is "surrounded by danger." What reasons does she give to show that she is in danger?

2. What is Dr. Roylott's motive (reason) for killing Julia?

3. Did you guess how the crime was carried out before it was revealed at the end? If so, what clues helped you?

4. "Elementary, my dear Watson," is a well-known saying. What does it mean?

5. Sherlock Holmes and Dr. Watson are one of the most famous pairs in all of literature. (a) Is Watson of any real use in solving the crime? (b) Did you figure out anything before Watson did? (c) What do you think is the author's main reason for including Watson in the story?

6. Holmes uses at least seven clues to solve the mystery. Name three or four of them.

7. At the end, Holmes states that Dr. Roylott's death isn't likely to "weigh very heavily on my mind." (a) What does he mean? (b) Why does he say this?

Inferences

Character Clues

In the study of literature, the word *character* has two meanings. One, as we know, is "a person in a story or a play." The other is "a person's nature, or the sum of all that person's qualities." When you write a paragraph about the kind of person you are, you are describing your *character*.

In a story, the author can tell us directly about a character's character. For instance, Character *X* can be described as "brave and powerful, but a little too stubborn." In a play, however, this kind of direct description is impossible. The author of a play must present the characters to the audience indirectly. To do this, the author provides hints as to character, or **character clues.** These clues include actions, speeches, and things the audience can see on the stage.

For instance, when we first see Helen Stoner, she is dressed in black and is wearing a veil. The black dress hints that she is sad. The veil hints that she is troubled enough to keep her face hidden from public view. Both of these turn out to be true in the first few minutes of the play.

Here are six character clues taken from the play. Answer the questions in complete sentences on a separate sheet of paper.

1. Among the items seen in Holmes's parlor are books, newspapers, and a violin. What sort of person does Holmes seem to be?
2. Helen Stoner "looks about 30, but her hair already shows traces of gray." What does the gray hair suggest?
3. Holmes's third speech is "Don't be afraid. Just leave everything to me." What does this remark show about Holmes's character?
4. Just before Dr. Roylott leaves Holmes's rooms, he picks up a heavy iron poker and bends it double. What does this action indicate about Roylott's character?
5. At the Roylott mansion, Holmes examines everything in great detail. He even uses his magnifying glass now and then. What does this search tell us about Holmes?
6. Even after observing Holmes's inspection, Watson declares that he doesn't "see anything odd." What does this remark suggest about Watson?

Sentence Meaning

Figurative Language

Figurative language (see page 161) has been simply defined as "words that do not mean exactly what they seem to say." In many cases, figurative language makes *comparisons* that, when taken word for word, are not really true. For instance, if you say you are "in the dark" about something, you are really saying that being ignorant can be compared to being in a dark place. However, ignorance means "lack of knowledge," which has nothing to do with dark places.

Here are five items from the play. Four contain figurative language. The other one does not. On a separate piece of paper, write the numerals of the items that *do* contain figurative language. Then explain what two things are being compared.

1. She [Helen Stoner] looks like a hunted animal.
2. "The [Roylott] family was once very rich."
3. "That's easy. It's [the story is] all burned in my memory."
4. "We're in deep waters here. Please tell us the rest."
5. "I think we can wrap things up along those lines."

Composition

Follow your teacher's instructions before completing *one* of these writing assignments.

1. Use the following vocabulary words from the play in five sentences of your own. Your sentences must be about the play, but do not simply copy from the book. The words are: (a) *mortgage* (page 164), (b) *coroner* (page 169), (c) *theory* (page 171), (d) *motive* (page 173), and (e) *logical* (page 184). When you have finished, check to be sure that your sentences are complete. Revise if necessary.

2. A newspaper story written to announce a person's death is called an *obituary* (oh BICH oo er ee). Use the character clues and information in the play to write an obituary for Dr. Grimesby Roylott. You should give some information about his past. You should also explain the manner in which he died. If you want, use obituaries in your local paper as models.

VOCABULARY AND SKILL REVIEW

Before completing the exercises that follow, you may wish to review the **bold-faced** words on pages 157 to 184.

I.
1. A *mortgage* on a house is a (a) description. (b) loan. (c) special chimney.
2. *Precise* measurements are (a) useless. (b) always metric. (c) very exact.
3. A *deep* problem is one that is (a) easy to solve. (b) found only in plays. (c) difficult to understand.
4. To *root* in a box is to (a) dig around. (b) pack carefully. (c) plant new roots.
5. You are most likely to *grope* your way in (a) a dark room. (b) a well-lighted room. (c) broad daylight.
6. A *coroner* deals with (a) bank loans. (b) dead bodies. (c) grammar and usage.
7. A *theory* about something is a (a) proven law. (b) reasonable guess. (c) wild or foolish idea.
8. A *meddler* (a) repairs metals. (b) cuts paper to size. (c) butts into other people's business.
9. To *treat* a subject is to (a) avoid it. (b) share it with a trusted person. (c) deal with it.
10. A *coincidence* is (a) the end or conclusion of a report. (b) the accidental happening of two related events at the same time. (c) a solution to a crime.

II. On a separate sheet of paper, write the term in each line that means the same, or nearly the same, as the term in *italics*.
1. *nerve:* sickness, courage, understanding, habit
2. *logical:* written, spoken, only, reasonable
3. *vague:* stylish, unclear, ugly, ill
4. *alteration:* change, kind of speech, beginning, agreement
5. *root:* keep calm, dig around, avoid danger, fall asleep
6. *motive:* opportunity, piece of luck, courage, reason
7. *brawl:* pointed tool, native, heat, noisy fight
8. *cheetah:* Indian dress, plaid material, wild cat, speckled snake
9. *vividly:* dishonestly, very fast, meanly, clearly
10. *elementary:* simple, young, educational, small

III. Sometimes whole sentences can be thought of as figurative language. Think about all the old sayings you have heard. What about "one rotten apple will spoil the barrel"? What about "a chain is no stronger than its weakest link"? What about "still waters run deep"? Do the meanings of these sentences really concern apples, chain links, and waters? What do the sentences *really* mean?

Here are some old sayings you have probably never heard. They were collected among rural (country) black Americans about 50 years ago. Each cleverly expresses a bit of folk wisdom. On a separate sheet of paper, explain the real meanings of at least five of the sayings. Use the numbers of the original sayings for your explanations.

1. If your coattail catches fire, don't wait till you see the blaze before you put it out.

2. The lean hound leads the pack when the rabbit is in sight.

3. Ripe apples make the tree look taller.

4. The noises of the wheels don't measure the load in the wagon.

5. Hogs that are getting fat aren't in for luck.

6. Life is short and full of blisters.

7. If you want to see how much folks are going to miss you, just stick your finger in the pond, then pull it out and look at the hole.

8. One person can thread a needle better than two.

9. The billy goat gets hit hardest when he looks like he's going to back out of a fight.

10. Nothing looks good on a miserable man.

Washington Irving (1783 - 1859)

Sunnyside—the Tarrytown, New York, home of Washington Irving

Washington Irving was born in New York City in 1783, toward the end of the American Revolution. In that year, the British forces finally left the streets, and George Washington's troops took over. Mrs. Irving promptly named her newborn child after the famous general. A few years later, George Washington came back to New York as the first president of the United States. On the street one day, he patted his young namesake on the head. From that moment on, Washington Irving's life seemed made.

Irving was the sort of man who charmed everyone he met and made a success of all he touched. He wrote humor, horror, history, travel books, and even a hit play. He served as a diplomat in Spain for many years, where he heard many old stories that he later wrote down for American readers. ("The Adventure of the Mason" is one such story.) Tales like the still-popular "Legend of Sleepy Hollow" and "Rip Van Winkle" made him America's first major author. The year he died, he finished a five-volume biography of—who else?—George Washington.

THE ADVENTURE OF THE MASON

by Washington Irving

▶ It's the middle of the night. There's a knock on the door. A stranger offers you a lot of money to do a job. Only, you've got to do it right away, and he's going to blindfold you. Will you do it? The poor bricklayer in this story does. What happens to him is beyond his wildest dreams.

Once upon a time there lived a poor mason, or bricklayer, in Granada. He kept all the saints' days and holidays. Yet, with all his good works, he grew poorer and poorer. At last he could scarcely earn enough bread for his large family.

One night he was aroused from his first sleep by a knocking at his door. He opened it, and saw before him a tall, spare, hungry-looking person.

"Hark ye, honest friend!" said the stranger. "I know that you are a good man and one to be trusted. Will you take on a job for me this very night?"

"With all my heart, sir, as long as I am well paid," replied the mason.

"That you shall be. But you must allow yourself to be blindfolded," said the visitor.

To this the mason did not object. So, with his eyes covered, he was led away by the stranger. They went through various rough lanes and winding passages. At last, they stopped before the door of a house. The stranger then used a key and turned a creaking lock. He opened what sounded like a heavy door. After they had entered, the door was closed and bolted. The mason was led through an echoing hallway to an inner part of the building. Here the bandage was removed from his eyes. He found himself in a large room, dimly lighted by a single lamp.

In the center was the dry basin of an old fountain. Under this, the stranger asked the mason to form a vault. Bricks and mortar were at hand for the purpose. He therefore began and worked all night, but without finishing the job. Just before dawn, the stranger put a piece of gold into his hand. Then, blindfolding the mason, he led him back to his house.

- **mason** (MAY sun) one who builds with stone or bricks
- Granada (gruh NAH duh) city in Spain
- spare (SPAIR) thin
- hark ye (HARK yee) listen (to me); pay close attention
- **mortar** (MOR tur) cement or lime mixed with sand and water for building

"Are you willing," said the stranger, "to return and complete your work?"

"Gladly, sir," said the mason, "as long as I am so well paid."

"Well, then, tomorrow at midnight I shall call again," said he, as he left.

The next night the stranger returned for the mason, and the vault was finished.

"Now," said the stranger, "you must help me to bring the bodies that will be buried in this vault."

The poor mason's hair rose on his head at these words. But he followed the stranger, with trembling steps. They came to a distant hall of the mansion. Here he was relieved to see three or four large jars standing in one corner. They were evidently full of money. It was with great labor that he and the stranger car-ried them and placed them in their tomb. The vault was then closed, and all traces of the work were covered up.

Again the mason was blindfolded. He was led forth by a route different from that by which he had come. After they had wandered for a long time through a maze of lanes and alleys, they stopped. The stranger put two pieces of gold into his hand.

"Wait here," said he, "until you hear the church bell toll for morning prayers. If you dare to uncover your eyes before that time, evil will befall you." So saying he left.

The mason waited faithfully. He amused himself by weighing the gold pieces in his hand and clinking them against each other. The moment the church bell rang, he uncovered his eyes. Finding himself on the bank of the river, he made his way home. For two whole weeks, he and his family had a good time on the profits of his two nights' work. Then he was again as poor as ever.

He continued to work a little, and to keep saints' days and holidays, from year to year. His family grew up thin and

- **evidently** (EV i dunt lee) **plainly; clearly**
- **trace** (TRAYS) **mark left by something**
- maze (MAYZ) **confusing network of paths**
- befall (bi FAWL) **happen to**

ragged. Then one evening, he was seated at the door of his house. Up came a rich, old miser. This man was noted for owning many houses, and he was known as a greedy landlord. The man of money eyed him for a moment from beneath a pair of shaggy eyebrows.

"I am told, friend," said he, "that you are very poor."

"There is no denying the fact, sir," replied the mason. "It speaks for itself."

"I presume, then," said the landlord, "that you will be glad of a job and will work cheaply."

"As cheap, my master, as any mason in Granada," he answered.

"That's what I want," said the landlord. "I have an old house fallen into decay. It costs me more money than it is worth to keep it in repair. Nobody will live in it. So I must patch it up as cheaply as possible."

The mason was therefore led to a large, empty house that was going to ruin. Passing through several halls, he entered an inner room. There his eye was caught by an old fountain. He paused for a moment. A dreaming memory of the place came over him.

"Pray," said he, "who lived in this house before?"

"A pest upon him!" cried the landlord. "It was an old miser. A man who cared for nobody but himself. He was said to be very rich. Since he had no relations, it was thought he would leave all

his treasures to the Church. He died suddenly, and nothing could be found but a few coins in a leather purse.

"The worst luck has fallen on me," he went on. "Since his death, the old fellow has stayed in this house without paying rent. There is no taking the law against a dead man. People say they hear the clinking of gold all night in the room where the old miser slept. It sounds as if he were counting over his money. Whether true or false, these stories have brought a bad name on my house. No one will live in it."

"Enough," said the mason. "Let me live in your house rent-free until you find a better tenant. I will put it in repair and quiet the troubled spirit that disturbs it. I am a poor but honest man. I will not be frightened off by the devil himself. Not even if he should come in the shape of a big bag of money!"

The offer of the honest mason was gladly accepted. He moved his family into the house. He did what he had promised. Little by little he restored the mansion to its former state. The clinking of gold was no more heard at night in the room of the dead miser.

But it began to be heard by day in the pocket of the living mason. In a word, his wealth grew rapidly, to the surprise of all his neighbors. He became one of the richest men in Granada. The secret of his wealth was never revealed until, on his deathbed, he told his son and heir.

- **heir** (AIR) one who will receive property and wealth upon the death of another person

193

ALL THINGS CONSIDERED

1. At first, the mason in the story is (a) poor. (b) lazy. (c) unmarried.

2. The first job the mason takes on is clearly unusual because the stranger (a) wears a mask. (b) must blindfold the mason. (c) swears the mason to secrecy.

3. The blindfold is used because the stranger (a) is really a ghost. (b) does not want to be recognized. (c) does not want the mason to find the house again.

4. The stranger wants the mason to make a (a) stone fountain. (b) gravestone. (c) vault.

5. The mason uses the money he gets for this job to (a) buy a house. (b) have a good time with his family. (c) feed the poor.

6. The second man who hires the mason is (a) miserly. (b) very kind. (c) very poor.

7. No one will live in the second man's house because it is (a) in a bad neighborhood. (b) thought to be haunted. (c) too expensive to rent.

8. The mason recognizes the house years later when he sees (a) a certain fountain. (b) a portrait of the stranger. (c) the lock on the front door.

9. The mason makes a deal with the landlord to (a) buy the house. (b) fix up the house and live there rent-free. (c) get rid of the ghost for a lot of money.

10. The mason becomes wealthy at the end because (a) the landlord pays him very well. (b) he fixes up the house and sells it. (c) he digs up the treasure that the stranger had buried.

THINKING IT THROUGH

Discuss the following items in class.

1. (a) What is the main surprise in the story? (b) Does the main surprise happen near the beginning, the middle, or the end?

2. Could everything in the story have really happened? Explain.

3. Some readers think the mason does a bad thing in not revealing the truth about the gold. (a) What do you think? (b) If the mason had told the truth, who or what would have ended up with the gold?

4. Review the story events. Think of a different ending for the story. Make it an ending that takes a sharp turn or a zigzag.

Relationships

Spatial Order

Paragraphs can be organized in several ways. One common way is the use of **spatial** (SPAY shul) **order,** or words that tell *where.* (The word *spatial* comes from the word *space.*) The following paragraph from the story is a good example of spatial order:

> To this the mason did not object. So, with his eyes covered, he was led away by the stranger. They went through various rough lanes and winding passages. At last, they stopped before the door of a house. The stranger then used a key and turned a creaking lock. He opened what sounded like a heavy door. After they had entered, the door was closed and bolted. The mason was led through an echoing hallway to an inner part of the building. Here the bandage was removed from his eyes.

Do any words in the first sentence tell *where?* No. Go on to the second sentence. One word tells *where.* That word is "away." Now try the third sentence. Can you find the string of seven words in the third sentence that tells *where?*

Go through the paragraph. Write all other words or word groups that tell *where.* Use one numeral for each word or word group. Use a separate sheet of paper for your answers.

Composition

Follow your teacher's instructions before completing *one* of these writing assignments.

1. Complete each of these sentences by including a word or a group of words that tells *where.* Underline the word or words in your sentence that tell *where.* Make sure you have written complete sentences. Write on a separate sheet of paper.
Example: The woman *lives in a huge mansion.*

   a. The party is _____.   c. The blackboard was _____.
   b. The car went _____.   d. The book fell _____.

2. Write directions that would enable someone who is visiting your school to walk or ride from your house to your school. Make your directions so complete that an ordinary person could not possibly go wrong. Read your directions. Revise if necessary.

THE MARK OF KONG-HU

retold by Virginia Johnson

▶ In this play from old China, a wise judge does some strange things to solve a mystery.

CHARACTERS

The Chorus, *introduces the scenes and comments on the action; very formal and polite*

The Property Person, *dressed in black; tries to stay in the background and not be noticed*

Ko-ning, *a young woman, a farmer*

The Judge, *old and wise beyond belief*

Three Guards

Three Merchants

Townspeople

The Gong Handler

> *There is no curtain. The* Property Person *sits at a table toward the left rear. On and near the table are all the properties [or items] to be used in the play. The* Gong Handler *sits in the right rear corner. Both remain on stage at all times. Scenes are started and ended by the sound of the gong. When possible, the actors enter from the left and exit to the right.*

Chorus (*Enters to stage left. Bows to greet the audience and presses hands together.*)**:** Welcome, gracious ladies and honorable gentlemen. Welcome to our play. First you must meet the humble players you have so kindly agreed to come and see. First, there is Ko-ning. (*She appears, bows, and remains center stage.*) She is the wife of Chang, who now, alas, is off fighting the emperor's wars. Ko-ning, you see, is very poor. She grows

---

- chorus (KOR us) in some plays, a person (or group) who stands apart from the action and comments on it; found most often in older plays
- **property** (PROP ur tee) any object used in a play
- **gracious** (GRAY shus) pleasant; courteous

196

garlic on Chang's tiny farm. Next, there is the judge, said to be the wisest man in all of China. (*The* Judge *enters, bows twice, and exits.*) We also have three guards (*They enter, bow, and exit.*) and three merchants (*Enter, bow, and exit*). There are other people in our play, too, but for now, we will take up the action.

Scene 1

(*The gong sounds. The* Property Person *places a few pieces of garlic before* Ko-ning.)

Chorus: Life is not easy for poor Ko-ning. The emperor has sent her husband off to fight in distant battles. She has only one little field. This year she has planted only garlic, which she hopes will bring a good price.

(Ko-ning *pretends to hoe the soil, then gets down on her knees to inspect the crop. She continues to act out the* Chorus's *words throughout the speech.*)

Chorus: But she worries that someone will steal her garlic in the night. She builds a little shack in the middle of the field.

(*The* Property Person *places two chairs back to back about two feet apart and sets a board across the top.*)

Chorus: There she can sleep and guard her crop. Nights pass, and the ground under Ko-ning gets harder and harder. She tosses and turns. Finally she decides that for just one night, she will leave the field and sleep in her own little bed.

(Ko-ning *exits stiffly. The* Property Person *removes the garlic quickly and starts sweeping the stage with a stiff broom, continuing till the gong sounds.*)

Chorus: But when Ko-ning returns to the field in the morning—
Ko-ning (*Entering*)**:** Oh, no! What has happened? Every last bit—stolen! Here, and here, and here. How will I live? What will I do? Look, not even a footprint. Whoever it was, they swept the earth to remove all traces. Who will help me? I must try to think calmly. Ah, I have heard that in the city there is an aged judge, the wisest man in all of China. So I will go to the city. Today. Right now!

(*She exits. The* Property Person *removes the "shack" as the gong sounds.*)

Scene 2

(*At the gong, the three* Guards *carry the* Judge *on stage in a big chair. They remain standing behind the chair, arms folded, very serious. The* Property Person *brings him a large, important-looking book.*)

Chorus (*To audience*)**:** The courtroom. (*To Judge*) You may begin.
Judge: Thank you.
Ko-ning (*Entering and kneeling*)**:** Your excellency.
Judge: Your name?
Ko-ning: Ko-ning, your honor.
Judge: Why do you come here, my little flower?
Ko-ning: Because, your honor, my garlic has been stolen.
Judge: From where, my child?
Ko-ning: From my field, your honor.
Judge: Then why did you not catch the thief?
Ko-ning: I was not there when the thief came.
Judge: Then why did you not bring me someone to tell me what the robber looked like?

Ko-ning: Because, your excellency, no one saw the thief.

Judge: Then why did you not bring me some clue, something the thief left behind, perhaps?

Ko-ning: Because, your honor, the thief left not even a footprint behind. This morning there was nothing in the field but my little shack, and it had been there before.

Judge: I see. I see. (*He presses his fingertips together and looks lost in thought.*) Ko-ning, you have told me little. But I think I can help you catch the thief.

Ko-ning: Honorable sir!

Judge: The facts in this case are clear. Your garlic has been stolen. A shack was the only thing in the field at the time. So the shack must have stolen the garlic.

Ko-ning: But sir—

Judge: Silence, my child! I must see the shack, and I am far too old to go to the field myself. I demand that you bring the shack to appear in this courtroom!

Ko-ning (*Confused.*)**:** Yes, your honor.

Judge (*Waving his hand.*)**:** Our patient audience, I am sure, will be glad to wait for your return.

(Ko-ning *exits an instant, then enters to the* Property Person's *table. The* Property Person *helps with the awkward load of the two chairs and the board.*)

Chorus: Ko-ning goes to her field, puts the shack on her back, and returns.

Ko-ning (*Assembling "shack" before* Judge.)**:** I have brought the shack, your excellency.

Judge (*Rising.*)**:** Tell me, Shack, did you or did you not steal the garlic belonging to Ko-ning? What! You refuse to answer? (*There are laughs in the audience.*) Order! Order!

Chorus: Order! Order, please!

Judge: I remind everyone in this room that this is a court of law! Any more of this laughing, and I will have you all put in jail! Now, if Shack will not speak, we shall make it speak.

(*He nods toward the* Property Person, *who quickly gives clubs to the three* Guards. *They pound away on the "shack" without mercy.*)

● **excellency** (EK suh lun see) title of great honor

Ko-ning (*To* Chorus)**:** What *is* this? Has he gone crazy?

Chorus: "Wise" is opposite of "crazy."

Ko-ning: Can't you do something?

Chorus (*Pointing* Ko-ning *back to her place*)**:** I am not in this play. *You* are in this play.

Ko-ning (*To* Judge)**:** Honorable sir—

Judge: Quiet! (*To audience.*) Order! I said no more laughing, and I meant it. Lock the door! (*Someone does so.*) You are all of you now under arrest. The charge—contempt of court. You will go to jail, each of you. And you will remain in jail until your fine has been paid. That fine is to be—one pound of garlic!

(*Gong. The* Property Person *removes the clubs and rearranges the chairs and board in front of the* Judge *so that they now form a table.* Ko-ning *exits.*)

Scene 3

Chorus: Do not be angry, honorable ladies and gentlemen. You are under arrest, that is true. But please remember that the Judge was and is and always will be the wisest man in all of China. If you think him mad, it is the madness of wisdom. And since you cannot leave this room, you have no choice but to remain and see how our little play works out. . . . Before long, relatives of the people put in jail begin to arrive to pay the fines of one pound of garlic each.

(*Gong. A* Townsperson *enters, takes a small paper bag from the* Property Person's *table and opens it up while crossing to the* Judge.)

Judge (*Examining the bag just handed him*)**:** And for whom do you come and pay this fine?

Townsperson (*Bowing*)**:** Fu-yen, your excellency. Wang Fu-yen.

Judge (*Taking a small piece of paper and a pencil from the* Property Person)**:** Now, write his name on one side of the tag. And on the other, write the name of the merchant from whom you bought the garlic.

• contempt (kun TEMPT) **rude behavior; lack of respect**

(*The* Townsperson *does so, bows, and exits. The* Judge *puts the piece of paper in the bag and places it on the "table.")*

Chorus: And so it goes all day, and all the next day. (*During this speech, a few other* Townspeople *enter and act out the bag and paper "fine paying.")* Before long, there is not a pound of garlic left to be found in the city. To buy it, people have to travel far into the countryside. But before the second night has come, all the fines have been paid.

(*The* Property Person *carries a large box of "garlic bags" to the* Judge's *feet.*)

Judge (*To a Guard*): Now, go and get Ko-ning. (*The* Guard *exits and returns immediately with* Ko-ning.)

Ko-ning (*Bowing*): Honorable sir.

Judge: Now, my apple blossom, you are to look at all these bags of garlic. Tell me when you find garlic that might be yours.

Ko-ning (*Looking in her third bag*): This! This must be from my little field!

Judge: How do you know?

Ko-ning (*Smelling it*): It is so fresh! Right from the earth. (*She reaches in the bag for a sample.*) And here, see? A little bit of reddish soil. My field is very red.

Judge: Give me the paper with the names. (*He takes it.*)

Chorus: The search through the bags takes only an hour.

(*During this speech,* Ko-ning *hurries with the bags, handing some slips of paper to the* Judge. *The* Property Person *helps her divide the bags into a large pile and a small pile.*)

Chorus: You see? Do you still think the Judge is mad? No, you are growing wise, like the Judge. You see that the Judge had the shack beaten only to make you laugh. He had you laugh only to arrest you. He had you arrested only to collect all the garlic for miles around.

Judge (*Rising, holding papers*): Ko-ning, all these papers name only three merchants. That means—

Ko-ning (*Interrupting*): That one of the three must have stolen my garlic!

Judge: Maybe, Ko-ning, maybe. It might have been one of them. Or it might have been two, or all three. Or it might have been someone who stole the garlic and then sold it to one, two, or three of these merchants.

Ko-ning (*Sadly*)**:** Oh.

Judge: But one thing is certain. At least one of these merchants must know who stole your garlic. And by tomorrow we will know, too. (*To* Guards.) Arrest these three merchants without delay. Bring them to the jail room in the cellar. I will be waiting for them. Now be off! (*All exit as the gong sounds.*)

Scene 4

(*The* Property Person *quickly removes the bags and moves the "table" to center stage. On it is placed a small carved statue of an ancient god of some kind. Finally, a long black cloth or screen is stretched across the rear of the stage. When all is ready, the gong sounds.*)

Chorus (*To* Gong Handler)**:** I was supposed to go first. (*To audience.*) Oh well, we beg your pardon for mixing things up. Where is the judge?

(*Claps hands once, waits, and then twice. The* Judge *enters, carrying a candle, and blinking as though the room is dark. The* Property Person *lights the candle, which the* Judge *leaves on the "table" as he crosses to stage right.*)

Chorus: Now, how many of you see how the judge will trap the thief? Watch closely. Our play is almost over.

Judge: Have the merchants brought in. (*The three* Merchants *enter, roughly handled by the* Guards.) Now then, we will make short work of this case. Do any of you know who stole the garlic belonging to Ko-ning?

Merchant 1: No, your excellency.

Merchant 2: On my word, sir, no.

Merchant 3: Not I, your honor.

Judge: No? No? No? You lie! At least one of you is lying. I ask you again: Who stole the garlic?

(*They remain silent, and the* Judge *continues the speech, pacing the floor and shouting into their faces.*)

Judge: Let me tell you something. I am called *wise* by many citizens throughout this land. Perhaps this is true; perhaps not. But wisdom is not all I have to help me. No, for many years I have had the help of this ancient god, a god of truth. His name is Kong-hu. (*He lifts up the god, then sets it down.*) I tell you, Kong-hu has never failed to catch the guilty person. Look at his eyes! Look, I said! Those are the eyes of truth. They can see right into you. At this moment, Kong-hu knows who is guilty. I give you one last chance to confess. (*Silence.*) All right, you will all spend the night right here in this jail cell. It will be dark. You will see nothing. But remember this: The eyes of truth do not need light to see. They have their own light. So if you stole Ko-ning's garlic, watch out, I tell you! Sometime in the night, Kong-hu will make a mark on your back. In the morning, we shall see this mark and all shall know who is guilty!

(*He takes the candle and stomps out, accompanied by* Guards. *The* Merchants *sit down tiredly, facing the audience.*)

Chorus: Now the night passes slowly.

(*There is a pause. The* Property Person *picks up a moon— a painted yellow moon on a short pole—and crosses the stage slowly. Then the* Property Person *puts the moon down and returns to the table.*)

Chorus: The moon shines all night, but inside the Judge's jail it is dark, dark, dark. And toward morning, we can hear the birds singing. Listen. Hear them? We can also hear the heavy feet of the Judge returning.

(*The* Judge *enters with* Ko-ning *and the* Guards. *The three* Merchants *have now shifted far from the god on the table, so that they sit nearer the rear wall. They look weary from their sleepless night. The* Judge *carries a candle, which the* Property Person *lights.*)

Ko-ning: Are these the three?

Judge (*To* Merchants)**:** Stand up, I tell you. (*They rise. The* Judge *picks up the god, Kong-hu.*) Tell me, now, did any of you feel it when Kong-hu put that mark on your back? (*The* Merchants *cannot help shaking their heads in disbelief.*) What? You doubt the power of this god? You doubt the eyes of Kong-hu? No, I tell you. At least one of you does not doubt. (*Loudly*) Turn around. (*They*

turn. Merchant 3 *has black smears on the back of his shirt.*) Now, turn back again. Face me. (*Pointing*) You, swine, you stole the garlic of Ko-ning!

Merchant 3: No, I am—

Judge: Silence! You are under arrest! (*The* Merchant *bolts, but all three* Guards *seize hold of him.*) For stealing the garlic, I give you a lifetime in jail. And for lying about it, I give you a second lifetime. Take him away! (*The* Guards *drag* Merchant 3 *off.*)

Ko-ning: How did—?

Judge (*To the other* Merchants): You are free to go. (*They exit.*)

Ko-ning: The god really left a mark!

Judge (*Laughing*): No, my rising moon. But the guilty merchant thought Kong-hu might leave a mark. You see, there is a wise old saying, "Guilt will out." The one who stole your garlic thought he might be marked, you see. To prevent that happening he spent the night with his back pressed against the wall. What he didn't know was—(*He runs a finger over the black rear wall, then holds it up. It is black.*)

Ko-ning: Why, *soot!*

Judge: Soot, indeed. I had it put on all four walls. (*Ko-ning kneels before him and takes his hand.*) Now, Ko-ning, you have your garlic back. In fact, for your pains, I will give you all the garlic here. You are now rich, my nightingale. (*Gong.*)

Chorus: That is our play, ladies and gentlemen. You may like to know that with her riches, Ko-ning bought her husband out of service. She and Chang lived a long and happy life. Thank you for coming, and may you continue to grow in wisdom.

- bolt (BOLT) **run away fast**
- **soot** (SOOT) **fine black powder from smoke**

ALL THINGS CONSIDERED

1. The play is unlike a modern American play because it has (a) scenes. (b) both male and female actors. (c) a chorus.

2. The Property Person in the play (a) directs the actors. (b) regulates the music. (c) sets the stage for each scene.

3. During the time of the play, Ko-ning's husband is off (a) fighting wars. (b) working in a city. (c) fighting the emperor.

4. Ko-ning's garlic is stolen when she (a) goes to the city. (b) suddenly falls ill. (c) goes to sleep in her little bed.

5. Ko-ning cannot understand why the Judge (a) asks her questions. (b) refuses to visit the field. (c) has the shack beaten.

6. It comes as a surprise when the Judge arrests (a) the three merchants. (b) Ko-ning. (c) the entire audience.

7. The Judge has the fines paid in garlic in order to (a) trace the thief. (b) increase its price. (c) make himself rich.

8. Ko-ning identifies her own garlic by the (a) freshness and the soil color. (b) freshness and the size. (c) soil color and the size.

9. Kong-hu, the small god, is said to have (a) the power of death. (b) eyes of truth. (c) an excellent memory.

10. The guilty merchant is caught by (a) Kong-hu, the god. (b) his own effort to appear innocent. (c) his own confession to the Judge.

THINKING IT THROUGH

Discuss the following items in class.

1. Question 1, above, suggests one difference between "The Mark of Kong-hu" and a modern American play. How many other differences can you think of? Try to give at least three.

2. Although "The Mark of Kong-hu" is first of all a mystery, it also has its funny moments. What would make you laugh the loudest if you saw the play on a stage?

3. You may have been confused when you started reading the play. But this confusion would work the other way, as well. If Chinese plays are confusing to you, what's there about American plays that might confuse a Chinese audience? Use the plays you have read in this book as examples.

4. Near the end of the play, the Judge quotes an old saying, "Guilt will out." (a) What does this mean? (b) How is it illustrated in the play?

Literary Skills

Subject and Theme

The *subject* of a piece of literature should not be confused with its *theme*. The **subject** is simply what the piece of literature is about. It can usually be expressed in a word or in just a few words. For instance, the subject of "The Mark of Kong-hu" might be said to be justice, theft, or guilt. A **theme** (THEEM), on the other hand, is an idea or a message. It usually takes a complete sentence to adequately express a theme. Of course, since a story or a play can contain more than one idea, it is possible to have several themes. Only one of these, however, is the main theme.

Here are five possible themes for "The Mark of Kong-hu." Which three do you think are really themes of the play? Of these, which is the main theme?

1. Modern judges have interesting ways of fining people.
2. Wisdom should be honored and respected.
3. Guilty people often make their guilt known when trying to hide it.
4. Married men should not be sent off to fight in wars.
5. People who have been wronged deserve to be helped by the legal system.

Composition

Follow your teacher's instructions before completing *one* of these writing assignments.

1. Below are five subjects (words) that might be used for five different stories. On a separate sheet of paper, turn each into a theme (sentence) that might be the main idea of the story. Use the following example as a guide:
   Subject: dogs
   Theme: A dog can be amazingly loyal to a good owner.
   (a) money (b) friends (c) honesty (d) beauty (e) love
2. Some stories have very strong themes. These stories seem to be written to get a certain idea across. Select any story you have read in this book that you think has a strong theme. First, tell what you believe the main theme to be. Then explain how the events in the story illustrate that theme.

VOCABULARY AND SKILL REVIEW

Before completing the exercises that follow, you may wish to review the **bold-faced** words on pages 191 to 204.

I. On a separate sheet of paper, mark each item *true* or *false*. If it is *false*, explain in your own words just what is wrong.
   1. A mark left by something is called a *trace*.
   2. A *theme* can usually be expressed in a word or two.
   3. Stage *property* is another name for a large stage.
   4. A bricklayer uses *mortar* to hold bricks together.
   5. "Your *excellency*" is a proper title for every government official.
   6. Wood is the main building material that a *mason* uses.
   7. A good hostess tries hard not to be *gracious*.
   8. *Soot* from factory smokestacks helps to pollute the air.
   9. *Spatial* order is organization according to time.
   10. This is *evidently* sentence number ten.

II. Each of the ten items below might be either the subject or the theme of a story. On your paper, write **S** (subject) or **T** (theme).
   1. A popular boy
   2. Hard work can lead to success.
   3. Bears in Glacier National Park
   4. A new teacher's first day
   5. A young boy learns to value friends more than money.
   6. Cheating does not pay off in the long run.
   7. A chase by night
   8. Hard work does not always bring success.
   9. Deer hunting
   10. Deer hunting should be stopped.

A SECRET FOR TWO

by Quentin Reynolds

▶ No one knew old Pierre's secret—until it suddenly became a surprise. . . .

Montreal is a very large city. But, like all large cities, it has some very small streets. Streets, for instance, like Prince Edward Street, which is only four blocks long. No one knew Prince Edward Street as well as did Pierre Dupin. For Pierre had delivered milk to the families on the street for thirty years now.

During the past fifteen years, the horse that drew the milk wagon used by Pierre was a large white horse named Joseph. In Montreal, especially in that part of Montreal that is very French, the animals, like children, are often given the names of saints. When the big white horse first came to the Provincale Milk Company, he didn't have a name. They told Pierre that he could use the white horse. Pierre stroked the softness of the horse's neck. He stroked the sheen of its splendid belly, and he looked into the eyes of the horse.

"This is a kind horse, a gentle and faithful horse," Pierre said. "I can see a beautiful spirit shining out of the eyes of the horse. I will name him after good St.

- Montreal (mon tree AWL) **city in eastern Canada that has French as its official language**
- sheen (SHEEN) **brightness; shininess**

Joseph, who was also kind and gentle and faithful and a beautiful spirit."

Within a year, Joseph knew the milk route as well as Pierre. Pierre used to boast that he didn't need reins—he never touched them. Each morning Pierre arrived at the stables of the Provincale Milk Company at five o'clock. The wagon would be loaded and Joseph hitched to it. Pierre would call, *"Bonjour, vieil ami,"* as he climbed into his seat. Joseph would turn his head, and the other drivers would smile and say that the horse would smile at Pierre. Then Jacques, the foreman, would say, "All right, Pierre, go on." Pierre would call softly to Joseph, *"Avance, mon ami."* And this splendid combination would stalk proudly down the street.

The wagon, without any direction from Pierre, would roll three blocks down St. Catherine Street, then turn right two blocks along Roslyn Avenue; then left, for that was Prince Edward Street. The horse would stop at the first house, allow Pierre perhaps thirty seconds to get down from his seat and put a bottle of milk at the front door, and would then go on, skipping two houses and stopping at the third. So down the length of the street. Then Joseph, still without any direction from Pierre, would turn round and come back along the other side. Yes, Joseph was a smart horse.

Pierre would boast, at the stable, of Joseph's skill. "I never touch the reins. He knows just where to stop. Why, a blind man could handle my route with Joseph pulling the wagon."

So it went on for years—always the same. Pierre and Joseph both grew old together, but gradually, not suddenly. Pierre's huge walrus mustache was pure white now. Joseph didn't lift his knees so high, or raise his head quite as much. Jacques, the foreman of the stables, never noticed that they were both getting old until Pierre appeared one morning carrying a heavy walking stick.

"Hey, Pierre," Jacques laughed. "Maybe you got the gout, hey?"

"Mais oui, Jacques," Pierre said a bit uncertainly. "One grows old. One's legs get tired."

"You should teach that horse to carry the milk to the front door for you," Jacques told him. "He does everything else."

He knew every one of the forty families he served on Prince Edward Street. The cooks knew that Pierre could neither read nor write. So instead of following the usual custom of leaving a note in an empty bottle if an additional quart of milk was needed, they would sing out when they heard the rumble of his wagon wheels over the cobbled street, "Bring an extra quart this morning, Pierre."

"So you have company for dinner tonight," he would call back gaily.

- stalk (STAWK) **walk in a stiff, proud way**
- gout (GOUT) **painful disease of the joints, usually of the feet and the hands**
- **cobbled** (KOB uld) **paved with stones—usually refers to a street (when used as an adjective)**

209

Pierre had a remarkable memory. When he arrived at the stable, he'd always remember to tell Jacques, "The Paquins took an extra quart this morning. The Lemoines bought a pint of cream."

Jacques would note these things in a little black book he always carried. Most of the drivers had to make out the weekly bills and collect the money. But Jacques, liking Pierre, had always excused him from this task. All Pierre had to do was to arrive at five in the morning, walk to his wagon, which was always in the same spot at the curb, and deliver his milk. He returned some two hours later, got down stiffly from his seat, called a cheery "Au'voir" to Jacques, and then limped slowly down the street.

One morning the president of the Provincale Milk Company came to inspect the early morning deliveries. Jacques pointed Pierre out to him and said, "Watch how he talks to that horse. See how the horse listens and how he turns his head toward Pierre? See the look in that horse's eyes? You know, I think those two share a secret. I have often noticed it. It is as though they both sometimes chuckle at us as they go off on their route. Pierre is a good man, Monsieur Président, but he gets old. Would it be too bold of me to suggest that he be retired and be given perhaps a small pension?" he added anxiously.

"But of course," the president laughed. "I know his record. He has been on this route now for thirty years and never once has there been a complaint. Tell him it is time he rested. His salary will go on just the same."

But Pierre refused to retire. He was panic-stricken at the thought of not driving Joseph every day. "We are two old men," he said to Jacques. "Let us wear out together. When Joseph is ready to retire—then I, too, will quit."

Jacques, who was a kind man, understood. There was something about Pierre and Joseph that made a man smile tenderly. It was as though each drew some hidden strength from the other. When Pierre was sitting in his seat, and when Joseph was hitched to the wagon, neither seemed old. But when they finished their work, then Pierre would limp down the street slowly, seeming very old indeed. The horse's head would drop, and he would walk very wearily to his stall.

Then one morning Jacques had dreadful news for Pierre when he arrived. It was a cold morning and still pitch-dark. The air was iced that morning. And the snow that had fallen during the night glistened like a million diamonds piled together.

Jacques said, "Pierre, your horse, Joseph, did not wake up this morning. He was very old, Pierre. He was twenty-five, and that is like being seventy-five for a man."

"Yes," Pierre said, slowly. "Yes. I am seventy-five. And I cannot see Joseph again."

"Of course you can," Jacques

• **Monsieur** (muh SYOOR) French for *Mister*
• **pension** (PEN shun) retirement pay

soothed. "He is over in his stall, looking very peaceful. Go over and see him."

Pierre took one step forward, then turned. "No . . . no . . . you don't understand, Jacques."

Jacques clapped him on the shoulder. "We'll find another horse just as good as Joseph. Why, in a month you'll teach him to know your route as well as Joseph did. We'll . . ."

The look in Pierre's eyes stopped him. For years Pierre had worn a heavy cap. The peak came low over his eyes, keeping the bitter morning wind out of them. Now Jacques looked into Pierre's eyes, and saw something that startled him. He saw a dead, lifeless look in them. The eyes were mirroring the grief that was in Pierre's heart and his soul. It was as though his heart and soul had died.

"Take today off, Pierre," Jacques said. But already Pierre was hobbling off down the street; and had one been near, one would have seen tears streaming down his cheeks and have heard half-smothered sobs. There was a warning yell from the driver of a huge truck that was coming fast. There was the scream of brakes. But Pierre apparently heard neither.

Five minutes later an ambulance driver said, "He's dead. Was killed instantly."

"I couldn't help it," the driver of the truck protested. "He walked right into my truck. He never saw it, I guess. Why, he walked into it as though he were blind."

The ambulance doctor bent down. "Blind? Of course the man was blind. See those cataracts? This man has been blind for five years." He turned to Jacques. "You say he worked for you? Didn't you know he was blind?"

"No . . . no . . . ," Jacques said softly. "None of us knew. Only one knew—a friend of his named Joseph. . . . It was a secret, I think, just between those two."

- **peak** (PEEK) front part of a cap
- **cataract** (KAT uh rakt) clouding of the eye's lens that can cause blindness

ALL THINGS CONSIDERED ──────────────

1. Joseph, the horse in the story, is named after (a) a saint. (b) the foreman. (c) Pierre's former horse.

2. When he starts driving Joseph, Pierre (a) is blind. (b) can see. (c) wears glasses for reading.

3. A remarkable thing about Joseph is that he (a) is blind. (b) often does the milk route without Pierre. (c) knows all the houses at which to stop.

4. A remarkable thing about Pierre is that he (a) never gets sick. (b) always rides backward. (c) has an excellent memory.

5. When Pierre is given a chance to retire on a pension, he (a) accepts eagerly. (b) demands more money. (c) refuses.

6. When Pierre is 75, Joseph is (a) 15. (b) 25. (c) 35.

7. Throughout his years as Joseph's driver, Pierre is helped by (a) the president of the company. (b) the foreman, Jacques. (c) the other drivers who know his secret.

8. The story ends just after (a) Jacques dies. (b) Pierre goes blind. (c) Jacques learns the truth.

9. The secret is finally revealed by (a) one of Pierre's customers. (b) a doctor. (c) Pierre.

10. The "secret for two" is: (a) Jacques knows that Pierre cannot read. (b) Pierre knows that his horse is too old to work. (c) The horse "knows" that his driver is blind.

THINKING IT THROUGH ──────────────

Discuss the following items in class.

1. (a) In your opinion, could the story have happened in real life? (b) What might have happened to reveal Pierre's secret before his death? Make up an event.

2. Why didn't people think it strange that Pierre never seemed to read anything in his latter years?

3. Turn back to the short paragraph on page 211 that begins, "Pierre took one step forward, then turned." (a) When you first read the paragraph, what did you think caused Pierre's actions and words? (b) How did your understanding change after you finished the story?

4. The paragraph referred to in question 3 is a good example of *foreshadowing* (see page 125). There are several other examples of foreshadowing in the story. What is one of them?

Relationships

Main Idea and Supporting Details

Most students have been doing main-idea exercises for years. They read a paragraph to find the sentence that gives the **main idea,** or the central thought. The remaining sentences provide **supporting details,** or reasons and examples upon which the main idea is based.

Main ideas and supporting details are not limited to paragraphs. An entire story can contain several main ideas. The supporting details for the ideas can be found anywhere in the story. For example, one main idea in "A Secret for Two" is this: "part of Montreal . . . is very French." The supporting details occur throughout the story: a) French customs in naming children and animals are followed; b) *Pierre Dupin* and *Jacques* are French names; c) Pierre speaks French; d) Pierre's customers have French names.

Examine each of the following three lists. On a separate sheet of paper, write the sentence that contains the main idea of the list.

1. a) Pierre serves the same milk route for over 30 years.
b) Pierre's customers stay in the same houses for years.
c) Things in this part of Montreal change very little over the years.
d) For at least 15 years, Jacques has been foreman.
e) The president of the company has long known of Pierre's good record.

2. a) Jacques excuses Pierre from keeping written records of sales.
b) Jacques asks the president to retire Pierre on a pension.
c) When Pierre says he wants to go on working, Jacques understands.
d) Jacques, the foreman, is very kind to Pierre.
e) When Joseph dies, Jacques suggests Pierre take the day off.

3. a) Pierre's mustache turns pure white.
b) After a time, Pierre starts carrying a walking stick.
c) Pierre states that his legs get tired.
d) As the story progresses, Pierre *limps* and then *hobbles*.
e) Slowly, Pierre gets old and feeble.

Inferences

Context Clues

An **inference,** you may remember, is a guess based on all the available facts. You also make inferences nearly every time you read. You often guess at the meaning of a word that may be new to you. What clues guide your guess? The *context,* of course, or all the words that surround the unknown word.

The context of a word is the same thing as its ambience. There! Did you have any trouble with *ambience,* a word most college seniors do not know? You could tell that *ambience* means "surroundings," or "environment." The **context clues** helped you.

How did you deal with the French words in "A Secret for Two"? Did you use context clues to make inferences as to their meaning? Look back at those terms now. (You can spot them easily because they are in *italics.*) Notice the context in which each is used. Then select the correct meaning for each term from the following items.

1. *Bonjour, vieil ami* (page 209): (a) Hello, old friend. (b) Alas, another day. (c) Goodbye, boss.
2. *Avance, mon ami* (page 209): (a) Wait up, old horse. (b) Goodbye, my foreman. (c) Go ahead, my friend.
3. *Mais oui* (page 209): (a) Certainly not. (b) I'm fine. (c) Oh, yes.
4. *Au'voir* (page 210): (a) Bad news. (b) Goodbye. (c) Oh, no.

Composition

Follow your teacher's instructions before completing *one* of these writing assignments.

1. Using the colored word-blocks on the bottoms of the pages following this one, find five words you think most members of your class would not know. Use each word in a sentence that makes the meaning clear from its context. Do *not* simply define the word; use it in a normal way that makes its meaning clear.
2. Although the story is called "A Secret for Two," Pierre and Joseph "understand" the secret in quite a different way. In your opinion, how much of Pierre's secret did Joseph really "understand"? Explain in a short paragraph. (Don't limit yourself to horse sense. For instance, in what way does a seeing-eye dog "understand" that its master is blind?)

LOOKING AT LIMERICKS

▶ A **limerick** (LIM ur ik) is a five-line poem with a particular pattern that involves syllables, rhyme, and rhythm. Most good limericks have a surprise in the last line. Here are a few examples.

There was a young man who said, "Why
Can't I look in my ear with my eye?
　　If I put my mind to it,
　　I'm sure I can do it.
You never can tell till you try."

There was a young lady of Niger
Who smiled as she rode on a tiger;
　　They came back from the ride
　　With the lady inside,
And a smile on the face of the tiger.

There once was a girl of New York
Whose body was lighter than cork;
　　She had to be fed
　　For six weeks upon lead,
Before she went out for a walk.

There was an old man of Peru
Who dreamed he was eating his shoe.
　　He awoke in the night
　　In a terrible fright
And found it was perfectly true!

There was a young lady of Lynn
Who was so uncommonly thin
　　That when she essayed
　　To drink lemonade,
She slipped through the straw and fell in.

WAYS OF KNOWING

1. (a) Of the five lines in a limerick, which two lines rhyme with line 1? (b) Which two lines rhyme with each other, but not with line 1?

2. Try to find the rhythm of a limerick by saying "da-da-da" instead of the words or syllables. Look at line 1 of any limerick. It goes "da DA da da DA da da DA (da)." (a) Which lines in a limerick (by number) follow the pattern of line 1? (b) What is the rhythm pattern of the other two lines?

3. Now that you know the pattern of a limerick, try writing one yourself. Start by thinking of a first line that ends in a word with many possible rhymes: *Paul, Jane, Kate,* etc.

- Niger　(NY jur)　**country in northwest Africa**
- essay　(es AY)　**try; make an effort**

215

SORRY, WRONG NUMBER

by Lucille Fletcher

▶ Have you ever overheard a conversation on the phone at the same time that you were using it? Many people have, if only faintly. But suppose you happened to hear two men planning a murder—in what sounded like your neighborhood! Suppose too that you are a sick person, confined to bed, and alone in the house. That's the way the plot starts moving in this thrilling radio play.

CHARACTERS

Mrs. Stevenson
Operator
(First) Man
Second Man (George)
Chief Operator
Second Operator
Sergeant Duffy
Third Operator
Western Union
Information
Woman

Act I

(**SOUND:** *Number being dialed on phone; busy signal.*)

Mrs. Stevenson (*a complaining, self-centered person*): Oh—dear!

(*Slams down receiver. Dials* Operator.)

Operator: Your call, please?

Mrs. Stevenson: Operator? I've been dialing Murray Hill 4—0098 now for the last three quarters of an hour, and the line is always busy. But I don't see how it *could* be busy that long. Will you try it for me, please?

Operator: Murray Hill 4—0098? One moment, please.

Mrs. Stevenson: I don't see how it could be busy all this time. It's my husband's office. He's working late tonight, and I'm all alone here in the house. My health is very poor—and I've been feeling so nervous all day—

Operator: Ringing Murray Hill 4—0098.

(**SOUND:** *Phone buzz. It rings three times. Receiver is picked up at other end.*)

Man: Hello.

Mrs. Stevenson: Hello? (*A little puzzled.*) Hello. Is Mr. Stevenson there?

Man (*into phone, as though he had not heard*): Hello. (*Louder.*) Hello.

Second Man (*slow, heavy voice, faintly foreign accent*): Hello.

First Man: Hello, George?

George: Yes, sir.

Mrs. Stevenson (*louder and more commanding, to phone*): Hello. Who's this? What number am I calling, please?

First Man: We have heard from our client. He says the coast is clear for tonight.

George: Yes, sir.

First Man: Where are you now?

- **self-centered** (SELF SEN turd) selfish; concerned with oneself
- **client** (KLY unt) person who pays for a duty performed

Note: The text of SORRY, WRONG NUMBER as it appears here has, with the author's permission, been slightly adapted from the original version.

George: In a phone booth.

First Man: Okay. You know the address. At eleven o'clock the private patrolman goes around to a place on Second Avenue for a break. Be sure that all the lights downstairs are out. There should be only one light visible from the street. At eleven fifteen a subway train crosses the bridge. It makes a noise in case her window is open and she should scream.

Mrs. Stevenson (*shocked*)**:** Oh—*hello!* What number is this, please?

George: Okay. I understand.

First Man: Make it quick. As little blood as possible. Our client does not wish to make her suffer long.

George: A knife okay, sir?

First Man: Yes. A knife will be okay. And remember—remove the rings and bracelets, and the jewelry in the bureau drawer. Our client wishes it to look like simple robbery.

George: Okay, I get—

(**SOUND:** *A soft buzzing signal.*)

Mrs. Stevenson (*clicking phone*)**:** Oh! (*Soft buzzing signal continues. She hangs up.*) How awful! How unspeakably—

(**SOUND:** *Dialing. Phone buzz.*)

Operator: Your call, please?

Mrs. Stevenson (*uptight and breathless, into phone*)**:** Operator, I—I've just been cut off.

Operator: I'm sorry, madam. What number were you calling?

Mrs. Stevenson: Why—it was supposed to be Murray Hill 4–0098, but it wasn't. Some wires must have crossed—I was cut into a wrong number—and—I've just heard the most dreadful thing—a—a murder—and—(*As an order*) Operator, you'll simply have to retrace that call at once.

Operator: I beg your pardon, madam—I don't quite—

Mrs. Stevenson: Oh—I know it was a wrong number, and I had no business listening—but these two men—they were

---

• **unspeakably** (un SPEEK uh blee) horribly; not to be spoken of

cold-blooded fiends—and they were going to murder some-body—some poor innocent woman—who was all alone—in a house near a bridge. We've got to stop them—we've got to—

Operator (*patiently*): What number were you calling, madam?

Mrs. Stevenson: That doesn't matter. This was a *wrong* number. And *you* dialed it. And we've got to find out what it was—immediately!

Operator: But—madam—

Mrs. Stevenson: Oh, why are you so stupid? Look, it was obviously a case of some little slip of the finger. I told you to try Murray Hill 4–0098 for me—you dialed it—but your finger must have slipped—and I was connected with some other number—and I could hear them, but they couldn't hear me. Now, I simply fail to see why you couldn't make that same mistake again—on purpose—why you couldn't *try* to dial Murray Hill 4–0098 in the same careless sort of way—

Operator (*quickly*): Murray Hill 4–0098? I will try to get it for you, madam.

Mrs. Stevenson: *Thank* you.

(*Sound of ringing; busy signal.*)

Operator: I am sorry. Murray Hill 4–0098 is busy.

Mrs. Stevenson (*madly clicking receiver*): Operator. Operator.

Operator: Yes, madam.

Mrs. Stevenson (*angrily*): You *didn't* try to get that wrong number at all. I asked explicitly. And all you did was dial correctly.

Operator: I am sorry. What number were you calling?

Mrs. Stevenson: Can't you, for once, forget what number I was calling, and do something specific? Now I want to trace that call. It's my civic duty—it's *your* civic duty—to trace that call—and to apprehend those dangerous killers—and if *you* won't—

- **cold-blooded fiend** (KOLD BLUD id FEEND) **very wicked person without mercy**
- explicitly (eks PLIS it lee) **very clearly**
- **specific** (spi SIF ik) **definite; exact**
- **civic** (SIV ik) **having to do with good citizenship**
- **apprehend** (ap ri HEND) **seize; arrest**

Operator: I will connect you with the Chief Operator.

Mrs. Stevenson: *Please!*

(*Sound of ringing.*)

Chief Operator (*a cool pro*)**:** This is the Chief Operator.

Mrs. Stevenson: Chief Operator? I want you to trace a call. A telephone call. Immediately. I don't know where it came from, or who was making it, but it's absolutely necessary that it be tracked down. Because it was about a murder. Yes, a terrible, cold-blooded murder of a poor innocent woman—tonight—at eleven fifteen.

Chief Operator: I see.

Mrs. Stevenson (*high-strung, demanding*)**:** Can you trace it for me? Can you track down those men?

Chief Operator: It depends, madam.

Mrs. Stevenson: Depends on what?

Chief Operator: It depends on whether the call is still going on. If it's a live call, we can trace it on the equipment. If it's been disconnected, we can't.

Mrs. Stevenson: Disconnected?

Chief Operator: If the parties have stopped talking to each other.

Mrs. Stevenson: Oh—but—but of course they must have stopped talking to each other by *now*. That was at least five minutes ago—and they didn't sound like the type who would make a long call.

Chief Operator: Well, I can try tracing it. Now—what is your name, madam?

Mrs. Stevenson: Mrs. Stevenson. Mrs. Elbert Stevenson. But—listen—

Chief Operator (*writing it down*)**:** And your telephone number?

Mrs. Stevenson (*more bothered*)**:** Plaza 4–2295. But if you go on wasting all this time—

Chief Operator: And what is your reason for wanting this call traced?

Mrs. Stevenson: My reason? Well—for heaven's sake—isn't it obvious? I overhear two men—they're killers—they're planning to murder this woman—it's a matter for the police.

Chief Operator: Have you told the police?

Mrs. Stevenson: No. How could I?

Chief Operator: You're making this check into a private call purely as a private individual?

Mrs. Stevenson: Yes. But meanwhile—

Chief Operator: Well, Mrs. Stevenson—I seriously doubt whether we could make this check for you at this time just on your say-so as a private individual. We'd have to have something more official.

Mrs. Stevenson: Oh, for heaven's sake! You mean to tell me I can't report a murder without getting tied up in all this red tape? Why, it's perfectly idiotic. All right, then. I *will* call the police. (*She slams down receiver.*) Ridiculous!

(*Sound of dialing.*)

Second Operator: Your call, please?

Mrs. Stevenson (*very annoyed*)**:** The Police Department—*please.*

Second Operator: Ringing the police department.

(*Rings twice. Phone is picked up.*)

Sergeant Duffy: Police department. Precinct 43. Duffy speaking.

Mrs. Stevenson: Police department? Oh. This is Mrs. Stevenson— Mrs. Elbert Smythe Stevenson of 53 North Sutton Place. I'm calling to report a murder.

Duffy: Eh?

Mrs. Stevenson: I mean—the murder hasn't been committed yet. I just overheard plans for it over the telephone . . . over a wrong number that the operator gave me. I've been trying to trace down the call myself, but everybody is so stupid—and I guess in the end you're the only people who could *do* anything.

Duffy (*not too impressed*)**:** Yes, ma'am.

Mrs. Stevenson (*trying to impress him*)**:** It was a perfectly *definite* murder. I heard their plans distinctly. Two men were talking, and they were going to murder some woman at eleven fifteen tonight—she lived in a house near a bridge.

Duffy: Yes, ma'am.

Mrs. Stevenson: And there was a private patrolman on the street.

> - **red tape**—overly complicated official rules
> - **precinct** (PREE singkt) division of a city for police control

221

He was going to go around for a break on Second Avenue. And there was some third man—a client—who was paying to have this poor woman murdered—They were going to take her rings and bracelets—and use a knife—Well, it's unnerved me dreadfully—and I'm not well—

Duffy: I see. When was all this, ma'am?

Mrs. Stevenson: About eight minutes ago. Oh . . . (*relieved*) then you *can* do something? You *do* understand—

Duffy: And what is your name, ma'am?

Mrs. Stevenson (*losing patience*)**:** Mrs. Stevenson. Mrs. Elbert Stevenson.

Duffy: And your address?

Mrs. Stevenson: 53 North Sutton Place. *That's* near a bridge, the Queensborough Bridge, you know—and *we* have a private patrolman on *our* street—and Second Avenue—

Duffy: And what was that number you were calling?

Mrs. Stevenson: Murray Hill 4–0098. But—that wasn't the number I overheard. I mean Murray Hill 4–0098 is my husband's office. He's working late tonight, and I was trying to reach him to ask him to come home. I'm an invalid, you know—and it's the maid's night off—and I *hate* to be alone—even though he says I'm perfectly safe as long as I have the telephone beside my bed.

Duffy (*trying to end it*)**:** Well, we'll look into it, Mrs. Stevenson, and see if we can check it with the telephone company.

Mrs. Stevenson (*using more patience*)**:** But the telephone company said they couldn't check the call if the parties had stopped talking. I've already taken care of *that.*

Duffy: Oh, yes?

Mrs. Stevenson (*getting bossy*)**:** Personally I feel you ought to do something far more immediate and drastic than just check the call. What good does checking the call do, if they've stopped talking? By the time you track it down, they'll already have committed the murder.

Duffy: Well, we'll take care of it, lady. Don't worry.

Mrs. Stevenson: The whole thing calls for a search—a complete

---

- unnerve (un NURV) **take away courage; terrify**
- **invalid** (IN vuh lid) **sick person**
- **drastic** (DRAS tik) **forceful; severe**

and thorough search of the whole city. I'm very near a bridge, and I'm not far from Second Avenue. And I know *I'd* feel a whole lot better if you sent around a radio car to *this* neighborhood at once.

Duffy: And what makes you think the murder's going to be committed in your neighborhood, ma'am?

Mrs. Stevenson: Oh, I don't know. The coincidence is so horrible. Second Avenue—the patrolman—the bridge—

Duffy: Second Avenue is a very long street, ma'am. And do you happen to know how many bridges there are in the city of New York alone? Not to mention Brooklyn, Staten Island, Queens, and the Bronx? And how do you know there isn't some little house out on Staten Island—on some little Second Avenue you've never heard about? How do you know they were even talking about New York at all?

Mrs. Stevenson: But I heard the call on the New York dialing system.

Duffy: How do you know it wasn't a long-distance call you overheard? Telephones are funny things. Look, lady, why don't you look at it this way? Supposing you hadn't broken in on that telephone call? Supposing you'd got your husband the way you always do? Would this murder have made any difference to you then?

Mrs. Stevenson: I suppose not. But it's so inhuman—so cold-blooded—

Duffy: A lot of murders are committed in this city every day, ma'am. If we could do something to stop 'em, we would. But a clue of this kind that's so vague isn't much more use to us than no clue at all.

Mrs. Stevenson: But surely—

Duffy: Unless, of course, you have some reason for thinking this call is phony—and that someone may be planning to murder *you?*

Mrs. Stevenson: *Me?* Oh, no, I hardly think so. I—I mean—why should anybody? I'm alone all day and night—I see nobody except my maid Eloise—she's a big two-hundred-pounder—she's

---

- **coincidence** (ko IN suh duns) **two or more related events accidentally happening at the same time**
- **vague** (VAYG) **unclear**

223

too lazy to bring up my breakfast tray—and the only other person is my husband Elbert—he's crazy about me—adores me—waits on me hand and foot—he's scarcely left my side since I took sick twelve years ago—

Duffy: Well, then, there's nothing for you to worry about, is there? And now, if you'll just leave the rest of this to us—

Mrs. Stevenson: But what will you *do?* It's so late—it's nearly eleven o'clock.

Duffy (*firmly*): We'll take care of it, lady.

Mrs. Stevenson: Will you broadcast it all over the city? And send out squads? And warn your radio cars to watch out—especially in suspicious neighborhoods like mine?

Duffy (*more firmly*): Lady, I *said* we'd take care of it. Just now I've got a couple of other matters here on my desk that require my immediate—

Mrs. Stevenson: Oh! (*She slams down receiver hard.*) Idiot. (*Looking at phone nervously.*) Now, why did I do that? Now he'll think I *am* a fool. Oh, why doesn't Elbert come home? *Why* doesn't he?

(*Sound of dialing operator.*)

Act II

(*Sound of dialing operator.*)

Operator: Your call, please?

Mrs. Stevenson: Operator, for heaven's sake, will you ring that Murray Hill 4–0098 number again? I can't think what's keeping him so long.

Operator: Ringing Murray Hill 4–0098. (*Rings. Busy signal.*) The line is busy. Shall I—

Mrs. Stevenson (*nastily*): I can hear it. You don't have to tell me. I know it's busy. (*Slams down receiver.*) If I could only get out of this bed for a little while. If I could get a breath of fresh air—or just lean out the window—and see the street— (*The phone rings. She answers it instantly.*) Hello. Elbert? Hello. Hello. Hello. Oh, what's the *matter* with this phone? *Hello? Hello?* (*Slams down receiver. The phone rings again, once. She picks it up.*) Hello? Hello—Oh, for heaven's sake, who *is* this? Hello, Hello, *Hello.* (*Slams down receiver. Dials operator.*)

Third Operator: Your call, please?

Mrs. Stevenson (*very annoyed and commanding*)**:** Hello, operator. I don't know what's the matter with this telephone tonight, but it's positively driving me crazy. I've never seen such inefficient, miserable service. Now, look. I'm an invalid, and I'm very nervous, and I'm *not* supposed to be annoyed. But if this keeps on much longer—

Third Operator (*a young, sweet type*)**:** What seems to be the trouble, madam?

Mrs. Stevenson: Well, everything's wrong. The whole world could be murdered, for all you people care. And now, my phone keeps ringing—

Operator: Yes, madam?

Mrs. Stevenson: Ringing and ringing and ringing every five seconds or so, and when I pick it up, there's no one there.

Operator: I am sorry, madam. If you will hang up, I will test it for you.

Mrs. Stevenson: I don't want you to test it for me. I want you to put through that call—whatever it is—at once.

Operator (*gently*)**:** I am afraid that is not possible, madam.

Mrs. Stevenson (*storming*)**:** Not possible? And why may I ask?

Operator: The system is automatic, madam. If someone is trying to dial your number, there is no way to check whether the call is coming through the system or not—unless the person who is trying to reach you complains to the particular operator—

Mrs. Stevenson: Well, of all the stupid, complicated—! And meanwhile *I've* got to sit here in my bed, *suffering* every time that phone rings, imagining everything—

Operator: I will try to check it for you, madam.

Mrs. Stevenson: Check it! Check it! That's all anybody can do. Of all the stupid, idiotic . . .! (*She hangs up.*) Oh—what's the use . . . (*Instantly* Mrs. Stevenson's *phone rings again. She picks up the receiver. Wildly.*) Hello. HELLO. Stop ringing, do you hear me? Answer me? What do you want? Do you realize you're driving me crazy? Stark, staring—

Man (*dull, flat voice*)**:** Hello. Is this Plaza 4–2295?

Mrs. Stevenson (*catching her breath*)**:** Yes. Yes. This is Plaza 4–2295.

- **inefficient** (in uh FISH unt) **wasteful of time or energy; poorly run**
- **stark** (STARK) **absolutely; totally**

Man: This is Western Union. I have a telegram here for Mrs. Elbert Stevenson. Is there anyone there to receive the message?

Mrs. Stevenson (*trying to calm herself*)**:** I am Mrs. Stevenson.

Western Union (*reading flatly*)**:** The telegram is as follows: "Mrs. Elbert Stevenson. 53 North Sutton Place, New York, New York. Darling. Terribly sorry. Tried to get you for last hour, but line busy. Leaving for Boston 11 P.M. tonight on urgent business. Back tomorrow afternoon. Keep happy. Love. Signed. Elbert."

Mrs. Stevenson (*shocked, to herself*)**:** Oh—no—

Western Union: That is all, madam. Do you wish us to deliver a copy of the message?

Mrs. Stevenson: No—no, thank you.

Western Union: Thank you, madam. Good night. (*He hangs up phone.*)

Mrs. Stevenson (*softly, to phone*)**:** Good night. (*She hangs up slowly, suddenly bursting into tears.*) No—no—it isn't true! He couldn't do it. Not when he knows I'll be all alone. It's some trick—some fiendish—(*She dials operator.*)

Operator (*coolly*)**:** Your call, please?

Mrs. Stevenson: Operator—try that Murray Hill 4—0098 number for me just once more, please.

Operator: Ringing Murray Hill 4—0098. (*Call goes through. We hear ringing at other end. Ring after ring.*)

Mrs. Stevenson: He's gone. Oh, Elbert, how could you? How could you—? (*She hangs up phone, sobbing with pity to herself, turning nervously.*) But I can't be alone tonight. I can't. If I'm alone one more second—I don't care what he says—or what the expense is—I'm a sick woman—I'm entitled—(*She dials Information.*)

Information: This is Information.

Mrs. Stevenson: I want the telephone number of Henchley Hospital.

Information: Henchley Hospital? Do you have the address, madam?

Mrs. Stevenson: No. It's somewhere in the seventies, though. It's a very small, private, and exclusive hospital where I had my appendix out two years ago. Henchley. H-E-N-C—

- fiendish (FEEN dish) **savagely cruel**
- **entitled** (en TY tuld) **have as a claim or right**
- **exclusive** (eks KLOO siv) **private and expensive;**

Information: One moment, please.

Mrs. Stevenson: Please—hurry. And please—what *is* the time?

Information: I do not know, madam. You may find out the time by dialing Meridian 7–1212.

Mrs. Stevenson (*angered*)**:** Oh, for heaven's sake! Couldn't you—?

Information: The number of Henchley Hospital is Butterfield 7–0105, madam.

Mrs. Stevenson: Butterfield 7–0105. (*She hangs up before she finishes speaking, and immediately dials number.*)

(*Phone rings.*)

Woman (*middle-aged, solid, firm, practical*)**:** Henchley Hospital, good evening.

Mrs. Stevenson: Nurses' Registry.

Woman: Who was it you wished to speak to, please?

Mrs. Stevenson (*bossy*)**:** I want the Nurses' Registry at once. I want a trained nurse. I want to hire her immediately. For the night.

Woman: I see. And what is the nature of the case, madam?

Mrs. Stevenson: Nerves. I'm very nervous. I need soothing—and companionship. My husband is away—and I'm—

Woman: Have you been recommended to us by any doctor in particular, madam?

Mrs. Stevenson: No. But I really don't see why all this catechizing is necessary. I want a trained nurse. I was a patient in your hospital two years ago. And after all, I *do* expect to *pay* this person—

Woman: We quite understand that, madam. But registered nurses are very scarce just now—and our superintendent has asked us to send people out only on cases where the physician in charge feels it is absolutely necessary.

Mrs. Stevenson (*growing very upset*)**:** Well, it *is* absolutely necessary. I'm a sick woman. I—I'm very upset. Very. I'm alone in this house—and I'm an invalid—and tonight I overheard a telephone conversation that upset me dreadfully. About a murder—a poor woman who was going to be murdered at eleven fifteen

- registry (REJ is tree) **department where registers, or lists, are kept**
- catechizing (KAT uh ky zing) **asking many questions**

227

tonight—in fact, if someone doesn't come at once—I'm afraid I'll go out of my mind—(*Almost off handle by now.*)

Woman (*calmly*): I see. Well, I'll speak to Miss Phillips as soon as she comes in. And what is your name, madam?

Mrs. Stevenson: Miss Phillips. And when do you expect her in?

Woman: I really don't know, madam. She went out to supper at eleven o'clock.

Mrs. Stevenson: Eleven o'clock. But it's not eleven yet. (*She cries out.*) Oh, my clock *has* stopped. I thought it was running down. What time is it?

Woman: Just fourteen minutes past eleven.

(*Sound of phone receiver being lifted on same line as* Mrs. Stevenson's. *A click.*)

Mrs. Stevenson (*crying out*): What's *that?*

Woman: What was what, madam?

Mrs. Stevenson: That—that click just now—in my own telephone? As though someone had lifted the receiver off the hook of the extension phone downstairs—

Woman: I didn't hear it, madam. Now—about this—

Mrs. Stevenson (*scared*): But *I* did. There's someone in this house. Someone downstairs in the kitchen. And they're listening to me now. They're—(*Hangs up phone. In a hushed voice.*) I won't pick it up. I won't let them hear me. I'll be quiet—and they'll think—(*with growing terror*) But if I don't call someone now—while they're still down there—there'll be no time. (*She picks up receiver. Soft buzzing signal. She dials operator. Ring twice*)

Operator (*a slow, lazy voice*): Your call, please?

Mrs. Stevenson (*a desperate whisper*): Operator, I—I'm in desperate trouble—I—

Operator: I cannot hear you, madam. Please speak louder.

Mrs. Stevenson (*still whispering*): I don't dare. I—there's someone listening. Can you hear me now?

Operator: Your call, please? What number are you calling, madam?

Mrs. Stevenson (*desperately*): You've got to hear me. Oh, please. You've got to help me. There's someone in this house. Someone who's going to murder me. And you've got to get in touch with the—(*Click of receiver being put down in* Mrs. Stevenson's *home. Bursting out wildly.*) Oh, there it is—he's put it down—

he's put down the extension—he's coming—(*She screams.*) He's coming up the stairs—(*Wildly.*) Give me the police department—(*Screaming.*) The police!

Operator: Ringing the police department.

(*Phone is rung. We hear sound of a subway train coming nearer. On second ring,* Mrs. Stevenson *screams again, but roaring of train drowns out her voice. For a few seconds we hear nothing but roaring of train, then dying away, phone at police headquarters ringing.*)

Duffy: Police department. Precinct 43. Duffy speaking. (*Pause.*) Police department. Duffy speaking.

George: Sorry. Wrong number. (*Hangs up.*)

ALL THINGS CONSIDERED

1. The murder that Mrs. Stevenson hears being planned is supposed to (a) be a joke. (b) look like part of a robbery. (c) take place on the street.

2. The "client" who wants the murder committed is probably (a) George. (b) Sergeant Duffy. (c) Mrs. Stevenson.

3. The telephone operators (a) are all rude in their refusal to help Mrs. Stevenson. (b) work closely with the police in emergencies. (c) try their best to help Mrs. Stevenson with the information they have.

4. Reading between the lines, we can tell that Sergeant Duffy (a) will probably do little or nothing to help Mrs. Stevenson. (b) already knows about the planned murder. (c) is not familiar with Mrs. Stevenson's area of the city.

5. A phone call from Western Union informs Mrs. Stevenson that (a) she should worry for her life. (b) her husband is returning from Boston. (c) her husband is leaving for Boston.

6. Toward the end of the play, Mrs. Stevenson (a) tries to get a nurse to stay with her. (b) begins to see strange things in her room. (c) sends a telegram to a Boston hotel.

7. Mrs. Stevenson knows that someone is in the house when she (a) sees a light turned off in the hall. (b) hears a click on the extension phone. (c) hears a whisper coming from the kitchen.

8. Mrs. Stevenson's last phone call is made to the (a) hospital. (b) chief operator. (c) police department.

9. We can conclude that at the end of the play, (a) Mrs. Stevenson faints with fright. (b) Mrs. Stevenson dials a wrong number. (c) George kills Mrs. Stevenson.

10. At the time the play ends, Mr. Stevenson probably (a) doesn't know that his wife is dead. (b) believes that his wife may be dead. (c) is rushing home to save Mrs. Stevenson's life.

THINKING IT THROUGH

Discuss the following items in class.

1. Just before the end of Act 1, Sergeant Duffy asks Mrs. Stevenson if she thinks *she* is going to be murdered. (a) What is her reply? (b) What did you, the reader, think at this point?

2. Early in Act 2, Mrs. Stevenson answers the phone twice, yet no one is on the line. (a) Who might be calling? and (b) for what purpose?

3. Mrs. Stevenson has a difficult time communicating her concerns to others. (a) How could she have gotten better results from people like the telephone operators, the woman at the hospital, and Sergeant Duffy? (b) Did her demanding tone have anything to do with the way others reacted to her? Explain.

4. Early in the play, George is said to have a "faintly foreign accent." Why did the author bother to include this detail? (Remember, this is a *radio* play.)

5. Why is "Sorry, Wrong Number" a particularly good play for radio?

6. Later, "Sorry, Wrong Number" was turned into a popular movie. (You may have seen it on TV.) What kinds of things could the writer of the movie add to the original play?

Relationships

Cause and Effect

A **cause** is an event or idea that leads to a certain result, which is called an **effect.** For example, Mrs. Stevenson's overhearing the murder plans (cause), results in her calling the operator and the police (effect). We find cause-effect relationships in everything we read. In fact, every time you answer a question beginning with a term like *Why . . .* or *For what reason . . .* , you are giving the cause of a certain effect.

Match the five causes on the left with the five effects on the right.

CAUSES	EFFECTS
Because—	
1. Mr. Stevenson feels he might need an alibi,	(a) . . . Mrs. Stevenson can't get help for the night.
2. registered nurses are in short supply,	(b) . . . we know who committed the murder.
3. Mrs. Stevenson hears a click on the phone,	(c) . . . Mrs. Stevenson's screams go unheard.
4. the subway crosses a nearby bridge,	(d) . . . a trip to Boston is arranged.
5. George's voice says the last three words,	(e) . . . she knows someone else is inside the house.

Composition

Follow your teacher's instructions before completing *one* of these writing assignments.

1. In two or three sentences, explain why you think it took so long for Mrs. Stevenson to realize that it was her own murder she overheard being planned, and not someone else's.

2. Rewrite the first page of the play as the beginning of a short story. You will probably want to include some of the spoken words. Also, you will have to add a description of the scene, descriptions of the characters, and action. You might want to begin as follows: *Mrs. Stevenson was worried. She had been calling her husband for nearly an hour, but the line was always busy.*

VOCABULARY AND SKILL REVIEW

Before completing the exercises that follow, you may wish to review the **bold-faced** words on pages 208 to 227.

I. On a separate sheet of paper, write the *italicized* term that best fills the blank in each sentence.

cataract	*vague*	*limerick*	*entitled*	*context*
specific	*peak*	*pension*	*red-tape*	*civic*

1. You may run into a lot of _____ when you try to get a driver's license in a large city.
2. You can often tell the meaning of a word from its _____.
3. The _____ of the mechanic's hat was soaked with oil.
4. A _____ always has five lines.
5. Ms. Avila had an operation to remove a _____ from her left eye.
6. Grandma gets a monthly _____ from the company she used to work for.
7. She is also _____ to a Social Security check each month.
8. _____directions can cause no end of confusion.
9. Voting in elections is an important _____ duty for most adults.
10. The writing teacher wanted lots of sharp, _____ details in our compositions.

II.
1. The word *cobbled,* nearly always refers to a (a) suit. (b) street. (c) stick.
2. Only a *fiend* would (a) star on a track team. (b) laugh at a joke. (c) poison dogs for fun.
3. A criminal lawyer's *client* would be (a) the person he or she is paid to represent in court. (b) a judge or jury. (c) anyone who opposes that lawyer in court.
4. An *invalid* might find it difficult to (a) move quickly around the house. (b) watch television. (c) read a book.
5. An example of a *coincidence* is (a) five straight days of rain. (b) a family of five or more people. (c) all members of a family having the same date of birth.
6. A city *precinct* is (a) the area surrounding a city. (b) a police district. (c) a run-off election.
7. The person most likely to *apprehend* someone would be a (a) police officer. (b) doctor or a nurse. (c) teacher.

8. When a school principal takes *drastic* action, he or she (a) awards the prizes in person. (b) is very concerned about a problem. (c) doesn't really care about the school.

9. *Inefficient* study habits would probably lead to (a) poor marks. (b) good athletic skills. (c) strong writing skills.

10. A person who is *unspeakably self-centered* is (a) quiet and shy. (b) inclined to be overly generous. (c) terribly selfish.

III. Read this short selection carefully before answering the questions that follow.

THE ARTIST

by Isabelle C. Chang

There was once a king who loved the graceful curves of the rooster. He asked the court artist to paint a picture of a rooster for him. For one year he waited and still this order was not fulfilled. In a rage, he stomped into the studio and demanded to see the artist.

Quickly the artist brought out paper, paint, and brush. In five minutes a perfect picture of a rooster emerged from his skillful brush. The king turned purple with anger, saying, "If you can paint a perfect picture of a rooster in five minutes, why did you keep me waiting for over a year?"

"Come with me," begged the artist. He led the king to his storage room. Paper was piled from the floor to the ceiling. On every sheet was a painting of a rooster.

"Your Majesty," explained the artist, "it took me more than one year to learn how to paint a perfect rooster in five minutes."

Life is short, art is long.

1. The context makes it clear that the word "emerged" (paragraph 2, line 3) means (a) *faded.* (b) *came forth.* (c) *proceeded awkwardly.*

2. The *cause* of the artist's work was (a) his knowledge of chickens. (b) the finished painting. (c) the king's first order.

3. The *result* of the artist's work was (a) his knowledge of chickens. (b) the finished painting. (c) the kings's first order.

4. The *main idea* of the selection is that (a) artistic skill that seems easy can take a long time to develop. (b) kings usually get what they want. (c) roosters are sometimes easy to paint.

5. A *supporting detail* for this main idea is the (a) king's angry face. (b) kind of brush used. (c) paintings piled to the ceiling.

UNIT REVIEW

I. Match the terms in Column A with their definitions in Column B.

<table>
<tr><td>A</td><td></td><td>B</td></tr>
</table>

A

1. spatial order

2. limerick

3. theme

4. figurative language

5. context

6. character clue

7. supporting detail

B

a) idea, or message, of a story or a play

b) all the words that surround a particular word

c) saying one thing and meaning another

d) five-line humorous poem

e) arrangement according to place

f) reason for or example of a main idea

g) hint as to the nature of a person in a story or a play

II. Here are eight statements about literature. Each of them might be called a *main idea* that covers a wide range of supporting details. Try to support each of the statements with a sentence or two referring to something in this unit. What you refer to may be as large as a whole selection or as small as a particular word. Start your support with the term *For example.* The first has been done as a sample. On a separate sheet of paper, do *at least five* of the others.

1. The theme of some stories seems to be very important. *For example, "The Adventure of the Mason" suggests that good luck may come to people who lead hard-working lives.*

2. The quality of a short story has little to do with its length.

3. The surprise in a short poem is best saved till the last line.

4. Different countries have different styles of presenting plays on stage.

5. The meaning of a word can often be understood from its context.

6. Zigzags have been popular in literature for hundreds of years.

7. Some poems depend on a certain pattern of rhyme and rhythm.

8. Stories are sometimes turned into plays.

SPEAKING UP

▶ At first glance, the 10 lines below certainly look like a short poem. When you read them, you will discover that they're really a short speech. What kind of person is speaking? To whom is the person talking? Do your best to read the lines as the speaker would have said them. Again, practice makes perfect.

MY RULES

by Shel Silverstein

If you want to marry me, here's what you'll have to do:

You must learn how to make a perfect chicken-dumpling stew.

And you must sew my holey socks,

And soothe my troubled mind,

And develop the knack for scratching my back,

And keep my shoes spotlessly shined.

And while I rest you must rake up the leaves,

And when it is hailing and snowing

You must shovel the walk . . . and be still when I talk,

And—hey—where are you going?

"My Rules" from WHERE THE SIDEWALK ENDS. The Poems and Drawings of Shel Silverstein Copyright © 1974 by Snake Eye Music, Inc. Reprinted by permission of Harper & Row, Publishers, Inc.

- **dumpling** (DUMP ling) *round piece of biscuit dough, cooked by boiling*
- **knack** (NAK) *special skill*

WRITING YOUR OWN DESCRIPTION

There's an old saying, "A picture is worth a thousand words." This saying is usually true. Certainly, it would take thousands and thousands of words to describe every detail shown in this photograph. Your job now is to write the clearest word picture you can in about 15 minutes.

Start your description with this sentence which gives the *main idea*: On a smog-free winter day, downtown Los Angeles looks spectacular against the backdrop of Mount Baldy.

Think about *supporting details* that will add to the main idea. What is pictured? What size are they in real life? What shape are they? What colors do you imagine them to be? What special features might they have? In some cases, how many are shown?

The most difficult part of the assignment will concern *spatial order*. It might be a good idea to start with the large, nearly square building in the center. Then go on to describe the view to the left and finally, the view to the right. Most of your sentences should contain phrases such as <u>on the edge</u>, <u>about halfway between</u>, and <u>in the distance</u>.

UNIT · 4

DISCOVERING THE SELF

An old poem goes like this:

> There were three girls walked down the road,
> As down the road walked she:
> > The girl she was,
> > The girl they saw,
> > The girl she wanted to be.

Me, myself, and I—are they three persons, or one person? Someone once said that the hardest person to get to know is yourself. You think of yourself as a certain kind of individual. Yet, what exactly is the "I" saying to the "Me" and to the "Myself"? What about yourself as you appear in the minds of other people? When you act in a certain way, do others always *see* your actions as you do? What about your secret thoughts? Should you— and do you—ever share them with other people? Problems such as these are the special topic of this unit.

THE GOLD MEDAL

by Nan Gilbert

▶ "They look at me—" she sobbed, "but they don't *see* me!"
"You see yourself, don't you?" the old man asked mildly.
"Well, then, what more do you need?"

The day had been too much for Amanda. It had started out bad and got no better, one thing piling on another all day long.

"That skirt is too short," her mother had frowned during this morning's last-minute inspection. "Did you scrub your teeth? Are your fingernails clean?"

"Mom, I'm not a *baby!*" Amanda had let out a hopeless squawk and fled. It was no use. When her mother looked at her, she didn't see Amanda—not really. She saw an Example to help show their new neighbors that the Dawsons were as clean and quiet and well-mannered as any family on the block.

"I'm not an Example!" grumbled Amanda rebelliously. "I'm *me!*"

Amanda Dawson—tall for her years, a little thin, leggy as a newborn colt. Flopping short black ponytail, jutting elbows, springy knees. Long feet that could trip her up—and frequently did.

Face plain and unremarkable except for large, liquid, chocolate-brown eyes, just one shade darker than her scrubbed, shining skin.

What did her mother see, if she didn't see Amanda? Amanda's quick imagination leaped to present her with the picture of a Proper Example: a spotlessly clean, tidy creature who kept her elbows in and her knees hidden . . . whose hair never worked loose from its tight rubberband . . . who didn't run or shout or use slang . . . whose name was always on the honor roll. . . .

"You there—shoo! Don't trespass! Keep to the sidewalk!"

Absorbed in her picture-making, Amanda had unthinkingly taken the shortcut across Mrs. Hawthorne's corner lot. Now the old lady had popped from her house like a cuckoo from a clock.

"Oh, woe!" muttered Amanda, retreating quickly. "Here we go again!"

- **rebelliously** (ri BEL yus lee) **?**
- **jutting** (JUT ing) **sticking out sharply**
- **absorbed** (ab SORBD) **deeply interested**

Notice that no definitions are given for some of the harder words. As you read, try to figure out any words you may not know. They will be discussed later.

The first time this had happened, Amanda had felt bewildered. The short-cut was worn bare by years of school-children's feet, and others seemed to be using it freely.

"I'm not hurting anything," she had said.

Her protest roused the old lady to a flurry of shrill bird-like cries. "This is private property—I have my rights!"

Now, loping back to the sidewalk, pursued by indignant chirps, Amanda told herself resignedly, "Mrs. Hawthorne doesn't see me either." When the old lady looked at Amanda, it was as though she saw not just one girl, but a whole regiment of Amandas, marching across her lot, crushing flowers and shrubs!

Amanda sighed. How did you make someone really *see* you? So they'd know you were *you?* Not a Regiment. Not an Example.

- **bewildered** (bi WIL durd) confused; puzzled
- **flurry** (FLUR ee) noisy confusion
- indignant (in DIG nunt) angry
- resignedly (ri ZY nid lee) without a struggle
- **regiment** (REJ uh munt) ?

Not a Gang of Hoodlums, either! That's what Mr. Grogan always saw when he looked at her, Amanda decided. By the time Amanda entered Mr. Grogan's store to buy a candy bar, her imagination was growing livelier by the minute.

Mr. Grogan was all smiles and jokes—"Well, well, what's it going to be this time? A nice big box of chocolates, maybe?" he asked.

But he watched Amanda carefully as she lingered over the candy display. When she brought her purchase to the counter, he made an excuse to peek into her lunch sack—"My, my, won't get any fatter on a diet like that!"

No need to look—I didn't steal anything! For a second, Amanda was afraid she had said the words out loud. Mom would split a seam if she even suspected Amanda of speaking up like that, pert and sassy! Hastily, Amanda grabbed her sack and ducked out of the store. Until she had her imagination under control, she'd better keep a close guard on her tongue!

Head down, Amanda scuffed slowly toward school. The day had hardly begun and already it rested heavily on her shoulders. Nor did she expect anything inside the walls of Jefferson School to lighten the load.

School was Amanda's greatest trial this fall. Instead of a familiar building filled with old friends, her family's move to a new home had made Amanda a stranger among strangers. As yet she had made no real friends to replace those she had lost. Though some of the girls were cordial and kind, nobody asked her home after school or stopped at Amanda's house for cookies and pop. And she knew there were others—or maybe it was their parents—who didn't like her being at Jefferson at all. This thought added to the day's accumulating weight of gloom.

During the noon break, Amanda avoided the lunchroom. She took her sack-lunch outside to a sheltered corner of the building. For some reason, today the sunny nook seemed lonely. Each bite Amanda swallowed had to fight its way past a great lump that unexpectedly blocked her throat.

When the bell summoned her back to class, Amanda reluctantly joined the hurrying, chattering crowds in the hall. Her next class was science, taught by Mr. Moore. Amanda thought Mr. Moore the nicest of all the teachers; for him she tried extra hard to do good work. Her first lonely, awkward day in Jefferson, Mr. Moore had welcomed her with genuine warmth. And he was always generous with his after-school time, ready to help her if there was something she didn't understand.

But now, slumped low in her back-row seat, with the lump still big in her

- pert (PERT) **?**
- **cordial** (KOR jul) **?**
- **reluctantly** (ri LUK tunt lee) **unwillingly; slowly**
- **genuine** (JEN yoo in) **?**

throat and a growing heaviness in her heart, Amanda thought, "He doesn't see me either. He'd treat *any* black kid the same way." Because he's kindhearted. Because he truly wants to help a black child fit into a white world. For him, she was the symbol of a cause he believed in. She wasn't herself at all.

Mr. Moore had to call her name twice before she realized he had asked her a question. Amanda stared at him somberly.

"I don't know," she said.

"Oh, come now, Amanda, of course you do. Remember, it's what we talked about yesterday—"

"I don't know!" The lump in Amanda's throat broke suddenly into a loud, dismaying sob. "Why is it so awful if *I* don't know? Lots of times *they* don't know, and you never look so—so—" It was Mr. Moore's look of hurt surprise that sent her dashing out of the room, that and the new and louder sob rising in her throat.

From the doorway she turned to face him. "I don't care—it's true!—I've got as much right to be st-stupid as anybody!" The second sob got away from her before she could slam the door. Humiliated, she pelted down the hall and out of the building.

The day was too lovely for gloom— an Indian summer afternoon, with rich golden warmth spread over the fields and hills like an eiderdown quilt. In spite of herself, her bowed shoulders lifted, her heart lightened. . . .

- **somberly** (SOM bur lee) **sadly; unhappily**
- **dismaying** (dis MAY ing) **?**
- pelt (PELT) **?**
- eiderdown quilt (I dur doun KWILT) **a comforter filled with soft duck feathers**

And she began to run. Running, to Amanda, was like flying. There was special joy in the clean rush of air against her upraised face, the pounding blood in her veins. When Amanda ran, she left all her coltish awkwardness behind. Her stride lengthened; her arms pumped; her long feet—that could trip her up when she walked—barely skimmed the ground.

Down the road she flew, and across a pasture where horses pricked their ears at her in mild amazement. She had to stop for breath—panting, laughing, giddy with this supercharge of oxygen— then she was off again. Up and over a gentle slope where a giant cottonwood offered an oasis of cool green shade she flew.

Too late Amanda saw the high heap of overturned earth below the tree. The springs in her tiring legs coiled and propelled her upward. Arms and legs stretched wide in a split. Thin body bent flat over her forward knee, Amanda cleared the pile of dirt—

But not the excavation behind it. Arms flailing, legs treading the air, she lunged for the far side, then fell back ingloriously into the hole.

"You hurt?" a voice asked with quavery concern.

Amanda sat up, dazed, and brushed dirt from her hands and skirt. Her startled brown eyes, almost level with the rim of hollowed-out earth, saw for the first time the bent figure of an old man under the tree.

"N-no," she said.

"That was mighty pretty running," the old man said with approval, "and as nice a hurdle as ever I've seen. I'm glad you didn't hurt yourself." After a moment, he added, "That's a grave you're settin' in."

Amanda squeaked and scrambled out onto the grass. "A—a *grave?*"

"Yep, for Chief. Chief's my dog."

"Oh—" Amanda cast about for words. "I—I'm sorry he's dead."

"He isn't. Not yet anyway." The old man struggled to his feet. He leaned heavily on his spade as he surveyed his handiwork. "Just about ready. Yep, a few more days and it'll be done. Wouldn't want anyone else to dig it—not for Chief. But if I was to do it, I figured I'd better get started. Can't turn more'n a few spadefuls a day."

- **giddy** (GID ee) **?**
- **cottonwood** (KOT un WOOD) **kind of wide-spreading tree**
- **propel** (pruh PEL) **?**
- **excavation** (eks kuh VAY shun) **hole made by digging**
- flailing (FLAYL ing) **waving wildly**
- treading (TRED ing) **stepping on**
- **lunge** (LUNJ) **?**
- ingloriously (in GLOHR ee us lee) **?**
- quavery (KWAY vur ee) **trembling; shaking**

244

Amanda looked at the excavation over which the old man was now pulling a piece of tarpaulin. "He—must be a big dog."

"He's that, all right. Used to be, anyway." The old man weighted the tarpaulin with a rock at each corner, then straightened slowly. "Kinda thin now, poor old boy. You want to come meet him? Chief was a runner, too, in his day— and his day lasted a lot longer than most."

Taking her consent for granted, he started down the other side of the slope toward a small house almost hidden behind a tangle of vines and shrubbery. Amanda looked a little wildly toward town, but an emotion much stronger than her alarm tugged her in the opposite direction. A runner, the old man had said—just like that. Here was someone who had looked at her and seen—not a Black Child or an Example or a Black Regiment, but Amanda herself—a runner. Wordless with upswelling gratitude, she followed the old man through a door. When Amanda's eyes adjusted to the dim light inside, she made out the form of a big black dog sprawled near the window in a dappling of green-filtered sunlight. Except for a single thump of tail, he didn't move. The old man stooped low, patted the black head

and scratched gently behind long velvety ears.

Cautiously, Amanda went nearer. She didn't know much about dogs; she was uncertain how to treat one that seemed so barely alive. "Is he—uh— pretty old?"

"Sixteen," the old man said. "Yep, that's pretty old for a dog. 'Specially a hunter like Chief . . . we've had some high times together, haven't we, old boy?"

The tail thumped once again. Amanda knelt gingerly and stroked the black coat; it was silky soft, but there seemed nothing between it and the bones beneath. To cover her dismay, she said hurriedly, "I guess a dog is a pretty good friend, isn't he?"

"The right kind of dog—yep, no better."

"You mean, like a hunter maybe?"

The old man snorted. "Breed's the least of it! Line up a hundred Labradors and, chances are, you wouldn't find another like Chief. Wasn't another in his own litter like him. I know—I had the pick of the litter."

Grunting a little with the effort, he straightened and moved to a chair by an ancient roll-top desk. "My friend couldn't figure why I took the pup I did. 'Sam,' he says, 'that's the runt of the lot! Look here—

- **tarpaulin** (TAR paw lin) **?**
- dappling (DAP ling) **group, or bunch, of spots**
- gingerly (JIN jur lee) **very carefully**
- Labradors (LAB ruh dorz) **breed of big dogs**
- **litter** (LIT ur) **young animals born at one time**

see how lively this one is!' But I held to my choice—yes siree, I knew I had a winner."

"How?" asked Amanda, fascinated.

"By the look in his eyes. There he sat, all paws and floppy head, as forlorn a pup as you'd see by any ash can, but those eyes were watching me. 'Believe in me,' they said, 'and I can do anything.'" The old man laughed. "Guess you think I'm a little foolish—well, maybe so. But I wasn't wrong about Chief, no sir! This proves it."

The old desk creaked as he rolled up the cover. In every pigeonhole within there was a ribbon—red ribbons, blue ribbons, purple ribbons, and a single gold medal. "Won 'em all, Chief did," the old man said proudly. He touched one after another. "Best working dog . . . best in class . . . best of show. . . ."

Out of curiosity, Amanda reached for the gold medal. "Why, it's a *runner's* medal!" she cried.

The old man took the medal from her and studied it fondly. "Yep, this was his first—bought it myself. Chief cried his heart out that day, wanted to do miracles for me but he just didn't have the know-how yet. 'Never you mind,' I told him. 'I know you're a champion.' Next time I went to town, I bought him a medal to wear till he'd proved himself to everyone else."

- **forlorn** (for LORN) **?**
- pigeonhole (PIJ un hohl) **small compartment in a desk**

246

As if he had followed their conversation, the black dog thumped his tail once more, and fleetingly raised his head. The old man nodded. "Yep, you're right, Chief. You showed 'em. Don't need this one anymore."

Unexpectedly, he extended it to Amanda. "*You* wear it, Sis. You got the look—just like Chief had. Wear it till you win your own."

Amanda gulped. She sniffed back tears and had to rub her nose childishly. "They look at me—" she sobbed, "but they don't *see* me!"

"You see yourself, don't you?" the old man asked mildly. "Well, then, what more do you need? A dream, and the ambition to work for it—enough for anybody." Gently he closed her fingers over the medal.

ALL THINGS CONSIDERED

1. In the first part of the story, Amanda feels that no one (a) is ever kind to her. (b) really knows how smart she is. (c) thinks of her as an individual.

2. Amanda is annoyed when Mr. Grogan, the store owner, (a) ignores her. (b) charges her too much. (c) suspects her of stealing.

3. Amanda's greatest trial is due to the fact that her (a) school is new to her. (b) mother doesn't care about her. (c) marks are dangerously low.

4. Amanda feels that Mr. Moore, the teacher, (a) calls on her too much. (b) treats her like a symbol, not as a person. (c) doesn't give her enough help.

5. Amanda leaves school (a) with her friends. (b) after she shouts at Mr. Moore. (c) because she's sent home.

6. Accidentally, Amanda runs into (a) an open grave. (b) an old dog. (c) an old friend.

7. Like Amanda, the old dog once (a) had a quick temper. (b) won many prizes. (c) was a good runner.

8. Like Amanda, Chief once (a) ran away from home. (b) attracted the old man's attention. (c) made the old man cry.

9. The old man tells about giving the dog a (a) large ham bone. (b) gold medal. (c) scolding for running away.

10. At the end of the story, the old man gives Amanda the gold medal because he (a) wants her to sell it. (b) believes she'll be a winner someday. (c) thinks she will help him bury Chief.

• fleetingly (FLEE ting lee) **quickly; briefly**

THINKING IT THROUGH

Discuss the following items in class.

1. (a) Why is it often hard to move to a new school? (b) What might the other students do to make Amanda's life in the new school easier? (c) What might Amanda do to make things easier for herself?

2. (a) What is Amanda's picture of a "Proper Example"? (b) Why does she suspect her mother wants her to be a "Proper Example"?

3. Because Amanda has a lively imagination, she also pictures other ways that people see her—as a Whole Regiment, a Gang of Hoodlums, and as a symbol of a cause. In your own words, tell what it is that *really* bothers Amanda.

4. Before the story is half over, Amanda is annoyed with her mother, with Mrs. Hawthorne, with the store owner, and with her science teacher. Yet two of these people really want to help Amanda. (a) Name the two people. (b) Tell how they try to help Amanda.

5. Amanda trusts the old man in the story, and she goes to his home to "meet" his dog, Chief. What advice would you give Amanda if the same thing happened today?

6. "Chief was a runner, too, in his day," the old man says (page 245). Why is Amanda pleased about this statement?

7. Look back at the advice the old man gives Amanda in the last paragraph (page 247). Do you think it is good advice—not only for Amanda but for anybody? Explain.

Inferences

More Context Clues

The *context* of a word might be said to be the words and sentences around it (see page 214). When you read "The Gold Medal," you found that no definitions were given for some of the words at the bottom of the pages. If you didn't know the meaning of those words before, you probably came to understand their meanings from the context.

Ten of the harder words from the story are given in context on page 249. On a separate sheet of paper, copy each **bold-faced** word and write its meaning.

1. Amanda grumbled **rebelliously** at her mother's morning inspection. (a) like a rebel; in protest (b) in absolute silence (c) jokingly; laughingly

2. Mrs. Hawthorne saw not just one girl but a **regiment** of Amandas. (a) couple (b) reference book (c) large army unit

3. Amanda wanted to speak up to the storekeeper in a **pert,** almost rude way. (a) cute; attractive (b) sassy; lively (c) unfair; demanding

4. Some of the new girls had been **cordial** and kind. (a) suspicious; doubtful (b) very loud; noisy (c) sincere; gracious

5. Mr. Moore had welcomed Amanda with **genuine** warmth. (a) sincere; honest (b) uncomfortable; uneasy (c) casual; incidental

6. Amanda **pelted** down the hall and out of the building. (a) threw something (b) raced; hurled herself (c) crept silently

7. Amanda felt **giddy** from a supercharge of oxygen after her long run. (a) calm (b) guilty (c) dizzy

8. Amanda **lunged** for the far side of the hole, but fell back into the hole. (a) glanced all around (b) hopped (c) pushed forward

9. The old man pulled a **tarpaulin** over the grave and weighted it with a rock at each corner. (a) heavy cloth or plastic cover (b) huge tombstone (c) mound of earth.

10. The old man had loved the **forlorn** little pup at once. (a) injured (b) expensive (c) lonely

Inferences

Symbolic Meanings

In literature as in life, a **symbol** is something that stands for something else. For instance, the United States uses the red, white, and blue flag as a *symbol*. In other words, the **symbolic** (sim BOL ik) **meaning** of a flag is the country for which it stands.

Literature is full of symbolic meanings. The following questions will help you think about the symbolic meanings in the story.

1. Amanda's mother wants Amanda to be neat, spotlessly clean, and properly dressed. What, in the eyes of other people, would be the symbolic meaning of Amanda's appearance?

2. Amanda is annoyed because Mr. Grogan's actions seem to say that he does not trust her ("... a Gang of Hoodlums.... That's what Mr. Grogan always saw when he looked at her."). What two things does Mr. Grogan do that are symbolic of mistrust?

3. The weather in stories often carries a symbolic meaning. (a) What is the weather like when Amanda leaves school? (b) How does it make her feel?

4. What is the symbolic meaning of all the ribbons Chief won that are now kept in the old man's desk?

5. (a) What is the special symbolic meaning of the gold medal? (b) How does this meaning differ from that of all the other prizes?

Composition

Follow your teacher's instructions before completing *one* of these writing assignments.

1. Look back at the words in the colored boxes at the bottom of the story's pages. Pick any five words that are *not* defined in the boxes. Using each word once, write five complete sentences of your own on a separate sheet of paper. When you have finished, underline the word from the colored box in each sentence. (Be sure the word is used in its proper context.)

2. The introduction to this unit starts with a short poem about a girl. It refers to the girl (1) as she is, (2) as other people see her, and (3) as she wants to be. Suppose this girl is Amanda. Write a paragraph describing the "three Amandas." For extra credit, write three paragraphs—one paragraph about *each* Amanda. Another careful reading of "The Gold Medal" will help you think of what to include.

Paul Laurence Dunbar (1872 - 1906)

The Paul Laurence Dunbar School in Baltimore, Maryland

Paul Laurence Dunbar was a famous American writer. There are probably more schools that are named after Dunbar than after any other author. Yet strangely, the books in many of these schools contain absolutely nothing written by Dunbar. Why? The reasons are interesting.

Dunbar's parents had been slaves, and he became the first black American to earn a living as an author. It is not surprising that many of his stories and poems deal with matters of race as they once were in a younger America. Also, Dunbar wrote in a style that now seems quite old-fashioned. Still, some of his writings have survived the test of time. Here is just one example.

SYMPATHY

by Paul Laurence Dunbar (excerpt)

I know why the caged bird sings, ah me,
   When his wing is bruised and his bosom sore,
When he beats his bars and he would be free;
It is not a carol of joy or glee,
   But a prayer that he sends from his heart's deep core,
But a plea, that upward to heaven he flings—
I know why the caged bird sings!

• **plea** (PLEE) appeal; request

251

DISCOVERING THE SELF

WAYS OF KNOWING

1. Dunbar says that the song of the caged bird is not a carol but a prayer, a plea. In two or more sentences, tell what you think the bird might prefer to be doing, rather than singing in a cage.

2. At first glance, "Sympathy" seems to be only about a bird in a cage. However, the poem has an important *symbolic meaning* (see page 249). Explain this symbolic meaning in your own words.

▶ Countée Cullen (1903–1946), another well-known poet, was a great admirer of Dunbar. Think about "Sympathy" as you read the poem below.

FOR PAUL LAURENCE DUNBAR

by Countée Cullen

Born of the sorrowful of heart
Mirth was a crown upon his head;
Pride kept his twisted lips apart
In jest, to hide a heart that bled.

WAYS OF KNOWING

1. The poem mentions (Dunbar's) heart, head, and lips. Find a word or a phrase used to describe each of these.

2. The poem also mentions Dunbar's mirth, or sense of humor. (Both as a person and as an author, Dunbar could be very funny.) How does Cullen's poem explain why Dunbar expressed both tears and laughter so well at different times?

3. Put the meaning of the poem "For Paul Laurence Dunbar" in a complete sentence of your own.

- mirth (MURTH) laughter; amusement
- **jest** (JEST) fun; sport

▶ If you're like most people, you find yourself something of a puzzle. One day, you're flying like a kite in a spring breeze. The next day, you feel like a flat tire. Here's how two gifted poets managed to catch these shifting moods and put them into words.

CHARLES

by Gwendolyn Brooks

Sick-times, you go inside yourself,
And scarce can come away.
You sit and look outside yourself
At people passing by.

HAPPY THOUGHT

by Jesús Papoleto Meléndez

have you ever been in a
crowded train
& thought
a happy thought
& it's slipped
from thought
to smile
& from smile
to giggle?

/people stare.

WAYS OF KNOWING

1. In which poem does the speaker seem almost to be in a little box, away from all other people?
2. In which poem does the speaker share some inner feelings with other people?
3. In "Charles," does the term "sick-times" refer only to physical illness? Explain.
4. In your opinion, does the speaker in "Happy Thought" really mind the fact that "people stare"? Give reasons for your answer.

TWICE I SAID
I LOVE YOU

by Teresa Giardina

▶ Barbie had said the words only once before. Now she decided to write them. She would express her feelings with those famous three little words.

My older sister Ellie once said that I'm not interested in boys and that it's not normal. I acted dumb and made believe I didn't have any idea what she was talking about. I mean, I didn't want to go into details. Because the truth of the matter is, I *am* interested in the opposite sex, very much interested. As a matter of fact, I'm ashamed to say how interested I really am. I could name lots of boys—men even—that I was interested in, although nothing ever came of it.

Once I got this crush on my teacher, Mr. Millerd. I began to think about him a lot. It got so I was always thinking of him. If I raised my hand and he didn't call on me, I was miserable. If he did call on me and I didn't know the answer, I was miserable. I couldn't even eat, and that's something because I like to eat.

I began to want to be alone all the time, and in my house there's no place to be alone. Annie has all her junk in our bedroom and is always playing dolls. The only place I could be alone was the bathroom. I used to invent these stories about Mr. Millerd and act them out in front of the mirror. I do that a lot, make up stories I mean. I can think of some pretty wild ones.

But with Mr. Millerd it was different. I never acted happy. I mean, no matter what I thought of, it was sad. I was always dying for him. Like we were on a sinking ship and there was only one place left in the lifeboat. Mr. Millerd wanted me to save myself but I wouldn't and we struggled with each other. Finally I hit him over the head with something and knocked him out and put him into the lifeboat as the water started to swirl and rise around my ankles.

• **crush** (KRUSH) short-lived but strong feeling of love

Or else I send him a lot of money. Where I get the money I don't know. But anyway, I send him all this money and he opens up a school of his own. And I get a job scrubbing floors in the school just to be near him, and he never knows that I sent him the money. For the rest of my life I scrub and scrub.

The funny thing is, I think some of this may be true. I mean, I think some day I will die for someone and it won't be necessary. I mean, no one wants me to die for them, but I think I will.

I don't understand it. I really don't. I mean, my friend Margie is always making up stories about boys, but she always comes out ahead. She makes up these stories where the boys are always doing things for her or giving her things or trying to kiss her and all, and she just can't stand them, which gives me a laugh. I don't know of *any* boy that Margie can't stand.

But anyway, I could never do this. I tried though. I tried to imagine it differently, where Mr. Millerd would be just crazy about me or we would be just crazy about each other, but it didn't come out right.

Then one day in school I did this crazy thing. I wish I didn't, but I did. It was study period and I was writing in my notebook. What I was doing, I was writing Mr. Millerd's name over and over again.

Then I took a clean sheet of paper and wrote, "Dear Mr. Millerd, I love you." I signed my name. I folded the paper and stuck it in my book. I felt funny writing it.

I never wrote those words before. It felt real funny. I never said it to anyone either. I mean not to any person. As a matter of fact, no one ever said it to me. I can't remember when anyone said, "Barbie, I love you."

What I mean about never saying it to a person is this. Ellie's husband, Frank, keeps a dog around the gasoline station, and when the dog had puppies Frank gave them all away. But there was this one nobody wanted. It was a shivery, puny kind of a dog. I guess that's why no one wanted him.

Anyway, Frank gave the pup to me. I called it Mickey. What a nuisance he was. I was always wiping up after him. He wouldn't train, not for a long time.

I kept hoping he'd get cute as he grew. He grew all right, but he

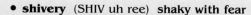

- **shivery** (SHIV uh ree) **shaky with fear**
- **puny** (PYOO nee) **small and weak**

remained just as shivery. And what trouble he used to get me in! I got in more fights over Mickey than anything.

You hear stories about dogs protecting their masters and all. Well, not Mickey. I never saw a dog that was so afraid. If I was walking with him, he'd never run away and sniff at things. He was afraid to leave my side. Boy, what a coward he was. Everyone on the block got to know what a coward Mickey was. The kids used to make fun of us. Especially this boy, Billy.

Billy and me never got along. Billy is one of those mean guys, and he had a dog that was just as mean. They used to wait for us. I swear, I think even his dog used to wait for Mickey and me to come down the block. Then they used to charge at us. Billy would be whooping and his mutt would be barking. Mickey was so afraid, he darn near used to climb up my leg. Sometimes I really had to carry him, and he wasn't exactly light either.

My mother began to complain about him. She said Mickey used to whine all the time I was in school. I couldn't go anywhere. I began to wish I didn't have him.

Anyway, this one day Mickey and I were walking along real quiet-like when a bottle fell from a garbage can. It dropped on the sidewalk and made this terrific noise. It happened so quick even I jumped.

Well, Mickey took off. Before I could catch him, he started to run across the street. I saw him zig-zagging between the cars. I closed my eyes just before a truck hit him.

When I got to him I knew he was dead. There was no blood or anything, but I knew Mickey was dead.

The driver got out of the truck and stood alongside of me and began to shout. "Get this straight. The dog ran in front of my truck. It wasn't my fault. Do ya hear? It wasn't my fault."

I didn't say anything. I bent down and fixed Mickey's ear. It was kind of folded up. I put it down nice and flat.

"Say . . . listen kid . . ." the driver said.

But I didn't look at him. I wasn't mad or anything. I knew it wasn't his fault.

"I love you, Mickey," I said very low. "I love you."

Well, anyway, that's the only time I ever said it and it was to a dead dog, so maybe it doesn't count.

Well, back to Mr. Millerd. After class I handed him the note and left. I didn't go home, though. My father was home and he was always banging on the bathroom door for me to "get out of there." And I wanted to dream. So I walked. I didn't go anywhere in particular. I just walked and walked.

When I got home, I locked myself in the bathroom. I was so mixed up I couldn't even act in front of the mirror or anything. And I hated myself. I really did. I kept wishing I hadn't written the note. I began to wish I were dead. I began to wish I could get sick, real sick, and die. I wanted to tell someone but I didn't know who. I wouldn't tell my father. That's out and I won't even go into why.

I couldn't tell my mother. She'd get all kinds of peculiar ideas and she'd probably ask me all kinds of peculiar questions. And even Ellie. If I told Ellie she'd laugh. Then she'd ask how tall Mr. Millerd was and the color of his eyes. Ellie always wants to know the color of people's eyes.

That's the trouble with people. If you tell them something, right away they give you advice. You should've done this or you shouldn't have done that. They just can't listen and let it go—always ready with advice. That's why I never tell anybody anything.

The next day Mr. Millerd didn't say anything when I came into the room. I didn't look at him much except when his back was turned.

But when class was over, he called me. He was sitting at his desk marking some papers. I kept looking at my feet.

"Barbie, about that note yesterday," he said. "I misplaced it even before I had a chance to read it."

I looked up quick. Then I went back to looking at my stupid feet.

"I'm afraid I've lost it. What was it about? Was it important?"

"No, no," I said. "Nothing important."

"Oh," Mr. Millerd said, and continued to mark the papers.

There didn't seem much else to say, so I left.

I don't know how I felt. I guess I was relieved. But yes . . . I don't know . . . somehow . . . it's funny, though, when you think of it.

Twice I said "I love you," and twice it didn't count.

ALL THINGS CONSIDERED

1. Of the following, the word that best fits Barbie is (a) *coward.* (b) *dreamer.* (c) *selfish.*

2. The event that happens first in time order is (a) the dog's death. (b) the writing of the note. (c) the conversation with Mr. Millerd.

3. To be alone, Barbie sometimes goes to (a) her room. (b) her sister's apartment. (c) the bathroom.

4. In the story, Barbie regrets (a) not taking care of her dog properly. (b) trying to share things with her father. (c) writing a note to Mr. Millerd.

5. Regarding Mickey, Barbie (a) hates him for being a coward. (b) has absolutely no complaints. (c) really loves him with all his faults.

6. Mickey is killed by (a) poison. (b) a truck. (c) a car.

7. Regarding her parents, Barbie (a) places too much trust in them. (b) finds it hard to communicate with them. (c) loves one but not the other.

8. Barbie doesn't like it when people (a) insist on giving her advice. (b) refuse to let her help them. (c) seem fearful of her.

9. At the end, Mr. Millerd tells Barbie that (a) he didn't read the note. (b) she did the wrong thing. (c) he liked the note.

10. At the end, Barbie feels (a) happy and comfortable. (b) angry and disappointed. (c) relieved but confused.

THINKING IT THROUGH

Discuss the following items in class.

1. If you were a friend of Barbie's, what kind of advice, if any, would you try to give her?

2. Look back at the paragraph about Margie's stories about boys (page 255). How do these stories contrast with the stories Barbie imagines about herself?

3. In your opinion, did Mr. Millerd handle the matter of the note well by saying he had not read it? Give reasons for your opinion.

Literary Skills

Point of View

Every story has to be written from a certain point of view. That is, someone, real or imagined, has to tell what's going on. The **point of view** is simply the position from which the story is told. Nearly all stories are told from either a *first-person* or a *third-person* point of view.

- **First person:** The storyteller, called the **narrator** or the *speaker,* is involved as a character in the story. This character refers to himself or herself as "I" and "me."

- **Third person:** The storyteller is *not* involved as a character in the story. The storyteller must refer to each character as "he" or "she."

Notice that the word *author* (or *writer*) has not been used so far. Study these two diagrams.

First-Person Point of View

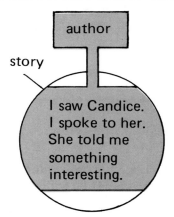

Third-Person Point of View

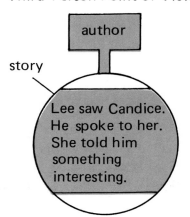

As the diagram shows, an author writing in the first person is involved in the story as the "I" character. Everything in the story is told from the "I" character's point of view and is limited to what that character could see, hear, think, or know. However, in third-person narration, the author is completely outside the story and is free to comment on anything.

Before you answer the following questions, be sure you know the terms *point of view, author, narrator, first person,* and *third person.*

1. What is the point of view of "Twice I Said I Love You"?
2. What is the name of the author of "Twice I Said I Love You"?
3. What is the narrator's name in the same story?
4. What is the point of view of "The Gold Medal" (page 240)?
5. Does "The Gold Medal" have a character who can be called the *narrator* of the story?
6. If you were keeping a diary or a journal, in which point of view would you be writing?
7. In which point of view is most of the news on the first page of your daily newspaper written?
8. Turn back to the first selection in this book, " 'I,' Says the Poem." Who is the author?
9. Is the narrator of " 'I,' Says the Poem" a first-person or a third-person narrator? Give reasons for your answer.
10. Do the words *author* and *narrator* mean exactly the same thing (yes or no)? Explain.

Bonus Question: In your opinion, which point of view, the first or the third person, tends to make a story more believable? Why?

Composition

Follow your teacher's instructions before completing *one* of these writing assignments.

1. Write five sentences altogether. In sentences one and two, use the first-person point of view. Then write two sentences using the third-person point of view. Finally, write the last sentence using the first-person point of view again, but write *a sentence that could not possibly be true of yourself.*
2. Write a paragraph summarizing the main events in "Twice I Said I Love You," using the third-person point of view.

VOCABULARY AND SKILL REVIEW

Before completing the exercises that follow, you may wish to review the **bold-faced** words on pages 240 to 259.

I. On a separate sheet of paper, write the term in each line that means the same, or nearly the same thing, as the term in *italics*.

1. *plea:* army unit, insects, request, type of skirt
2. *forlorn:* happy, lonely, musical, antique
3. *bewildered:* supported, made angry, made mountainous, confused
4. *puny:* small and weak, smelly, hard to see, nervous
5. *excavation:* meeting, punctuation mark, excuse, large hole
6. *regiment:* rule book, priest's garment, army unit, box or case
7. *giddy:* dizzy, healthy, unconscious, powerful
8. *humiliated:* promoted, raised up, shamed, aired out
9. *cordial:* awful, rude, dishonest, friendly
10. *reluctantly:* tiredly, unwillingly, quickly, too late

II. On a separate sheet of paper, mark each item *true* or *false*. If it is *false*, explain in your own words just what is wrong.

1. A boxer should be *shivery* when he climbs into the ring for a fight.
2. If you have a *crush* on a teacher, you should certainly tell everyone, including the teacher.
3. The "I" in a *first-person* story refers to the narrator.
4. A *cottonwood* is a good shade tree.
5. Bad winter storms sometimes start as a *flurry* of light snow.
6. Mother cats often have a *litter* of one.
7. A *genuine* smile is a good thing for a politician to have as she or he greets the public.
8. A *tarpaulin* can be made of either steel or plastic.
9. *Absorbed* students and teachers make for interesting classes.
10. *Dismaying* news is often told *somberly.*

III. Read the poems below carefully before you answer the questions that follow.

A bee thumps against the dusty window,
falls to the sill,
climbs back up, buzzing;
falls again;
and does this over and over.
If only he would climb higher!
The top half of the window is
open.

—Robert Sund

CONVERSATION WITH MYSELF

by Eve Merriam

This face in the mirror
stares at me
demanding *Who are you? What will you become?*
and taunting, *You don't even know.*
Chastened, I cringe and agree
and then
because I'm still young,
I stick out my tongue.

1. Which poem is written in the first-person point of view?
2. Which poem is written in the third-person point of view?
3. The first poem, as a complete poem, seems to have much symbolic meaning. What is this symbolic meaning? (Hint: Ask yourself, What does the bee represent, or stand for?)
4. Both poems have something to say about the *self,* the theme of this unit. Choose either poem and, in a sentence or two of your own, explain what that poem says about the self.

- taunting (TAWNT ing) **teasing**
- chastened (CHAY sund) **corrected; punished**
- cringe (KRINJ) **shrink away**

IV. A **haiku** (HY koo) is a three-line poem that has long been popular in Japan. Many, but not all, works of haiku have a 5—7—5 pattern—5 syllables in the first line, 7 syllables in the second line, and 5 syllables in the third. Most haiku refer to or describe something in nature. They also have some important symbolic meaning.

Here are four haiku. Those on the left are ancient haiku from Japan. Those on the right are by Richard Wright, an American. First, read each haiku for what it describes. Try to see this picture clearly in your mind's eye. Do this immediately. (Read the haiku now. Then, read the paragraph that follows this one.)

Now reread each of the haiku for its symbolic meaning. What does each poem say about *people?* More important, what does it say about *you?* For instance, the first poem suggests that if you talk too much, you may show others how little you really know. Try to put the symbolic meaning of at least two of the other haiku in your own words.

UNTITLED HAIKU

FRIEND, THAT OPEN MOUTH
REVEALS YOUR WHOLE INTERIOR . . .
SILLY HOLLOW FROG!

> **—Anonymous**

I am nobody
A red sinking autumn sun
Took my name away

> **—Richard Wright**

AH ME! I AM ONE
WHO SPENDS HIS LITTLE BREAKFAST
MORNING GLORY GAZING

> **—Basho**

Make up your mind snail!
You are half inside your house
and halfway out!

> **—Richard Wright**

CHAIR

by Cheryl Miller Thurston

▶ Imagine yourself in a wheelchair. How would you like to be treated by others? This short play will teach you something about people who have handicaps—and about yourself.

CHARACTERS

Narrator 1

Narrator 2

Michael, *a new student, in a wheelchair*

Mrs. Rizzuto, *a history teacher*

Joe ⎫
Leslie ⎪
Elena ⎪
Marian ⎬ *students*
Laura ⎪
Kevin ⎭

Joe: I'm hungry. There's Chair over there. Let's get him and go down to the lunchroom.

Leslie (*shocked*): Joe! You shouldn't call Michael "Chair."

Joe: Why not?

Leslie: It's . . . well, it's not very nice. He's handicapped!

Joe (*shrugging*): So am I. He can't walk; I can't spell.

Leslie: That's not a handicap.

Joe: That's easy for *you* to say. You've never in your whole life forgotten to "drop the *e* when adding *-ing.*"

Leslie: I still don't think that's a handicap. It's not physical.

Joe: What about these? (*He points to his glasses.*) I can't see two feet in front of me without them. If you don't think that's a handicap, you haven't seen me try to swim without them. I butterfly-stroked right into a cement wall last summer and nearly knocked myself out. I could have drowned!

Leslie: But being in a wheelchair is different, more serious.

Joe: It depends on how you look at it. I'll bet Chair doesn't run into cement walls.

Leslie: His name is *Michael!* You're so dense. Can't you see you shouldn't make fun of him?

- **physical** (FIZ i kul) **of the body**
- dense (DENS) **stupid**

264

Joe: Who's making fun of him? (Michael *approaches*.) Hi, Chair!

Michael: Hi, Metal Mouth.

Joe (*to* Leslie): Aha! I forgot another handicap: crooked teeth.

Leslie (*shaking her head in disgust*): I give up. (*to* Michael) Hello, Michael.

Michael: Hi, Leslie.

Leslie: How are you today?

Michael: Fine, thank you. And you?

Leslie: Fine. It's sure is a nice day out, isn't it?

Michael: It sure is.

Leslie: Don't you just love this nice weather? I can hardly wait to get out of school. A bunch of us are going over to the park and play Frisbee tonight. You ought to join us . . . (*She remembers his wheelchair.*) Oh, I'm sorry!

Joe (*laughing*)**:** You blew it! And you were trying to be so nice!

Leslie: Drop dead! (*to* Michael) I *am* sorry, Michael. Forgive me.

Joe: "Forgive me"? Do you believe that? *Nobody* says, "Forgive me." Hurry up, Chair. Forgive her and let's go eat lunch. I'm starved.

Michael: You're forgiven, Leslie, but you really didn't do anything. I play Frisbee, too, you know. Maybe not as well as you, but I'm not bad, considering this machinery I've got to lug around with me.

Leslie: Thank you for being so understanding, Michael. (*to* Joe) As for you, Mr. Metal-Mouth Wise Guy, I hope you lose your glasses and run into another cement wall—harder this time so that you might knock some manners into that thick skull of yours! (*She turns and leaves.*)

Michael: What did you do to her?

Joe: She's mad because I call you "Chair." Thinks I'm insulting you.

Michael: Typical. I get so sick of . . .

Joe: I know, I know. We went through all that last month, remember? So spare me the lecture and lend me a quarter. I don't have enough lunch money.

Michael: If I *did* have a quarter, I wouldn't lend it to you. You remember to pay people back like you remember to do your homework.

Joe: Some friend you are. I think I'll take you over to the gym and roll you into the swimming pool.

Michael (*cheerfully*)**:** I'm scared. I think I might even faint.

Joe: Do it after lunch. I'm too hungry to hang around here with smelling salts. Besides, I've still got to find a quarter. Here comes Elena. I'll bet she's got more sympathy than you do.

Narrator 1: Elena approaches, and Joe gives her a big grin.

Joe: Elena! You certainly look nice today!

Elena (*suspiciously*)**:** What do you want?

Joe: Who says I want anything?

Elena: No one. I just know you. Besides, my hair is dirty, and I spilled Coke on my shirt this morning. I know I don't look nice. What do you want?

Joe: A quarter. For lunch. Can't you see I need nourishment?

Elena: You need *something*, but I'm not sure it's nourishment.

Michael: What are we having today, anyway?

Elena: Something called "Autumn Delight," according to the announcements.

• **typical** (TIP i kul) like others in a certain group; being a type of something

Joe: Oh, no. That means we're having leftovers stirred together and given a cute name. Wait till you've been here awhile, Chair. By Halloween the stuff's turned yellow, and they call it "Goblin's Goulash." In February it's gone past yellow to red and it's "Valentine Variety." And by May it's green with mold, and the name is "Springtime Stew."

Michael: I hate to ask, but what's it like by the end of school?

Joe: By then it's turned so many colors they call it "Rainbow Revenge." Anyone who eats it falls into a faint and doesn't wake up until school starts again.

Michael: And that's our lunch?

Joe: Look at it this way—better to eat it now and break your stomach in easy. Come on, Elena, lend me a quarter.

Elena: No. Sorry.

Joe: You're heartless.

Elena: *Smart* is a better word for it.

Joe: I guess I'd better try somebody else. Be back in a minute, I hope. (*He hurries off.*)

Elena: Good luck! (*to* Michael) So how's it going, Mike?

Michael: OK. A lot better, actually.

Elena: Are you feeling more at home here?

Michael: Yes. At least I have one class now where I feel pretty normal—and where there are some decent people like you and Joe and the others.

Elena: We're not any different from anyone else in school—well, maybe Joe is. (*She laughs.*) He's pretty weird. But the others mean well. They just need to be taught, I guess, like we were.

Michael: I don't know how to teach them. That outburst last month just sort of happened.

Elena: And it's a good thing it did. Boy, were you ever awful! Remember how you snapped at everyone?

Narr 2: We go back to Michael's first day at the new school. Mrs. Rizzuto is introducing him to her history class.

Mrs. Rizzuto: Class, this is Michael Holmes. He just moved here from Oregon, and I hope you'll make him feel welcome. Joe, would you move up so he can get his chair behind your desk?

• **goulash** (GOO lash) kind of stew

Joe: Sure.

Narr 2: Mike wheels down the side of the room and stops behind Joe. Everyone stares.

Mrs. R: I've just given an assignment, Michael. Marian, please show Michael what we're doing. The rest of you, get busy.

Narr 1: Marian reaches across the aisle and hands Mike a textbook.

Marian: We're answering the questions here on page 128. (*She opens the book for him.*) One through ten. (*She points to the questions.*) These right here. Do you understand?

Michael: Of course.

Marian: Good. What part of Oregon are you from?

Mike (*glaring at her and rudely pulling the book away from her*)**:** What difference does it make to you? I've got to get busy.

Marian (*looking surprised*)**:** Well, let me know if you need some help.

Mike: I won't!

Narr 2: Mike begins reading. Marian looks hurt and turns back to her book. The bell rings, and everyone gets up to go.

Kevin (*to* Mike)**:** Want me to carry your books or push you or anything? It's pretty crowded in the halls—gets rough sometimes.

Mike (*rudely*)**:** No.

Narr 1: Kevin shrugs and leaves with everyone else.

Narr 2: Now it is the day after Mike has met the class. As Mrs. Rizzuto's class begins, Joe accidentally knocks his pen off his desk. Michael sees it fall, reaches over the side of his wheelchair, and picks it up.

Kevin: Did you get those questions answered, Joe?

Joe: Yes. Wait—I forgot; I still have to write out the answer to number 10. I'd better hurry. (*He sits down and reaches for his pen.*) Where's my pen? (*He looks around.*) Hey, you guys! I put my pen down here just a minute ago. Now where is it?

Laura: You probably lost it.

Joe: No, I had it. I'm sure of it! (*loudly*) Somebody ripped off my pen. And it was a *good* one—cost me a buck!

Kevin: You just want an excuse not to do your homework.

Joe: No, I had it, I tell you. (*He sees* Michael *holding the pen.*) You've got it!

Michael: I don't see your name on it.

Joe: But it's my pen. I must have just knocked it on the floor.

Michael: How am I supposed to know if it's yours? I found it; it's mine.

Joe (*angrily*)**:** Who are you to say it's yours just because I took my hand off it for a second? Now give me my pen.

Michael: Just try and make me!

Joe: I'm going to count to ten, and I'd better have that pen back by the time I'm finished!

Elena (*warning*)**:** Joe . . .

Kevin: Come on, just forget it, Joe. He can't . . .

Joe: One . . . two . . .

Laura: Stop it, Joe.

Kevin: Leave him alone.

Joe: Leave *him* alone! I didn't take *his* pen! Three . . . four . . .

Narr 1: The bell rings, and Mrs. Rizzuto enters. Joe glares at Mike and takes his seat, along with the rest of the class.

Narr 2: Now it is Michael's third day at school. Joe goes to his seat in history and sees his pen on his desk. He glances at Mike, who stares down at a book. Mrs. Rizzuto starts class.

Mrs. R: All right. Yesterday we were talking about the Declaration of Independence, and I asked you to think about where it says, "All men are created equal." What do you think? Do you think that statement is true?

Laura: Of course. The Declaration says so, so it must be true.

Joe: Come on! It can't be true. Just look at you compared to me. We sure weren't born equal, at least when it comes to math. You get straight A's without half trying, and I only get C's even if I study my brains out.

Mrs. R: What do the rest of you think? Are we equal?

Elena: No. I mean, we all have things we're good at, things we're bad at. I think it means we're just equal in *rights*. (*Many students nod.*)

Mrs. R: I agree. I think we all have different strengths, different weaknesses. Take me, for example. I'm good at . . . let's see . . . I'm good at playing Scrabble. But I'm terrible at cooking. Luckily, my husband makes all our meals, so we don't starve. What about the rest of you? What are you bad at, good at?

Narr 2: Michael raises his hand and then speaks slowly and carefully.

Michael: Well, I'm bad at walking, obviously—I can't do it at all. And what am I good at? I guess I'm good at being rude.

Mrs. R (*looking puzzled*): Rude?

Michael: Yes. I think I owe the class an apology, especially Joe. I've been pretty obnoxious. I did take your pen, Joe, and I had no right to.

Joe: You didn't think that yesterday. What made you change your mind?

Michael: You.

Joe: How?

Michael: You insisted on treating me just like you treat anybody else. You had a *right* to be mad at me, and you said so. Most people won't do that. They think because I'm handicapped they should treat me differently.

Mrs. R: Differently? How, Michael?

Michael: Well, take Marian, for example. Not to hurt your feelings, Marian, but I think you should know you hurt mine the other day. That's why I was so rude.

Marian: I did? What did I do?

Michael: You opened my book for me to show me the assignment. Then instead of just saying "Do 1–10 on page 128," you pointed out the exercise and repeated, "These right here." Then you

---

● obnoxious (ub NOK shus) **very disagreeable**

even asked me if I understood—just like I was a first grader or something. My legs may not work, but there's nothing wrong with my *brains.*

Marian: I was only trying to be nice . . . .

Michael: Everyone's always trying to be nice to me. But they're not looking at me and seeing if I *deserve* it. Even if I'm awful, they're still nice. I wish people would see *me,* not the chair. *Me,* not my hardware. I wish they'd treat me like a person, like everyone else. Do you know that no one in any school I've gone to has ever even given me a nickname?

Elena: What's that got to do with anything?

Michael: When people call you by nicknames—I mean friendly nicknames—it shows that they accept you, that they like you. I heard Kevin call you "Beautiful" all the time, Elena. And you call him "Prez" because he's president of the class. Marian's called "Short-Stuff," and Joe—well, I've heard him called all *kinds* of names!

Joe: Lucky me . . . "Motor Mouth," "Pizza Face," "Frankenstein," "Creep" . . .

Michael: But people call you those things just to tease you—they know you can take it. Everyone's always so formal with me. I don't even get called "Mike" at school. It's always "Michael."

Joe: Tell you what. I'll call you "Mike," and I'll give you a nickname, too. Let's see. You're not short, so it can't be "Short Stuff." You're not beautiful—no offense—and you're not president of anything, yet. *I know!* I hereby appoint you class leader so I can call you "Chairman Mike." Get it?

Narr 1: He laughs along with Mike and the rest of the class.

Narr 2: Now we return to the present, several weeks after Mike had explained his feelings. Michael and Elena continue their conversation in the hall.

Michael: So now I'm stuck with "Chair" for a nickname, at least from Joe. And you know what? I like it! He doesn't mean it in a nasty way; he means it in a friendly, belonging sort of way.

Elena: I know . . . and here he comes again. I wonder if he got his quarter.

• **offense** (uh FENS) insult

Joe (*triumphantly*): I got it—and from *Leslie!*

Michael: Leslie!

Joe: Yes! She said she'd give me the quarter if I promised to stop calling you "Chair"!

Michael (*angrily*): She what?

Elena: Calm down, Mike.

Michael: See what I mean? How can I ever be normal with people like *her* around?

Elena: Why don't you tell her how you feel?

Michael (*loudly*): I will! I'll go tell *her* a thing or two!

Elena: Not like that. Yelling at her won't make her understand. Why don't you try explaining honestly?

Michael (*after a pause*): OK. What have I got to lose? Let's go eat.

Narr 1: They all go to the lunchroom and take their trays to Leslie's table.

Joe: Hi, Leslie. Mind if Elena and "Wheels" and I join you?

Leslie: Joe! You promised!

Joe: Only about "Chair." I didn't say I wouldn't call him something else.

Michael: Leslie, I think I should tell you that what you did makes me—well, makes me mad. Or maybe *insulted* would be a better word.

Leslie: Insulted? How did I insult you?

Michael: You were *paying* Joe to be nice to me! You wouldn't think of doing that with anyone else.

Leslie: I didn't mean anything . . . .

Michael: I know. But I don't need special treatment. Well, maybe I need some physically—I have to use elevators instead of stairs, for example. But I don't need to be treated special in other ways. I want to be treated the way I *deserve* to be treated, according to the way I act. Try looking at me, Leslie, not this wheelchair. See *me!* (*He smiles.*) I'm not so bad, really.

Joe: Don't believe him. He's got a wart on his left earlobe.

Leslie (*shocked*): Joe! (*She remembers, stops, and peers at* Mike.) I guess you do, don't you? How disgusting! (*She smiles.*) You know what? I've got one on my left elbow. Look. (*She sticks her elbow out and shows him her wart.*)

Joe: How romantic. You two were made for each other.

Leslie: That does it. Mike, grab his right arm; Elena, his left. (*She grins wickedly.*) And I'll get the Jell-O.

Narr 2: Leslie balances a square on her fork and quickly drops the Jell-O inside Joe's shirt front. Joe yells as it slithers down his chest.

Leslie (*smiling*)**:** Doesn't it feel great to be part of a team effort, Mike? You're one of us!

Elena (*seeing the principal approach*)**:** That may not be such a great thing. This is one team that I'm afraid is about to get in a lot of trouble . . . .

Michael (*smiling*)**:** Oh, well. I think it's probably worth it. (*to Joe*) And sorry it had to be lime, Joe. I know how you hate green!

• slither (SLITH ur) **slip and slide**

273

ALL THINGS CONSIDERED

1. The action of the play takes place on (a) one day only. (b) four days. (c) at least ten days.

2. The first person to treat Mike as a normal person is (a) Marian. (b) Kevin. (c) Joe.

3. The history class seems to agree that all people should be equal in (a) wealth. (b) ability. (c) rights.

4. Marian insults Mike by (a) explaining a simple assignment in too much detail. (b) insisting on pushing the wheelchair. (c) calling him "Chair."

5. Mike says that he (a) is better at Frisbee than anyone else. (b) prefers to be called "Michael." (c) has never had a nickname.

6. Mike feels insulted when Leslie (a) offers to carry his books. (b) pays Joe not to call him "Chair." (c) spins his chair around in the hall.

7. A student who is *not* in Mrs. Rizzuto's history class is (a) Marian. (b) Elena. (c) Leslie.

8. The student who learns a lesson near the end of the play is (a) Laura. (b) Elena. (c) Leslie.

9. The play ends with a piece of Jell-O (a) on the floor. (b) in Elena's purse. (c) inside Joe's shirt.

10. After the play ends, it is likely that the nickname "Chair" will be used by (a) more people. (b) fewer people. (c) no one.

THINKING IT THROUGH

Discuss the following items in class.

1. On Mike's first day in school, both Marian and Kevin make him feel uncomfortable. (a) What does each do that bothers Mike? (b) What is the reason for their actions?

2. What joke does Joe make using the word "chairman"? Explain fully.

3. Mike learns a lesson when he says, "OK. What have I got to lose?" (page 272) What lesson has he learned?

4. The play has one strong *theme,* or idea. Express this theme in a complete sentence of your own.

Relationships

Chronological Order

The term **chronological** (kron u LOJ i kul) **order** simply means in the order of time: *yesterday, today, tomorrow; noon, afternoon, evening.* The events in most stories and plays take place in chronological order. "The Gold Medal" (page 240) is a good example.

Flashback

Sometimes, the events are not presented in exact chronological order. In "Chair," the first scene takes place on a certain day in school. The next scene happens several weeks earlier. The middle section of the play skips—or "flashes"—back to previous time periods. A **flashback** interrupts the normal chronological order to show events that happened earlier. The middle section of "Chair" is a series of three flashbacks.

Here are some events from "Chair." On a separate sheet of paper, write them in chronological order—the order in which they would happen in real life. Then write *Flashback* before each event that is part of a flashback in the play. You may wish to look through the play to check your answers.

a) Marian insults Michael by offering him too much help.
b) Leslie learns the truth about Michael's feelings.
c) Michael picks up Joe's pen and starts an argument.
d) Joe asks people for a quarter for lunch.
e) Michael is introduced to the history class.

Composition

Follow your teacher's instructions before completing *one* of these writing assignments.

1. Suppose Michael were going to visit your class tomorrow. Write five questions you would like to ask him. Make them meaningful questions about the feelings, thoughts, and experiences of a student who has spent many years in a wheelchair.
2. Write one meaningful question Michael would really enjoy answering. Then, answer the question as you think Michael might respond. Include at least two reasons or examples.

▶ What can result from taking crazy chances? Some people don't learn the answer—until it's too late.

Dear Readers: Today's column is dedicated to that beautiful guy, Paul "Bear" Bryant, the "winningest coach" from the University of Alabama. The Bear, who died last Jan. 26, used to read this column to every freshman class on opening day.

It would be lovely if Ray Perkins, the Bear's successor, carried on the tradition. Bryant loved his kids and he wanted them to stay alive.

DEAD AT SEVENTEEN

Agony claws my mind. I am a statistic. When I first got here I felt very much alone. I was overwhelmed with grief, and I expected to find sympathy.

I found no sympathy. I saw only thousands of others whose bodies were as badly mangled as mine. I was given a number and placed in a category. The category was called "Traffic Fatalities."

The day I died was an ordinary school day. How I wish I had taken the bus! But I was too cool for the bus. I remember how I wheedled the car out of Mom. "Special favor," I pleaded. "All kids drive." When the 2:50 bell rang, I threw my books in the locker . . . free until tomorrow morning! I ran to the parking lot, excited at the thought of driving a car and being my own boss.

It doesn't matter how the accident happened. I was goofing off—going too fast, taking crazy chances. But I was enjoying my freedom and having fun. The last thing I remember was passing an old lady who seemed to be going awfully slow. I heard a crash and felt a terrific jolt. Glass and steel flew everywhere. My whole body seemed to be turning inside out. I heard myself scream.

Suddenly, I awakened. It was very quiet. A police officer was standing over me. I saw a doctor. My body was mangled. I was saturated with blood. Pieces of jagged glass were sticking out all over. Strange that I couldn't feel anything. Hey, don't pull that sheet over my head. I can't be dead. I'm only 17. I've got a date tonight. I'm supposed to have a wonderful life ahead of me. I haven't lived yet. I can't be dead.

Later I was placed in a drawer. My folks came to identify me. Why did they have to see me like this? Why did I have to look at Mom's eyes when she faced the most terrible ordeal of her life? Dad suddenly looked very old. He told the man in charge, "Yes—he is our son."

The funeral was weird. I saw all my relatives and friends walk toward the casket. They looked at me with the saddest eyes I've ever seen. Some of my buddies were crying. A few of the girls touched my hand and sobbed as they walked by.

Ann Landers

Please—somebody—wake me up! Get me out of here. I can't bear to see Mom and Dad in such pain. My grandparents are so weak from grief they can barely walk. My brother and sister are like zombies. They move like robots. In a daze. Everybody. No one can believe this. I can't believe it, either.

Please, don't bury me! I'm not dead! I have a lot of living to do! I want to laugh and run again. I want to sing and dance. Please don't put me in the ground! I promise if you give me just one more chance, God, I'll be the most careful driver in the whole world. All I want is one more chance. Please, God, I'm only 17.

Vocabulary words appear at the bottom of page 277.

ALL THINGS CONSIDERED ⸻

1. Paul "Bear" Bryant's purpose in reading aloud the column was clearly to (a) save lives. (b) make students write better. (c) show his interest in subjects other than football.
2. The teenage narrator makes it clear that the accident (a) was his fault. (b) was caused by a slow driver. (c) involved more than one car.
3. The incident is told as if it is the time (a) between the funeral and the burial. (b) before the funeral. (c) after the burial.
4. The narrator regrets most not being allowed to (a) live a full life. (b) graduate from high school and college. (c) become a teacher.
5. The wishes the narrator expresses in the last paragraph (a) will never be fulfilled. (b) might come true. (c) seem selfish after what has happened.

THINKING IT THROUGH ⸻

Discuss the following items in class.

1. The column cannot really be true, since no one can write a column after death. Yet in a way, every word seems to ring true. Do any of the narrator's thoughts strike you as false or artificial? Support your answer with reasons.
2. A group of high-school students insisted that this Ann Landers column be printed in this book. (a) In your opinion, what made the column so meaningful to them? (b) Do you share their feelings? Explain why, or why not.

- successor (suk SES ur) **one who follows another in a certain job**
- **agony** (AG uh nee) **great suffering of body or mind**
- statistic (stuh TIS tik) **one counted among many**
- **mangled** (MANG guld) **horribly damaged**
- **category** (KAT uh gohr ee) **class of objects; defined group**
- **fatality** (fay TAL i tee) **accidental death**
- wheedle (HWEED ul) **coax; persuade by smooth words**
- **saturated** (SACH uh ray tid) **soaked**
- **ordeal** (or DEEL) **severe trial or test**

▶ What do you do when you find yourself confused and sad? Some people talk to friends or parents. Other people write to newspaper experts like Ann Landers. If you're truly in a tizzy, you might try—*Miss Piggy*.

DEAR MISS PIGGY

by Moiself

Dear Miss Piggy,

For some reason, my garden this year produced a bumper crop of cabbages, and I don't know what to do with them all. Are there any good cabbage recipes?

Green Thumb

Dear Green Thumb,
No.

♥ ♥ ♥

Dear Miss Piggy,

Whenever I cook spaghetti, it always gets all tangled up into clumps. What am I doing wrong?

Frustrated

Dear Frustrated,
I am not sure, but you might try a light cream rinse, followed by a quick once-over with a blow-dryer.

♥ ♥ ♥

Dear Miss Piggy,

Is there anything you can do with the ends you cut off asparagus stalks? Asparagus isn't cheap, and it seems like you're throwing half of it away.

Thrifty

Dear Thrifty,
Well, I guess you could dye them and thread a string through them and hang the whole mess up somewhere, or maybe just stick a lot of toothpicks in them and make . . . look, is it really that important? Can't you just stick them in a bag and then, when you have forgotten all about it, just toss them out?

- tizzy (TIZ ee) **very excited and not knowing what to do next**
- bumper (BUM pur) **very large**
- frustrated (FRUS tray tid) **blocked from reaching some goal**
- **sash** (SASH) **window that slides up and down**

Dear Miss Piggy,

All of my plants, which were once so nice and green, have turned brown and died. What should I do?

Bereft

Dear Bereft,

That is truly sad. And green is such a pretty color. . . . But cheer up. Plants are just like lamps. You plug them in, and they turn right on. When they stop working, just unplug them, throw them away, and plug in another.

❤ ❤ ❤

Dear Miss Piggy,

My car engine turns over, but it won't start. I've checked the plugs, the points, the condenser, the coil, and the distributor, and I even sprayed carburetor cleaner in the carb, but no dice. What gives?

Stuck

Dear Stuck,

It sounds to me like your car is broken. If you need it soon, I would get it fixed.

Dear Miss Piggy,

I have a couple of old-fashioned sash windows that have a large gap where the two halves meet. When there's a wind, they rattle all night, and in winter there is a terrible draft. What can I do?

Rattled

Dear Rattled,

An interesting problem. You know what you might try? Take a handful of cut-off asparagus spear ends and work them into the cracks. Not only will this eliminate that annoying rattle and stop up the draft, but it will give you something useful to do with the otherwise wasted halves of what is, after all, a rather costly vegetable.

❤ ❤ ❤

Dear Miss Piggy,

If a base runner is struck by a foul ball that bounces off a wall into fair territory and hits him, is he out?

Bleacher Bum

Dear Bleacher Bum,

Well, I don't know. I suppose if it hit him in the head, he would at the very least be woozy for a bit. What is this person running from? And what is so "foul" about that ball? Did someone drop it in something messy? Moi needs facts.

- bereft (bi REFT) **deprived; saddened, usually by a death**
- condenser (kun DEN sur) **part of gasoline motor that stores electricity for the spark plugs**
- distributor (di STRIB yuh tur) **part of motor that sends electricity to the plugs**
- moi (MWAH) **French for** *me*

Dear Miss Piggy,

My hinges squeak, and the sound is driving me bananas. Is there anything I can do?

Unhinged

Dear Unhinged,

Try hammering a prune into them. If the problem persists, add honey.

Dear Miss Piggy,

I have had very bad luck with pets— three little doggies all ran away, and I would hate to suffer such a loss again— but if I don't have something around the house to keep me company, I get lonely. Help!

Doggone

Dear Doggone,

I know what you mean. My darling little Foo-Foo is a source of great joy to me. You might try a more stationary pet, like a clam or a potato. If you prefer something more in the furry line, mink coats make excellent pets.

Dear Miss Piggy,

Your book was excellent, splendid, superior, first-rate, top-notch, a classic, superb, magnificent, marvelous, wonderful, sensational—the best! I'm sorry to see it end.

Synonymous

Dear Synonymous,

And so is moi! Au revoir, God bless and . . .

- **persist** (pur SIST) **keep going**
- **stationary** (STAY shuh ner ee) **not moving; standing still**
- **synonymous** (si NON uh mus) **having the same meaning**
- **au revoir** (oh ruh VWAR) **French for *goodbye***

ALL THINGS CONSIDERED

1. The context makes it clear that the term "Green Thumb" (first letter on page 278) means (a) *jealous husband.* (b) *giant who grows cabbages.* (c) *good gardener.*
2. Miss Piggy does not seem to know the meaning of the term (a) *sash window.* (b) *foul ball.* (c) *bumper crop.*
3. To sound knowing, Miss Piggy likes to use (a) names of famous people. (b) quotations from poetry. (c) French words.
4. "Synonymous" is a good way for the person to sign the last letter because he or she (a) has used 12 terms that mean almost the same thing. (b) likes to make up words. (c) is certainly wise.
5. The word that best describes Miss Piggy's advice is (a) *practical.* (b) *silly.* (c) *useful.*

THINKING IT THROUGH

Discuss the following items in class.

1. In your opinion, why don't people who write to Miss Piggy use their real names to sign the letters?
2. Finish this sentence in your own words: *Most of Miss Piggy's advice is funny because . . .*
3. Did you think about other possible answers as you read the letters? Choose the letter you found most interesting. Then try to write a *funnier* answer than Miss Piggy's.

TA-NA-E-KA

by Mary Whitebird

▶ Mary Whitebird is 11 years old. She's turned out of the house to survive on her own—for five days. It's all part of an old Native American custom—a test of whether a young person is ready to be an adult.

As my birthday drew closer, I had awful nightmares about it. I was reaching the age at which all Kaw Indians had to take part in Ta-Na-E-Ka. Well, not all Kaws. Many of the younger families on the reservation were beginning to give up the old customs. But my grandfather, Amos Deer Leg, stood by the old traditions. He still wore handmade beaded moccasins instead of shoes. He kept his iron-gray hair in tight braids. He could speak English, but he spoke it only with white men. With his family he used a Sioux dialect.

Grandfather was one of the last living Indians who actually fought against the U.S. Cavalry. Not only did he fight, he was wounded in a skirmish at Rose Creek. This was the famous battle in which the well-known Kaw chief Flat Nose lost his life. At the time, my grandfather was only eleven years old.

Eleven was a magic word among the Kaws. It was the time of Ta-Na-E-Ka, which means "flowering of adulthood." My grandfather had told us about it hundreds of times. It was the age, he said, "when a boy could prove himself to be a warrior. And a girl can take the first steps to womanhood."

"I don't want to be a warrior," my cousin, Roger Deer Leg, confided to me. "I'm going to become an accountant."

"None of the other tribes make girls go through the survival ritual," I complained to my mother.

"It won't be as bad as you think, Mary," my mother said. "Once you've gone through it, you'll never forget it. You'll be proud."

I even complained to my teacher, Mrs. Richardson. I felt that, as a white woman, she would side with me.

She didn't. "All of us have rituals of

- **dialect** (DY uh lekt) local manner of speaking
- **skirmish** (SKUR mish) minor battle in a war
- **confide** (kun FYD) tell as a secret
- ritual (RICH oo ul) ceremony; tradition

one kind or another," Mrs. Richardson said. "And look at it this way: How many girls have the chance to compete on equal terms with boys? Don't look down on your heritage."

Heritage, indeed! I didn't plan to live on a reservation for the rest of my life. I was a good student. I loved school. My favorite stories were about knights in armor and fair ladies and dragons. I had never once thought that being Indian was exciting.

But I've always thought that equal rights for women started with the Kaw. No other Indian tribe treated women more "equally" than the Kaw. Unlike most other Sioux tribes, the Kaw allowed men and women to eat together. And hundreds of years ago, a Kaw woman had the right to reject a man chosen for her—even if her father had arranged a marriage.

The wisest women (usually the old ones) often sat in tribal councils. Furthermore, most Kaw legends are about "Good Woman," a kind of super person. Good Woman led Kaw warriors into battle after battle, which they always seemed to win.

And girls as well as boys were required to go through Ta-Na-E-Ka.

The actual ceremony varied from tribe to tribe. But since the Indians' life on the plains depended on survival,

Ta-Na-E-Ka was a test of survival.

"Endurance is the highest virtue of the Indian," my grandfather explained. "To survive, we must endure. When I was a boy, Ta-Na-E-Ka was more than just the symbol it is now. We were painted white with the juice of a sacred herb. Then we were sent naked into the wilderness, without so much as a knife. We couldn't return until the white had worn off. It wouldn't wash off. It took almost eighteen days.

- **heritage** (HER i tij) what is handed down to a person from ancestors
- **endurance** (en DOOR uns) ability to withstand hardship; survival
- **virtue** (VUR choo) good quality

"During that time," he went on, "we had to stay alive. We did it by trapping food, eating insects and roots and berries, and watching out for enemies. And we did have enemies—both the white soldiers and the Omaha warriors. They were always trying to capture Kaw boys and girls going through their endurance tests. It was an exciting time."

"What happened if you couldn't make it?" Roger asked. He was born only three days after I was, and we were being trained for Ta-Na-E-Ka together. I was happy to know he was frightened, too.

"Many didn't return," Grandfather said. "Only the strongest and shrewdest. Mothers were not allowed to weep over those who didn't return. If a Kaw couldn't survive, he or she wasn't worth weeping over. It was our way."

"What a lot of hooey," Roger whispered. "I'd give anything to get out of it."

"I don't see how we have any choice," I replied.

Roger gave my arm a little squeeze. "Well, it's only five days."

Five days! Maybe it was better than being painted white and sent out naked for eighteen days. But not much better.

We were to be sent, barefoot and in bathing suits, into the woods. Even our very traditional parents put their foot down when Grandfather suggested we go naked. For five days we'd have to live off the land. We'd have to keep warm as best we could and get food where we could. It was May. But on the northernmost shores of the Missouri River, the days were still chilly and the nights fiercely cold.

Grandfather was in charge of the month's training for Ta-Na-E-Ka. One day he caught a grasshopper. Then he showed us how to pull its legs and wings off in one flick of the fingers. And how to swallow it.

I felt sick, and Roger turned green. "It's a darn good thing it's 1947," I told Roger teasingly. "You'd make a terrible warrior." Roger just made a face.

I knew one thing. This was one Kaw Indian girl who wasn't going to swallow a grasshopper—no matter how hungry she got. And then I had an idea. Why hadn't I thought of it before? It would have saved nights of bad dreams about squooshy grasshoppers.

I headed straight for my teacher's house. "Mrs. Richardson," I said, "would you lend me five dollars?"

"Five dollars!" she exclaimed. "What for?"

"You remember the ceremony I talked about?"

"Ta-Na-E-Ka. Of course. Your parents have written and asked me to excuse you from school so you can take part in it."

"Well, I need some things for the ceremony," I said, in a half-truth. "I don't want to ask my parents for the money."

"It's not a crime to borrow money, Mary. But how can you pay it back?"

- **shrewdest** (SHROOD est) cleverest
- **traditional** (truh DISH uh nul) following old customs

"I'll baby-sit for you ten times."

"That's more than fair," she said. She went to her purse and handed me a crisp, new, five-dollar bill. I'd never had that much money at once.

"I'm happy to know the money's going to be put to a good use," Mrs. Richardson said.

A few days later, Ta-Na-E-Ka began. First came a long speech from my grandfather. It was all about how we had reached the age of decision, how we now had to take care of ourselves. We had to prove that we could survive the most horrendous of ordeals.

All the friends and relatives gathered at our house for dinner and made jokes about their own Ta-Na-E-Kas. They all advised us to fill up now, since for the next five days we'd be eating crickets. Neither Roger nor I was very hungry.

"I'll probably laugh about this when I'm an accountant," Roger said, trembling.

"Are you trembling?" I asked.

"What do you think?"

"I'm happy to know boys tremble, too," I said.

At six the next morning, we kissed our parents and went off to the woods. "Which side do you want?" Roger asked. According to the rules, Roger and I would stake out "territories" in separate areas of the woods. We weren't to communicate during the whole ordeal.

"I'll go toward the river, if it's okay with you," I said.

"Sure," Roger answered. "What difference does it make?"

To me, it made a lot of difference. There was a marina a few miles up the river, and there were boats anchored there. At least I hoped so. I figured that a boat was a better place to sleep than under a pile of leaves.

"Why do you keep holding your head?" Roger asked.

"Oh, nothing. Just nervous," I told him. Actually, I was afraid I'd lose the five-dollar bill, which I had tucked into my hair with a bobby pin. As we came to a fork in the trail, Roger shook my hand. "Good luck, Mary."

"N'ko-n'ta," I said. It was the Kaw word for *courage*.

The sun was shining and it was warm. But my bare feet began to hurt right away. I saw one of the berry bushes Grandfather had told us about. "You're lucky," he had said. "The berries are ripe in the spring, and they are delicious and nourishing." They were orange and fat and I popped one into my mouth.

Argh! I spat it out. It was awful and bitter. Even grasshoppers were probably better tasting. However, I never intended to find out.

I sat down to rest my feet. A rabbit

- **horrendous** (ho REN dus) horrible; awful
- **ordeal** (or DEEL) severe test; harsh experience
- stake out (STAYK out) mark the limits of
- **marina** (muh REE nuh) large area set up for docking boats

285

hopped out from under the berry bush. He nuzzled the berry I'd spat out and ate it. He picked another one and ate that, too. He liked them. He looked at me, twitching his nose. Then I watched a red-headed woodpecker tap on an elm tree. I caught a glimpse of a skunk waddling through some twigs. All of a sudden, I realized I was no longer frightened. Ta-Na-E-Ka might be more fun than I'd expected. I got up and headed toward the marina.

"Not one boat," I said to myself, depressed. But the restaurant on the shore, "Ernie's Riverside," was open. I walked in, feeling silly in my bathing suit. The man at the counter was big and tough-looking. He wore a sweatshirt with the words "Fort Sheridan, 1944," and he had only three fingers on one of his hands. He asked me what I wanted.

"A hamburger and a milk shake," I said. I held the five-dollar bill in my hand so he'd know I had money.

"That's a pretty heavy breakfast, honey," he said.

"That's what I always have for breakfast," I lied.

"Forty-five cents," he said, bringing me the food. (Back in 1947, hamburgers were twenty-five cents and milk shakes were twenty cents.) "Delicious," I thought. "Better'n grasshoppers. And Grandfather never once said that I couldn't eat hamburgers."

While I was eating, I had a grand idea. Why not sleep in the restaurant? I went to the ladies' room and made sure the window was unlocked. Then I went back outside and played along the riverbank. I watched the water birds, trying to identify each one. I planned to look for a beaver dam the next day.

The restaurant closed at sunset, and I watched the three-fingered man drive away. Then I climbed in the unlocked window. There was a night light on, so I didn't turn on any lights. But there was a radio on the counter. I turned it on to a music program.

It was warm in the restaurant, and I was hungry. I helped myself to a glass of milk and a piece of pie. But I meant to keep a list of what I'd eaten, so I could leave money. I also meant to get up early. Then I could sneak out through the window and head for the woods before the three-fingered man returned. I turned off the radio. I wrapped myself in the man's apron. And, in spite of the hardness of the floor, I fell asleep.

"What the heck are you doing here, kid?"

It was the man's voice.

It was morning. I'd overslept. I was scared.

"Hold it, kid. I just wanna know what you're doing here. You lost? You must be from the reservation. Your folks must be worried sick about you. Do they have a phone?"

"Yes, yes," I answered. "But don't call them."

I was shivering. The man, who told me his name was Ernie, made me a cup of hot chocolate. Meanwhile, I explained

---

• nuzzle (NUZ ul) **nudge with the nose**

about Ta-Na-E-Ka.

"Darndest thing I ever heard," he said, when I was through. "Lived next to the reservation all my life, and this is the first I've heard of Ta-Na whatever-you-call-it." He looked at me, all goose bumps in my bathing suit. "Pretty silly thing to do to a kid," he muttered.

That was just what I'd been thinking for months. But when Ernie said it, I became angry. "No, it isn't silly. It's a custom of the Kaw. We've been doing this for hundreds of years. My mother and my grandfather and everybody in my family went through this ceremony. It's why the Kaw are great warriors."

"Okay, great warrior," Ernie chuckled, "suit yourself. And if you want to stick around, it's okay with me." Ernie went to the broom closet and tossed me a bundle. "That's the lost-and-found closet," he said. "Stuff people left on boats. Maybe there's something to keep you warm."

The sweater fitted loosely, but it felt good. I felt good. And I'd found a new friend. Most important, I was surviving Ta-Na-E-Ka.

My grandfather had said Ta-Na-E-Ka would be filled with adventure. I was certainly having my fill. And Grandfather has never said we couldn't accept hospitality.

I stayed at Ernie's Riverside for the whole five days. In the mornings, I went into the woods. There I watched the animals and picked flowers for each of the tables in Ernie's. I had never felt better. I was up early enough to watch the sun rise on the Missouri, and I went to bed after it set. I ate everything I wanted—insisting that Ernie take all my money for the food.

"I'll keep this in trust for you, Mary," Ernie promised. "In case you are ever desperate for five dollars."

I was sorry when the five days were over. I'd enjoyed every minute with Ernie. He taught me how to make western omelets and Chili Ernie Style. (That's still one of my favorite dishes.) And I told Ernie all about the legends of the Kaw. I hadn't realized I knew so much about my people.

But Ta-Na-E-Ka was over. As I neared my house, at about nine-thirty in the evening, I became nervous all over again. What if Grandfather asked me about the berries and the grasshoppers? And my

---

- **omelet** (OM uh lit) eggs beaten up, fried, and folded in half when done

feet were hardly cut. I hadn't lost a pound, and my hair was combed.

"They'll be so happy to see me," I told myself hopefully, "that they won't ask too many questions."

I opened the door. My grandfather was in the front room. He was wearing the ceremonial beaded deerskin shirt which had belonged to *his* grandfather.

"N'g'da'ma," he said. "Welcome back."

I hugged my parents warmly. Then I let go when I saw my cousin Roger sprawled on the couch. His eyes were red and swollen. He'd lost weight. His feet were an unsightly mass of blood and blisters. And he was moaning: "I made it, see. I made it. I'm a warrior. A warrior."

My grandfather looked at me strangely. I looked clean, well fed, and radiantly healthy. My parents got the message. My uncle and aunt gazed at me with hostility.

Finally my grandfather asked, "What did you eat to keep you so well?"

I sucked in my breath and blurted out the truth: "Hamburgers and milk shakes."

"Hamburgers!" my grandfather growled.

"Milk shakes!" Roger moaned.

"You didn't say we *had* to eat grasshoppers," I said meekly.

"Tell us about your Ta-Na-E-Ka," my grandfather commanded.

I told them everything, from borrowing the five dollars, to Ernie's kindness, to watching the beaver.

"That's not what I trained you for," my grandfather said sadly.

I stood up. "Grandfather, I learned that Ta-Na-E-Ka *is* important. I didn't think so during training. I was scared stiff of it. I handled it my way. And I learned I had nothing to be afraid of. There's no reason in 1947 to eat grasshoppers when you can eat a hamburger."

Inside, I was shocked at my own boldness. But I liked it. "Grandfather, I'll bet you never ate one of those rotten berries yourself."

Grandfather laughed! He laughed aloud! My mother and father and aunt and uncle were all dumbfounded. Grandfather never laughed. Never.

"Those berries—they are terrible," Grandfather admitted. "I could never swallow them. On the first day of my Ta-Na-E-Ka, I found a dead deer—shot by a soldier, probably. It kept my belly full for the entire period of the test!"

Grandfather stopped laughing. "We should send you out again," he said.

I looked at Roger. "You're pretty smart, Mary," Roger groaned. "I'd never have thought of what you did."

"Accountants just have to be good at arithmetic," I said comfortingly. "I'm terrible at arithmetic."

Roger tried to smile, but couldn't. My

- **hostility** (hos TIL i tee) dislike; unfriendliness
- **blurt** (BLURT) say suddenly
- **dumbfounded** (DUM found ud) astonished

grandfather called me to him. "You should have done what your cousin did. But I think you are more aware of what is happening to our people today than we are. I think you would have passed the test under any circumstances, in any time. Somehow, you know how to live in a world that wasn't made for Indians. I don't think you're going to have any trouble surviving."

Grandfather wasn't entirely right. But I'll tell about that another time.

ALL THINGS CONSIDERED

1. Ta-Na-E-Ka is an Indian (a) warrior. (b) traditional dance. (c) test of survival.

2. As both Mary and her cousin Roger prepare for Ta-Na-E-Ka, Roger is (a) confident. (b) scared. (c) jealous of Mary.

3. Roger and Mary are taught about Ta-Na-E-Ka by (a) Chief Flat Nose. (b) Mary's grandfather. (c) the teacher, Mrs. Richardson.

4. Mary prepares in a secret way by (a) borrowing money. (b) hiding food in a tree trunk. (c) building a treehouse.

5. Mary says that the Kaw tribe gave women equal rights. As one example, she tells that women (a) took part in tribal government. (b) managed some of the local stores. (c) hunted deer.

6. During Ta-Na-E-Ka, Mary survives by eating (a) grasshoppers. (b) hamburgers. (c) berries.

7. She sleeps in a (a) boat. (b) cave. (c) restaurant.

8. Ernie helps Mary survive, but he does *not* give her (a) money. (b) food. (c) a sweater.

9. When Mary tells the family about her Ta-Na-E-Ka, her grandfather (a) gets angry. (b) shakes his head and says she will never be a warrior. (c) admits he never ate wild berries either.

10. Grandfather decides that Mary passed the test because she (a) showed her complete respect for the old ways. (b) tried her best. (c) knew how to survive in the modern world.

THINKING IT THROUGH

Discuss the following items in class.

1. By taking part in Ta-Na-E-Ka, Mary is performing a Kaw ritual. However, she goes about it in a new way. At the end of the story, do you think Mary has more or less respect for her heritage?

2. Mary's Ta-Na-E-Ka differs from her grandfather's. Think about it. In what ways were the Ta-Na-E-Ka's different?

• **circumstance** (SUR kum stans) **condition**

Inferences

Fact and Opinion

A **fact** is something known to be true. It can be checked and proved. *It is a fact that this sentence is printed in italic type.* It is also a fact that you just read a sentence in italic type.

An **opinion** is what a person thinks or believes about something. It may be your opinion that italic type is easier to read than regular type. It may be another person's opinion that italic type is harder to read. Even though many people may agree on a certain opinion, no one can *prove* it to be true.

Especially when reading nonfiction, it is important to keep the difference between fact and opinion in mind.

Here are five sentences from the selection. In some, the narrator is stating facts. In others, she is expressing opinions she had at the time of the events described. On your paper, write *fact* or *opinion* for each sentence.

1. I felt that, as a white woman, she would side with me.

2. It [the berry] was awful and bitter.

3. I went to the ladies' room and made sure the window was unlocked.

4. "It's a custom of the Kaw."

5. My grandfather asked, "What did you eat to keep you so well?"

Composition

Follow your teacher's instructions before completing *one* of these writing assignments.

1. Write six sentences about the selection. In three of your sentences, state facts. In the other three sentences, express your opinions. Here are two examples:
Fact: Ta-Na-E-Ka was a five-day ritual.
Opinion: Ernie, the man in the restaurant, did the right thing in helping the girl.

2. Write a paragraph at least 150 words long describing yourself. That's not hard. The difficult part is this: you must write only facts, not opinions. Try to avoid words that even suggest opinions. For instance, you may think you have a "neat" haircut, but how would you describe it *in fact?*

VOCABULARY AND SKILL REVIEW

Before completing the exercises that follow, you may wish to review the **bold-faced** words on pages 262 to 289.

I. On a separate sheet of paper, write the *italicized* term that best fills the blank in each sentence.

physical	*heritage*	*goulash*	*marina*	*hostility*
blurt	*horrendous*	*endurance*	*virtue*	*typical*

1. Honesty is thought to be a _____ by almost everybody.
2. You should get some _____ exercise every day.
3. Dad doesn't like _____ unless it contains lots of meat.
4. Radio station WSNG wanted a _____ student from our school for an interview.
5. The hurricane destroyed many boats in the _____ .
6. "Part of my _____ is my beautiful southern dialect," she said.
7. Mr. Gold's long illness was a _____ experience for all.
8. Some students get in trouble when they _____ out remarks in class.
9. _____ is the opposite of "friendliness."
10. The Boston Marathon requires tremendous _____ .

II. 1. A *dialect* is a way of (a) thinking about life. (b) talking. (c) reaching an agreement.
2. An *omelet* requires (a) sugar. (b) green vegetables. (c) eggs.
3. If you *confide* something to a person, you (a) tell it privately. (b) hand a person something. (c) probably dislike the person.
4. A *skirmish* in a war would probably involve (a) entire armies. (b) thousands of soldiers. (c) a few troops.
5. No one likes to go through a long (a) *flashback.* (b) *ordeal.* (c) *circumstance.*
6. The word *stationary* means (a) not movable. (b) note paper. (c) any paper.
7. A *saturated* dish towel would be (a) nearly new. (b) black with dirt. (c) very wet.
8. A traffic *fatality* is a traffic (a) jam. (b) death. (c) long news broadcast.

291

9. To put something in a *category* is to place it in a (a) safe place. (b) kind of vehicle. (c) group of similar things.

10. A *sash* is part of a (a) book. (b) window. (c) drama.

III. Read the poem carefully before you answer the questions.

MY PEOPLE

by Bernice George

I am a Navajo; the Navajos are my people.
They live in the hogans upon the dry desert,
With a little shade house and a sheep corral.
It is nice and peaceful there away
From the city street.
There were the sad, dark years for my people,
But my people didn't disappear.
They started rebuilding, increasing
In population.
I am proud that the desert floor,
The lonely hogans,
Have made me thoughtful and
Respectful of my people.
I am proud to be born in my people's land.
I shall never forget my home and people.

1. Even a short poem can contain a flashback. Examine the poem to find its eight sentences (count the periods). Which two sentences, by number, form a flashback?

2. Most of the poem consists of facts about the Navajo people. Yet the poem does use a few words that are opinions. Write at least two of these "opinion words" on your paper.

Bonus question: The feelings Bernice George expresses about the Navajos are not exactly the same as those expressed by Mary Whitebird about the Kaw people. What does Mary Whitebird say in "Ta-Na-E-Ka" that Bernice George does *not* say in the poem?

● **hogan** (HOH gun) a Navajo house, made of branches, clay, and sod

Langston Hughes (1902-1967)

A writer with world-wide appeal

One evening in 1925, a well-known poet named Vachel Lindsay was going to read his poetry at the Wardman Park Hotel in Washington, D.C. As Lindsay sat in the hotel dining room just before the reading was to begin, a busboy in a clean white jacket came up to him. The young man placed three of his own neatly copied poems on the table. Would Mr. Lindsey be good enough to look at them?

The next morning, the busboy woke up to find his name in the newspaper. More than that, when he got to the hotel, he found reporters and photographers waiting for him. What had happened? He learned that Lindsay had read all three of his poems to an eager audience the evening before. The discovery of the unknown genius was big news.

The meeting with Lindsay was the spark that sent Hughes's career zooming upward. First came a poetry prize. Then came his first book, *The Weary Blues.* This was followed by a B.A. degree from Lincoln University. Then came book after book after book—39 in all. Hughes successfully wrote poems, stories, novels, essays, operas, musicals, translations, biographies, and his autobiography. He combined a deep love and sympathy for common people with a sense of humor that the public loved. One of his famous poems appears below.

DREAMS

Hold fast to dreams
For if dreams die
Life is a broken-winged bird
That cannot fly.

Hold fast to dreams
For when dreams go
Life is a barren field
Covered with snow.

THANK YOU, M'AM

> ► Langston Hughes once said that in every race and in every country where he had been, *most* people were generally good. This faith in people is shown in the story that follows.

She was a large woman with a large purse that had everything in it but hammer and nails. It had a long strap and she carried it slung across her shoulder. It was about eleven o'clock at night, and she was walking alone, when a boy ran up behind her and tried to snatch her purse. The strap broke with the single tug the boy gave it from behind. But the boy's weight, and the weight of the purse combined caused him to lose his balance so, instead of taking off full blast as he had hoped, the boy fell on his back on the sidewalk, and his legs flew up. The large woman simply turned around and kicked him right square in his blue-jeaned sitter. Then she reached down, picked the boy up by his shirt front, and shook him until his teeth rattled.

After that the woman said, "Pick up my pocketbook, boy, and give it here."

She still held him. But she bent down enough to permit him to stoop and pick up her purse. Then she said, "Now ain't you ashamed of yourself?"

Firmly gripped by his shirt front, the boy said, "Yes'm."

The woman said, "What did you want to do it for?"

The boy said, "I didn't aim to."

She said, "You a lie!"

By that time two or three people passed, stopped, turned to look, and some stood watching.

"If I turn you loose, will you run?" asked the woman.

"Yes'm," said the boy.

"Then I won't turn you loose," said the woman. She did not release him.

• **slung** (SLUNG) hung; made to swing loosely

"I'm very sorry, lady, I'm sorry," whispered the boy.

"Um-hum! And your face is dirty. I got a great mind to wash your face for you. Ain't you got nobody home to tell you to wash your face?"

"No'm," said the boy.

"Then it will get washed this evening," said the large woman starting up the street, dragging the frightened boy behind her.

He looked as if he were fourteen or fifteen, frail and willow-wild, in tennis shoes and blue jeans.

The woman said, "You ought to be my son. I would teach you right from wrong. Least I can do right now is to wash your face. Are you hungry?"

"No'm," said the being-dragged boy. "I just want you to turn me loose."

"Was I bothering *you* when I turned that corner?" asked the woman.

"No'm."

"But you put yourself in contact with *me*," said the woman. "If you think that that contact is not going to last awhile, you got another thought coming. When I get through with you, sir, you are going to remember Mrs. Luella Bates Washington Jones."

• **frail** (FRAYL) weak

Sweat popped out on the boy's face and he began to struggle. Mrs. Jones stopped, jerked him around in front of her, put a half nelson about his neck, and continued to drag him up the street. When she got to her door, she dragged the boy inside, down a hall, and into a large kitchenette-furnished room at the rear of the house. She switched on the light and left the door open. The boy could hear other roomers laughing and talking in the large house. Some of their doors were open, too, so he knew he and the woman were not alone. The woman still had him by the neck in the middle of her room.

She said, "What is your name?"

"Roger," answered the boy.

"Then, Roger, you go to that sink and wash your face," said the woman, whereupon she turned him loose—at last. Roger looked at the door—looked at the woman—looked at the door—*and went to the sink.*

"Let the water run until it gets warm," she said. "Here's a clean towel."

"You gonna take me to jail?" asked the boy, bending over the sink.

"Not with that face, I would not take you nowhere," said the woman. "Here I am trying to get home to cook me a bite to eat and you snatch my pocketbook! Maybe you ain't been to your supper either, late as it be. Have you?"

"There's nobody home at my house," said the boy.

"Then we'll eat," said the woman. "I believe you're hungry—or been hungry—to try to snatch my pocketbook."

"I wanted a pair of blue suede shoes," said the boy.

"Well, you didn't have to snatch *my* pocketbook to get some suede shoes," said Mrs. Luella Bates Washington Jones. "You could of asked me."

"M'am?"

The water dripping from his face, the boy looked at her. There was a long pause. A very long pause. After he had dried his face and not knowing what else to do dried it again, the boy turned around,

- half nelson (HAF NEL sun) **wrestling hold on back of neck**
- **whereupon** (hwair uh PON) **after which**
- **suede** (SWAYD) **soft leather with a velvet-like surface**

wondering what next. The door was open. He could make a dash for it down the hall. He could run, run, run, run, *run!*

The woman was sitting on the daybed. After a while she said, "I were young once and I wanted things I could not get."

There was another long pause. The boy's mouth opened. Then he frowned, but not knowing he frowned.

The woman said, "Um-hum! You thought I was going to say *but,* didn't you? You thought I was going to say, *but I didn't snatch people's pocketbooks.* Well, I wasn't going to say that." Pause. Silence. "I have done things, too, which I would not tell you, son—neither tell God, if He didn't already know. So you set down while I fix us something to eat. You might run that comb through your hair so you will look presentable."

In another corner of the room behind a screen was a gas plate and an icebox. Mrs. Jones got up and went behind the screen. The woman did not watch the boy to see if he was going to run now, nor did she watch her purse which she left behind her on the daybed. But the boy took care to sit on the far side of the room where he thought she could easily see him out of the corner of her eye, if she wanted to. He did not trust the woman *not* to trust him. And he did not want to be mistrusted now.

"Do you need somebody to go to the store," asked the boy, "maybe to get some milk or something?"

"Don't believe I do," said the woman, "unless you just want sweet milk yourself. I was going to make cocoa out of this canned milk I got here."

"That will be fine," said the boy.

She heated some lima beans and ham she had in the icebox, made the cocoa, and set the table. The woman did not ask the boy anything about where he lived, or his folks, or anything else that would embarrass him. Instead, as they ate, she told him about her job in a hotel beauty shop that stayed open late, what the work was like, and how all kinds of women came in and out, blondes, redheads, and Spanish. Then she cut him a half of her ten-cent cake.

"Eat some more, son," she said.

When they were finished eating she got up and said, "Now, here, take this ten dollars and buy yourself some blue suede shoes. And

---

• plate (PLAYT) **small burner for cooking**

next time, do not make the mistake of latching onto *my* pocketbook *nor nobody else's*—because shoes come by devilish like that will burn your feet. I got to get my rest now. But I wish you would behave yourself, son, from here on in."

She led him down the hall to the front door and opened it. "Goodnight! Behave yourself, boy!" she said, looking out into the street.

The boy wanted to say something else other than, "Thank you, m'am," to Mrs. Luella Bates Washington Jones, but he couldn't do so as he turned at the barren stoop and looked back at the large woman in the door. He barely managed to say, "Thank you," before she shut the door. And he never saw her again.

ALL THINGS CONSIDERED

1. The time period of the story is (a) late afternoon. (b) early evening. (c) between eleven o'clock and midnight.
2. After snatching the purse, the boy falls because (a) the woman pushes him to the sidewalk. (b) he is off balance. (c) he trips over the purse.

- **barren** (BAR un) dull; uninteresting
- **stoop** (STOOP) front step

3. The boy probably tells a lie when he says that (a) he would run away if released. (b) he didn't mean to snatch the purse. (c) his name is Roger.

4. Roger goes with Mrs. Jones because (a) she drags him with a wrestling hold. (b) he wants something to eat. (c) he wants her to like and trust him.

5. When they arrive at Mrs. Jones's room, she first orders him to (a) eat something. (b) go to the store. (c) wash his face.

6. Roger says he snatched the purse to get money (a) to buy food. (b) for carfare home. (c) to buy a pair of shoes.

7. According to the woman, she has (a) lived a spotless life. (b) also done things that were not right. (c) raised several boys to be honest men.

8. While they eat, Mrs. Jones (a) avoids asking questions that might embarrass Roger. (b) continues to scold Roger. (c) watches the news on TV.

9. After the meal, Mrs. Jones (a) gives Roger money. (b) takes the boy's money as punishment. (c) calls Roger's parents.

10. At the end of the story, Roger's attitude toward Mrs. Jones is one of (a) anger. (b) envy. (c) gratefulness.

THINKING IT THROUGH

Discuss the following items in class.

1. Do you believe the story could have really happened? Why, or why not?

2. The story is unusual because the characters are not often called by their names. Instead, the author uses "the woman" and "the boy" over and over. Why might he have done this?

3. At one point, Roger asks, "You gonna take me to jail?" Mrs. Jones does not answer directly. In your opinion, why doesn't she call the police?

4. At another point, Roger offers to go to the store. In your opinion, would he have returned? Support your answer by referring to a sentence or two in the story.

5. At the end, Roger wants to say more than a simple *thank you*. What would he have said if he had managed to put his true feelings into words?

Sentence Meaning

Denotation and Connotation

Good authors choose their words with great care. They know that words often have two kinds of meanings. One kind of meaning is a word's **denotation** (dee noh TAY shun), or the meaning given in the dictionary. The other is a word's **connotation** (kon uh TAY shun), or the meaning a word suggests or brings to mind. Think about the following pairs of words: *slender-skinny, home-house, wealthy-rich, officer-cop, thrifty-cheap.* In each pair the denotations, or dictionary meanings, would be nearly the same. However, the connotations—what the words suggest—are quite different. For example, *slender* might suggest a person who is attractive. The word *skinny* might suggest an unattractive person.

Here are four items from "Thank You, M'am." Answer the questions that follow each item.

1. She was a large woman with a large purse. . . . (How would the connotation change if *fat* were used for the first *large?*)
2. ". . . you are going to remember Mrs. Luella Bates Washington Jones." (Why not simply *remember me?* What do the last five words in the quotation suggest?)
3. ". . . shoes come by devilish like that will burn your feet." (What does *devilish* suggest that *dishonestly* does not? What is the connection between *devilish* and *burn your feet?*)
4. "But I wish you would behave yourself, son, from here on in." (Read the sentence again, using *kid* or *boy* for *son.* What does *son* suggest that the other words do not?)

Composition

Follow your teacher's instructions before completing *one* of these writing assignments.

1. Imagine you were the author, Langston Hughes. Which part of the story did you enjoy writing most? Tell why.
2. Imagine you were Roger, the boy in the story. After receiving the money, would you have written a thank-you note, seen the woman again, paid the money back, or thanked her in some other way? Explain.

▶ "Hold fast to your dreams," wrote Langston Hughes. That's good advice. Without goals, a person's life just drifts in different directions. Once the goals are in sight, *getting there* becomes the job. *Getting there* is the special subject of this tall, thin poem.

- **spikes** (SPYKS) **spiked running shoes**
- **cinders** (SIN durz) **coal ashes used on running tracks**
- **catapult** (KAT uh pult) **rush headlong; shoot forward**
- lurch (LURCH) **move suddenly**
- sinew (SIN yoo) **cord that connects muscle to bone**
- **ecstasy** (EK stuh see) **supreme joy; great thrill**
- **ecstatic** (ek STAT ik) **joyful; very happy**
- **hurtling** (HURT ling) **rushing wildly; dashing against**

TO JAMES

by Frank Horne

Do you remember
How you won
That last race . . . ?
How you flung your body
At the start . . .
How your spikes
Ripped the cinders
In the stretch . . .
How you catapulted
Through the tape . . .
Do you remember . . . ?
Don't you think
I lurched with you
Out of those starting holes . . . ?
Don't you think
My sinews tightened
At those first
Few strides . . .
And when you flew into the stretch
Was not all my thrill
Of a thousand races
In your blood . . . ?
At your final drive
Through the finish line
Did not my shout
Tell of the
Triumphant ecstasy
Of victory . . . ?
Live
As I have taught you
To run, Boy—
It's a short dash
Dig your starting holes
Deep and firm
Lurch out of them
Into the straightaway
With all the power
That is in you
Look straight ahead
To the finish line
Think only of the goal
Run straight
Run high
Run hard
Save nothing
And finish
With an ecstatic burst
That carries you
Hurtling
Through the tape
To victory . . .

301

WAYS OF KNOWING

1. The poem is addressed "To James" by a speaker referred to as "I." (a) Does this speaker seem to be older or younger than James? (b) Who might the speaker be? That is, what is the speaker's past relationship with James?

2. There is a line in the poem that contains only one word. (a) What is this word? (b) How is the part of the poem that follows this word different from the part that comes before the word?

3. The speaker advises James to run "straight," "high," and "hard." What does he mean by each of these three words?

4. Suppose that a teacher, using words from the poem, told you, "Right now you are digging your starting holes." What would this teacher mean?

5. Why, do you think, is the poem written in a tall, thin column, rather than in wide lines that reach farther across the page?

VOCABULARY AND SKILL REVIEW

Before completing the exercises that follow, you may wish to review the **bold-faced** words on pages 292 to 301.

I. On a separate sheet of paper, mark each item *true* or *false*. If it is *false*, explain what is wrong with the sentence.

1. A *suede* jacket would probably cost a good deal of money.
2. Athletes tend to be healthy and *frail.*
3. The *denotation* of a word is its dictionary meaning.
4. The *connotation* of a word is its dictionary meaning.
5. A *hogan* is a small city in the desert.
6. Birds may injure themselves *hurtling* against window panes.
7. Track stars usually feel *ecstatic* when they come in last.
8. The *stoop* of a house can be found in the cellar.
9. Lazy people often *catapult* their way as they move along.
10. Actors probably enjoy a few moments of *ecstasy* when the audience cheers.

II. Here are eight pairs of words. On your paper, write the word in each pair that has the more favorable connotation.

Example: *skinny-slender.* You would write *slender,* since the word carries favorable connotations. *Slender* is used as a compliment. *Skinny,* however, is usually used as an insult.

1. curious-nosy
2. stubborn-firm
3. stern-cruel
4. smell-fragrance

5. loaded-wealthy
6. puny-dainty
7. custodian-janitor
8. idling-resting

A BONUS SELECTION

▶ People sometimes discover important things about themselves when being tested under pressure. The author of this true story is just such a person. As a young woman, she agreed to join her husband for a few months of adventure. They were to trap muskrat and other animals for fur, in Canada's Far North. But when the deep snows came, they found that they were trapped themselves.

Years later, when she was in her 60s and living comfortably in British Columbia, Olive A. Fredrickson sat down to write the amazing story of what happened in that

STARVATION WILDERNESS

by Olive A. Fredrickson

Our scow was heavy. It was an old 30-footer that we had bought at Fort Fitzgerald. But with only two grown-ups, a baby, and a pair of sled dogs on board, it rode high. The steady current of the Slave River pushed us north far faster than anyone could have walked on shore.

We had oars, and now and then my young husband, Walter, used them for a short distance. But there was no need for it. Mostly he just steered. We watched the early-fall scenery slip past or played with our six-month-old daughter, Olive. When we weren't cuddling her, she slept as contented as a kitten in the small cardboard box that was her crib.

Muskrat sign was plentiful along the river. Wherever there was green grass along the shore, snow geese pastured by the hundreds. We were rarely out of hearing of their wild voices. We had come to a land of plenty, Walter and I agreed. It was a dream country for a young trapper and his wife.

The time was late August of 1922. The trip had come about when Walter met two trappers, Nels Nelson and Pete

- muskrat (MUSK rat) **brown animal that lives in and near water, about two feet long; also called** *marsh rat* **and** *rat* **in the selection**
- scow (SKOU) **barge; tub-like boat for carrying cargo**
- cuddling (KUD ling) **holding and petting**

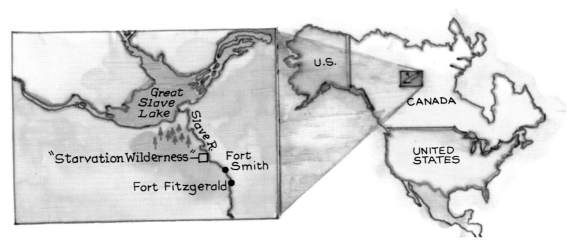

Anderson, at Fort Fitzgerald. They had trapped the fall before down the Slave in Northwest Territories. They had come out before Christmas, they said, with 1,600 muskrat skins that brought $1.50 apiece. There were lakes all over the country, they told Walter, and every one of those lakes crawled with marsh rats.

My husband was a trapper at heart, above everything else. For him stories of that kind were like wild tales of gold to other men. He gave up then and there all thought of going to Fort McMurray, where I had been looking forward to the presence of other women, a few comforts, and a doctor in case the baby or I needed one. The three of us, Walter decided, would spend the winter trapping on those rich fur grounds.

We bought the scow and 34 single-spring traps. We also bought 400 pounds of flour, 50 pounds of white sugar, and four 50-pound sacks of potatoes. I remember that we paid $12 for each of those sacks. Coal oil was $2 a gallon at Fitzgerald. We completed our grub list with beans, rice, salt pork, oatmeal, baking powder, salt, and tea—and cornmeal for the dogs.

We loaded the scow and shoved off on August 23 for the trip down the Slave to our trapping grounds. We were in completely unfamiliar country. It was the first time either of us had been that far north. We were on our way into what Walter had been told was good fur country. He was completely happy. I'll confess that I wasn't quite so cheerful as he was about wintering with a child not yet a year old hundreds of miles from the nearest doctor.

Nels and Pete had told us to look for an old sawdust pile on the west shore of the river. We should settle down around there, they had said. We passed the sawdust pile on our fourth day of floating. We tied up the scow, let our two dogs loose for a run, got the tent up, and carried our supplies up the bank. It was close to midnight when we finished. We tied the dogs to trees and turned in.

After we had gotten to sleep, I was awakened by some animal gnawing on the salt pork we had brought into the tent. At first I thought one of the dogs had gotten loose. But as my eyes grew accustomed to the dim light in the tent I made out a large skunk.

The tent was only 9 × 12 feet. That skunk was working on the pork within three feet of my face. I shook Walter awake. We tried to drive the skunk off, but it wouldn't budge.

"I'll have to shoot it or we won't have any pork," Walter finally said. We knew it wasn't a very good idea, but we had no choice.

Shooting a skunk inside a tent is a big mistake. Whoever invented tear gas simply copied something that skunks have used for thousands of years. It wouldn't be truthful to say the air turned blue, but it certainly turned something. Our eyes started to water. We were almost blinded. We began to gag. I grabbed the baby and fumbled my way outside. After a minute or so, Walter stumbled out behind me, dragging the dead skunk. He threw it over the river-

bank. We hauled our bedding outside and spent the rest of the night in the open. We were tired enough to sleep anywhere. The next morning I told Walter that his way of saving our salt pork was no good. The pork smelled almost as bad as the tent.

Next we started work on a cabin for our winter home. We planned to live in it only until November, when the lakes would freeze and we'd have to quit trapping. So we threw it up hurriedly. It was built of small green logs. It was soon finished, and about October 1 we put our traps out.

As it happened, we stayed on in that rough cabin until spring. For one thing, there was a lot of fur, mink as well as muskrat. There was also firewood handy. The cabin stood in a thick grove of spruces, where it was sheltered from the wind.

We had torn our scow apart to make doors and windows. I suggested to Walter that he build a boat. It was a clumsy boat, for we had no way to bend the heavy boards of the scow.

The trapping looked good, but now we faced another problem. Wild meat was so scarce that we got worried. There wasn't a moose or deer track anywhere. Before winter closed in on us, we had named that belt of timber and swampy

- salt pork—fat pork cured with salt to keep fresh
- tear gas—kind of gas that burns the eyes, sometimes used to control riots
- gag (GAG) **cough with a sick feeling**
- belt (BELT) **area; region**

lakes Starvation Wilderness. Snow came to stay on October 10. After that the whole country was white and lifeless.

Trapping was good. We were looking at our traps twice a day. We'd hike out to the lakes together. Then I'd take Olive and the dog team with a small toboggan and cover half the line. Walter would go over the other half. We'd meet at midday. On the way back to camp, he covered my end of the line and I took his.

We both trapped until the first of November. Then the lakes were frozen. The temperature had dropped too low for us to be out in the wind and cold. From December until the end of March, the temperature rarely climbed as high as 10° below zero. There were days when it went to 65° below. The wind cut like a knife. We huddled in our shack and tried to keep warm.

Spruce pitch dripped from the roof poles and matted my long curls that Walter liked so much. In desperation I finally took the scissors one day when he was out looking at fox traps and cut my hair as short as I could. He was so upset when he came home that his face turned gray.

We got through that bitter winter until February. By then we knew we'd run out of food long before June, when we had planned to catch the first steamboat coming up the Slave. We had known since October that I was pregnant. Our

second baby would be born in July. We didn't dare to wait for the boat, knowing that before the end of winter we'd have nothing to eat.

We were in no shape for the 60-mile trip out to Fort Smith. Our two dogs were old and not strong enough to pull Olive and me on the sled. The baby could ride, but I'd have to walk. We didn't have suitable clothing for cold of 40° and 50° below zero. What we lacked were fur parkas and fur-lined moccasins. But as our food dwindled, we made ready for the trip. Walter would leave Olive and me at Fort Smith and come back in time to trap again as soon as the lakes opened.

We put hot water in the water bottle, and we heated stones. We wrapped the baby in our whole bedroll of four blankets with the stones and water bottle beside her, and struck out up the Slave. The empty toboggan with Olive aboard was all our dogs could pull.

It was bitterly cold, probably around 40° below. The going was hard. We made poor time. The dogs pulled willingly enough for a while. But the heavy going was too much for them. We had traveled about 15 miles when they began to give out. They stopped frequently. More than once they lay down in the snow. Walter urged them on and pushed all he could on the toboggan handles to help them. But we both knew we weren't going to go much farther.

- toboggan (tuh BOG un) **large, flat sled**
- parka (PAR kuh) **fur jacket with a hood**
- dwindle (DWIN dul) **become less and less**
- bedroll (BED rohl) **role of blankets or other bedding**

The winter days are very short there in the North. By 3:30 in the afternoon, dusk was beginning to come down. Across the river there was a little cabin with smoke curling out of the chimney. I can't remember that I was ever gladder to see a human habitation.

The cabin belonged to two young trappers. We pulled in thinking we could stay the night. But there wasn't room to walk between the stove, beds, and table. It was plain that they couldn't put us up. They told us that four miles farther up the Slave another trapper, Bert Bennett, had a comfortable cabin. We rested a little while, and started for Bennett's place with the early dark thickening over the frozen snowy wilderness. I didn't feel as if I could go 500 feet, much less four miles.

That was one of the worst hikes I've ever had. Each mile of the four seemed like 10. The dogs stopped every few yards to lie down. Walter went ahead to break trail and pull them along with a short length of rope. I pushed on the toboggan handles for a change. It was too dark for Walter to see where he was putting his snowshoes, and he must have fallen 100 times. I had pain in every inch of the legs, my back, and all through my body. I finally realized I was leaning on the toboggan handles more than I was pushing. It seemed to me that the easiest thing to do would be to walk off into the snow and lie down and sleep forever.

But there was Olive to think of, I reminded myself. I could hear her whimper now and then, and wondered if she was freezing. There was nothing I could do about it if she was. I didn't dare open the bedroll she was wrapped in to look at her. I just kept putting one foot ahead of the other, stumbling and staggering along, terribly cold, until I lost all track of time and place.

A shout from Walter brought me out of my stupor. "Hello, there!" he yelled. I looked ahead and could see a square of light shining out of a window. Oh, what a welcome sight!

I don't remember Bennett opening the door, or Olive and me being carried into the warmth of the cabin. The first thing I recall was Walter pulling off my coat. Then somebody set a bowl of hot soup in front of me and shook me and told me to eat.

- habitation (hab i TAY shun) **a building to live in**
- stupor (STOO pur) **dazed or dull state; loss of feeling**

fore in deep snow. When Bennett looked at his thermometer that morning it was 61° below. The wonder was that the three of us had not frozen to death on the trail.

We realized then that we could not make it to Fort Smith. It was dangerous and foolhardy to try. Luckily, Bennett had extra supplies that he could spare. He sold us flour and beans enough to see us through, and even lent Walter 24 good muskrat traps.

We stayed three days with Bennett. I regained my strength. At the end of the three days I was as good as new. The dogs were in better shape than when we'd begun our terrible trip up-river. We were ready to go back to our cabin and see the winter out. With muskrat at $1.50 each, there was more good money to be made as soon as the lakes started to open. When the first boat came up the Slave, we would be waiting for it.

We started out on a clear morning with the sun shining. Wind had drifted and packed the snow solidly enough that we seldom broke through. The dogs and Walter and I all had easy going. We pulled up in front of our lonely little cabin just as it was coming full dark.

In a daze I watched Bennett take off Olive's rabbit-skin coat and start to feed her. They told me afterward that I cried out, "No, don't take her coat off. She'll freeze!" But I have no memory of that. I did not even realize that we were safe and warm inside four walls. The next thing I remember, Walter was telling me to get up for breakfast.

I was too stiff and sore to make it. But he pulled me out of bed and made me move my legs and body. It's surprising how much power of recovery you have at 21. I was four months pregnant, and I had run and walked 23 miles the day be-

We did not see or hear a living thing except each other, the dogs, and three foxes that Walter trapped, until the end of March. It seemed as if all the game, even rabbits, had died off or left the country. Neither of us had ever seen a winter wilderness so lifeless and still.

• foolhardy (FOOL har dee) **foolishly risky; much too bold**

We fed the three fox carcasses to the dogs. They were starved enough to gulp them down. The beans and flour Bert Bennett had sold us were running low, and we were eating less than half of what we wanted.

Toward the first of April, we decided to start our mink and muskrat trapping, even though the lakes were still covered with three feet of ice. It wasn't so much that we wanted fur. We needed the muskrats as food for ourselves and the dogs. Things had reached a point where I hated to eat because we had almost nothing for the dogs. None of us would last much longer without meat.

We made a trip to the nearest lake where we had trapped before freeze-up. We found the shallow lake frozen solid. Not a muskrat was left. When we turned the dogs back toward camp that afternoon, Walter and I were about as worried as two people could get.

A few days after that we packed up the little food we had left. We took our tent, bedding, and traps, and went eight miles west to some bigger lakes that Walter had found earlier.

We put up the tent at the first lake. We found water under the ice, cut into muskrat houses, and caught a few muskrat. They eased the pinch of our hunger, but we were not taking enough for ourselves and the dogs.

At last Walter made the unhappy announcement that the dogs would have to be destroyed. I realized that was kinder than letting them starve. But the idea of it almost broke my heart. It had to be done, but I cried until I was sick.

Less than a week after that the weather broke in our favor. The sun came out warm and bright. The snow started to melt, and the lakes opened up around the shores. We began trapping muskrats by the dozens. If the night was cold and ice formed, our luck fell off. Some days we took only five or six pelts, but one day we took 70. We were living on muskrat meat, and for the first time that winter we had enough to eat. I boiled it and gave Olive the broth in her bottle. She thrived on it.

When spring comes to the North it comes with a rush. Suddenly it is sunny day after day. The days are long and warm. But the short dark hours of the spring nights are often cold. It was hard to keep warm in our tent, even with a fire in the tiny stove. That stove was to cause the worst disaster of all.

We continued trapping while the snow melted and the creeks rose and became little rivers. Walter and I agreed that we'd stay camped at the lake until May 10. Then we'd hike back to our cabin. We'd go up the Slave to Bert Bennett's place in our rowboat, and there catch the first steamer of the season to Forth Smith. But things don't always go as people plan them.

- carcass (KAR kus) **body of dead animal**
- thrive (THRYV) **grow healthy and strong**

On the morning of May 2, I was in the tent baking bannock in the little stovepipe oven. I stepped outside to look for Walter and saw him coming a quarter-mile up the lake. I took Olive by the hand and walked to meet him. She was toddling all over by then. When we met, I took part of his load of fresh pelts and the three of us started back.

All of a sudden we heard ammunition exploding at a terrible rate. Then smoke and flames rolled up around the tent. Walter dropped his sack of fur and ran. I grabbed Olive and hurried after him as fast as I could. When I got to the tent my husband was dragging out charred food and burning pieces of blankets. I grabbed the things as he pulled them out and doused them in the lake.

It was all over in 10 minutes. A tent burns fast.

What we had saved would have made a very small bundle. There were two or three half-burned pieces of blanket. There were the few matches in our pockets and in a waterproof container. Walter's .22 was safe. There were four shells in it, and Walter had a box in his pocket. The rest of our ammunition was gone. Most of the rat pelts had been hanging in a tree outside the tent and were safe.

Of our food, we had about four cups of flour, wet and mixed with cinders, and a pound or so of beans. For Olive, luckily, there were a few undamaged cans of milk.

With muskrat meat, that handful of supplies would have to see us through until we could reach Bennett's cabin. That meant a hard hike of 8 or 10 miles through difficult country, and then 23 miles by rowboat against the spring current of the mighty Slave. Worst of all, we knew we could not make the trip up-river until the Slave broke up. We had no idea when that would happen.

Things looked pretty grim. I was expecting a second baby in less than two months, and we knew we had a very rough time ahead. But there was no use sitting beside the ruins of our tent and worrying. The thing was to get started.

We hung our traps in trees where we would be able to find them the following fall. We ate our bannock and a good meal of muskrat we had roasted earlier, rolled Olive in the patches of bedding, and lay down under a tree to rest for a few hours. We did not dare to use a match for a fire. We had to hoard them for times of need.

When we awoke we made up our loads and were ready to start. I wrapped Olive in the blanket pieces. I'd carry her on my back. She was so thin she wasn't very heavy. I rolled one cooking pot, knives, forks, spoons, a cup, and the baby bottle in a scrap of blanket and tied it all on my back behind her. Walter's

- bannock (BAN uk) **kind of flat bread**
- charred (CHARD) **partly burned**
- douse (DOUS) **soak with water**
- hoard (HOHRD) **store away; save**

load consisted of the dry muskrat pelts, about 250 in all, our stove—it weighed only about 10 pounds—and three lengths of stovepipe.

We left the burned-out camp with me carrying all I could handle and Walter packing a load of about 110 pounds. Every creek was roaring full and was two or three times as wide as usual. Many times Walter had to make three trips through the swollen and icy creeks, one with his pack, one with Olive and my load, and a third to help me across.

It took two days of the hardest kind of travel to get back to our cabin. At the end of the first day we stopped and made a camp under a clump of spruces. We roasted a muskrat we had brought along. We went without breakfast and our noon meal the second day. But in the middle of the afternoon, I shot a small muskrat. It wasn't big enough to make a good meal for one hungry person, let alone three. But we stopped and cooked it on the spot and divided it up.

It was midnight when we trudged up to our cabin. We were tired, discouraged, and hungry. But at least we had a roof over our heads again and four walls to keep out the cold at night. We didn't mind too much going to bed without supper.

When daylight came, I got up and scraped each empty flour sack for the little flour that remained in it. One look at the Slave that morning confirmed our worst fears. Water was running between the ice and shore. We couldn't get out on the river. We wouldn't have dared. There was no hope of following the shore up to Bennett's place either, because of the many large creeks that flowed into the river. We had no choice but to wait for the ice to go out.

The 11 days between May 10 and the time when the ice finally went out of the Slave were a nightmare of hunger and worry—mostly hunger.

Because we were so short of matches, we kept plenty of wood on hand and fed the fire. We never let it go out.

I found a roll of wire and set snares for ducks, rabbits, muskrats—anything. In all, I snared two red squirrels and a blackbird. We pulled up dead grass along the edge of the water and ate the tender yellow shoots below. One day I saw a fool hen—a spruce grouse—perched on a low branch of a tree. I hurried to rig a snare on a pole. I reached up and dropped it over her head and jerked her to the ground. That was the best meal we had all that time. For once poor little Olive got all the broth she wanted.

Hunger cramps kept us awake at

- confirm (kun FURM) **prove true**
- snare (SNAIR) **loop or noose for catching small animals or birds**
- shoot (SHOOT) **first part of growing plant to appear**
- grouse (GROUS) **kind of wild bird, a little smaller than a chicken**

night, and when we slept we dreamed troubled dreams of food. In my own case, being seven months pregnant didn't make things any better. Right then I needed to eat for two. Each night we slept less. Each day we got weaker. The baby's whimpering for food tore us apart. Walter cursed himself over and over for bringing Olive and me down the Slave.

If we had brought a few traps back from our tent camp, we could have caught muskrats or ducks. But we'd left all the traps behind. For three days our only food was what we called spruce tea. I stripped green needles off and boiled them. We drank a few spoonfuls every couple of hours. It eased the hunger cramps and seemed to give us some strength.

Olive was no longer running around the cabin. She sat quiet and played with whatever was at hand. There was no color in her lips and cheeks. Her eyes looked hollow and dull. I can't put into words how worried and afraid Walter and I were.

We made crude hooks by bending safety pins and tried fishing in the open water along the shore of the river, using pieces of red yarn for bait. Our catch totaled one very small jackfish. I tapped a small birch tree (they were few and far between in that area) for sap. It tasted good, but we had only half a cup to divide among the three of us.

At last, at 10 o'clock on the morning of May 21, the ice in the Slave began to move. By midnight it was gone, and the water was rolling past our door. At 3:00 in the morning of the 22nd we shoved our little boat into the river and were on our way to Bennett's.

It was dangerous to try traveling so soon after the ice went out. Chunks of ice weighing many tons kept sliding off the banks and drifting down with the current, but we had no choice.

Walter rowed, and I sat in the stern and paddled and steered us away from

floating ice. It was killing work. Our closest call came that first day. Rowing close to shore, we saw a huge block of ice come sliding off a pile 40 feet high. It crashed into the water almost alongside us. The force of it lifted our rowboat into the air and sent it flying. We wound up 150 feet out in the swiftest part of the current, right side up only because we had happened to be pointed in the right direction when the ice thundered down.

Walter and I drank spruce tea and gathered and ate grass roots. We also drank water often because it seemed to ease our hunger. We just kept rowing until we gave out. Then we'd rest, and then we'd row some more.

It took us six days to make the 23-mile trip up the Slave to Bert Bennett's cabin. They were as dreadful as any days I can remember. We pulled up to shore at his place at midnight on May 27—dirty, ragged, starving, and so burned by wind and sun that we hardly knew our own reflections when we looked in a mirror. In those six days we had eaten nothing but spruce tea, grass roots, and the inner bark of trees.

A Mr. and Mrs. King from Fort Smith were at Bennett's. They had come down on the ice in March. She gave us each half a biscuit and a couple of spoonfuls of stewed apricots, but the food was too much for our stomachs. We awakened three hours later with dreadful cramps and were miserably sick for the next 12 hours. It was four days before I was well enough to be out of bed. Mrs. King fed me a few spoonfuls of canned soup and cream every hour, and at the end of that time I felt fine. By then Walter and Olive had bounced back too.

Bennett and the Kings fixed us up with some clothing. We waited out a comfortable and happy month until the Miss Mackenzie came up the Slave on her first trip of the year. We boarded her near the end of June, and the trip to Fort Smith was lovely.

We sold our furs in Fort Smith. We had 560 muskrat pelts, 27 mink, three red foxes, four skunks, and a few weasels. The fox pelts brought $25 each, the mink $10. We paid off our debts and had $1,060 left in cash. We had never had money that came harder.

Our second daughter, Vala, was born on July 18. Vala was a scrawny, blue-gray baby, weighing only 3½ pounds. For three weeks my doctor did not think either she or her mother would live. But we made it, and Vala grew to be a healthy, pretty girl.

Walter went back to his trapline in the fall, but I'd had enough of the North. It's a place of great beauty, and the winter stillness is spellbinding, but it can also be terribly cruel. I knew I would never winter in a trapper's shack with my two little girls if I could help it. I stayed behind.

- scrawny (SKRAW nee) **thin and wiry**
- spellbinding (SPEL bynd ing) **fascinating; very interesting**

ALL THINGS CONSIDERED

1. The trip down the Slave River to the camping grounds was made (a) in a rowboat. (b) in an old scow. (c) on a trail by the water's edge.

2. Most cheerful about the idea of the camping trip was (a) Olive A. Fredrickson, the writer. (b) Walter, the husband. (c) Olive, the child.

3. An adventure early in the selection concerned (a) trapping a fox. (b) snaring a grouse. (c) shooting a skunk.

4. At one point, the writer cut off her hair because (a) lice were a problem in the crude cabin. (b) she gave up trying to look pretty. (c) it was matted with pitch from the roof poles.

5. When they tried to escape the wilderness by walking 60 miles to Fort Smith, the young couple (a) turned back after a mile or two. (b) made it only to Bennett's cabin, less than halfway. (c) nearly made it.

6. Toward spring, the *greatest* problem became (a) getting enough to eat. (b) keeping warm. (c) getting little Olive to a doctor.

7. Luckily, the tent fire did *not* destroy (a) any matches or ammunition. (b) the blankets. (c) canned milk for little Olive.

8. Toward the end, the trip out of the wilderness was delayed by (a) river ice and swollen creeks. (b) bitter cold. (c) darkness.

9. When the young couple finally reached other people, they met with (a) dishonest trading. (b) human kindness. (c) human cruelty.

10. After the experience, the writer decided that (a) Walter should give up trapping. (b) she'd like to do it again, but with better equipment. (c) she'd never do it again.

THINKING IT THROUGH

1. The writer says little directly about the feelings between herself and Walter during the period described. (a) What were these feelings? (b) How can you tell?

2. Walter lost his life five years later when a canoe he was paddling alone tipped over on a windy lake. (a) Does this fact surprise you? (b) Why, or why not?

3. As the writer would certainly admit, she and her husband did some things that were clearly foolish. What was one of these things? Explain.

4. What do you think the writer learned from her experiences? Try to answer this question in at least two ways.

UNIT REVIEW

I. Match the terms in Column A with their definitions in Column B.

A

1. context
2. symbol
3. first-person narrative
4. third-person narrative
5. chronological order
6. flashback
7. fact
8. opinion
9. denotation
10. connotation

B

a) arrangement according to time
b) told as if by one of the characters (with "I")
c) dictionary meaning of a word
d) a sudden switch back to an earlier period in time
e) idea or judgment about a fact or facts
f) all the words that surround a certain word
g) something that stands for or suggests something else
h) the meaning a word suggests
i) told by a narrator who keeps out of the story (no "I")
j) something that is true or that has definitely happened

II. If you want to discover what another person is really like, ask that person to name a favorite story—or book, movie, TV show, etc. The answer to that question will often tell you more than the person would reveal—or even know—about himself or herself.

Try this method of discovery right now—on yourself. First turn back to the table of contents. Look at all the titles under UNIT IV: DISCOVERING THE SELF. Write the selection you liked best at the top of a sheet of paper. Write the selection you liked least at the bottom. Then go on to arrange all the other titles in your own preferred order.

When this is done, think about the titles near the top. (It is often helpful to pretend that someone else had written the list.) Do they reveal anything about you as a person? For instance, if you liked "Ta-Na-E-Ka" best, you might be a bit of a rebel yourself. "Chair" might show a sympathy for others, or, if you read it aloud in class, a need to do things with other people. Remember, if you liked one selection much better than some others, *there must be a reason.*

Write a short paper telling what your top two or three selections tell about you. You can think about those at the bottom of your list as well, but the top choices usually reveal more.

▶ Can you feel lonely even in a large city? Of course you can. Langston Hughes made friends easily and knew hundreds of people. Yet he also knew the feeling of being all, all alone.

The poem is an excellent one for you to practice reading aloud. Notice that five different sounds are given in the first six lines. Notice too that the word *lonely* is heard ten times (including the title). Stress the sad long ō in that word so it sounds like what it means.

LONELY HOUSE

by Langston Hughes

At night when everything is quiet
This old house seems to breathe a sigh.
Sometimes I hear a neighbor snoring,
Sometimes I hear a baby cry,
Sometimes I hear a staircase creaking,
Sometimes a distant telephone.
Then the quiet settles down again,
The house and I are all alone.
Lonely house! Lonely me!
Funny with so many neighbors
How lonely it can be.
Oh, lonely street! Lonely town!
Funny you can be so lonely
With all these folks around.
I guess there must be something
I don't comprehend—
Sparrows have companions,
Even stray dogs find a friend.
The night for me is not romantic.
Unhook the stars and take them down.
I'm lonely in this lonely house
In this lonely town.

• **comprehend** (kom pri HEND) **understand**

WRITING YOUR OWN NEWS STORY

The photograph shows a split-second slice of an important 100-meter hurdle race. Imagine that you witnessed the event. Now you are preparing to write a news story for a daily paper.

Start by asking yourself some questions. Where did the race take place? Did the girls represent different schools or clubs? What are the girls' names? If you can, invent some problem that made the race interesting. For instance, the two girls may have told you that they are good friends; yet, they had to race against each other in a final heat. Or, perhaps the expected winner might have tripped over the last hurdle and fell. Decide who will finally win the race. Make up other *facts* for the news story. However, you can add an *opinion* of your own, too.

Begin your news story with a dateline, such as CHICAGO, May 18, 19——. Your first paragraph should be a short summary. The rest of the paragraph should also be short. Use *chronological order* to tell about the events of the big race.

317

U N I T · 5

WHAT IS A HERO?

What is a hero? Think about that question. Why should any man or woman deserve to be raised above others and respected as a special kind of human being? For example, think about kings, queens, and generals of long ago. They may have been heroes to some, but were they heroes to the people they defeated and conquered? Now think about famous explorers, inventors, and scientists. Were they thought of as heroes? Do you think of some of these people as heroes still?

Think about heroes today. For example, do the superstars deserve the attention they get? If so, why? What about the many unsung heroes—the men and the women who rise to heroic acts with never a thought of fame or money?

In this unit, you'll be asked to think about some "heroes" of fact and fiction. You'll start by reading about a high school girl who found the inner courage to risk her own life to save a baby's life. You'll go on to consider other types of heroes, from the ancient Greek warrior Ulysses to modern America's Dr. Martin Luther King, Jr. You'll learn that becoming a hero is not always the same thing as winning the fight or the battle. At the end, you'll be asked the question again: *What is a hero?*

TERROR IN THE NORTH

by Eloise Engle

▶ *What is a hero?* The girl's teacher talked about just that question. Little did anyone imagine that the "moment of truth" was only hours away.

"*S*ometime during our lives," said the history teacher, "we all face our moment of truth."

Stina Olson sat up straight in her seat. How did he know that a problem like this had been troubling her? Could he tell just by looking at her that she was questioning what kind of person she really was?

"As history shows," he continued, "few people really know how they will behave under extreme stress. Heroism often appears in wartime. Or sometimes we find heroic deeds in peacetime, when the enemy is fire, flood, hurricane, or earthquake."

Stina Olson relaxed again. He's certainly not talking about me, she thought. I'm the world's greatest coward.

About four o'clock on the afternoon of March 27, 1964, Stina decided she would *not* go along with the others from school. They were going to help clean and paint their town, Seward, Alaska. Seward was scheduled to receive the All-American Cities Award in just one week. There were plenty of last-minute jobs to be done before tourists from all over flocked in. But this was not her concern. She was not an Alaskan in any sense of the word. She had, in fact, arrived only a few months before, to live with her aunt and uncle after her mother had died. Living in Seattle, she had always felt close to the 49th state. But now things were different. Being an Alaskan, she had learned, meant far more than just living here. Oh, it was all

- **extreme** (ik STREEM) very great
- **stress** (STRES) pressure; uncomfortable strain
- Seattle (see AT ul) city in the state of Washington, the most northwestern of the "lower 48" states and the closest to Alaska

mixed-up. But it had something to do with a pioneer spirit, a love for the wilderness, and a little thing called "guts." No matter how hard she tried, she could not find these things within herself. So lately she had simply given up the idea of ever fitting in.

It wasn't that the people of Seward hadn't been friendly when she first arrived—the adults, that is. But the kids had a kind of "show me" attitude. At least it seemed that way to Stina. She had always been self-conscious about being shorter and more slender than other girls her age. This, along with her blonde hair, blue eyes, and fair skin, took at least two years off her 16. Not being very good at sports was another mark against her.

There was the time when Dan Darby had asked her to go along with the gang on a hiking trip. She had packed a lunch and climbed into her heaviest jeans and boots. Then she started out, only nearly to collapse from fright when they reached the top of a cliff that dropped straight down into Resurrection Bay. Dan, who was almost six feet tall and just about the best-looking boy in town, just shook his head in wonder. "Boy, they sure grow 'em frail in the 'Lower 48' these days."

She forced herself to sneak another look. The city below jutted out into the turquoise-blue water. Colorful fishing boats sailed in and out of the bay. The sun shone down on the sparkling water, and Stina had to agree to the country's beauty. But that didn't help that little cowardly streak running up her spine.

"I . . . I'm going to start back down," she murmured.

"Okay, okay." Dan took her arm and guided her along the dangerous mountainside. He was quiet for quite a while. Then he said, "You'll get used to it . . . eventually . . . I think."

But she didn't. She went fishing for silver salmon and wound up seasick.

Now, at five o'clock, she headed for the Stetson house. She was to baby-sit for their three-month-old infant. She thought that she was at least freeing two adults for the clean-up job. *I'm the one*

- **self-conscious** (SELF KON shus) very aware of oneself; embarrassed or shy
- **frail** (FRAYL) weak
- jut (JUT) stick out
- **eventually** (i VEN choo uh lee) in the end; at some time

behind the one behind the gun, she told herself grimly. *Even if I don't fit in here, I can do something calm and simple like baby-sitting.*

The Stetsons' house had been built only two years before. It was one of the nicest in town. Stina truly enjoyed being there because of the wide view of the harbor from the living-room window.

"The baby has been fed and he's just about ready to fall asleep," Mrs. Stetson told Stina. "There are sodas in the refrigerator, and . . . oh yes, some delicious roast moose. Help yourself."

After they left, Stina settled down in an easy chair by the window. She began looking through a magazine. For some strange reason she couldn't concentrate, not even on the pictures. Her whole body felt tense. She didn't know why. Was it because twilight was now creeping over the bay? Or was it simply because she was alone and mad at herself? No, there was something more.

She shuddered and tried to think of something pleasant. But it was no use. She pushed up her sweater sleeves and saw the goose-bumps on her arms. *Now, why do I feel this way?* She glanced at her watch. Five thirty. *Something is happening somewhere . . . I know it!*

Something *was* happening somewhere. About 150 miles south-east, and about 12 miles beneath the icy green waters of Prince William Sound, powerful forces were at work on the earth's crust. Twisting, straining layers of rock began to move. The raging forces beneath the thin, rocky crust would not be stilled. The tremendous power, held back for centuries, could no longer be kept in harness. The largest single catastrophe ever to hit any state in the union began a rampage that would affect one million square miles. . . .

"Who's there?" Stina called out in answer to a pounding at the door.

"It's me. Dan." He hurried into the room carrying a large paper sack. "I can only stay a minute. I brought you some of the gang's

- **grimly** (GRIM lee) **harshly; sternly**
- **concentrate** (KON sun trayt) **pay close attention**
- **catastrophe** (kuh TAS truh fee) **sudden, horrible disaster**
- **rampage** (RAM payj) **wild outbreak**

leftover hot dogs." He looked through the bag. "And here are some potato chips and cake."

Stina was more ashamed than ever. She forced herself to laugh. "You're great, Dan. Now I won't have to eat moose for supper."

He started toward the door. "I'll try to stop in later. That is . . . if you want me to."

"Oh, I do," she blurted out. "I . . . I really don't mean to seem unfriendly. I honestly like it here but . . ." *There was that strange feeling again!* "Dan, don't go. Please stay and have a soda."

She hurriedly poured some soda over ice. Then she set the glasses on the coffee table. But they did not stay put. The ice tinkled as the fizzing soda danced over the rims of the glasses. Stina frowned. She looked in puzzlement at Dan. Then she looked past him at the china figurines on the bookcase. These, too, were bouncing up and down. Suddenly, there was a strange and terrible sound, a sort of "Vroooooo." It came from far away or under the earth. Stina's whole body stiffened. "What . . . what was that?" she gasped.

Dan shrugged his shoulders and laughed lightly. "Oh, probably just a little earthquake. We have 'em all the time. Alaskans get used to 'em. Sit tight, and don't be afraid."

The whole house began to shake violently. Furniture fell over and slid around the room. The chimney on the roof crumbled, and now Stina began to feel seasick. "Oh, no . . . no!" she screamed, as she almost fell to the floor.

Dan wasn't laughing anymore. "It's a good strong one, I'll say that for it," he said. He grabbed her arm and pushed her toward the doorway where there would be support from overhead. "Don't panic now."

Now the pictures on the wall began to crash to the floor. Lamps sailed across the room. The floor beneath them cracked and groaned. The kitchen cupboard doors swung open, emptying dishes, silverware, canned foods, pots, and pans onto the floor. Flour, sugar, milk, syrup all crashed into a huge heap. The shattering glass and splintering house joints roared in her ears as she jerked free from Dan.

"Let go of me!" she screamed. "I've got to get out of here." This

- **blurt** (BLURT) **say suddenly**
- **figurine** (fig yuh REEN) **small statue**

must be a nightmare. It couldn't be real. But even as she tried to get to the front door, her feet flew from under her.

It was probably less than a minute since the horrible shaking began, but it seemed as if it would never end. "Please stop," she cried. "Please!" Looking out the window she could see trees crashing down. Huge cracks ripped open the earth and horrible black mud squirted up. The ground itself was rolling in waves. In the distance she could see the dock area. "Look, Dan!" she gasped.

They stared, horror-stricken. The entire waterfront north of Washington Street slid into the bay. With it went the dock, warehouse, and huge fuel-storage tanks of an oil company. And then the other waterfront buildings north to San Juan dock, the small boat harbor—everything in sight—slipped away in underwater slides. Almost immediately, the lid blew off in another oil-storage tank area. Orange flames leaped into the air as eight tanks exploded. And in back of the flames, speeding down the bay at hundreds of miles an hour, was a huge tidal wave of sea water.

Dan grabbed Stina's arm. "We've got to get out of here. That wave is coming inland!" Somehow Stina managed to follow Dan out of the house. They scrambled up on top of some oil barrels and

• **tidal wave** (TYD ul WAYV) huge, destructive ocean wave

324

from there onto a neighbor's garage. "This will never hold," Dan yelled. "Here, we'll have to jump over to the housetop."

He went first, then braced himself to catch Stina. "Hurry!" he called.

She bent down to leap—and then she remembered! Oh no! Oh no! "Dan, I forgot about the baby. I've got to go back for him!"

"You can't, Stina! There isn't time! You'll be killed!"

But she could hear nothing except the pounding of her own heart. It was as if suddenly tons of strength had been pumped into her trembling body. She did not look back to the safety of the rooftop. Nor did she glance outward to the Bay, with the wall of water racing nearer and nearer. She thought only of the helpless infant whose life would be gone if she could not reach him in time. As she struggled up the broken steps of the house, she remembered the words of the history teacher. . . . Something about a "moment of truth." Yes, this was her moment of truth. She was terrified. But she was not running from her responsibility in order to save her own skin. This discovery about herself seemed to pour into her even more strength. Stumbling past broken furniture, upturned chairs, and falling plaster, she reached the bedroom. Then she snatched up the baby, wrapped him in a blanket, and ran out of the house again.

"Over here, Stina. Hurry!" Dan yelled.

Stina's throat was hot and dry. But her legs could still move, and that was what counted. She handed Dan the baby and began to climb up onto the rooftop. She saw the towering wall of water bearing down on them. Two minutes later it struck the Stetsons' house, tearing it to pieces. The garage they had been on top of, only minutes before, went next.

Beneath her, she felt the porch of the house being torn away. The bedrooms, splintering and swirling, went next. The baby, now in Stina's arms, was crying. As long as he was crying, there was strength and life in his tiny form. Stina was grateful that he could not know of his nearness to death.

"Hang on tight," Dan ordered. Suddenly the rooftop raft sailed dizzily away in the swirling water. There was nothing left of the house but the living room beneath them. As they sped on through the muddy water, she saw a raging fire in the distance. She dimly wondered if its fiery fingers would reach as far inland as their rooftop perch.

• bearing (BAIR ing) **pressing; advancing rapidly**

They bumped into trees, parts of houses, and buildings. It seemed certain their raft would split wide open. Unbelievable minutes, that seemed like an entire lifetime, went by. At last they found themselves caught between trees. Dan leaped into action. He tied the roof to the trees with the television wires. Now, at least, they were anchored to something. But the waves reached as high as the attic and lapped at the roof itself.

The sixth and last of the tidal waves finally fell back. Only then did Dan risk lowering himself into the house. Stina, holding the baby, sat tight. "Be careful, Dan," she yelled.

As she waited, darkness fell. She could still see familiar objects sailing by. The moonlight reflected on a car. As it floated by like a toy, it flipped over on its side. Minutes later, the bodies of two dogs came near. She almost cried out because she thought she recognized one of them as her family's pet.

It seemed as if Dan had been gone forever. What could he be doing? "Dan, are you all right?" she called out.

"I'm coming," he answered, and swung himself onto the rooftop again. "We're in luck . . . two candles, a lighter, and a can of juice for Junior."

Stina was grateful for them. But as the heavy chill in the air grew sharper, she shivered more and more.

"Do you suppose there's some kind of insulation in the roof?" she asked. "If we could get at it, it might help to keep us warm."

"Good idea," Dan said. He began pulling up shingles and tearing out insulation with which they could wrap themselves for warmth. Then there was nothing to do except . . . wait.

"Somebody will rescue us," he comforted Stina. "Our best bet is to stay put."

"I know. I'm not afraid anymore."

"So I noticed," Dan said, smiling. "And I take back any kidding I ever did about you. Just wait till word gets around."

Down at the waterfront, the raging fires had been carried back to sea by the returning waves. Dock pilings that had been snapped off were floating upright. Coated with tar, their top sections were aflame. They looked like candles floating in the night all over the bay.

- piling (PY ling) **huge wooden pole driven into the ground to form part of a wall or a foundation**

What seemed hours dragged by. Then Stina's heart leaped as she saw the beautiful gleam of approaching flashlights. There were sounds of human voices calling. "You up there. Are you all right?"

Dan cupped his hands to his mouth and shouted, "We're fine."

He peeked inside the blanket to look at the baby. Then he put his arm around Stina. "All three of us are okay," he said huskily, "thanks to you, Stina."

Stina managed a smile. Then she bent forward to yell as loudly as she could, "There are three wet, cold Alaskans up here. Come and get us!"

ALL THINGS CONSIDERED

1. Early in the story, Stina is (a) very angry at her history teacher. (b) beginning to like Alaska better. (c) self-conscious and lonely.

2. Stina thinks she is a coward because of something that happens during (a) a hike to the top of a cliff. (b) a fishing trip in Seattle. (c) a baby-sitting job.

3. One reason Stina particularly likes the Stetsons' house is the (a) delicious food. (b) adorable baby. (c) view of the harbor.

4. Stina is embarrassed when (a) Mrs. Stetson questions her abilities. (b) Dan brings her leftover food. (c) a neighbor hears the baby crying.

5. Dan's first reaction to the earthquake is to (a) laugh it off. (b) get Stina out of the house. (c) get his camera ready.

6. Dan decides to leave the house when he (a) turns on the radio. (b) smells the fires. (c) sees the tidal wave.

7. Stina feels that she has inner strength when she (a) calms Dan down. (b) phones the Stetsons about the danger. (c) returns to save the baby.

8. For some time they drift about on a raft made of (a) a doghouse. (b) some living-room furniture. (c) a roof and the room under it.

9. The raft finally comes to rest (a) on top of a cliff. (b) between trees. (c) near an oil-storage tank.

10. At the end, Stina is most happy to see the (a) approaching flashlights. (b) insulation. (c) juice for the baby.

THINKING IT THROUGH

Discuss the following items in class.

1. At the beginning of the story, the teacher speaks of "our moment of truth." (a) What does this term mean? (b) What "moment of truth" does Stina discover halfway through the story?

2. Scientists know that people and animals behave differently before an earthquake actually happens. (a) What details seem to show that Stina senses a coming disaster? (b) Why is Dan well prepared to deal with an earthquake?

3. The story is based on a real disaster that happened more than 20 years ago. (a) What was this real disaster? (b) Could the story have really happened? Explain.

4. How does Dan's view of Stina change from the time the story begins to when the story ends?

5. Right at the end, Stina yells, "There are three wet, cold Alaskans up here." Why does she say *Alaskans,* not *people?*

6. Does Stina fit your idea of a "hero"? Explain.

Literary Skills: Review

If you wish to review the meaning of any term in *italics* in this exercise, refer to the Glossary of Terms.

I. On a separate sheet of paper, write complete sentences by choosing the correct endings for the statements.

1. The main *conflict* in the *plot* of "Terror in the North" occurs (a) between people. (b) between people and nature. (c) within a single person.

2. The *point of view* of the story is (a) *first person.* (b) *second person.* (c) *third person.*

3. The *climax* of the story comes when (a) Stina hikes to the top of the cliff. (b) the tidal wave is first seen. (c) Stina and Dan reach safety near the end.

II. Answer these questions on a separate sheet of paper. You should use at least one complete sentence for each item.

1. Although most of the story is *fiction,* some parts are *nonfiction.* What is one part that can correctly be called nonfiction?

2. The story has several *plot questions.* In your opinion, what is the main plot question?

3. What natural event is a very important part of the *setting* of "Terror in the North"?

4. The story has several *themes.* In your opinion, what is the main theme? (Hint: Think about what Stina learns from her experiences.)

5. Does the author use all four methods of *characterization* for Stina? Prove your answer with additional sentences taken directly from the story.

Composition

Follow your teacher's instructions before completing *one* of these writing assignments.

1. Imagine you are a TV reporter who is rushed by helicopter to Seward, Alaska. You meet Stina Olson the morning after the disaster. What three important questions would you ask her?

2. Evaluate the story using the ten questions on page 150.

FOUL SHOT

by Edwin A. Hoey

▶ Two seconds of torture—and a hero is born.

With two 60's stuck on the scoreboard
And two seconds hanging on the clock,
The solemn boy in the center of eyes,
Squeezed by silence,
5   Seeks out the line with his feet,
Soothes his hands along his uniform,
Gently drums the ball against the floor,
Then measures the waiting net,
Raises the ball on his right hand,
10   Balances it with his left,
Calms it with fingertips,
Breathes,
Crouches,
Waits,
15   And then through a stretching of stillness,
Nudges it upward.

The ball
Slides up and out,
Lands,
20   Leans,
Wobbles,
Wavers,
Hesitates,
Exasperates,
25   Plays it coy
Until every face begs with unsounding screams—

And then

And then

And then,

30   Right before ROAR-UP,
Dives down and through.

- **solemn** (SOL um) very serious
- **waver** (WAY vur) move in an unsteady way
- **exasperate** (ig ZAS puh rayt) annoy greatly; make angry
- **coy** (KOI) pretending to be shy

WAYS OF KNOWING

1. When the poem begins, what is the score of the game? How much time is left?

2. Although the words "silence" and "stillness" are used in the poem, there *are* a few sounds. (a) What are these sounds? (b) Which sound is the loudest?

3. The first part of the poem (lines 1–16) is full of figurative language (see page 161). What are at least two examples?

4. Look at line 11. (a) What does "it" refer to? (b) What is really being made calm here?

5. In the second part of the poem (lines 17–26), the ball is made to seem almost human. Show how this is done. List the words that help.

6. Lines 19 through 24 consist of single words. Why might the poet have done this, rather than putting the six words on one line?

7. The poet uses the term "unsounding screams." These words seem to mean the opposite of each other. How does the phrase make sense in the poem?

8. (a) How do you imagine the boy feels at the end of the poem? (b) How do *you* feel?

THE
BACKGROUND

The Setting: Washington, D.C. A hot August afternoon in 1963. About 200,000 freedom marchers stand in the scorching sunlight in front of the Lincoln Memorial. Most are restless, waiting for the day's big event. From time to time they glance at a group of well-known black leaders high on the Memorial steps. Finally, one of the group steps forward into a wave of applause and cheers. In a rich rolling voice he begins: "Five score years ago, a great American, in whose symbolic shadow we stand, signed the Emancipation Proclamation."

The moments that followed have gone down in history. Martin Luther King, Jr., delivered the best-known speech of the last 50 years. Here are some excerpts from that famous address.

- **score** (SKOR) group of 20
- **symbolic** (sim BOL ik) serving as a symbol; standing for the real thing
- emancipation (i man suh PAY shun) act of setting free
- proclamation (prok luh MAY shun) official announcement

"I HAVE A DREAM...."

by Martin Luther King, Jr. (excerpts)

I say to you today, my friends, that in spite of the difficulties and frustrations of the moment I still have a dream. It is a dream deeply rooted in the American dream. I have a dream that one day this nation will rise up and live out the true meaning of its creed: "We hold these truths to be self-evident—that all men are created equal." . . .

I have a *dream* today. . . .

This is our hope. . . . With this faith we will be able to work together, pray together, struggle together, go to jail together, stand up for freedom together, knowing that we will be free one day.

This will be the day when all of God's children will be able to sing with new meaning "My country 'tis of thee, sweet land of liberty, of thee I sing. Land where my fathers died, land of the pilgrims' pride, from every mountainside let freedom ring." And if America is to be a great nation this must become true. So let freedom ring from the prodigious hilltops of New Hampshire. Let freedom ring from the mighty mountains of New York. . . . But not only that; let freedom ring from Stone Mountain of Georgia. Let freedom ring from Lookout Mountain of Tennessee. . . . From every mountaintop, let freedom ring.

When we let freedom ring, when we let it ring from every village and every hamlet, from every state and every city, we will be able to speed up that day when all of God's children, black men and white men, Jews and Gentiles, Protestants and Catholics, will be able to join hands and sing in the words of the old Negro spiritual, "Free at last! Free at last! Thank God almighty, we are free at last!"

- frustration (fruh STRAY shun) **unhappy feelings that come from not being able to reach one's goal**
- **creed** (KREED) **formal statement of belief**
- **self-evident** (self EV i dunt) **needing no proof; obviously true**
- prodigious (pruh DIJ us) **great; huge**
- hamlet (HAM lit) **very small village**
- Gentile (JEN tyl) **person who is not Jewish**

ALL THINGS CONSIDERED

1. The speech was given (a) on the Gettysburg battlefield about 50 years ago. (b) during the Freedom March on Washington over 20 years ago. (c) at the United Nations about ten years ago.
2. Behind King as he spoke was a statue of (a) George Washington. (b) Abraham Lincoln. (c) Dwight D. Eisenhower.
3. King made it very clear that his dream was (a) for minorities only. (b) next to impossible. (c) part of the American dream.
4. King wanted freedom to ring from mountaintops (a) in both the North and the South. (b) mainly in the South. (c) mainly in the North.
5. One thing that was *not* mentioned in the speech was the need for (a) faith. (b) working together. (c) money.

THINKING IT THROUGH

Discuss the following items in class.

1. Early in the speech, King spoke of "the difficulties and frustrations of the moment." (a) What did he mean? (b) If the speech were given today, do you think he would use the same words? Explain.
2. Like many great speakers, King knew the value of repeating words and phrases. What are three examples of this use of repetition?
3. King also knew the power of a good quotation. What are three examples, and from where do they come?
4. When King reached the end of his speech, many people in the crowd had tears on their cheeks. Soon after, the same thing happened to millions—people of different races and religions—as the speech was shown on TV. What, do you think, caused people to react in this way?
5. Exactly what was the "dream" of Martin Luther King, Jr.? Try to put the idea in a complete sentence of your own.

Sentence Meaning: Review

If you wish to review the meaning of any term in *italics* in this exercise, refer to the Glossary of Terms.

I. Answer these questions on a separate sheet of paper. You should use at least one complete sentence for each item.

1. The word "dream" has *multiple meanings*. (a) What is the most common meaning of the word? (b) What meaning does it have in King's famous speech?

2. Consider the sentence, "It is a dream deeply rooted in the American dream." Which word, besides "dream," has a *figurative* meaning?

3. One example of *figurative language* is used seven times in the speech. What is this term?

4. (a) In your *opinion,* to which of the five senses (see page 48) does the speech appeal most? (b) What other sense is involved?

5. Consider the sentence, "Here are some excerpts from that famous address." What does the word "excerpts" mean? Use *context clues* to help you decide.

II. Think about the following items in terms of *denotation* and *connotation*. In each case, explain why the term used is better than the possible replacement.

Example: Term used: in the *scorching* sunlight (page 332). Possible replacement: in the *hot* sunlight. Possible answer: *Scorching* is better than *hot* because it suggests real discomfort, even agony. It shows how much the people at the Freedom March wanted to hear Martin Luther King, Jr.

Term Used	Possible Replacement
1. In a *rich* rolling voice	1. In a *heavy* rolling voice
2. I Have a *Dream*	2. I Have a *Wish*
3. *Martin Luther King, Jr.*	3. *Martin L. King* (Think— what connotations are added by using the full name?)
4. "Land where *my fathers* died"	4. "Land where *people of the past* died"
5. When we let freedom *ring*	5. When we let freedom *spread forth*

335

Bonus question: (a) What has happened to the denotation of the word *men* since the speech was written (or in the more than 200 years since the Declaration of Independence was written)? (b) If Dr. King were writing the last paragraph today, what change would he probably make?

Composition

Follow your teacher's instructions before completing *one* of these writing assignments.

1. Using King's ideas, write three sentences beginning "I have a dream *that* . . ." Try to express three "dreams" that you have for America. You may use some of the ideas of Martin Luther King, Jr., but use your own words.

2. Pretend you were a top TV news reporter. You've just witnessed King's performance, and now it's time to write the story. Write the words that you will read to millions of viewers on the evening news. Try to include some description of the crowd as well as a summary of the speech. On-the-air time limit: one minute.

VOCABULARY AND SKILL REVIEW

Before completing the exercises that follow, you may wish to review all the terms presented in the text.

I. On a separate sheet of paper, write the term in each line that means the same, or nearly the same, as the term in *italics:*

1. *solemn:* foolish, serious, diseased, wealthy
2. *blurt:* make unclear, wink at, say suddenly, choke
3. *extreme:* kind, frightful, very great, not enough
4. *exasperate:* annoy greatly, be short of breath, plan, think or reason
5. *grimly:* with a smile, in a harsh way, while chewing, seeming old
6. *catastrophe:* kind of boat, end, disaster, honor or award
7. *stress:* pressure, strong beam, unit of electricity, smoke
8. *frail:* chubby, weak, old, wise
9. *figurine:* number, tiny person, small statue, princess or queen
10. *eventually:* in the end, never, illegally, seldom

II. Match the terms in Column A with their definitions in Column B.

A	B
1. narrator	a) exciting part of a story near the end
2. autobiography	b) true; real
3. climax	c) saying one thing and meaning another
4. theme	d) point of view using "I" and "me"
5. nonfiction	e) person or character who tells a story
6. figurative language	f) feeling a piece of literature gives the reader
7. first person	g) unreal and weird story
8. coincidence	h) idea, or message, or a work of literature
9. fantasy	i) two or more related events accidentally happening at the same time
10. mood	j) a person's account of his or her own life

ON THE LEDGE

by Thompson Clayton

▶ Who become heroes? Sometimes ordinary people develop courage quite suddenly—and everything changes.

Sergeant Gray leaned out a sixth-floor window. Eight feet to his left, on a narrow ledge, stood a young man with frightened eyes. The young man's back was flat against the building. His arms were spread wide. His fingers gripped the edges of the rough bricks.

Gray looked down and swallowed hard. Six floors below, a crowd had gathered. Somewhere down on the street a siren screamed.

If I go out there, Gray thought, *I'll fall for sure.* High places had always scared Gray. He looked over at the young man. The youth's open shirt was wet with sweat. A strong wind blew his pants tight against his legs.

"Take it easy, fella," Gray said. The youth was about the size of his own 17-year-old son. "There's a lot of people down there you could hurt if you fall."

The young man looked down. His eyes seemed to be completely white. He said nothing.

"What's your name, pal?" asked Gray.

The boy swallowed and answered. "Walt," he said. "Walter Whitfield."

"Walt, you've got a lot of guts to go out there. More than I have. You must have a big problem. You want to talk about it?"

"You a cop?" asked Walter.

"I try to be," said Gray.

"Then I don't want to talk to you," said Walter.

Gray took off his cap and mopped his forehead. His head was wet and sticky. His damp shirt stuck to his back.

"Would you talk to someone else, Walter?" Gray asked.

"Maybe."

"Who, Walter? Your mother?"

"My mother's dead," Walter said. His voice shook.

"I'm sorry, Walter. Would you talk to your girlfriend then?"

"No!" Walter said angrily.

"Your brother?"

Once again Walter swallowed hard. "I might," he answered.

"What's his name?" asked Gray.

"John—John Whitfield."

"Does he live in town?"

"He has an office on Belton Street."

"Know his phone number?" Gray asked.

"No, it's in the book."

"Get it," Gray said over his shoulder to a policeman named Morely.

Morely reached for a phone book. "I'll have it in a minute," he said.

"We're calling him, Walter," Gray said with a smile. He looked down at the street. A long silver-and-red fire truck was backing into a space cleared by the police.

"I'll jump," said the boy. His teeth showed white against his tanned face. "If they raise a ladder, I'll jump."

Gray leaned out and signaled the firefighters below. They stopped and looked up. Gray waved his arms to show the firefighters they were to stop.

"All right, Walter. They won't raise it," Gray said.

"I've got Walt's brother on the phone," said Morely. "He says he's on his way."

"Your brother's coming," said Gray. "Think you can hold on?"

"I can make it." The burning noonday sun was now full on the youth's face. He licked his lips.

"Can I get you a drink?" asked Gray.

"No!"

"Anything else?"

"Only my brother," Walter replied.

Gray watched the boy's face. In the last minute the color had drained away. "You feeling OK, Walter?"

"Dizzy," Walter answered.

Gray swung around to Morely. "You think you could go out there?"

"Just thinking about it scares me half to death," said Morely.

Gray's eyes looked over the small group in the room. "Any of you done any high climbing? We need somebody to go out to help that kid. He might faint."

The men looked away. Two or three young office girls looked at him with wide eyes. There were no takers. Gray turned to the window again.

Looking at the youth, Gray was surprised at the sudden change. Walter's face now looked gray. His knees were shaking.

"Hang in there, Walter," Gray said. He tried to keep his voice calm. He wished now that they had put up the ladder. Maybe Walter wouldn't have jumped.

Down in the street the crowd had grown. Besides the fire truck, there were three police cars and an ambulance.

Gray looked over at Walter again. The boy started to lean outward—away from the building. For a moment he seemed about to fall. But then he caught himself, grabbing at the brick wall. His fingers showed white under the strain.

Gray could see that Walter was about to give up. "Morely," he called, "that boy's not going to make it!"

"What are we going to do?" Morely asked, fear in his voice.

"If you'll hold on to me, I'll try to reach him," Gray answered.

Slowly, carefully, he climbed over the windowsill and out onto the ledge.

"Walter, I'm coming to help you," he said softly. Walter's mouth opened, but no sound came out.

Morely reached out the window and grabbed Gray's left leg. Gray knelt on a ledge just six inches wide. He did not look down. He began inching his way toward Walter.

Gray could see that Walter was shaking with fear. Gray had to calm him somehow.

"Walter, can you move a little closer . . . so I can reach your hand?" Gray said softly. "Take it easy . . . a little at a time."

Walter said nothing. But he was slowly trying to slide his foot toward Gray. He stretched out his hand, trying to touch Gray's. They were still two feet apart.

"I can't," Walter said, his voice shaking.

"Hold on," said Gray. His mouth felt dry. "I'm coming." He moved closer to Walter. Morely could no longer hold him.

Making a quick move, Gray reached for Walter's shaking hand. Then suddenly Gray's knee slipped. Six floors

below the watching crowd gasped. Gray tried to regain his balance. He wavered back and forth. He was going over—

Suddenly he felt a hard hand. Somehow, in that terrible moment, Walter had found the strength and courage to save him.

Slowly the two made their way back to the window. Inside, they lay on the floor, drained of all strength.

"Sergeant," Walter said softly.

"Yeah, kid," Gray answered.

"I'm sorry," Walter said. Gray smiled.

It was then that he knew Walter Whitfield was going to make it.

• **waver** (WAY vur) move in an unsteady way

ALL THINGS CONSIDERED

1. The young man has climbed out on the ledge (a) to show off. (b) because of an argument with his girlfriend. (c) for a reason not fully explained in the story.

2. Sergeant Gray is (a) head of the Police Rescue Squad. (b) afraid of heights. (c) an expert on ropes and knots.

3. When Gray offers to talk to Walter, the youth (a) at first refuses. (b) asks for a friend on the police force. (c) tells his troubles quickly.

4. After a time, Walter (a) agrees to see his brother. (b) waves away the safety net below. (c) starts moving farther away from the window.

5. The appearance of a fire truck and ladder makes (a) Gray sigh with relief. (b) the crowd shout at Walter. (c) Walter threaten to jump.

6. Gray becomes more worried when Walter (a) shouts at the crowd. (b) says he's dizzy. (c) takes small steps along the ledge.

7. Finally, Gray (a) follows an order to climb out on the ledge. (b) finds the courage within himself to climb out. (c) holds out a stick for Walter to grab.

8. Gray further shows courage by (a) moving beyond Morely's reach. (b) standing up on the ledge. (c) saving Walter from a bad slip.

9. When Gray starts to waver, he is saved by (a) Morely. (b) Walter. (c) his own quick thinking.

10. The story contains (a) only one hero. (b) two heroes. (c) many heroes.

THINKING IT THROUGH

Discuss the following items in class.

1. The story is told in a very simple style—short words, short sentences, short paragraphs. Why is this particular style well suited to this kind of story?

2. In your opinion, about how long has the young man been on the ledge when the story starts? Explain your answer.

3. (a) In your opinion, does Gray say and do the right things in the situation? (b) What might he have done or said that would have caused problems?

4. If you had to pick the most heroic person in the story, who would it be? Why?

5. Look back at the last paragraph in the story. In your opinion, what do the last four words mean? Explain fully.

Inferences: Review

If you wish to review the meaning of any term in *italics* in this exercise, refer to the Glossary of Terms.

Answer the questions in complete sentences on a separate sheet of paper.

1. The author never states directly that the ledge is part of a certain kind of building. Yet by *reading between the lines,* you can tell. What kind of building is it? Tell why you think so.

2. What *inferences* can you make about Walter's brother? For instance, is he older or younger than Walter?

3. Early in the story, you probably made a *prediction* that Walter would or would not make it. Explain that prediction and your reasons.

4. The story is full of *character clues.* For instance, on page 338 you read, "Gray took off his cap and mopped his forehead. His head was wet and sticky. His damp shirt stuck to his back." How does Sergeant Gray feel at this time?

5. (a) Write one sentence stating a *fact* taken from the story. (b) Then write a sentence containing an *opinion* about the story.

Composition

Follow your teacher's instructions before completing *one* of these writing assignments.

1. Here are five pairs of words from the story. Use each pair in a complete sentence of your own. Write on a separate paper.
   (1) *crowd, ledge*   (2) *problem, talk*   (3) *brother, phone*
   (4) *dizzy, climb*   (5) *courage, window*

2. Here's a real challenge! First, write ten three-digit numerals on your paper (such as 285 or 694). Do not repeat the same numeral in any of them (such as 2<u>8</u>2 or 6<u>9</u>9). Do this now.

   After you have written your numerals, refer to the numbered words below. Try to use the three words indicated by your first three-digit number in a sentence. Then go on to your second number. How many of the ten can you do?
   Example: 285—(2) *ledge,* (8) *climb,* (5) *brother*
   Sentence: Walter's *brother* was called a short while before Sergeant Gray decided to *climb* out on the *ledge.*
   (0) window (1) crowd (2) ledge (3) problem (4) talk (5) brother
   (6) phone (7) dizzy (8) climb (9) courage

▶ Does a hero have to achieve victory after victory to go on being a hero? Of course not. The literature of heroism is full of terms like *fallen leader* and *lost cause*. The following poems show how, long ago, four Native American warriors bravely faced fear, defeat, and even death.

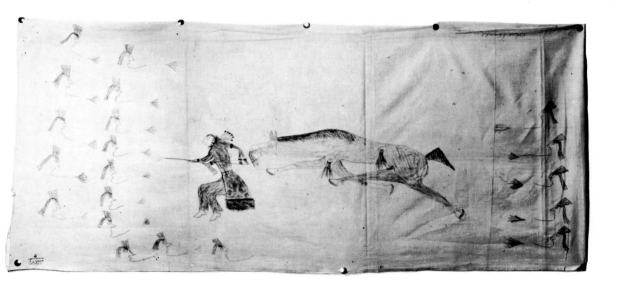

SONG OF FAILURE

(Teton Sioux)

A wolf
I considered myself.
But the owls are hooting
And the night
I fear.

WAR SONG

(Teton Sioux)

Soldiers,
You fled.
Even the eagle dies.

WARRIOR SONG I

(Omaha)

No one has found a way to avoid death,
To pass around it;
Those old men who have met it,
Who have reached the place where death stands waiting,
Have not pointed out a way to circumvent it.
Death is difficult to face.

WARRIOR SONG II

(Omaha)

I shall vanish and be no more,
But the land over which I now roam
Shall remain
And change not.

WAYS OF KNOWING

1. (a) In "Song of Failure," how did the speaker think of himself at first? (b) What does he now realize about himself?
2. How does the speaker in "War Song" manage to make defeat seem less painful?
3. The last two poems are about death. Yet in one of the poems, the speaker ends with a comforting thought. (a) Which poem is this? (b) What is that comforting thought—in your own words? (c) Do you think that the comforting thought turned out to be true? Explain your answer.

• circumvent (sur kum VENT) get around; avoid

344

Louisa May Alcott (1832 - 1888)

The Alcott family enjoy music and dancing in their home.

When Louisa May Alcott was in her early 20s, her father took some stories she had written and showed them to a friend of his who ran a well-known magazine. The editor read the stories. "Tell your daughter . . . she's never going to be a writer."

However, Louisa May Alcott was not the sort of person who easily took *no* for an answer. Her father was a starry-eyed genius—at everything but supporting a family. Since her teens, Louisa had worked to help put food on the table. She'd been a maid. She'd done sewing. She'd looked after children and older people. In spite of the fact that she had little schooling herself, she'd been a teacher. Most of all, she wanted to write. She turned out weird tales with fantastic plots and sent them to magazines, using pen names. Some stories were printed, but the big break never seemed to come. The family's debts continued to pile up.

Then, when Louisa was 35, an editor in nearby Boston asked her to write "a book for girls." At first she disliked the idea. "A book for girls" just wasn't her style. But money was needed. So she sat down to give it a try. For characters, she used herself, her sisters, her mother, and other people she knew, all under different names. The result was the famous *Little Women.*

Little Women not only paid off the Alcotts' debts, but went on selling to make the author rich and famous. Today it ranks as one of America's all-time best-sellers. (When you read it, remember that Louisa herself is the stormy "Jo.") Many other books followed, among them *Little Men, Eight Cousins,* and *Spinning-Wheel Stories,* from which "Tabby's Tablecloth" is taken.

TABBY'S TABLECLOTH

by Louisa May Alcott

▶ The famous "shot heard round the world" was fired on April 19, 1775. It was aimed at British soldiers, known as redcoats. The shot was fired by brave American minutemen. As much as any other single event, it set off the Revolutionary War.

Here is a less-known part of that story. What could a *tablecloth* have to do with the Revolution? Read on to find out.

On the 20th day of March, 1775, a slender girl was walking along a country road. She had a basket of eggs on her arm. She seemed to be in a great hurry and looked anxiously about her as she went, for those were dangerous times.

Tabitha Tarbell lived in Concord, Massachusetts, a town that took a famous part in the Revolution. She was a bright-eyed girl of 14, full of vigor and patriotism. Just then she was excited by rumors that the British were coming to Concord to destroy the supplies sent there for safekeeping while the enemy occupied Boston. Tabby glowed with anger at the idea, and felt like shaking her fist at King George of England.

- **minuteman** (MIN it man) a civilian who was armed and prepared to fight during the American Revolution
- **vigor** (VIG ur) energy; strength

In nearly every house something valuable was hidden: powder, axes, tents, guns, and cartridges. Cannons were hidden in the woods. Firearms were being manufactured at Barrett's Mills. A guard of ten men patrolled the town at night. The brave farmers were making ready for what they felt must come.

There were Tories in the town who gave the enemy all the information they could gather. Therefore, much caution was necessary in making plans. Passwords and secret signals were used. Messages were sent from house to house in all sorts of strange ways. Such a message now lay hidden under the eggs in Tabby's basket. The girl was going on an important errand from her uncle, Captain David Brown, to Deacon Cyrus Hosmer, who lived at the other end of town. She had been employed several times before in the same way and had done her job well. Once she had run all the way to Captain Barrett's, in the night, to warn him that Dr. Lee, the Tory, had been seen sending certain secret plans to the enemy.

Suddenly Tabby's cheeks turned pale. Her heart gave a thump as two men came in sight and stopped suddenly on seeing her. They were strangers. Although nothing in their dress indicated it, the girl quickly knew that they were British soldiers. They exchanged a few whispered words. Then they came on, swinging their sticks. One kept a lookout along the lonely road before and behind them.

"My pretty lass, can you tell me where Mr. Daniel Bliss lives?" asked the younger, with a smile.

Tabby was sure now that they were British. The man they wanted was a well-known Tory. But she showed no sign of alarm, beyond the slight color in her cheeks. She answered politely, "Yes, sir, over yonder a piece."

"Thanks and a kiss for that," said the young man, bending down to present his gift. But he got a box on the ear, and Tabby ran off in a fury.

With a laugh they went on, never dreaming that the girl was going to turn spy herself and get the better of them. She hurried away to Deacon Hosmer's and did her errand. She added the news that strangers were in town. "We must know more of them," said the deacon. "Put a different suit on her, wife, and send her with the eggs to Mrs. Bliss. Tabby can look around while she rests and gossips

• Tory (TOR ee) **citizen who stayed loyal to England during the American Revolution**

347

over there. Bliss must be looked after, for he is a Tory and will do us harm."

Away went Tabby in a blue cloak and hood. Coming to the Tory's house about noon, she smelled the odor of roasting meat and baking pies.

Stepping softly to the back door, she peeped through a small window. Mrs. Bliss and her maid were cooking away in the big kitchen. They were too busy to notice the little spy, who slipped around to the front of the house before she went in. All she saw made her suspicious. In the dining room a table was set forth in great style, with the best china and a fine long tablecloth. Still another peep through the bushes by the living room windows showed her the two strangers with Mr. Bliss. All talked seriously, but in too low a tone for a word to reach even her sharp ears.

"I *will* know what they are at. I'm sure it's bad, and I won't go home with only my walk for my pains," thought Tabby. Marching into the kitchen, she presented her eggs with a message from Madam Hosmer.

"They are mighty welcome, child. I've used a lot for my custards, and I need more. We've company to dinner unexpected, and I'm much put about," said Mrs. Bliss. Tabby thought the woman seemed to be worried about something besides the dinner.

"Can I help, ma'am? I'm a good hand at beating eggs, Aunt Hitty says. I'm tired, and wouldn't mind sitting a bit if I'm not in the way," said Tabby, bound to discover something more before she left.

"But you be in the way," said old Puah, the maid. "We don't want any help; so you'd better be steppin' along home, else suthin' besides eggs may git whipped. Talebearers ain't welcome here."

"Good day, old crab apple," answered Tabby. Catching up her basket, she marched out of the kitchen with her nose in the air.

But as she passed the front of the house, she could not resist another look at the fine dinner table. One window stood open. As the girl leaned in, something moved under the long tablecloth that swept the floor. It was not the wind, for the March day was still and sunny. In a minute out popped a gray cat's head. Then the cat came purring to meet the newcomer.

"Where one tabby hides, another can. Do I dare to do it? What

---

• **talebearer** (TAYL bair ur) a gossip; person who carries stories

will happen to me if they find me? How wonderful it would be if I could hear what these men are plotting! I will!"

A sound in the next room decided her. Putting the basket among the bushes, she leaped lightly in. She vanished under the table, leaving the cat calmly washing its face on the window sill.

Tabby's heart began to flutter. It was too late to retreat; at that moment, in hurried Mrs. Bliss. The poor girl could only make herself as small as possible, quite hidden under the long folds that fell on all sides from the wide, old-fashioned table. But by the time the guests were called in, Tabby was calm enough to have all her wits about her.

For a time the hungry gentlemen were too busy eating to talk much. But when Mrs. Bliss went out, they were ready for business. The window was shut. The talkers drew closer together and spoke so low that Tabby could only catch a sentence now and then. But she heard enough to prove that she was right. These men were Captain Brown and Ensign De Bernicre of the British Army. They had come to learn where the supplies were stored and how well the town was defended.

- **wits** (WITS) **good sense**
- **ensign** (EN sun) **low-ranking military officer**

"These people won't fight, will they?" asked Ensign De Bernicre.

"There goes a man who will fight you to the death," answered Mr. Bliss, pointing to a man passing outside.

The ensign swore. He gave a stamp that brought his heavy heel down on Tabby's hand as she leaned forward. The blow nearly forced a cry from her. But she bit her lips and never stirred, though faint with pain. When she could listen again, Mr. Bliss was telling all he knew about the hiding places of the powder, cannons, and other things the enemy wished to capture and destroy.

Tabby very nearly had a chance to fight or flee. Just as they were preparing to leave the table, a sudden sneeze nearly undid her. She thought she was lost. She hid her face, expecting to be dragged out—to instant death, perhaps.

"What's that?" exclaimed the ensign, as a sudden pause followed the sneeze.

"It came from under the table," added Captain Brown. A hand lifted a corner of the cloth.

A shiver went through Tabby. She held her breath, with her eye upon that big, brown hand. But the next moment she could have laughed with joy, for the cat saved her. The cat had come to doze on her warm skirts. Now, when the cloth was raised, thinking she was to be fed, the cat rose and walked out purring loudly, tail straight up, with its white tip waving like a flag of truce.

"'Tis but the old cat, gentlemen. A good beast, and luckily for us, unable to report our talk," said Mr. Bliss with a sigh of relief.

Then they left the room, and after some delay the three men set off for Boston. But Tabby had to stay in her hiding place till the table was cleared. Then the spy crept out softly. Raising the window with great care, she ran away as fast as her stiff legs would carry her.

By the time she told her tale, however, the British soldiers were well on their way to Boston. So they escaped, but the warning was given. Tabby received great praise for her hour under the table. The people had time to remove the most valuable supplies to nearby towns. They got their cannons ready and drilled their minutemen. Those brave farmers meant to fight, and the world knows how well they did it when the hour came.

- **truce** (TROOS) short halt to fighting (a truce flag is white)

CHECKPOINT

> *Stop here and consider what you have read so far.*
> *Choose the answer that best completes each of the following statements.*
>
> 1. The setting of the story is the Massachusetts town of (a) Lexington. (b) Concord. (c) Boston.
> 2. Tabby's purpose in carrying eggs around town was to (a) help support her aunt and uncle. (b) meet boys. (c) carry secret messages.
> 3. Tabby knew the two strangers were British soldiers when (a) they asked about the house of a well-known Tory. (b) they both tried to kiss her. (c) she saw their military shoes.
> 4. The idea of hiding under the tablecloth came to Tabby from (a) Captain Brown. (b) a story she suddenly remembered. (c) a cat.
> 5. One thing that did not bother Tabby during her hour under the table was (a) a foot stamping down. (b) sleepiness. (c) a sneeze.

Such an early spring had not been known for years. By the 19th of April, fruit trees were in bloom and the elms were budding fast. It seemed a pity that such a lovely world should be disturbed by war. But the people leaped from their beds when young Dr. Prescott came, riding for his life, with the message Paul Revere brought from Boston in the night:

"Arm! Arm! The British are coming!"

Like an electric spark, the news ran from house to house. The men made ready to fight. A little later, word came that the British were at Lexington. Blood had been shed. By sunrise a hundred men stood ready, with good Parson Emerson at their head. More men were coming in from other towns.

Tabby stood at the door looking across the river to the town. Drums were beating, bells ringing, and people hurrying here and there.

"I can't fight, but I *must* see," she said. Catching up her cloak, she ran over the North Bridge, promising her aunt to return as soon as the enemy appeared.

• **parson** (PAR sun) minister

"What news? Are they coming?" called the people from the few houses that stood along the road. But Tabby could only shake her head and run faster. Soon she reached the middle of the town. She found that the little local army had gone along the Lexington road to meet the enemy. Then she hurried in that direction. Climbing a high bank, she waited to catch a glimpse of the British redcoats, of whom she had heard so much.

About seven o'clock they came. The sun glittered on the arms of 800 English soldiers marching toward the hundred local farmers.

"Let us stand our ground. And if we die, let us die here," said brave Parson Emerson, still among his people. He was ready for anything but surrender.

"Nay," said a cautious man, "it will not do for us to *begin* the war."

So they reluctantly fell back to the town. The British followed slowly, being tired from their seven-mile march over the hills from Lexington. Coming to a little brown house on the hillside, one of the thirsty officers saw a well. A bucket was swinging at the end of a long pole. Running up the bank, he was about to drink. But suddenly a girl, who was crouching behind the well, sprang up. She flung the bucket of water in his face, crying:

"That's the way we serve spies!"

Before Ensign De Bernicre—for it was he—could clear his eyes, Tabby was gone over the hill with a defiant laugh toward the red-coats below.

Pleased with herself, Tabby darted about the town, watching the British at their work. They cut down and burned the liberty pole. They broke open sixty barrels of flour. They set the courthouse on fire. Other troops were ordered to different parts of the town to search houses and destroy all the supplies they found.

Captain Parsons was sent to take possession of the North Bridge. De Bernicre led the way, for he had taken notes on his former visit and was a good guide. As they marched, a slim scarlet figure went flying on before them. It was Tabby, hurrying home to warn her aunt.

"Quick, put on this gown and cap and hurry into bed. These snooping soldiers will surely have pity on a sick girl, and respect this

- **reluctantly** (ri LUK tunt lee) **unwillingly**
- **defiant** (di FY unt) **disobedient; showing refusal to obey**

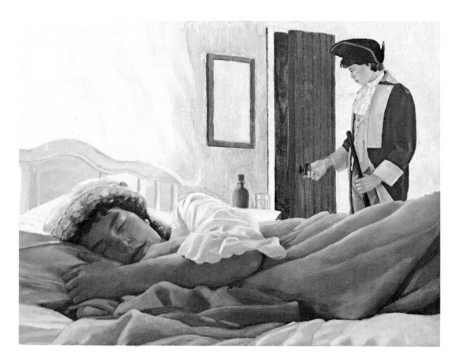

room if no other," said Mrs. Brown. She helped Tabby into a short nightgown and round cap, tucking her in well when she was laid down. Between the fat feather mattresses were hidden many muskets, the most precious of their supplies. Aunty Brown put medicine bottles and glasses on the table. Then she set some evil-smelling herbs to simmer on the fire.

By and by the soldiers came. It was well for Tabby that the ensign remained below to guard the doors while the men searched the house from attic to cellar. He might have recognized the lively girl who had twice treated him badly.

"Step softly, please," Mrs. Brown said as the soldiers neared the bedroom. "You wouldn't harm a poor, sick girl. The doctor thinks it is smallpox, and a fright might kill her. I keep the room as fresh as I can with herbs, so I guess there isn't much danger of catching it."

The men reluctantly looked in. They saw a flushed face on the pillow (for Tabby was red with running, and her black eyes wild with excitement). They took a sniff at the herbs. Then, with a quick glance into a closet or two, they left the room.

• **flushed** (FLUSHT) reddened; glowing

They would have been disgusted at the trick played on them if they had seen the sick girl fly out of bed and dance with joy as they tramped away. But the joy soon left Tabby as she watched the minutemen gather by the bridge. She saw the British march down on the other side. For a little while shots rang out and smoke rose. Shouts were heard as red and blue coats struggled for the bridge. Then the British fell back, leaving two dead soldiers behind them.

No need to tell more of the story of that day. Most people know it. Many have made the trip to see the bronze Minuteman standing on a stone pedestal that marks the spot where the brave Concord farmers fired the shot that made the Old North Bridge famous.

We must follow Tabby, and tell how she got her tablecloth. When the fight was over, the dead buried, and the wounded cared for, the Tories were punished. Dr. Lee was ordered to stay on his own farm, on penalty of being shot if he left it. The property of Daniel Bliss was taken by the government. Some things were sold at auction, and Captain Brown bought the tablecloth. He gave it to Tabby, saying, "There, my girl, that belongs to you. You may well be proud of it. Thanks to your quick eyes and ears, we were not taken by surprise, but sent the redcoats back faster than they came."

And Tabby *was* proud of it. She kept it carefully, displaying it whenever she told the story. Years later, it covered the table when her wedding supper was spread. She got it out for many dinners at Thanksgiving and Christmas through the happy years of her married life. She lived to be over 90.

Then it was kept by her daughters as a souvenir of their mother's youth. The well-worn cloth still appeared on great occasions till it grew too thin for anything but careful keeping. Years later, it still served to illustrate the story so proudly told by Tabby's grandchildren.

• pedestal (PED i stul) **base on which a statue stands**

ALL THINGS CONSIDERED

1. The "shot heard round the world" (a) was fired in Boston. (b) began the American Revolution. (c) occurred before the time of the story.

2. At the time of Tabby's adventure, Massachusetts was ruled by (a) England. (b) Paul Revere. (c) a group of American minutemen.

3. Tabby's family and friends were worried because the Torries (a) spied for the British. (b) treated redcoats badly. (c) had too many arms hidden.

4. Tabby's news enabled the citizens to (a) attack the British first. (b) move war supplies to nearby towns. (c) capture the two British soldiers.

5. Paul Revere's message was (a) "The British are coming!" (b) "Blood has been shed at Lexington!" (c) "Live free or die."

6. One of Tabby's defiant acts was to (a) splash a British soldier with water. (b) paint slogans on a barn. (c) hurl stones at the advancing troops.

7. When the British soldiers came to Concord, they (a) arrested all spies. (b) burned the liberty pole and the courthouse. (c) marched on toward Lexington.

8. To escape the redcoats' notice, Tabby (a) dressed up like a Tory. (b) pretended to be sick. (c) fled into the hills.

9. The tablecloth was (a) burned by the British. (b) bought at an auction. (c) used to bury a Tory spy.

10. The selection last mentions that Tabby's story was proudly told by (a) Captain Brown, Tabby's uncle. (b) the British soldiers. (c) Tabby's grandchildren.

THINKING IT THROUGH

Discuss the following items in class.

1. "Tabby's Tablecloth" is history—but with a difference. How does this story about part of the American Revolution differ from something you might read in a history book?

2. (a) Was the chief British purpose in marching on Concord to engage the minutemen in battle? (b) If not, what was it?

3. Why was Tabby better suited to be a spy than any of the men mentioned in the story?

4. At one point in the story, Tabby told herself, *Where one tabby hides, another can.* What did she mean?

5. Is it possible that Louisa May Alcott, the author, may have met Tabby in person? Prove your answer.

Inferences: Review

If you wish to review the meaning of any term in *italics* in this exercise, refer to the Glossary of Terms.

Answer the questions in complete sentences on a separate sheet of paper.

1. Explain how *context clues* would help you figure out the meaning of "pedestal" in this sentence: "Many have made the trip to see the bronze Minuteman standing on a stone pedestal that marks the spot where the brave Concord farmers fired the shot that made the Old North Bridge famous."

2. Every year, thousands and thousands of tourists go to Concord to see the famous bronze Minuteman. What is the *symbolic meaning* of this statue?

3. Tabby's children and grandchildren kept the tablecloth because of its *symbolic meaning.* What was this meaning?

4. (a) What *prediction* did you make when Mrs. Brown made it look as though Tabby had smallpox? (b) Was your prediction correct?

5. The author, Louisa May Alcott, might have chosen to stick to the *facts* of the story. Instead, she felt free to give her *opinions* from time to time. What is one of these opinions? It can be something stated directly or something you read *between the lines.*

Composition

Follow your teacher's instructions before completing *one* of these writing assignments.

1. Write three complete sentences on a separate sheet of paper. Sentence 1 should reveal an *opinion* of Tabby's. Sentence 2 should tell an *opinion* of the story's narrator. Sentence 3 should give an *opinion* of your own about the story.

2. A little more than a hundred years went by between the events described in the selection and the time of writing (1884). A similar period has now gone by from the time the selection was written to the present time. Suppose a modern author decided to write the story of "Tabby's Tablecloth." How might a modern retelling of the story differ from Louisa May Alcott's? Try to think of at least three possible differences.

VOCABULARY AND SKILL REVIEW

Before completing the exercises that follow, you may wish to review all the terms presented in the text.

I. On a separate sheet of paper, mark each item *true* or *false.* If it is *false,* explain in your own words just what is wrong.

1. The timid diver might *waver* at the edge of the diving board.
2. A *flushed* face is often a sign of embarrassment.
3. People who lack *vigor* should consider themselves lucky.
4. Parents seldom want their children to be *defiant.*
5. You can always trust your secret to a *talebearer.*
6. Orders to work harder or longer are often obeyed *reluctantly.*
7. People who drive at night should have their *wits* about them.
8. *Minutemen* were thieves who robbed stagecoaches and trains.
9. News of a *truce* would probably be greeted with relief by soldiers in battle.
10. A person who stayed loyal to England during the Revolution was called a *parson.*

II. Match the terms in Column A with their definitions in Column B.

A	B
1. foreshadowing	a) all the words that surround a particular word
2. opinion	b) any understanding of something not stated directly
3. context	c) providing hints about what might happen
4. prediction	d) statement made about what will happen in the future
5. inference	e) idea or judgment about a fact or set of facts

Homer (eighth century B.C.)

Homer as he recites one of his poems for a group of listeners

The author of the next two selections may not have been able to read or write! He is called Homer. He lived nearly 3,000 years ago in Greece. We know very little about Homer's life. Legends say that he was a blind poet. His friends are supposed to have led him from city to city.

In those days, stories were listened to, not read. Long stories were often put into rhyme, or poetry form, to make them easier to remember. Traveling poets like Homer told tales that had been handed down for generations. From those who came before him, Homer learned many familiar rhymes and plots for his poems. He changed and improved the old tales and made up new ones, too.

Finally, someone—maybe one of Homer's listeners—wrote down two long poems as Homer told them.

These works are called the *Iliad* and the *Odyssey*. They are considered to be the beginning of Western literature. They tell of the adventures of the Greek hero Ulysses (also called Odysseus) in the Trojan War around 1200 B.C. and his long journey home after the war.

The next two selections—in story form rather than in poetry form—come from Homer and his followers.

Homer kept his audiences spellbound for hours. So sit back and imagine that a traveling poet is telling you of amazing deeds that were done a long, long time ago.

ULYSSES AND THE TROJAN HORSE

by Homer
retold by Alice Delman

▶ What would you do if you were fighting a battle that seemed to go on forever? The war between Greece and Troy was in its tenth year. Then one side came up with a trick that turned the tide.

Across the sea from Greece, in what is now Turkey, there was once a fair, rich city, the most famous in the world. This city was called Ilium by its own people. In story and song, it is known as Troy. It stood on a sloping plain some distance back from the shore. Around the city were high, strong walls that no enemy could climb or batter down.

Inside the gates were the homes of the people. There was also a fine stone palace for the king and his sons, and a beautiful temple of Athena. Athena was the goddess who watched over the city. Outside the walls were gardens and farms and woodlands. Far in the distance rose the rocky heights of Mount Ida.

Troy was a very old city. For hundreds of years it had been growing in power and pride. "Ilium will last forever," the Trojans used to say as they looked at its solid walls and noble buildings. They

• Trojan (TROH jun) **of Troy; also people of Troy**

were wrong. Sad changes began to take place, and cruel war cut down the pride of Troy.

The Greek armies came across the sea. They came to conquer the city. The reason was this: one of the princes of Troy, Paris by name, had done a grave wrong to Greece. He had stolen and carried away the most beautiful of all Greek women, Helen, the wife of Menelaus of Sparta. The Greeks cried for revenge. Heroes and warriors from every Greek city and town joined hands against Troy.

Of all the Greek heroes, the wisest and shrewdest was Ulysses, the young king of Ithaca. Yet he did not go willingly to war. No, he would rather have remained at home with his good wife, Penelope, and his son, Telemachus. He was far happier pruning his grapevines and plowing his fields than he could ever be in the turmoil of battle. But the princes of Greece demanded his help. Rather than be thought a coward, he agreed.

"Go, Ulysses," said Penelope. "I'll keep your home and kingdom safe until you return."

And so he sailed away. Forgetting the quiet delights of home, he turned all his thoughts to war.

Ulysses and his Greek warriors came to Troy in a thousand little ships with sails and oars. They landed on the beach at the foot of the plain. They built huts and tents along the shore. They kindled fires. Around their camp, they threw up a wall of earth and stones. Then they dared the warriors of Troy to come out and meet them in battle.

So the siege began. For more than nine years, the city was surrounded by determined foes. But the walls were strong, and the Trojans were brave. Fierce battles were fought outside the gates. Some were won by the Greeks, some by the Trojans. But neither side could gain a final victory. The Trojans could not drive the invaders from their shores. And the Greeks could not force their way into the city.

"Athena protects us," said the hopeful people of Troy. "While the Palladium is with us, our city can't be taken."

The Palladium was a beautiful statue that stood in the temple of Athena. The Trojans believed that it had a strange power to protect its friends.

"It's useless for us to fight longer," said some of the Greeks. "We can never win while the Palladium is in Troy."

"We've already stayed too long," said others. "Let's abandon this hopeless siege and go home."

But Ulysses wouldn't give up. On a dark and stormy night, he stole into the city. He got past the guards unseen. He crept into the temple of Athena while all the watchers were asleep. There he seized the Palladium and carried it in triumph to the Greek camp.

"Now we'll surely win," said the Greeks.

But still the Trojans persevered. Their

- **shrewdest** (SHROOD est) cleverest, often in a tricky way
- **turmoil** (TUR moil) disorder; unrest
- **siege** (SEEJ) continued military attack; blockade

gates were well guarded, and the siege went on.

One morning in the early summer, all Troy was awakened at daybreak. The guards on the walls were shouting: "They're gone! The Greeks are gone!"

Soon a hundred eager men, women, and children were standing on the wall. They strained their eyes in the gray light of dawn, trying to make out the hated tents by the beach and the dark ships along the shore.

"They're not there," said a guard. "There's no sign of the Greeks. Thanks to Athena, they've left us at last." Suddenly the guard pointed toward the shore and cried, "Look! There's a strange, dark object among the reeds. It's by the inlet where the boys used to go swimming. What is it?"

Everyone looked. Sure enough, there was something among the reeds. It was smaller than a ship and larger than a man. In the dim light of morning, it looked like a sea monster lately emerged from the waves.

Just then the sun rose above Mount Ida, casting a rosy golden light on sea and shore. It made every object on the beach plainly visible. There was no longer any doubt about the strange thing in the reeds.

"It's a horse!" shouted one and all.

"But not a real horse," said the guard. "It's much too large. It's a huge, ill-made image that the Greeks have left behind—perhaps to frighten us. And now I remember! For several days, there

- persevere (pur suh VEER) **keep going without giving up**
- **reed** (REED) **tall grass that grows in a marsh**
- **emerge** (i MURJ) **come out**
- **image** (IM ij) **copy; likeness**

361

was something unusual going on behind the reeds and bushes there—workmen hurrying back and forth, and much noise of hammering. They were building this thing."

Just then Laocoön, a prince of Troy, joined them. He was an old man, wrinkled and gray—a priest of Apollo, wiser than most of his fellows. After looking long and carefully at the strange image, he turned to the crowd. "It's a trick," he said. "My children, beware of the cunning Greeks. They've made this image to fool you. I warn you to have nothing to do with it."

About the middle of the morning, Priam, the old king of Troy, issued an order. It was announced in all the streets. "Our enemies have gone," it said. "Peace and safety are ours once again. At noon the gates of the city shall be opened. At that time, our people may return to their peaceful occupations."

Then there was great joy in every corner of the city. It was as though day had dawned after a long and fearful night. How sweet it was to feel free from dread! How good to go about one's business in peace!

The women talked and sang as they began to clean their houses. The shopkeepers brought out their goods and offered fine bargains to the first buyers. The blacksmiths lighted fires in their forges, and began to hammer old spears into peacetime tools. The fishermen mended their nets. The farmers counted their rakes and hoes and plows. Everyone talked about the fine crops they would have on lands that had been idle so long.

But not all the people were so busy. Long before noon, a great crowd had gathered before the gate on the seaward side of town. They were anxious to get out of the long-surrounded city. No sooner was the gate opened than there was a wild rush across the plain toward the shore. Men as well as boys were eager to see whether the Greeks had left anything valuable behind.

They wandered along the beach, looking in every corner of the old camp. But all they found were a few bits of pottery, a broken sword or two, and a few cheap trinkets.

They kept well away from the inlet where the reeds grew. Even the boldest wouldn't go near the huge wooden horse. For Laocoön, the priest, had warned them again to beware of it. So they just stood at a distance and gazed at the strange, unshapely thing. What evil trick, they wondered, were the Greeks plotting?

Suddenly on the other side of the camp a great shouting was heard. Some Trojans who had been hunting in the marshes were seen approaching with a prisoner.

"A Greek! A Greek!" was the shout. Men and boys ran forward to see the

- **cunning** (KUN ing) clever in a tricky way; sly
- forge (FORJ) furnace used to heat metal
- **idle** (EYE dul) unused; not busy

captive and join in cursing him. The poor fellow was led by a leather thong twisted around his neck. As he stumbled along over the sand, the crowd jeered. They hit him with sticks and sand and anything they could lay hold of. The blood was trickling down his face. His eyes were swollen. But his persecutors, as they saw his wounds, only shouted louder. "A Greek! A Greek! Get rid of him!"

Then all at once the uproar stopped. Silence fell upon the crowd. For standing in his chariot nearby was one of the officers of the king.

"What prisoner is this? Why are you abusing him?" he asked.

"We think he's a Greek," answered the hunters. "We found him in the tall grass by the marshes. He was already wounded and half-blind. So it was easy for us to take him."

"Already wounded!" said the officer. "That's strange." Then turning to the prisoner, he asked, "How is this? Tell me whether you're a Greek or a friend of Troy. What's your name, and your country?"

"My name," said the prisoner, "is Sinon. By birth I'm a Greek, yet I have no country. Until ten days ago, I called myself a friend of Greece. I fought bravely alongside her heroes. But see these wounds. Can I remain friendly to those

who maimed me and would have taken my life, too?"

"Tell us about it," said the officer. "And tell us truly. Have the Greeks sailed home for good?" He told the hunters to loosen the thong about the prisoner's neck.

"Yes, I'll tell you," answered Sinon. "And I'll be brief. When Ulysses stole the Palladium from your temple, the Greeks felt sure the city was about to fall. Then day after day passed, and they didn't win a single fight. So they began to despair. A council was held. It was decided to give up the siege and sail for home. But great storms arose on the sea. The south wind never let up. No ship could put to sea."

"But what about the horse?" cried the Trojans. "The horse!"

"The horse," said Sinon, "was built on the advice of the soothsayer, Calchas. He told the Greeks, 'Athena is angry because her statue, the Palladium, was stolen from her temple. That's why the storms rage so fiercely. And they'll go on raging until you make a statue of a horse and leave it on this shore as a sign of your shame and repentance. Never can your ships return to Greece until that is done.'

"So the statue was built. The soothsayer said it would carry prosperity and peace wherever it went. But the Greeks

- thong (THAWNG) strip of leather
- **jeer** (JEER) make fun of in a nasty way
- maim (MAYM) injure badly; cripple
- **soothsayer** (SOOTH say ur) one who foretells the future
- **repentance** (ri PEN tuns) feeling of sorrow about one's bad deeds; regret
- **prosperity** (pro SPER i tee) wealth; success

didn't want it to be a benefit to Troy. That's why they built it so wide and high that it can't be taken through your gates. They placed it among the reeds by the shore. They hoped the waves might carry it out to sea."

"Ah, so that's their plan, is it?" cried the excited Trojans. "Well, we'll see about that!" And, forgetting about Sinon, the whole company and the king's officer rushed madly to the great horse.

"Beware, my countrymen, beware!" cried the voice of old Laocoön. He struggled through the crowd. "This is a trick of the Greeks. The horse won't bring you happiness and prosperity, but misery and ruin. Throw it into the sea, or burn it to ashes. But don't receive it into the city."

With these words, he hurled his spear at the huge image. The weapon struck it full in the chest. Those who stood nearest swore that they heard deep, hollow groans and a sound like the rattle of shields coming from the monster's throat.

"To the sea with it! The sea!" cried a few who believed in the old priest.

But most shouted, "To the city with it! The city! We'll outwit the Greeks yet!"

Some ran to the city for ropes and wheels. Others hurried to make a breach in the wall large enough for the monster to pass through. Ropes were tied to its neck and forelegs. Wooden rollers were put under the platform on which it stood.

Men with axes and hoes ran forward to clear a path across the plain. Then the strongest and most willing seized hold of the long ropes and began to pull. Others pushed from behind. Still others prayed to Athena.

So they tugged and sweated, and finally the huge image began to move. The wheels creaked and groaned. The shouts of the Trojans were so loud that the sound was heard far out to sea.

Slowly but steadily, the crowd advanced, dragging the wonderful horse that they believed would bless the city. The sun had set before they passed through the breach in the wall. Darkness was beginning to fall when the groaning wheels stopped. The great horse came to a standstill in a quiet corner close by the temple of Athena.

"My friends," said the king's officer, "we've done a fine day's work. Athena's horse rests near the place where it will stay. Now the happiness of Troy is certain. Go home. Tonight, for the first time in ten years, we can sleep secure."

With joyful shouts and friendly good nights, the crowd broke up. Every man went quietly to his own house. Soon the city was dark. The streets were silent and empty. And Athena's horse stood huge and wooden beside the temple wall.

About midnight, a man started to sneak out of the temple. He crept to the breach in the wall. In one hand he carried a basket of tar. In the other was a small torch that he had lighted at the temple fire. Carefully, he climbed to the top of the wall. Then he sat still and waited. Soon the sky began to grow lighter and

---

• breach (BREECH) **broken place; gap**

the shadows in the city less dark. The moon rose, bright and round. The rooftops, the city wall, the plains, and the sea—all were silvered over with soft moonbeams.

The man on the wall looked eagerly toward the sea. What were those dark objects moving swiftly over the water toward the shore? A thousand ships. The cunning Greeks had not started for home, as the Trojans had thought. They had gone only to the island of Tenedos. There they had lain all day, hidden in coves and inlets. Soon their vessels would again be beached in their old places by the empty camp.

The man on the wall was ready. He lifted his torch and dropped it carefully into the basket of tar. A bright flame rose up. It lit up the plain and the wall and the man's face. His eyes were red, his face wounded and swollen. It was Sinon.

Lights were soon seen on the ships. Then Sinon hurried down to the spot where the great horse was standing. With the flat edge of his sword, he struck its foreleg three times. There was a noise like the rattling of armor. Then a panel in the horse's chest slid aside. A man's head, in a gleaming helmet, appeared.

"Is all well, Sinon?" asked a deep voice.

"All's well, Ulysses. Our ships have landed, and our friends are marching across the plain. The foolish Trojans lie sleeping in their homes, little dreaming of what awaits them."

A rope ladder was let down, and

Ulysses descended to the ground. Then fifty other heroes followed him, glad to be in the open air again. All was going the way Ulysses had imagined it would when he had planned the Trojan Horse.

"Sinon," said Ulysses, "what are those scars on your face? Did the Trojans abuse you?"

"They abused me, but they didn't make these wounds," answered Sinon. "I made them myself, so I could persuade the Trojans to fall into our trap."

"I understand, Sinon," said Ulysses.

• **cove** (KOHV) small inlet or bay

"People call me the man of wiles! But now that title must be yours. And now, for the ending of the whole business! Follow me, my men. Let fire and sword do their worst!"

The Trojans awoke from their dreams of peace to see their homes in flames. They heard the shouts of the triumphant Greeks. They knew that nothing was left for them but captivity or death. So the long siege came to an end, and the fair rich city beyond the sea was overthrown.

Ten years had passed since the siege began. When the city lay in ashes, the Greeks set out in their ships. All sought to return to their native lands. Fondly, then, the thoughts of Ulysses turned to his beloved wife, Penelope, and his child, and the rugged hills and shores of Ithaca.

"Spread the sails, my men, and row hard," he said. "For Penelope waits at home for my return, and keeps my kingdom for me."

But scarcely were his little ships well out to sea when fearful storms arose. The vessels were tossed now this way, now that. They were at the mercy of winds and waves that drove them far, far off course. Soon they were sailing by savage shores and strange lands where wild men lived.

● wile (WYL) **trick meant to trap or deceive**

ALL THINGS CONSIDERED

1. The Greeks attack Troy because one Trojan (a) has great wealth. (b) stole a famous Greek statue. (c) carried off a Greek woman.

2. The Greeks have difficulty attacking Troy because (a) the city is surrounded by a strong wall. (b) the Trojans outnumber the Greeks. (c) food and water are scarce.

3. The Trojans are protected by (a) the prayers of their priest, Laocoön. (b) a statue of Athena. (c) a statue of a horse.

4. When the Greeks suddenly leave Troy, the Trojans (a) are not surprised. (b) open the gates of the city. (c) build a horse to thank the gods.

5. Sinon is a Greek soldier who (a) joins the Trojan side. (b) pretends to join the Trojan side. (c) builds the wooden horse.

6. To set his trap, Sinon (a) captures a few Trojans. (b) steals the Palladium. (c) injures himself on purpose.

7. Some Trojans do not want to take the wooden horse into the city because (a) the priest warns them that it is a Greek trick. (b) the priest warns them that the gods will be angry. (c) the king, Priam, thinks that moving the horse is a waste of time.

8. The Trojans bring the horse into the city because it (a) is supposed to bring good fortune. (b) is made of gold. (c) contains Greek prisoners.

9. The Greek army is (a) inside the horse. (b) in ships nearby. (c) inside the horse and in ships nearby.

10. The Greeks finally win the long war through (a) trickery. (b) long and hard fighting. (c) the help of many gods.

THINKING IT THROUGH

Discuss the following items in class.

1. Ulysses says that Sinon should be called "man of wiles," or tricks. Name at least two things Sinon does that show his cleverness.

2. The Trojans make several mistakes that lead to their defeat. (a) Name at least two. (b) Which do you think is their worst mistake? Why?

3. There is a saying that "All is fair in love and war." (a) What do the Greeks do that is not "fair"? (b) Do you agree with the saying? Explain your answer.

4. (a) Why, do you think, did the people of ancient Greece admire a character like Ulysses? (b) In your opinion, would people like Ulysses and Sinon attract such hero worship today? Explain.

Relationships: Review

If you wish to review the meaning of any term in *italics* in this exercise, refer to the Glossary of Terms.

I. Match the four *causes* on the left with the four *effects* on the right.

CAUSES	EFFECTS
Because—	
1. one Trojan had stolen and carried away Helen,	a) . . . the Trojans think they have won the war.
2. the Greek tents and ships seem to be gone,	b) . . . they tow it through the wall and into Troy.
3. the Trojans think the huge horse will bless the city,	c) . . . the Greeks set out to conquer and punish Troy.
4. Ulysses and 50 other Greek soldiers hide in the horse,	d) . . . they are able to help overcome and burn Troy with ease.

II. The famous Trojan War was fought over 3,000 years ago. Most modern readers cannot help noting *contrasts* between that ancient age and ours. For instance, would people today pull and push a huge statue into a city? There are *comparisons* as well. For example, then as now, small events can trigger major wars.

On a separate sheet of paper, list two other *contrasts* and two other *comparisons.* They can concern anything mentioned in or inferred from the selection.

Composition

Follow your teacher's instructions before completing *one* of these writing assignments.

1. Any complete sentence containing the word *because* must contain a cause and an effect. Using *because* in each, write three original sentences about the story. Then underline the causes with one line and the effects with two lines.

2. Write a paragraph describing an ancient Greek hero. Use people like Ulysses and Sinon as examples. Begin the first sentence, "To the ancient Greeks, a hero was a person who . . ."

ULYSSES MEETS THE CYCLOPS

by Homer
Adapted by Alice Delman

▶ The Greeks may have won the Trojan war, but their troubles were far from over. In this tale, Ulysses tells about one *big* problem. He and his men are trapped in a cave—with a giant who eats people!

They were giants, oafs. Living on a large island of their own, they knew no law. They went by the name of Cyclops—it means "eye like a wheel." Each of the monsters had only one—a huge, round eye in the middle of its forehead.

The mouth of a cave gaped above the water. This was the home of one Cyclops. As we rowed nearer to land, we saw him, taking his sheep out to graze. He seemed no man at all. No, he looked like a hairy mountain, rising up all alone on a plain.

We beached our ship. "Stay here and be on the lookout," I told the crew. Taking my twelve best fighters, I went ahead. With me, I brought food and wine. This was no common wine. It was a ruby-red brandy given me by the gods. I thought we might need a powerful drink like this. In fact, I knew it in my bones. We were setting foot in the lair of a beast—a wild man, all power and no law.

- **oaf** (OHF) stupid, awkward person
- **gape** (GAYP) open wide; yawn
- **lair** (LAIR) resting place of a wild animal; den

We scampered up to the cave. The Cyclops was still out with his sheep. So inside we went and feasted our eyes on his treasure—cheese, lambs and goats, bowls of milk.

My men crowded around me. They begged me, "Let's make off with the goats and the cheese. We ought to get back on the open seas while we can!"

Now I know they were right, but I didn't listen at that time. I wanted to see the caveman—and find out what gifts he might have for a guest like me. So we saw him. For some of my friends, it was an awful sight.

But we built a fire, ate some cheese, and waited. Towards evening, the Cyclops came back. A load of firewood was on his shoulder. He dumped it with a crash that echoed off the walls of the cave. In an instant, we all scurried to the far corner.

Next, he brought in the sheep he was going to milk. Then he picked up a huge rock and jammed it in the mouth of the cave. Two dozen wagons pulled by sweating horses could not have budged that rock.

He did his chores and fed the fire. As flames lit up the cave, his eye saw us. "Strangers," he said, "who are you? Are you good trading men? Or are you pirates?" His deep voice thundered against our hearts.

I answered, "We are soldiers on our way home. We ask your help. Our gods teach us to honor strangers. We beg you, great sir—do the same. Take care to please the gods, or Zeus will be angry."

From his savage chest came the answer. "You are a nitwit, trying to scare me with your gods," he said. "A Cyclops doesn't give a fig for any of them. We're more powerful. I'd never let you go for fear of Zeus—unless I felt like it. Tell me now, where did you leave your ship? Nearby?"

That was what he wanted to know! But I was too clever for him, and I lied boldly. "My ship?" I said. "It broke against the rocks of your shore. We are the only men left."

We got no pity from him. He grabbed at us. His hands caught two of my friends like squealing puppies. He beat their brains out and cut them up for his supper. He gobbled the meat like a hungry

- **scurry** (SKUR ee) **move quickly**
- Zeus (ZOOS) **chief of the Greek gods**

lion. We cried out to Zeus. But the Cyclops went on filling his giant belly.

Finally, having eaten enough, he lay down to sleep. Now I had the chance to act! Drawing my sword, I crept up close to him. I picked out the spot where I'd stab him. But I was stopped by a sudden thought. If I killed him, we'd all die. We could never push aside the huge rock that blocked the door. No, all we could do was moan and twiddle our thumbs till morning.

Soon after dawn, he did his chores. He snatched up another two men for breakfast. Then, gathering the sheep, he flicked aside the rock and went out. But in an instant, he had popped the rock back in again. He did it as easily as you'd stick the stopper in a bottle. We could hear him whistle as he climbed with his flock. Then there was silence.

What could we do? I looked around. Inside the cave lay the trunk of a fallen tree. The log was as long and thick as the mast of my ship. I chopped off a six-foot section and let my men scrape it smooth.

Next, I carved one end into a pointed spear. This my men and I plunged deep in the fire till it was as tough as iron. Finally, we dragged the weapon well back in the cave. Under one of the dung piles that lay everywhere, we hid it.

Just before evening, the Cyclops came back with his flock. Once inside, he wedged his stony door into place. He milked the sheep. He did his evening chores, caught two more men, and ate dinner.

• **plunge** (PLUNJ) push something quickly into something else

Now was the time. I stepped forward, holding out a bowl. In it was the wine I'd brought with me.

"Here, Cyclops," I said, "have a little wine. You'll see what fine things we had in the hold of our ship."

He grabbed the bowl and drank. The drink pleased him so much that he had to have more.

"Give me another, please," he said. "And tell me your name. I'll give you a gift that will make you happy. Even a Cyclops knows grape juice from a heavenly drink like this!"

Three times I filled the bowl, and three times he emptied it. When he had gotten slow and silly, I called out to him. I spoke in friendly tones.

"Cyclops, you ask my name? My name is NOBODY. That's what my mother, my father, and all my friends call me."

"Then I'll eat NOBODY last—his friends come first. That's my gift to you."

Even as he spoke, he stumbled. He fell back and lay there with his giant head leaning to one side. Sleep captured him like any of us. Drunk, he lay there. He hiccupped. Wine dribbled from his lip, and bits of human meat stuck to his chin.

Now we drew out the rough-hewn spear. Again we thrust it in the fire. I whispered brave words to my men, urging them to get up their courage. As we pulled the spear out of the flames, it glowed red-hot. We dashed forward, raised the spear, and rammed it into the Cyclops's eye. Leaning on the spear, I twirled it till it was spinning like a drill. The eyeball sizzled. The veins popped. And the eye rolled down the giant's cheek.

Now the Cyclops roared so wildly that the cave walls shook. Full of fear, we scattered to the corners of the cave. The Cyclops yanked out the bloody spear and flung it to the ground. Then he began to roar, calling for the other Cyclops, who lived in caves nearby. Hearing him, they came and crowded round outside the cave door.

"What's wrong?" they called to him. "Why such a loud cry on this starry night? We can't get any sleep. Is someone stealing your flock? Has someone tricked you or hurt you?"

From inside the cave, the giant bellowed, "NOBODY! NOBODY'S tricked me! NOBODY'S hurt me!"

"Oh, well," they answered. "If nobody's hurt you, then we can't help." And they all went back to bed.

I was almost bursting with laughter. The name had fooled them! But now the Cyclops, groaning with pain, staggered to the door. He groped blindly and clawed away the boulder. Then he sat down in the doorway. His arms were spread wide to catch any fool who tried to escape. He was hoping I might try it. I wasn't going to. Instead, I plotted and planned. How could I outwit death?

Here's the plan I liked best: The giant's sheep were big and fat, with heavy wool. The Cyclops could see nothing. So I took some cords of willow from his bed. Standing the sheep three abreast, I tied them together. Under each three, I tied a man. Tucked up below the middle sheep, he was protected on both sides.

Last of all, I took the fattest ram, the finest of the whole flock. Myself I hid under his belly, snuggling up to his woolly curls. With the fleece wound around my fingers, I hung on. So we all breathed hard and waited for dawn.

- rough-hewn (RUF HYOON) **roughly made; not polished**
- **thrust** (THRUST) shove
- **grope** (GROHP) feel about with the hands
- **ram** (RAM) male sheep

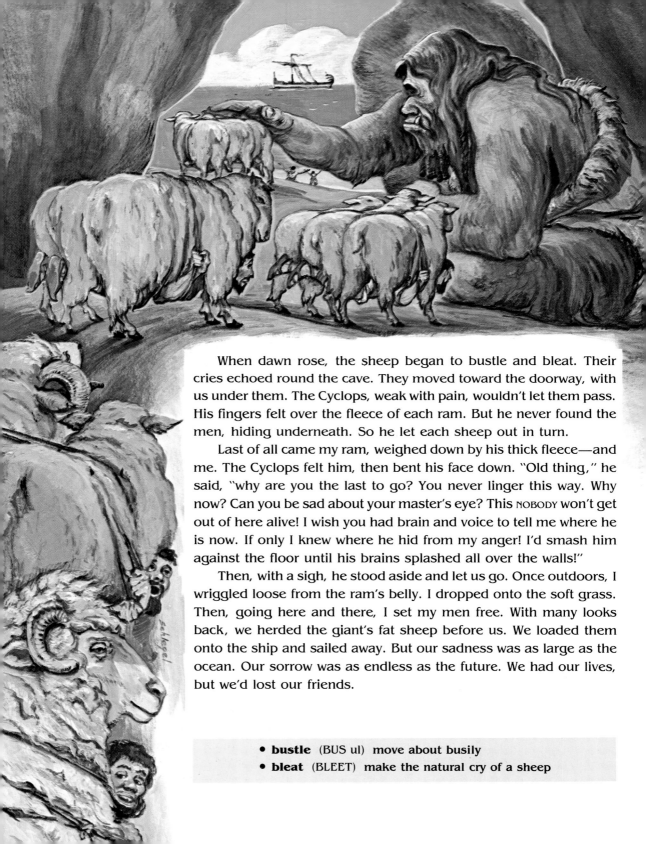

When dawn rose, the sheep began to bustle and bleat. Their cries echoed round the cave. They moved toward the doorway, with us under them. The Cyclops, weak with pain, wouldn't let them pass. His fingers felt over the fleece of each ram. But he never found the men, hiding underneath. So he let each sheep out in turn.

Last of all came my ram, weighed down by his thick fleece—and me. The Cyclops felt him, then bent his face down. "Old thing," he said, "why are you the last to go? You never linger this way. Why now? Can you be sad about your master's eye? This NOBODY won't get out of here alive! I wish you had brain and voice to tell me where he is now. If only I knew where he hid from my anger! I'd smash him against the floor until his brains splashed all over the walls!"

Then, with a sigh, he stood aside and let us go. Once outdoors, I wriggled loose from the ram's belly. I dropped onto the soft grass. Then, going here and there, I set my men free. With many looks back, we herded the giant's fat sheep before us. We loaded them onto the ship and sailed away. But our sadness was as large as the ocean. Our sorrow was as endless as the future. We had our lives, but we'd lost our friends.

- **bustle** (BUS ul) move about busily
- **bleat** (BLEET) make the natural cry of a sheep

ALL THINGS CONSIDERED

1. *Cyclops* means (a) "giant." (b) "eye like a wheel." (c) "man with no law."

2. Ulysses and his men are (a) soldiers. (b) pirates. (c) traders.

3. Ulysses leads his men to the Cyclops's cave because (a) their ship is wrecked. (b) they want to buy food. (c) he wants to see more of the giant.

4. Ulysses first tries to win the Cyclops's friendship by (a) giving him wine. (b) asking for help in the name of the gods. (c) offering money.

5. The Cyclops shows that he is a monster by (a) eating raw sheep. (b) eating people. (c) breathing fire.

6. On the first night, Ulysses and his men are stuck in the cave because (a) a huge rock blocks the doorway. (b) the Cyclops blocks the doorway with his body. (c) the men are tied up.

7. Ulysses gives the Cyclops wine (a) to try to win the giant's friendship. (b) so he can attack while the giant is drunk. (c) so he and his men can escape while the giant sleeps.

8. When he attacks the giant, Ulysses uses (a) a sword. (b) a rock. (c) a tree trunk.

9. The Greeks finally escape from the cave by (a) killing the Cyclops. (b) moving the rock. (c) hiding underneath the sheep as they go out.

10. Ulysses beats the giant because he, Ulysses, (a) is stronger. (b) is trickier. (c) has the gods on his side.

THINKING IT THROUGH

Discuss the following items in class.

1. Whose side did you take as you read the story? (Some modern readers tend to sympathize with the Cyclops and dislike Ulysses. After all, the Cyclops is living peacefully in his own land before Ulysses comes.)

2. Do you like this kind of story? (a) To what kinds of modern movies could you compare it? (b) Which story do you like better, this one or the "Trojan Horse"? Give reasons for your answers.

3. In your opinion, what two adjectives (words that describe) best suit a person like the ancient hero Ulysses? Choose your adjectives with care before discussing them with other class members.

Relationships: Review

If you wish to review the meaning of any term in *italics* in this exercise, refer to the Glossary of Terms.

I. Examine the following group of five sentences. One of the sentences gives the *main idea* of the entire group. The other sentences contain *supporting details.* On a separate sheet of paper, write the sentence that states the main idea.

Ulysses splits his forces, leaving some on the beach while taking the others to the cave.
Ulysses tells the Cyclops that his name is NOBODY.
Ulysses blinds the Cyclops with a spear.
Ulysses is a clever hero.
Ulysses and his men escape on the undersides of sheep.

II. 1. On your paper, arrange the following events in order to show what happens first in the story, what happens next, and so on.

Ulysses and his men leave the island in sadness.
Other Cyclops gather around the mouth of the cave.
The soldiers beg Ulysses to return to the safety of the ship.
Ulysses gives the Cyclops a lot of wine.
The twelve men and Ulysses enter the Cyclops's cave.

2. Now answer this question: Did you arrange the five sentences above in *spatial order* or in *chronological order?*

Composition

Follow your teacher's instructions before completing *one* of these writing assignments.

1. Write three sentences that say something about the *spatial order* revealed in the story. Consider using *sea, island, beach,* and *cave* as key words.

2. The Cyclops is one of the first make-believe monsters in literature. What do you think of Homer's monster? Maybe you can do better! Think about other descriptions of monsters. Use your imagination. Put scary parts together. Try to write a paragraph that would scare even Homer himself. You might use "My Favorite Monster" as a title.

VOCABULARY AND SKILL REVIEW

Before completing the exercises that follow, you may wish to review all the terms presented in the text.

I. On a separate sheet of paper, write the *italicized* term that best fills the blank in each sentence.

siege	*image*	*lair*	*bleat*	*scurry*
grope	*emerge*	*cove*	*jeer*	*cunning*

1. Cats *meow,* dogs *bark,* cows *moo,* and sheep _____.
2. The ship sailed into a _____ to escape the storm.
3. The enemy laid _____ to the castle.
4. As we approached the rabbits, they began to _____ away.
5. I sat quietly, waiting for them to _____ from their hiding places.
6. The fox hunted all night and then returned to its _____.
7. Foxes are known as very _____ animals.
8. Maria began to _____ in the dark for the light switch.
9. The baseball fans began to _____ at the tired pitcher.
10. The mirror shows you a reversed _____ of your face.

II.
1. A *soothsayer* (a) murmurs prayers. (b) foretells the future. (c) makes political speeches.
2. You might see a *ram* (a) through a microscope. (b) deep under water. (c) on a western ranch.
3. An *idle* farm is (a) a busy farm. (b) an experimental farm. (c) a farm that is not being used.
4. To *bustle* about is to (a) move busily. (b) feel very tired. (c) make many mistakes.
5. An example of a *turmoil* is (a) a sly fox. (b) the scene after a major earthquake. (c) a traitor to one's country.
6. You might find a *reed* in a (a) swamp or marsh. (b) secretary's desk. (c) school kitchen.
7. *Gape* means to (a) open wide. (b) scratch one's head. (c) move one's feet.
8. To *thrust* something means to (a) nibble it. (b) sit on it. (c) push it quickly.
9. If you feel *repentance,* you might (a) burst into laughter easily. (b) tell someone you're sorry. (c) beat your fists against a wall.
10. During a period of *prosperity* (a) most people go hungry. (b) jobs are hard to find. (c) many people are making money.

III. Match the terms in Column A with their definitions in Column B.

A	**B**
1. effect	a) having to do with space
2. contrast	b) central thought of a paragraph or a
3. chronological	selection
4. spatial	c) difference
5. main idea	d) the result of a cause
	e) having to do with time

IV. Explain the cartoon below in terms of (a) cause-effect and (b) comparison-contrast.

"Go! Go! Go! Go!"

Drawing by C. Barsotti; © 1973 The New Yorker Magazine, Inc.

Piri Thomas (born 1928)

The popular writer in a relaxed pose

Quick!—Name an American author who learned to write stories while serving a prison term.

Many high-school students would have no trouble with the answer. O. Henry, of course (see page 2). O. Henry's three years in jail gave him his start as a writer.

But which *other* American author learned to write stories while serving a prison term? The answer: Piri Thomas.

Piri Thomas grew up in New York City. In 1950, he was sent to jail for attempted armed robbery. He served seven years. In prison, he began to write stories. He wanted to tell the truth about the Puerto Rican and black people he knew so well. He also wanted to find out who he really was,

inside. In a way, he used his writing as an escape from prison life.

When he finally got out of prison, Piri Thomas got a job working with young people, many of whom were headed for trouble. He also worked with drug addicts. Meanwhile, he kept on writing. His book *Down These Mean Streets* (1967) made him a well-known author. Other books, plays, and articles followed.

AMIGO BROTHERS

by Piri Thomas

▶ A chance at the Golden Gloves was up for grabs, and both boys thought they could take it. However, each fighter had the same problem. To be a hero, he would have to whip his best friend. If that happened, could he ever be a hero to himself?

Antonio Cruz and Felix Varga were both seventeen years old. They were so together in friendship that they felt themselves to be brothers. They had known each other since childhood, growing up on the lower east side of Manhattan in the same tenement building on Fifth Street between Avenue A and Avenue B.

Antonio was fair, lean, and lanky, while Felix was dark, short, and husky. Antonio's hair was always falling over his eyes, while Felix wore his black hair in a natural Afro style.

Each youngster had a dream of someday becoming lightweight champion of the world. Every chance they had the boys worked out, sometimes at the Boy's Club on 10th Street and Avenue A and sometimes at the pro's gym on 14th Street. Early morning sunrises would find them running along the East River Drive, wrapped in sweat shirts, short towels around their necks, and handkerchiefs Apache style around their foreheads.

While some youngsters were into street negatives, Antonio and Felix slept, ate, rapped, and dreamt positive. Between them, they had a collection of *Fight* magazines second to none, plus a scrapbook filled with torn tickets to every boxing match they had ever

- amigo (uh MEE goh) friend(ly) (**A Spanish word. Other Spanish words in the story add flavor to the text but will not be defined. You will know some of them.**)
- tenement (TEN uh munt) **low-grade housing**
- Apache (uh PACH ee) **Native American group of the Southwest**
- negative (NEG uh tiv) **bad habit or behavior**

attended, and some clippings of their own. If asked a question about any given fighter, they would immediately zip out from their memory banks divisions, weights, records of fights, knockouts, technical knockouts, and draws or losses.

Each had fought many bouts representing their community and had won two gold-plated medals plus a silver and bronze medallion. The difference was in their style. Antonio's lean form and long reach made him the better boxer, while Felix's short and muscular frame made him the better slugger. Whenever they had met in the ring for sparring sessions, it had always been hot and heavy.

Now, after a series of elimination bouts, they had been informed that they were to meet each other in the division finals that were scheduled for the seventh of August, two weeks away—the winner to represent the Boys Club in the Golden Gloves Championship Tournament.

The two boys continued to run together along the East River Drive. But even when joking with each other, they both sensed a wall rising between them.

One morning less than a week before their bout, they met as usual for their daily workout. They fooled around with a few jabs at the air, slapped skin, and then took off, running lightly along the dirty East River's edge.

Antonio glanced at Felix who kept his eyes purposely straight ahead, pausing from time to time to do some fancy leg work while throwing one-twos followed by upper cuts to an imaginary jaw. Antonio then beat the air with a barrage of body blows and short devastating lefts with an overhand jaw-breaking right.

After a mile or so, Felix puffed and said, "Let's stop a while, bro. I think we both got something to say to each other."

Antonio nodded. It was not natural to be acting as though nothing unusual was happening when two ace-boon buddies were going to be blasting . . . each other within a few short days.

- bout (BOUT) **fight**
- medallion (muh DAL yun) **large medal**
- sparring (SPAR ing) **practice boxing with another**
- elimination (i lim uh NAY shun) **in a tournament, dropped after one loss**
- barrage (buh RAJ) **huge number, as of bombs or blows**
- devastating (DEV uh stay ting) **carrying destruction**

They rested their elbows on the railing separating them from the river. Antonio wiped his face with his short towel. The sunrise was now creating day.

Felix leaned heavily on the river's railing and stared across to the shores of Brooklyn. Fnally, he broke the silence.

"Gee . . . man. I don't know how to come out with it."

Antonio helped. "It's about our fight, right?"

"Yeah, right." Felix's eyes squinted at the rising orange sun.

"I've been thinking about it too, *panin*. In fact, since we found out it was going to be me and you, I've been awake at night, pulling punches on you, trying not to hurt you."

"Same here. It ain't natural not to think about the fight. I mean, we both are *cheverote* fighters and we both want to win. But only one of us can win. There ain't no draws in the eliminations."

Felix tapped Antonio gently on the shoulder. "I don't mean to sound like I'm bragging, bro. But I wanna win, fair and square."

Antonio nodded quietly. "Yeah. We both know that in the ring the better man wins. Friend or no friend, brother or no . . . "

Felix finished it for him. "Brother. Tony, let's promise something right here. Okay?"

"If it's fair, *hermano*, I'm for it." Antonio admired the courage of a tug boat pulling a barge five times its welterweight size.

"It's fair, Tony. When we get into the ring, it's gotta be like we never met. We gotta be like two heavy strangers that want the same thing and only one can have it. You understand, don'tcha?"

"*Si*, I know." Tony smiled. "No pulling punches. We go all the way."

"Yeah, that's right. Listen, Tony. Don't you think it's a good idea if we don't see each other until the day of the fight? I'm going to stay with my Aunt Lucy in the Bronx. I can use Gleason's Gym for working out. My manager says he got some sparring partners with more or less your style."

Tony scratched his nose pensively. "Yeah, it would be better for our heads." He held out his hand, palm upward. "Deal?"

"Deal." Felix lightly slapped open skin.

"Ready for some more running?" Tony asked lamely.

- welterweight (WEL tur wayt) **boxer in a lighter-weight division**
- pensively (PEN siv lee) **thoughtfully**

"Naw, bro. Let's cut it here. You go on. I kinda like to get things together in my head."

"You ain't worried, are you?" Tony asked.

"No way, man." Felix laughed out loud. "I got too much smarts for that. I just think it's cooler if we split right here. After the fight, we can get it together again like nothing ever happened."

The amigo brothers were not ashamed to hug each other tightly.

"Guess you're right. Watch yourself, Felix. I hear there's some pretty heavy dudes up in the Bronx. *Sauvecito,* okay?"

"Okay. You watch yourself too, *sabe?*"

Tony jogged away. Felix watched his friend disappear from view, throwing rights and lefts. Both fighters had a lot of psyching up to do before the big fight.

The days in training passed much too slowly. Although they kept out of each other's way, they were aware of each other's progress via the ghetto grapevine.

The evening before the big fight, Tony made his way to the roof of his tenement. In the quiet early dark, he peered over the ledge. Six stories below the lights of the city blinked and the sounds of cars mingled with the curses and the laughter of children in the street. He tried not to think of Felix, feeling he had succeeded in psyching his mind. But only in the ring would he really know. To spare Felix hurt, he would have to knock him out, early and quick.

Up in the South Bronx, Felix decided to take in a movie in an effort to keep Antonio's face away from his fists. The flick was *The Champion* with Kirk Douglas, the third time Felix was seeing it.

The champion was getting . . . beat, . . . his face being pounded into raw wet hamburger. His eyes were cut, jagged, bleeding, one eye swollen, the other almost shut. He was saved only by the sound of the bell.

Felix became the champ and Tony the challenger.

The movie audience was going out of its head, roaring in blood lust at the butchery going on. The champ hunched his shoulders grunting and sniffing red blood back into his broken nose. The challenger, confident that he had the championship in the bag, threw a

---

- psyching up (SY king UP) **getting into shape mentally (slang)**
- mingle (MING gul) **mix**
- lust (LUST) **powerful desire**

left. The champ countered with a dynamite right that exploded into the challenger's brains.

Felix's right arm felt the shock. Antonio's face, superimposed on the screen, was shattered and split apart by the awesome force of the killer blow. Felix saw himself in the ring, blasting Antonio against the ropes. The champ had to be forcibly restrained. The challenger was allowed to crumble slowly to the canvas, a broken bloody mess.

When Felix finally left the theater, he had figured out how to psyche himself for tomorrow's fight. It was Felix the Champion vs. Antonio the Challenger.

He walked up some dark streets, deserted except for small pockets of wary-looking kids wearing gang colors. Despite the fact that he was Puerto Rican like them, they eyed him as a stranger to their turf. Felix did a fast shuffle, bobbing and weaving, while letting loose a torrent of blows that would demolish whatever got in its way. It seemed to impress the brothers, who went about their own business.

Finding no takers, Felix decided to split to his aunt's. Walking the streets had not relaxed him, neither had the fight flick. All it had done was to stir him up. He let himself quietly into his Aunt Lucy's apartment and went straight to bed, falling into a fitful sleep with sounds of the gong for Round One.

Antonio was passing some heavy time on his rooftop. How would the fight tomorrow affect his relationship with Felix? After all, fighting was like any other profession. Friendship had nothing to do with it. A gnawing doubt crept in. He cut negative thinking real quick by doing some speedy fancy dance steps, bobbing and weaving like mercury. The night air was blurred with perpetual motions of left hooks and right crosses. Felix, his *amigo* brother, was not going to be Felix at all in the ring. Just an opponent with another face.

- superimposed (soo pur im POHZD) **placed on top of**
- awesome (AW sum) **causing fear and wonder**
- restrain (ri STRAYN) **hold back**
- wary (WAIR ee) **on guard; watchful**
- torrent (TOR unt) **rushing stream or downpour**
- fitful (FIT ful) **uneasy; very restless**
- perpetual (pur PECH oo ul) **never stopping; without pause**

Antonio went to sleep, hearing the opening bell for the first round. Like his friend in the South Bronx, he prayed for victory, via a quick clean knockout in the first round.

Large posters plastered all over the walls of local shops announced the fight between Antonio Cruz and Felix Vargas as the main bout.

The fight had created great interest in the neighborhood. Antonio and Felix were well liked and respected. Each had his own loyal following. Betting fever was high and ranged from a bottle of soda to cold hard cash on the line.

Antonio's fans bet with unbridled faith in his boxing skills. On the other side, Felix's admirers bet on his dynamite-packed fists.

Felix had returned to his apartment early in the morning of August 7th and stayed there, hoping to avoid seeing Antonio. He turned the radio on to *salsa* music sounds and then tried to read while waiting for word from his manager.

The fight was scheduled to take place in Tompkins Square Park. It had been decided that the gymnasium of the Boys Club was not large enough to hold all the people who were sure to attend. In Tompkins Square Park, everyone who wanted could view the fight, whether from ringside or window fire escapes or tenement rooftops.

The morning of the fight Tompkins Square was a beehive of activity with numerous workers setting up the ring, the seats, and the guest speakers' stand. The scheduled bouts began shortly after noon and the park had begun filling up even earlier.

• unbridled (un BRYD uld) **uncontrolled**

The local junior high school across from Tompkins Square Park served as the dressing room for all the fighters. Each was given a separate classroom with desk tops, covered with mats, serving as resting tables. Antonio thought he caught a glimpse of Felix waving to him from a room at the far end of the corridor. He waved back just in case it had been him.

The fighters changed from their street clothes into fighting gear. Antonio wore white trunks, black socks, and black shoes. Felix wore green trunks, white socks, and white boxing shoes. Each had dressing gowns to match their fighting trunks with their names neatly stitched on the back.

The loudspeakers blared into the open windows of the school. There were speeches by dignitaries, community leaders, and great boxers of yesteryear. Some were well prepared, some improvised on the spot. They all carried the same message of great pleasure and honor at being part of such a historic event. This great day was in the tradition of champions emerging from the streets of the lower east side.

Interwoven with the speeches were the sounds of the other boxing events. After the sixth bout, Felix was much relieved when his trainer Charlie said, "Time change. Quick knockout. This is it. We're on."

Waiting time was over. Felix was escorted from the classroom by a dozen fans in white T-shirts with the word FELIX across their fronts.

Antonio was escorted down a different stairwell and guided through a roped-off path.

As the two climbed into the ring, the crowd exploded with a roar. Antonio and Felix both bowed gracefully and then raised their arms in acknowledgment.

Antonio tried to be cool, but even as the roar was in its first birth, he turned slowly to meet Felix's eyes looking directly into his.

- blare (BLAIR) **make a loud noise**
- dignitary (DIG ni ter ee) **important person**
- improvised (IM pruh vyzd) **made up quickly, without planning**
- emerging (i MURJ ing) **coming out of**
- interwoven (in tur WOHV un) **mixed with**
- acknowledgment (ak NOL ij munt) **recognition; thanks**

Felix nodded his head and Antonio responded. And both as one, just as quickly, turned away to face his own corner.

Bong—bong—bong. The roar turned to stillness.

"Ladies and Gentlemen, *Señores y Señoras.*"

The announcer spoke slowly, pleased at his bilingual efforts.

"Now the moment we have all been waiting for—the main event between two fine young Puerto Rican fighters, products of our lower east side."

"*Loisaida,*" called out a member of the audience.

"In this corner, weighing 134 pounds, Felix Vargas. And in this corner, weighing 133 pounds, Antonio Cruz. The winner will represent the Boys Club in the tournament of champions, the Golden Gloves. There will be no draw. May the best man win."

The cheering of the crowd shook the window panes of the old buildings surrounding Tompkins Square Park. At the center of the ring, the referee was giving instructions to the youngsters.

"Keep your punches up. No low blows. No punching on the back of the head. Keep your heads up. Understand. Let's have a clean fight. Now shake hands and come out fighting."

• bilingual (by LING gwul) **able to use two languages**

Both youngsters touched gloves and nodded. They turned and danced quickly to their corners. Their head towels and dressing gowns were lifted neatly from their shoulders by the trainers' nimble fingers. Antonio crossed himself. Felix did the same.

BONG! BONG! ROUND ONE. Felix and Antonio turned and faced each other squarely in a fighting pose. Felix wasted no time. He came in fast, head low, half hunched toward his right shoulder, and lashed out with a straight left. He missed a right cross as Antonio slipped the punch and countered with one-two-three lefts that snapped Felix's head back, sending a mild shock coursing through him. If Felix had any small doubt about their friendship affecting their fight, it was being neatly dispelled.

Antonio danced, a joy to behold. His left hand was like a piston pumping jabs one right after another with seeming ease. Felix bobbed and weaved and never stopped boring in. He knew that at long range he was at a disadvantage. Antonio had too much reach on him. Only by coming in close could Felix hope to achieve the dreamed-of knockout.

Antonio knew the dynamite that was stored in his *amigo* brother's fist. He ducked a short right and missed a left hook. Felix trapped him against the ropes just long enough to pour some punishing rights and lefts to Antonio's hard midsection. Antonio slipped away from Felix, crashing two lefts to his head, which set Felix's right ear to ringing.

Bong! Both *amigos* froze a punch well on its way, sending up a roar of approval for good sportsmanship.

Felix walked briskly back to his corner. His right ear had not stopped ringing. Antonio gracefully danced his way toward his stool none the worse, except for glowing glove burns, showing angry red against the whiteness of his midribs.

"Watch that right, Tony." His trainer talked into his ear. "Remember Felix always goes to the body. He'll want you to drop your hands for his overhand left or right. Got it?"

- nimble (NIM bul) **quick and accurate**
- pose (POHZ) **position; way of standing**
- counter (KOUN tur) **act against**
- coursing (KOHR sing) **running or flowing**
- dispelled (di SPELD) **driven away; ended**

Antonio nodded, sprayed water out between his teeth. He felt better as his sore midsection was being firmly rubbed.

Felix's corner was also busy.

"You gotta get in there, fella." Felix's trainer poured water over his curly Afro locks. "Get in there or he's gonna chop you up from way back."

Bong! Bong! Round two. Felix was off his stool and rushed Antonio like a bull, sending a hard right to his head. Beads of water exploded from Antonio's long hair.

Antonio, hurt, sent back a blurring barrage of lefts and rights that only meant pain to Felix, who returned with a short left to the head followed by a looping right to the body. Antonio countered with his own flurry, forcing Felix to give ground. But not for long.

Felix bobbed and weaved, bobbed and weaved, occasionally punching his two gloves together.

Antonio waited for the rush that was sure to come. Felix closed in and feinted with his left shoulder and threw his right instead. Lights suddenly exploded inside Felix's head as Antonio slipped the blow and hit him with a pistonlike left, catching him flush on the point of his chin.

Bedlam broke loose as Felix's legs momentarily buckled. He fought off a series of rights and lefts and came back with a strong right that taught Antonio respect.

Antonio danced in carefully. He knew Felix had the habit of playing possum when hurt, to sucker an opponent within reach of the powerful bombs he carried in each fist.

A right to the head slowed Antonio's pretty dancing. He answered with his own left at Felix's right eye that began puffing up within three seconds.

Antonio, a bit too eager, moved in too close and Felix had him entangled into a rip-roaring, punching toe-to-toe slugfest that brought the whole Tompkins Square Park screaming to its feet.

Rights to the body. Lefts to the head. Neither fighter was giving an inch. Suddenly a short right caught Antonio squarely on the chin.

- feint (FAYNT) **move to trick; pretend**
- flush (FLUSH) **straight; even with**
- bedlam (BED lum) **confusion**
- momentarily (moh mun TAIR uh lee) **for an instant**

His long legs turned to jelly and his arms flailed out desperately. Felix, grunting like a bull, threw wild punches from every direction. Antonio, groggy, bobbed and weaved, evading most of the blows. Suddenly his head cleared. His left flashed out hard and straight catching Felix on the bridge of his nose.

Felix lashed back with a haymaker, right off the ghetto streets. At the same instant, his eye caught another left hook from Antonio. Felix swung out trying to clear the pain. Only the frenzied screaming of those along ringside let him know that he had dropped Antonio. Fighting off the growing haze, Antonio struggled to his feet, got up, ducked, and threw a smashing right that dropped Felix flat on his back.

Felix got up as fast as he could in his own corner, groggy but still game. He didn't even hear the count. In a fog, he heard the roaring

- flail (FLAYL) **wave or beat aimlessly**
- evading (i VAYD ing) **avoiding**
- frenzied (FREN zeed) **very excited**
- game (GAYM) **ready and willing**

of the crowd, who seemed to have gone insane. His head cleared to hear the bell sound at the end of the round. He was . . . glad. His trainer sat him down on the stool.

In his corner, Antonio was doing what all fighters do when they are hurt. They sit and smile at everyone.

The referee signaled the ring doctor to check the fighters out. He did so and then gave his okay. The cold water sponges brought clarity to both *amigo* brothers. They were rubbed until their circulation ran free.

Bong! Round three—the final round. Up to now it had been tic-tac-toe, pretty much even. But everyone knew there could be no draw and that this round would decide the winner.

This time, to Felix's surprise, it was Antonio who came out fast, charging across the ring. Felix braced himself but couldn't ward off the barrage of punches. Antonio drove Felix hard against the ropes.

The crowd ate it up. Thus far the two had fought with *mucho corazón*. Felix tapped his gloves and commenced his attack anew. Antonio, throwing boxer's caution to the winds, jumped in to meet him.

Both pounded away. Neither gave an inch and neither fell to the canvas. Felix's left eye was tightly closed. Claret red blood poured from Antonio's nose. They fought toe-to-toe.

The sounds of their blows were loud in contrast to the silence of a crowd gone completely mute. The referee was stunned by their savagery.

Bong! Bong! Bong! The bell sounded over and over again. Felix and Antonio were past hearing. Their blows continued to pound on each other like hailstones.

Finally the referee and the two trainers pried Felix and Antonio apart. Cold water was poured over them to bring them back to their senses.

They looked around and then rushed toward each other. A cry of alarm surged through Tompkins Square Park. Was this a fight to the death instead of a boxing match?

- clarity (KLAR i tee) clearness
- claret red (KLAR it RED) **deep purplish red**
- **mute** (MYOOT) **unable to talk; quiet**

The fear soon gave way to wave upon wave of cheering as the two *amigos* embraced.

No matter what the decision, they knew they would always be champions to each other.

BONG! BONG! BONG! "Ladies and Gentlemen. *Señores* and *Señoras.* The winner and representative to the Golden Gloves Tournament of Champions is . . . "

The announcer turned to point to the winner and found himself alone. Arm in arm the champions had already left the ring.

ALL THINGS CONSIDERED

1. The time period covered in the story is (a) about two weeks. (b) two days. (c) one day.
2. The two boys differ most in their (a) ability in the ring. (b) friendship. (c) appearance.

• embrace (em BRAYS) hug

3. Early every morning, the boys (a) deliver papers. (b) head for the gym. (c) go running together.

4. The boy described as the powerful slugger, rather than as the skillful boxer, is (a) Antonio. (b) Felix. (c) neither, since both fight the same way.

5. A big decision the boys make early in the story is (a) to stop being friends. (b) to speak both Spanish and English. (c) that they will not see each other before the fight.

6. The evening before the fight, Felix (a) goes to a movie. (b) invites friends to a party. (c) becomes very ill.

7. The fight is held (a) in a junior high school. (b) in the Boys Club gym. (c) outdoors.

8. Among the people at ringside is (a) Antonio's mother. (b) a doctor. (c) a reporter from the *Post*.

9. The surprise at the end is that (a) the reader is never told who the winner is. (b) the fight is only three rounds long. (c) a draw is declared.

10. The four short paragraphs at the end leave little doubt that the main message of the story concerns (a) the joy of victory. (b) the will to fight to the death. (c) brotherhood.

THINKING IT THROUGH

Discuss the following items in class.

1. Piri Thomas, the author, knows his subject matter well. The story is full of details about the streets of New York City. Give at least two of these details that make the story seem real.

2. Much is made of *psyching up* for the big fight. (a) What does the term mean? (b) How do the boys go about it?

3. Both boys hope for quick victory in the first round. Why is this their wish?

4. Most readers find the fight scene exciting. This is because the author keeps it going with a *barrage* of action words: *barrage, bobbed, weaved, charging*. What are two other words that make the fight scene really come alive?

5. The author deliberately chooses to have his fight story end in a rather odd way. Why does he use this particular ending? In other words, what is he trying to suggest between the lines to the reader?

UNIT REVIEW

I. *What is a hero?* This unit has asked you to think about this important question. As you may have realized, there are many kinds of heroes. Which kind do you prefer? sports stars? great warriors? famous people or "unsung heroes"? those people who help others? or those who become hero models because of their individual achievement?

Use "What is a Hero?" as the title of a paragraph of your own. Think seriously about the question: What person—or what kind of person—truly deserves the title "hero"? Mention at least one example, taken either from this unit or from your other reading.

II. You have probably written book reports. This assignment is easier than writing a book report, but you should go about it in the same way.

There are six selections in this unit that are over two pages long. Choose the one you liked best. Write a "story report," keeping in mind the following *do's* and *don'ts.*

DO'S

1. Do give a general idea of what the selection is about. Is it fiction or nonfiction? Who is the main character? What problems does the main character face?

2. Do comment on the way the author writes. For instance, does the author use interesting figurative language? What is the mood of the story? Does the setting seem real? Explain and give examples.

3. Do explain how the author changed your way of thinking, or at least what you were made to think about.

4. Do tell what kind of readers would probably like the story and what kind would not.

DON'TS

1. Don't begin with a sentence such as "I liked 'Terror in the North' because it was interesting." The second half of that sentence really says nothing. If you "liked" something, of course you found it "interesting"!

2. Don't use words like "fantastic" or "boring" without explaining the reasons for your opinions.

3. Don't devote more than half your report to telling what happened in the story. Of course, you have to tell something about the characters and their problems. Remember though, that a good report is much more than a summary.

4. Don't reveal the ending if it should come as a surprise to other readers.

SPEAKING UP

▶ Martin Luther King, Jr., was killed by an assassin's bullet on April 4, 1968. A few days later, the poet Nikki Giovanni put her feelings into words. Now try to put her words into sound patterns that add sincere feeling to the poem.

THE FUNERAL OF MARTIN LUTHER KING, JR.

by Nikki Giovanni

His headstone said
FREE AT LAST, FREE AT LAST
But death is a slave's freedom
We seek the freedom of free men
And the construction of a world
Where Martin Luther King could have lived and preached
   non-violence

                     Atlanta, April 9, 1968

Before you practice your reading, think about these questions and try to answer them.

1. (a) Where do the words "FREE AT LAST" come from? (b) What did they mean when Dr. King spoke them? (c) What additional meaning did they get after his death?
2. What is the difference in meaning between the "freedom" of line 3 and the "freedom" of line 4?
3. (a) How serious is the poet about the last three lines of the poem? (b) How can you make your voice reflect her feelings?

WRITING YOUR OWN EXPLANATION

This photograph appeared in newspapers across the country. An explanation of what was happening appeared along with the photograph. Your job now is to make up your own interesting explanation about the photograph. For example, you might tell *how* the trash cans were decorated, *why* the couple like the cans, or *what* use the cans have.

You take it from there. Be as creative and clever as you can. Start by asking yourself some questions. Did the two people pictured decorate the trash cans for each other? If so, why? How did they decorate them? If the couple didn't decorate the cans, who gave the cans to them? For what reason? Are the cans really intended to hold trash? If not, what do they hold?

Make as many notes as you wish. Then choose the type of explanation you will give. Will it be a *how*, *why*, or *what* explanation? The choice is yours. Write a good, clear explanation.

Glossary of Terms

This glossary defines terms that you have studied. The page references shown with the terms indicate where the terms are first defined and discussed. Turn to those pages if you need to review the lessons.

Autobiography p. 73 An *autobiography* is a person's account of his or her own life.

Cause and Effect p. 232 A *cause* is an event or idea that leads to a certain result, which is called an *effect.*

Character Clues p. 186 An author often must show what the characters in a story or a play are like in an indirect way. To do this, the author provides hints as to the character, or *character clues.* These clues include actions, speeches, and, in a play, things the audience can see on stage.

Characterization p. 91 The word *characterization* means the ways in which authors bring the people in their stories to life. There are four main methods of characterization: (1) the direct statements made by the author, (2) the speeches and the thoughts of the character, (3) the actions of the character, and (4) the reactions of other characters to the character.

Choral Reading p. 140 *Choral reading* is reading aloud together, with groups or individuals sometimes taking different parts. Narrative poems like "The Listeners" are best when they're read aloud to bring out the sounds.

Chronological Order p. 275 The term *chronological order* simply means in the order of time: yesterday, today, tomorrow; breakfast, lunch, supper; noon, afternoon, evening. The events in most stories and plays take place in chronological order.

Climax p. 47 The *climax* of a story is the most exciting part at or near the end. The action at the climax involves the solution to the final plot problem.

Coincidence p. 12 A *coincidence* occurs when two or more related events accidentally happen at the same time.

Comparison p. 64 A *comparison* usually shows how two (or more) things are alike. (See also *Contrast.*)

Conflict p. 31 A *conflict* develops when two opposite forces meet. There are four kinds of conflicts. A story can contain more than one kind, but usually only one is the *main* conflict. The four kinds are (1) conflict between people, (2) conflict within a single person, (3) conflict between people and things, (4) and conflict between people and nature.

Connotation p. 300 Words often have two kinds of meanings. One kind of meaning is a word's *connotation,* or the meaning a word suggests or brings to mind. (See also *Denotation.*)

Context Clues p. 214 *Context clues* are all the surrounding words that help the reader guess the meaning of an unknown word.

Contrast p. 64 A *contrast* shows how two (or more) things are different. (See also *Comparison.*)

Denotation p. 300 Words often have two kinds of meanings. One kind of meaning is a word's *denotation,* or the meaning given in the dictionary. (See also *Connotation.*)

Fact p. 290   A *fact* is something known to be true. It can be checked and proved. *For example, it is a fact that this sentence is printed in italic type.*

Fantasy p. 148   A *fantasy* is a very strange tale that could probably not happen in real life. Writers of fantasies tend to follow a two-part rule: (1) There must be only *one* impossible element in a fantasy. (2) Other than that, the story must be as realistic as possible.

Fiction p. 11   A piece of *fiction* is a made-up story. (See also *Nonfiction.*)

Figurative Language p. 161   In *figurative language,* the words do not mean exactly what they seem to say. For instance, did you ever really "die laughing"? Of course not!

First Person p. 259   In the *first person* point of view, the storyteller, called the narrator or the speaker, is involved as a character in the story. The character refers to himself or herself as "I" and "me." (See also *Third Person* and *Point of View.*)

Flashback p. 275   A *flashback* interrupts the normal chronological order to show events that happened earlier. (See also *Chronological Order.*)

Foreshadowing p. 125   *Foreshadowing* is the providing of hints or clues as to what might happen in a story or a play. Good foreshadowing prepares the reader to accept the event or surprise when it finally comes.

Haiku p. 263   A *haiku* is a type of three-line poem that has long been popular in Japan. Many, but not all, works of haiku have a 5–7–5 pattern—5 syllables in the first line, 7 syllables in the second line, and 5 syllables in the third. Most haiku refer to or describe something in nature. They also have some important

symbolic meaning. (See also *Symbolic Meaning.*)

Inference p. 74   An *inference* is an understanding of, or an idea about, something that is not stated directly by the writer. In other words, it is a guess based on all the available facts. It is reading between the lines.

Limerick p. 215   A *limerick* is a five-line poem with a particular pattern that involves syllables, rhyme, and rhythm. Most good limericks have a surprise in the last line.

Main Idea p. 213   The *main idea* of a paragraph is the central thought. It is often stated in a sentence. An entire story can contain several main ideas.

Melodrama p. 50   A *melodrama* is a play in which everything is exaggerated. The plot is fast and thrilling—but completely impossible. The characters are a standard lot: the villain, the heroine, and the hero.

Monologue p. 81   A *monologue* is an entertaining talk by a single speaker.

Mood p. 112   The *mood* of a story is the feeling it gives the reader. Some stories make us laugh and laugh. These put the reader in a happy, fun-filled mood. Other stories create a mood of fear, or even terror. Still others put the reader in a sorrowful mood.

Multiple Meanings p. 113   Some words in sentences can have more than one meaning, or *multiple meanings.* For instance, in the sentence "Wait till he brings it up," on page 101, the right meaning is "Wait till he suggests it." In a different context, the meaning might be "Wait till he carries or lifts it up."

Narrator p. 259   The *narrator* is a storyteller. Sometimes a narrator is involved as a character in a story.

Nonfiction p. 11 Stories about events that happened in real life are usually called true stories, or *nonfiction*. (See also *Fiction*.)

Opinion p. 290 An *opinion* is what a person thinks of believes about something. Even though many people may agree on a certain opinion, no one can prove it to be true.

Oral Interpretation p. 63 Reading aloud with expression is called *oral interpretation*. (Of course, when the words cannot be actually said aloud, a person can manage to have the words ringing in his or her mind's ear.)

Paragraph Signals p. 134 When some sort of change is taking place in a story, a writer uses *paragraph signals*. The changes signaled by the start of a new paragraph usually include one or more of the following: (1) a change in subject or idea, (2) a different person speaking or thinking, or (3) a jump from one time period to another.

Plot p. 11 The events in a story or a play are called the *plot*. The plot holds things together. Think of the plot as a series of problems that the main character has to overcome.

Plot Question p. 11 A *plot question* is a problem that keeps the reader interested. Most stories and plays have a series of plot questions. For instance: (1) Will Jill sign up for the big race? (2) Will Jill win the race? (3) What will happen now that Jill has defeated her best friend Janet, the track star?

Point of View p. 259 Every story has to be written from a certain *point of view*. that is, someone, real or imagined, has to tell what's going on. The point of view is simply the position from which the story is told. (See also *First Person* and *Third Person*.)

Prediction p. 134 A *prediction* is a judgment about what will happen in the future. Sometimes the purpose of foreshadowing is to enable the reader to make predictions while reading a story. (See also *Foreshadowing*.)

Reading Between the Lines p. 74 The term *reading between the lines* is a figurative way of saying "making inferences." (See also *Inference*.)

Rising Action p. 47 Writers know that each plot problem must be more interesting than the last. This kind of increasing excitement is called *rising action*.

Setting p. 97 The *setting* is where a story or a play takes place. The setting includes the time, since the same place can differ greatly from one time period to another. It also includes certain natural events, such as the weather, a mountain slide, or a tree falling across the road.

Short Story p. 11 The term *short story* really defines itself. A short story is simply a story that is short. A short story is usually a made-up story, or a piece of fiction.

Spatial Order p. 195 Paragraphs can be organized in several ways. One common way is the use of *spatial order,* or a series of terms that tells *where*.

Subject p. 206 The *subject* of a piece of literature should not be confused with its *theme*. The subject is simply what the piece of literature is about. It can usually be expressed in a word or in just a few words, such as *baseball* or *hidden treasures*. (See also *Theme*.)

Supporting Details p. 213 The *supporting details* in a paragraph or in a story are the reasons or examples upon which the main idea is based.

Suspense p. 112 *Suspense* is a condition of doubt or uncertainty. A story with suspense keeps you wondering what will happen next. Detective stories, for instance, nearly always have a mood of suspense.

Symbol/Symbolic Meaning p. 249 In literature as in life, a *symbol* is something that stands for something else. For instance, the United States uses the red, white, and blue flag as a symbol. In other words, the *symbolic meaning* of a flag is the country for which it stands. In the same way, a gold medal (a symbol) in a story can stand for a feeling of pride (a symbolic meaning).

Theme p. 206 A *theme* is an idea or a message in a story or a play. It usually takes a complete sentence to express a theme adequately. It is possible for a story or a play to have several themes. Only one of these, however, is the main theme. (See also *Subject.*)

Third Person p. 259 In the *third person* point of view, the storyteller is *not* involved in the story. The storyteller must refer to each character as "he" or "she." The storyteller cannot be involved as an "I" or a "me" in the story. (See *First Person* and *Point of View.*)

Index of Authors and Titles

Page numbers in **bold-faced** type indicate profiles (short biographies).

ACKNOWLEDGMENTS

We thank the following authors, agents, and publishers for their permission to reprint copyrighted material:

BARLENMIR HOUSE, PUBLISHERS—for "Happy Thought" from *Street Poetry and Other Poems* by Jesús Papoleto Meléndez. Copyright © 1972 by Barlenmir House, Publishers.

CHAPPELL & CO., INC.—for "Lonely House" by Kurt Weill and Langston Hughes. Copyright © 1946 by Kurt Weill and Langston Hughes. Copyright renewed, assigned to Chappell & Co., Inc. and Hampshire House Publishing Corp., for the U.S.A. only. All rights outside the U.S.A. controlled by Chappell & Co., Inc. International copyright secured. All Rights Reserved. Used by permission.

DON CONGDON ASSOCIATES, INC.—for "Of Missing Persons" by Jack Finney. Copyright © by Don Congdon Associates, Inc.

CROWN PUBLISHERS, INC.—for "Starvation Wilderness." Adapted from *The Silence of the North* by Olive A. Fredrickson and Ben East. Copyright © 1972 by Olive A. Fredrickson and Ben East. Used by permission of Crown Publishers, Inc.

THE CURTIS PUBLISHING COMPANY—for "Nab Blonde, 8, as Porridge Thief." Reprinted from *The Saturday Evening Post*. Copyright © 1967 by The Curtis Publishing Company—for "The Getaway" by John Savage. Reprinted from *The Saturday Evening Post*. Copyright © 1966 by The Curtis Publishing Company.

DELACORTE PRESS—for "Up on Fong Mountain." Excerpted from the book *Dear Bill Remember Me? and Other Stories* by Norma Fox Mazer. Copyright © 1976 by Norma Fox Mazer. Reprinted by permission of Delacorte Press.

DRAMATISTS PLAY SERVICE, INC.—for *Sorry, Wrong Number*. Copyright © 1952, 1948 by Lucille Fletcher. Reprinted by permission of the Dramatists Play Service, Inc. and the author.

E. P. DUTTON, INC.—for "My People" by Bernice George, from *Here I Am!* Copyright © 1969 by Virginia Olsen Baron. Reprinted by permission of E. P. Dutton, Inc.

FIELD NEWSPAPER SYNDICATE, ANN LANDERS—for "Dead at Seventeen" from the Ann Landers column. Copyright © Ann Landers, Field Newspaper Syndicate, and *The Waterbury Republican*.

CLAY FRANKLIN—for "The Cradle Will Rock" by Clay Franklin, from *Ten Plays of Terror*. Copyright © by Clay Franklin.

SAMUEL FRENCH, INC.—for "He Ain't Done Right By Nell" by Wilbur Braun. Copyright © 1935, by Samuel French. Copyright © 1962 (in renewal) by Samuel French. *CAUTION:* Professionals and amateurs are hereby warned that "He Ain't Done Right By Nell," being fully protected under the copyright laws of the United States of America, the British Commonwealth countries, including Canada, and the other countries of the Copyright Union, is subject to a royalty. All rights, including professional, amateur, cablevision broadcasting, and the rights of translation into foreign languages are strictly reserved. For royalty information concerning this play, producers must apply to Samuel French, Inc., at 45 West 25th Street, New York, N.Y. 10010, or at 7623 Sunset Blvd., Hollywood, Calif. 90046, or if in Canada, to Samuel French (Canada) Ltd., at 80 Richmond Street East, Toronto M5C 1P1. Copies of this play, in individual paper covered acting editions, are available from Samuel French, Inc., 45 West 25th St., New York, N.Y. 10010 or 7623 Sunset Blvd., Hollywood, Calif. 90046 or in Canada, Samuel French (Canada) Ltd., 80 Richmond Street East, Toronto M5C 1P1, Canada.

GIRL SCOUTS OF THE U.S.A.—for "Terror in the North" by Eloise Engle. Copyright © Girl Scouts of the U.S.A. From *American Girl*, March 1966. Reprinted as adapted by permission.

HARCOURT BRACE JOVANOVICH, INC.—for from *The People, Yes* by Carl Sandburg. Copyright 1936 by Harcourt Brace Jovanovich, Inc.; renewed 1964 by Carl Sandburg. Reprinted by permission of the publisher.

HARPER & ROW, PUBLISHERS, INC.—for "For Paul Laurence Dunbar" from *On These I Stand* by Countée Cullen. Copyright 1925 by Harper & Row, Publishers, Inc. Renewed 1953 by Ida M. Cullen.—for "My Rules" from *Where the Sidewalk Ends: The Poems and Drawings of Shel Silverstein*. Copyright © 1974 by Snake Eye Music, Inc.—for "Andre," (page 76), "Charles" (page 253), "Otto" (page 76) from *Bronzeville Boys and Girls* by Gwendolyn Brooks. Copyright © 1956 by Gwendolyn Brooks Blakely.—for from Chapter 2, "Where Are You Now, William Shakespeare?" (pp. 35–43, with deletion), in *Me, Me, Me, Me, Me: Not a Novel* by M. E. Kerr. Copyright © 1983 by M. E. Kerr. Reprinted by permission of Harper & Row, Publishers, Inc.

RONALD HOBBS LITERARY AGENCY—for "Christmas morning i" by Carol Freeman. Used with permission of the Ronald Hobbs Literary Agency.

VANESSA HOWARD—for "Reflections" by Vanessa Howard.

VIRGINIA JOHNSON—for "The Mark of Kong-Hu" by Virginia Johnson.

ALFRED A. KNOPF, INC.—for "Dreams" from *The Dream Keeper and Other Poems* by Langston Hughes. Reprinted by permission of the publisher—for "Amigo Brothers" from *Stories from El Barrio* by Piri Thomas. Copyright © 1978 by Piri Thomas—for from *Miss Piggy's Guide to Life* by Miss Piggy as told to Henry Beard. Copyright © 1981 by Henson Associates, Inc. Reprinted by permission of Alfred A. Knopf, Inc.

ALFRED A. KNOPF AND HENSON ASSOCIATES INC.—for "Dear Miss Piggy." Copyright © 1981 by Henson Associates, Inc. Reprinted by permission of Alfred A. Knopf and Henson Associates, Inc.

LITTLE, BROWN AND COMPANY—for "Southbound on the Freeway." Copyright © 1963 by May Swenson. First appeared in *The New Yorker*.

MACMILLAN PUBLISHING CO., INC.—for "I Stood Upon a Star" from *Collected Poems* by Sara Teasdale. Copyright 1930 by Sara Teasdale Filsinger, renewed 1958 by Morgan Guaranty Trust Co. of New York.—for "What Is Once Loved" from *Alice-All-by-Herself* by Elizabeth Coatsworth. Copyright 1937 by MacMillan Publishing Co., Inc., renewed 1965 by Elizabeth Coatsworth Beston.—for "Some People" from *Poems* by Rachel Field. (New York: Macmillan, 1957). Reprinted with permission of Macmillan Publishing Co., Inc.

EVE MERRIAM—for "'I,' Says the Poem," from *It Doesn't Always Have to Rhyme* by Eve Merriam. Published by Atheneum. Copyright © 1964 by Eve Merriam.—for "Conversation with Myself" from *It Doesn't Always Have to Rhyme* by Eve Merriam. Copyright © 1964 by Eve Merriam. Both reprinted by permission of the author.

WILLIAM MORROW & COMPANY, INC.—for "The Funeral of Martin Luther King, Jr.," from *Black Feeling, Black Talk, Black Judgement* by Nikki Giovanni. Copyright © 1968, 1970 by Nikki Giovanni. By permission of William Morrow & Company.

THE NEW YORKER—for the drawing by C. Barsotti. Copyright © 1973 by The New Yorker Magazine, Inc.

HAROLD OBER ASSOCIATES—for "Thank You, M'am" by Langston Hughes. Reprinted by permission of Harold Ober Associates Incorporated. Copyright © 1958 by Langston Hughes.

PETER PAUPER PRESS, INC.—for two untitled haiku beginning "Friend, that open mouth . . ." and "Ah me! I am one . . ." by Basho. Copyright © by Peter Pauper Press, Inc.

THE PUTNAM PUBLISHING GROUP—for "Wait Till Martin Comes." Reprinted by permission of Philomel Books, a division of Putnam Publishing Group, from *The Thing at the Foot of the Bed and Other Scary Tales.* Copyright © 1959 by Maria Leach.

RANDOM HOUSE, INC.—for "The Artist," from *Tales from Old China* by Isabelle Chang.—for "Greyday" from *Oh Pray My Wings Are Gonna Fit Me Well* by Maya Angelou. Both reprinted by permission of Random House, Inc.

PAUL R. REYNOLDS, INC.—for two haiku poems beginning "I am nobody . . ." and "Make up your mind snail!" Copyright © by Richard Wright. Reprinted by permission of Paul R. Reynolds, Inc., 12 East 41st Street, New York, N.Y. 10017.

FREDERICK H. ROHLFS/QUENTIN REYNOLDS—for "A Secret for Two." Copyright © 1936 by Crowell-Collier Publishing Company. Reprinted by permission of the Estate of Quentin Reynolds.

SCHOLASTIC INC.—adapted from "Ta-Na-E-Ka" by Mary Whitebird, from Scholastic *Voice,* December 1973. Copyright © 1973 by Scholastic Inc. Reprinted by permission—for "Boy in the Shadows" from *House of Evil* by Margaret Ronan. Copyright © 1977 by Scholastic Inc. Reprinted by permission of the publisher.

SCOTT MEREDITH LITERARY AGENCY—for "Appointment at Noon" by Eric Frank Russell.—for "The Gold Medal" by Nan Gilbert. Reprinted by permission of the author and the author's agents, Scott Meredith Literary Agency, Inc., 845 Third Avenue, New York, New York 10022.

THE SOCIETY OF AUTHORS—for "The Listeners" by Walter de la Mare. The Literary Trustees of Walter de la Mare and The Society of Authors as their representative.

SOUTHERN MUSIC PUBLISHING CO. INC.—for "I Dream a World" from *Troubled Island* by Langston Hughes & William Grant Still. Copyright © 1976 by Southern Music Publishing Co. Inc. Used by permission. All rights reserved.

STERLING PUBLISHING CO., INC.—for from *Monologues for Teens* by Vernon Howard. Copyright © 1957 by Sterling Publishing Co., Inc., New York, N.Y.

UNIVERSITY OF WASHINGTON PRESS—for the untitled poem beginning "A bee thumps . . ." by Robert Sund from *Bunch Grass.* Copyright © University of Washington Press.

XEROX EDUCATION PUBLICATIONS—for "Chair" by Cheryl Miller Thurston from *Read* Magazine. Reprinted by permission of *Read* magazine. Copyright © 1981 by *Weekly Reader* Publications.—for "Foul Shot" by Edwin A. Hoey. Reprinted by permission of *Read* magazine, published by Xerox Education Publications. Copyright © 1962 by Xerox Corp.—for "On the Ledge" by Thompson Clayton. Special permission granted by Pal Paperbacks, published by Xerox Education Publications. Copyright © 1976.

The following selections have been slightly adapted for the modern reader by Globe Book Company: Louisa May Alcott, "Tabby's Tablecloth"; Arthur Conan Doyle, "Sherlock Holmes and the Speckled Band"; O. Henry, "A Retrieved Reformation"; Homer, "Ulysses and the Trojan Horse" and "Ulysses Meets the Cyclops"; Washington Irving, "The Adventure of the Mason"; Edgar Allan Poe, "The Oval Portrait"; and Ann Radcliffe, "The Provençal Tale."

Every effort has been made to locate Carole Gregory Clemmons to obtain permission to reprint her poem "Spring"; Teresa Giardina to obtain permission to reprint her story "Twice I Said I Love You"; Zachary Gold to obtain permission to reprint his story "Spring over Brooklyn"; and Frank Home to reprint his poem "To James." If either the authors or heirs are located subsequent to publication, they are hereby entitled to due compensation.

Photo Acknowledgments

Bosworth Lemere, APSA/Freelance Photographers Guild: 136 (right); Brown Brothers: 2 (left), 92, 116 (left), 136 (left), 190, 251 (left); California Institute of Technology: 137; R. B. Chapman/Paul Laurence Dunbar Community School/Dr. Elze Gladden, Principal: 251 (right), Culver Pictures: 116 (right), 358; Frost Publishing Group: 345 (right); Harper and Row: 65; Henson Associates © 1981: 280; Historical Pictures Service, Chicago: 345 (left); Louise E. Jefferson/The Schomburg Center/New York Public Library: 293 (right); Alfred A. Knopf: 379; Frederic Lewis: 13 (left); Los Angeles County Museum of Natural History: 2 (right); Museum of the American Indian/Heye Foundation: 343; NASA: 33; National Park Service, Dept. of Interior: 13 (right); Ontario Science Centre: 155; Photofile International: 318; H. Armstrong Roberts: xii, 76, 84, 154, 238; The Schomburg Center/New York Public Library: 293 (left), 379; Shostal Associates: 331; UPI/Bettmann Archive: 75, 83, 237, 276, 332, 396; Wide World: 153, 317.

Illustrators

Bill Angresano: 93, 94, 283, 287, 292   Ted Burwell: 14, 78, 79, 128, 131, 304   Peter Catalanatto: 381, 385, 387, 390, 392   Rick Cooley: 67, 68, 70, 241, 243, 246   Anna De Vito: 98, 99, 100   Mel Erikson: 47, 107, 189, 259   Allan Eitzen: 208, 211, 338, 340   Julie Evans: 4, 7, 9, 139   Joe Forté: 163, 168, 172, 176, 179, 182   Ken Hamilton: 117, 121, 122, 216, 221, 224, 229, 323, 324, 327, 359, 361, 365, 366   Mary Lopez: 346, 349, 353   Glee Lo Scalzo: 263   Zig Makariwicz: 301   Neal McPheeters: 87, 89   Linda Miyamoto: 197, 199, 200, 203, 204   Charles Molina: 152, 192   Joanne Pappas: 17, 19, 20, 24, 28, 295, 298   Don Schlegel: 156, 158, 369, 371, 372, 374   Dennis Schofield: 265, 268, 273   Gerald Smith: 50, 52, 53, 54, 55, 57, 59, 307, 308, 312   Samantha Smith: 103, 105, 109   Deb Troyer: 255, 257   Kimanne Uhler: 143, 145   Kevin Walter: 115   Lane Yerkes: 36, 38, 42, 44